Ambushed
Under the
Southern Cross

To President Dane Sergent,
A MMV Rogue Valley Chapter.
In honor of the remaining
members of the
Rogue Valley Chapter.
Cordially!
Capt. George W. Duffy
September 2013.
"Steady as she goes!"

Other literary works by author

Editor, the *Bulletin*, Massachusetts Maritime Alumni Association. Monthly, circa 1960-1965.

Editor and advertising manager, Boston Shipping Association, Boston, Massachusetts.

Port of Boston Handbook
Volume I, 1975-1976.

Port of Boston Handbook
Volume II, 1977-1978.

Port of Boston Handbook
Volume III, 1979-1980.

Port of Boston Handbook
Volume IV, 1982-1983.

Port of Boston Handbook
Volume V, 1984-1985.

Editorial page column As I See It, the *Daily News*, Newburyport, Massachusetts. Sixty-two articles, between September 1994 and June 2002.

Thirteen articles from the *Daily News*, expanded and with graphics by webmistress Toni Horodysky (http://www.usmm.org).

Ambushed

Under the

Southern Cross

*The Making of an
American Merchant Marine Officer
and His Ensuing Saga
of Courage and Survival*

Capt. George W. Duffy

To order additional copies of this book, contact:
Xlibris Corporation
1-888-795-4274
www.Xlibris.com
Orders@Xlibris.com
38228

CONTENTS

Dedication

To Margaret, with love.

INTRODUCTION

By J. Revell Carr, former president and director of Mystic Seaport, America's leading maritime museum.

It has been said that "the sea connects all things," and while one can certainly make that case, I take a different perspective. In fact, the sea separates and isolates, creating awesome barriers. Man, over millennia, has confronted the rivers, bays, and oceans that have stood as barriers, and through his ingenuity and courage found ways to cross those bodies of water and transform the barriers into aquatic highways linking peoples and cultures. When the world's maritime history is considered, it is the story of the sea, but more importantly it is the story of men and women, who over thousands of years have shaped that history with their creativity, their daring and their endurance. While the seas have played critical roles in wars during the last several thousand years, the far greater story is that of those who have used the sea for commerce. The ships and the sailors of the merchant ships have carried not only cargoes of food, produce and manufactured goods over the years, but they have carried civilization itself—people, ideas, music, art, literature, and all the other elements of human endeavor.

As historians classify their subjects, those who have performed this service to mankind have been called merchant mariners, and the service in which they applied their skills, the merchant marine. In times of war the merchant marine is called on to carry out their already dangerous mission under conditions of greatly increased peril as the belligerent's naval forces seek to hunt down and destroy their enemy's merchant ships, cutting off vital supplies to the battle front and the home front. History has failed to do full justice to the heroes of the merchant marine, but this book adds one more important contribution to the literature that tells that story. This is the story of one young merchant marine officer, his incredible experiences during World War II, and the unlikely friendships that later developed.

George Duffy was serving his nation and its allies, along with tens of thousands of other courageous merchant mariners, as the turmoil of war engulfed Europe. He witnessed Japanese attacks in the Pacific just days after Pearl Harbor. George

Duffy's life changed that December. The peacetime merchant marine of the normally neutral United States in which he was serving suddenly became a wartime service, and his life was in far greater danger.

Though only nineteen, George was third officer in a fine new cargo ship, the *American Leader* of the American Pioneer Line. He carried on his young shoulders the responsibility to safely con the sleek new ship with its tons of valuable cargo and its peace-time crew of forty-nine through the oceans of the world. It was during his second voyage in *American Leader* that the ship had a fateful encounter that had all the drama of a swashbuckling sea tale, but it was a sea tale that was all too real and deadly. The *American Leader* was spotted, shadowed, and violently attacked by a sea raider that traveled the oceans flying false colors. To those who saw her in daylight, she appeared to be a cargo vessel from a neutral country, but heavy guns, torpedo tubes, and a well-trained crew of German navy officers and sailors were concealed behind the apparently benign exterior.

The tradition of ships sailing or steaming in disguise and flying the colors of other nations had gone on for centuries and had been practiced even by American ships as far back as the colonial era, but it was always a questionable practice. The fine line of "legality" rested on the raider dropping its disguise, hauling down the false colors and breaking out their true ensign before initiating an attack. The concept of converting merchant ships into heavily armed and well-manned warships and sending them to sea in WWII was controversial. The British and Americans did it in World Wars I and II with Q-ships, which played the very dangerous game acting as a decoy, looking like lone merchant ships and hoping to lure German U-boats into an attack. The Q-ships cruised along, carrying a buoyant cargo, anticipating an attack and prepared not only to absorb the first torpedo, but also to act confused and in panic, so the U-boat skipper, watching the scene through his periscope, would feel sufficiently confident to surface and finish the stricken ship with the U-boat's deck gun. It was then that the Q-ship dropped its disguise and unleashed the full fury of its hidden weapons on the vulnerable U-boat.

While the Q-ships functioned in an essentially defensive mode and only attacked enemy naval vessels, the disguised raiders of Germany during the world wars were aggressive fleets of powerful warships that wreaked havoc on Allied merchant ships, cargo and passenger, on all the world's oceans. In September 1942, George Duffy's *American Leader* endured a brutal attack by one of these German raiders under the command of the notorious *Kapitän zur See* Hellmuth Max von Ruckteschell, who had been highly decorated for his particularly successful and ruthless cruise in his first raider. He virtually wore that ship out, and in his second command he sought to enhance his reputation with further successes including the sinking of the *American Leader*. Ultimately, von Ruckteschell would be called to account for his brutality, but that did not help the survivors of the attack on the *American Leader*. George Duffy endured a fearful ordeal during the remainder of the war, but was among the fortunate since fewer than half of the *American Leader* crew survived to return home.

The tale of heroism and endurance that George Duffy tells in this book should be an education and inspiration to all who read it. Most inspirational is the fact that during the month he was prisoner aboard the German raider, he was treated well and that paved the way for unexpected friendships that would later develop. Years after the war, he was contacted by one of the officers of the ship in which he had been held prisoner, and this reacquaintance would develop into a warm, life-long friendship. This relationship grew out of the shared experience as past enemies and mutual respect that each individual held for the other. The shared ordeal of warfare would bring fine men from both sides together as close friends, healing the wounds of war.

Few stories of the war and its aftereffects have the power that George Duffy is able to impart through his vivid recollections, his secret journal, and his remarkable sketches that survived the war with him. This volume brings that story to life and creates an important document on the role of the merchant marine in World War II and the sacrifice the merchant mariners made.

PROLOGUE

And some there be, which have no memorial; who are perished, as though they had never been; and are become as though they had never been born.

—Ecclesiasticus 44:9

In the course of the World War II, according to the Web site http://www.usmm.org, an estimated 9,521 American merchant seamen died when their 1,554 ships, 733 of which were over 1,000 gross tons, were lost or damaged. Enemy action caused most of those losses, but marine casualties—collisions with other vessels, accidents, storms, and groundings—involved 79 vessels incurring the deaths of about 478 of the 9,521 total.

The use of approximate figures in the above paragraph may seem odd. The truth is, there is no one, no government agency, no records center, no one at all who knows precisely how many American merchant seamen died in the war. Other than a book under a glass case at the United States Merchant Academy, which is admittedly incomplete, and the newly constructed addition (2003) to the American Merchant Marine Veterans Memorial at San Pedro, California, there is no public display of the names of the merchant mariners who are on their last voyage. The San Pedro Memorial was as accurate as it could be on the date of the dedication. The above-mentioned Web site has been updated as of February 12, 2007.

How did this state of affairs come to be?

First, it must be realized many of the "between the wars era" merchant seamen were unmarried loners—nomads, men without family ties, or with families in Europe. When such a seaman was lost, who was to be notified other than a lady friend is some port? Who wondered, or called, or wrote if perchance he faded from sight? When war broke out the situation was exacerbated. Second, was the practice followed between the wars by many American shipping companies whereby they registered their vessels in foreign countries, Panama in

CAPT. GEORGE W. DUFFY

particular, and manned them with German crews. This was prevalent among the multinational oil companies. I still recall my reaction in 1939, standing on the deck of the school ship *Nantucket*, watching an Esso tanker named *Heinrich von Riedemann*, flying the flag of Panama, moving slowly through Boston harbor. Prior to the outbreak of war in 1939, in anticipation of the conflict, Germany called its seamen home, resulting in the crewless ships being temporarily laid up in American ports. On April 17, 1942, the *Riedemann*, still flying the Panamanian flag, was sunk in the Caribbean by the German U-66. When the tanker went down, who was manning her? Americans! Where else could Esso have recruited her master, mates, engineers, and crew? For the record, her German crew had left her at Baltimore on September 2, 1939, the day before hostilities commenced in Europe. Seven days after her sinking, much further south in the Atlantic Ocean, the German commerce raider *Michel*, using her torpedo boat, attacked and sank the five-year-old *Connecticut* operated by The Texas Company (Texaco), also registered in Panama. Incredibly, her entire crew, including a sixteen-man United States Navy gun crew, were Americans! The twenty-seven American merchant seamen who were killed presumably were not on record with any branch of the United States government.

The third reason why seamen have disappeared from the records is the matter of the shipping articles, the articles of agreement Between the Ship's Master and Seamen In the Merchant Service of the United States. This contract applies to foreign voyages only, and is administered by a shipping commissioner. It becomes a solid, witnessed record of the ship's complement. If the planned voyage is coastwise, i.e., between United States ports, a simpler agreement is utilized, and sometimes ignored, allowing the possibility of no one knowing exactly who is on board. As these agreements are generally not entered into until the vessel is ready to sail, although the crew is aboard and working, opportunity for confusion could exist. Thus it was with the SS *E. A. Bryan* and the SS *Quinault Victory*. On July 17, 1944, while loading ammunition in Port Chicago CA, the *Bryan* exploded, taking the Victory ship with her. Every person on board both vessels was killed, forty-four in the *E. A. Bryan* and sixty-two in the *Quinault Victory*. (These numbers include U.S. Navy Armed Guard personnel.) Generally, a Liberty ship (the *Bryan* was of that class) would be manned by thirty-nine to forty-five or so officers and unlicensed personnel. A Victory ship would carry as many as fifty-two to fifty-six men. So, were the two ships short-handed? The *Quinault Victory*, fresh out of her builder's yard, arrived at Port Chicago only a few hours before the explosion. Her casualty list shows what appears to be a complete Deck Department: master, four officers, and twelve seamen. The Engine Department consisted of a chief engineer, six assistant engineers, but only two oilers and two wipers where there should have been a dozen or more unlicensed men. The Steward's Department is most interesting, consisting of only the chief steward and five messmen. No cooks or room stewards. As for the *Bryan*, other than her master who was ashore, she had no third officer, second assistant engineer, chief steward, and was missing several unlicensed engine room crew. Were those empty billets actually filled by unsigned and thus unknown seamen? How good were records maintained by the unions who were filling the shipping companies' orders for personnel? And if a homeless seaman simply disappeared, who really cared or counted?

This brings up the subject of vessels sunk with all hands. In World War II, the United States suffered the loss of forty-five vessels and their *entire crews* totaling 1,788 seamen. With the number of lost crew in parenthesis—first number is merchant crew, second number is other persons on board, e.g., Navy Armed Guard, troops, and passengers—they were

Albert F. Paul (8-0)
Arthur R. Middleton (44-36)
Astral (37-0)
Azalea City (38-0)
Charles Henderson (39-13)
Coamo (133-53)
Cynthia Olson (33-2)
E. A. Bryan (31-13)
Edward B. Dudley (41-27)
Esso Williamsburg (42-18)
Frances Salman (28-0)
Harry Luckenbach (53-26)
James McKay (46-25)
James Sprunt (46-28)
John Burke (46-28)
John Harvey (38-28)
John Morgan (42-25)
John Winthrop (39-15)
L. J. Drake (35-6)
Lake Oswaya (30-9)
La Salle (40-17)
Lewis L. Dyche (41-30)
Louise Lykes (50-34)
Louisiana (41-8)

Major Wheeler (35-0)
Margaret (29-0)
Mariana (35-0)
Mary Luckenbach (41-24)
Meriwether Lewis (44-28)
Muskogee (34-0)
Norlavore (28-0)
Norvana (29-0)
Paul Hamilton (47-533)
Quinault Victory (36-26)
Rawleigh Warner (33-0)
Robert Gray (39-23)
Robin Goodfellow (41-19)
Samuel Heintzelman (42-19)
Suffolk (37-6)
Sumner I. Kimball (39-24)
Sun Oil (43-16)
Tillie Lykes (28-4)
West Ivis (35-9)
West Portal (40-12)
Wichita (40-10)

In addition, the Esso tanker *C. J. Barkdull*, flying the Panamanian flag, with a thirty-eight man American crew, plus twenty U.S. Navy gunners, on December 13, 1942, fell behind convoy UGS.3s and was never seen again. This brought the total losses to forty-six ships and 1,826 merchant mariner casualties.

There were, at one point, a few very lucky people aboard some of those ships. When the *Charles Henderson*'s cargo of munitions blew up in Bari, Italy, on April 29, 1945, her chief engineer was ashore. The captain of the *E. A. Bryan*, as was pointed out, also had left his ship before the cargo exploded, and a cadet and an able seaman from the *John Harvey* had gone into Bari on December 2, 1943, when that ship fell victim to a German air raid. Three members of the *Arthur Middleton*'s Armed Guard detachment, who happened to be on the stern of the vessel when she was torpedoed by the U-173 three miles off Oran, Algeria, on January 1, 1943, were the Liberty's only survivors. Similarly, three other gunners were the only survivors of the *John Morgan* when it collided with the Texaco tanker *Montana* off the Chesapeake Capes on June 1, 1943.

Also deserving to be recognized in this treatise are four sole survivors of the following vessels:

Atlantic Sun (46-19), Ordinary Seaman William Golobich*
Puerto Rican (39-25), Fireman/Watertender August Wallenhaupt
Steel Age (34-0), Able Seaman Jose Muniz*
W. D. Anderson (35-0), Unidentified.

* These men were taken prisoner by the German U-boats which sank their ships.

In addition were the following:

R. P. Resor (40-8), Able Seaman John J. Forsdal and Coxswain Daniel Hey, USN, being the only survivors.
Jacksonville (48-30), Fireman/Watertender Frank B. Hodges and an unidentified navy gunner, the only survivors.

Several ships sunk by the German raiders *Michel* and *Stier* were for varying lengths of time considered to have been lost with all hands. They were the author's *American Leader* (24-6), the previously mentioned *Connecticut* (27-11), the *Sawokla* (16-4), and the *Stanvac Calcutta* (16-0). Survivors were taken prisoner aboard the raiders and ultimately handed over to the Japanese, who eventually allowed them to write brief letters which were broadcast by a Tokyo radio station. One exception was a survivor of the *Stanvac Calcutta* who was taken to Europe by a German blockade runner and whose letter to Socony-Vacuum alerted the company to the fact that their ship was not lost with all hands. Two Japanese raiders, the *Hokoku Maru* and the *Aikoku Maru*, sank the *Malama* (2-0) and the *Vincent* (2-0), taking the crews of both ships prisoners. Three other ships were destroyed in the Far East: the *Admiral Y. S. Williams* (5-0), the *Capillo* (5-0), and the *President Harrison* (16-0). It is not known if any of the survivors of all five were classified as missing in action. What is known is the *Harrison's* unlicensed crew members lived free in Shanghai for ten months before being incarcerated. Funds for their living expenses were provided by the Swiss consulate, so it is probably safe to say word of their situation soon reached their next of kin.

Later in this book, the question of wages for seamen whose ships were sunk is discussed. For the moment, however, it should be pointed out, a great disparity existed for a considerable length of time between the treatment of shipwrecked American seamen in American-flagged vessels and American seamen in flag-of-convenience vessels. All in all, we in the ships knew little or nothing of the carnage being wreaked on the high seas and in our coastal waters. Nor were we aware of the shaky legal situation in which we were placed by the United States government's confiscation of the American merchant marine. Had we known the facts, why would we ever had gone to sea, particularly in 1942 and 1943? But the merchant marine was our calling and our livelihood. It was all we knew. And if nothing else, we were patriots.

CHAPTER ONE

Massachusetts Nautical School

In 1891, the Massachusetts legislature in its wisdom, upon observing that the State of Massachusetts was educating young men at the college level for careers in agriculture and the textile industry, established the Massachusetts Nautical Training School. Prior to that the United States Congress had in 1877 passed an act encouraging certain states, Massachusetts included, to create such maritime educational institutions. In spite of the law's authorization of the secretary of the navy to furnish the state with a suitable training vessel and to maintain it, the legislature dithered for fourteen years before acting.

The first class of cadets entered the school in April 1893, and a second class followed in October. Henceforth, that system stood in place until the early days of World War II. The course of education was two years. The campus was a ship, at first the USS *Enterprise*, then in 1909 the 1876-built USS *Ranger*. This latter vessel was a three-masted barque. A barque carries square sails on the fore and main masts and fore-and-aft sails on the mizzen mast. In today's vernacular, she'd be called a "tall ship." For propulsion in light winds and for maneuvering in and out of port, the *Ranger* was equipped with a double expansion, horizontal engine powered by steam from four coal-burning Scotch boilers. Her hull was Swedish iron; displacement 1,291 tons; length 202 feet; beam 32 feet; draft 15 feet. From the waterline to the top of the main mast measured 117 feet. In March 1913 the Massachusetts General Court changed the school's name to Massachusetts Nautical School, and in 1918 the navy renamed the ship *Rockport* and later *Nantucket*. May to September was spent at sea enabling the cadets who aspired to deck officer positions to learn practical seamanship and navigation, while those who sought out engineering careers were engaged in shoveling coal, making steam, oiling bearings, and whatever else goes on below decks. Prior to 1940, a typical training cruise would encompass Plymouth and London in England, Antwerp in Belgium, Le Havre in France, Lisbon in Portugal, the Azores when eastbound and Madeira westbound, plus several U.S. ports.

In the winter, the ship would be berthed in Boston. A portion of the rigging would be removed and a tarpaper-covered prefab "shack" erected over the weather deck. Here, ensconced in tablet armchairs, the cadets did their evening studies. Depending on the nearby shore facilities, particularly if the ship was tied up in Charlestown Navy Yard and space was available, mornings were spent in the classroom environment. Practical work in the yard's sail loft and the ship's engine room occupied the afternoons. There was little spare time and no extracurricular activities, although in some years a basketball team had been organized, and on the summer training cruises baseball was played on an informal basis wherever a diamond could be located and an opponent found. Physical fitness was maintained in the winter by means of running in formation, carrying rifles, around the navy yard before breakfast. There was also swimming at the Charlestown YMCA pool, and one of the eight-oared cutters was always ready to challenge the cadets' backs and arms. At sea in the summer, the strenuous activity of setting sails, trimming sails, furling sails, hoisting boats, coaling ship, rowing liberty party cutters, scrubbing decks, and all the numerous tasks involved in getting from one port to the next were more than enough to keep the 120 cadets in tip-top shape.

In a cadet's first year, he was classified as a nautical cadet, and his course of instruction covered all aspects of shipboard management: mathematics and physics, practical seamanship, practical engineering, electricity, and navigation. There were no language courses, no history, no English. What one had learned of those subjects in high school had to suffice. After twelve months, he opted for his major—marine engineering or seamanship and navigation. Graduation was the qualification to be examined for license as third assistant engineer for steam vessels of any horsepower or third mate for steam and motor vessels of any tonnage upon oceans. Pretty heady stuff for a nineteen or twenty year old young man!

All of that was accomplished for the total cost of $300 for the first year and $150 for the second! Uniforms, room, board, and tuition.

To graduate from Newburyport (Massachusetts) High School (NHS) in 1939, as I and 141 other young men and women did, was not an exalting experience. The future was bleak because jobs were few and money was scarce. Hope and ambitions for most of us were exercises in frustration. As an example, of those 142, merely 43 received diplomas indicating they had completed the Latin or scientific courses of study, the preparatory tracks for higher education. Imagine that! Only 30 percent were thinking of going to college, and I am sure to most of them those thoughts were in the form of dreams. As to exactly how many were enrolled in an institution of higher learning the following September, I cannot tell you, but a quick run through the 1939 year book indicates it was not more than the proverbial baker's dozen. There just wasn't any money. Families tended to be large and wages, if indeed the breadwinner had steady employment, were low. Scholarships, compared to the plethora of funds available to a high school graduate today, were practically nonexistent. What there was tended to be discriminatory. Furthermore, there were no guidance counselors, nor any particular advice from the teachers. I had done well at the Immaculate Conception (IC) grammar school in Newburyport, winning one of the two boys' prizes at graduation. As a result, somebody steered me into the scientific course at NHS. Was it the sister superior? Or my parents? I don't remember. What I do recall is we had sixty-three youngsters in that IC class. Four years later, only two of us completed the scientific course, and eight received Latin course diplomas. The climate of opinion in those days certainly did not encourage any education beyond reading, writing, and 'rithmatic. Frankly, I literally stumbled through my four years at NHS. I didn't receive many As, but no Fs. Some teachers discriminated along social and religious lines when report cards were issued, and I have long harbored the resentment of imagining I was an occasional victim. Nevertheless, I was well taught. What Ed Wilder, "Pa" Chittenden, Ed Spaulding, and, in particular, my English teacher Pauline Watts expounded stuck with me.

As I progressed through those years, three facts became crystal clear. One, I had to get out of Newburyport. Two, I had to go to college. Three, I had no money. The United States Naval Academy and the United States Coast Guard Academy were obvious solutions. On my own, I sought out Congressman George J. Bates seeking an appointment to either institution, and he started me through the process. Meanwhile, an alternative choice came over the horizon. One of my father's sisters, then living and working in Haverhill, Massachusetts, had a business associate whose son Francis J. Gallison graduated from the Massachusetts Nautical School in 1937. "Why don't you consider that school?" she suggested. At about the same time, the girls' physical education teacher at NHS, Anna Dyer, married Harold Sholes of nearby Rowley, Massachusetts, who was a nautical school graduate of 1936, and they moved into an apartment on High Street, just a few houses from the Duffy residence. Now I had advice. I applied to the nautical school and was conditionally accepted pending the result of a physical examination and my ranking in a comprehensive written test. Of the 130 (more or less) young men who took the test, I ranked tenth! NHS had done the job! What about the service academies? I fell by the wayside early on, flunking the government's medical exam. Inexplicably, the same doctor, several months later, passed me when as a cadet in the nautical school I was being enlisted in the United States Naval Reserve. Money remained a big obstacle. The nautical school wanted $300. Fortunately, another of my aunts was married to a successful industrialist named Colley B. Court, who was a philanthropist as well. He staked me for both years. Less than six months after graduation, I paid him off.

Louis Pasteur is quoted as saying, "In the fields of observation, chance favors only the mind that is prepared." It goes beyond "fields of observation" as this tale of my youth relates.

None of my ancestors had gone to sea for a living. They were Irish, although I was in my early forties when I became aware of the full facts. Edward Lanen and Mary Bray, my maternal great-grandparents, both from Kilkenny, married in 1847, and by 1855, the year they came to America, four children had been born to them. The youngest, George, born in 1854, was to become my grandfather. Of my paternal great-grandparents, Peter Duffy and Bridget Janings of County Mayo, I know little. They did have a son, Michael Duffy, born in 1855, a year later than George Lanen. He, at an early age, emigrated, but to Hawick, Scotland, to work in its woolen mills. There he met Mary Hanagan, the daughter of Patrick Hanagan and Mary Melvin, also of Mayo. They married in 1882 and ultimately became my paternal grandparents. Before coming to America they had two children, Patrick and Katherine. Patrick died in 1934, his obituary gave his birthplace as Scotland, so I at the age of twelve assumed I was of Scottish descent. No one told me anything different until one of my father's sisters died in 1983. I inherited her trove of family papers and artifacts, and learned I was 100 percent Irish!

In May 1886, the small Michael Duffy family arrived at Boston in the SS *Kansas*, settling in South Groveland, Massachusetts where the Lanen family had resided for twenty-six years after having previously lived five years in Lawrence, Massachusetts. By the time the Michael Duffys arrived, the Lanen family had added five more children, the youngest of whom was twenty-two. In contrast with George Lanen, I have learned nothing of Michael Duffy's brothers and sisters, if indeed there were any.

There are some small parallels, however. Michael Duffy and Mary Hanagan married in Ireland when Michael was twenty-seven years old. George Lanen was twenty-five when he married Kate Murphy in 1879. They had no children until 1887 when their daughter, also named Kate, was born. Unfortunately, both mother and baby died at the child's birth. A little over a year later George married Sarah Marrs Murphy, who was the widow of Kate's brother Henry. Their first child, Grace, was born on May 3, 1889. On December 5, 1890, they became parents of twin daughters, Alice and Florence. Thirty-two years later, I became Alice's first born. In February 1892, Michael and Mary Duffy's fourth child, George was born, and he was destined to be my father.

———

Author's mother at right, with her twin sister. Circa 1910.

South Groveland's attraction was its shoe shops and woolen mills, and the oldest three of the Lanen boys worked in the latter industry. Two were weavers, and one is listed as being a "Mill overseer." Their early and long residency in the town must have earned them a great deal of respect and admiration. George Lanen probably began his working life in the mills, but eventually became an entrepreneur, opening a grocery store in the village. A portion of the store was rented by the United States Postal Service as the town's Post Office. The postmaster was Edward Lanen, a little over two years younger than George. Their younger sister Julia, who was almost twenty-two years younger than George, was the store's bookkeeper. In 1892, George purchased a lot of land in the center of South Groveland, called Parker's Corner. He erected a substantial three-story building on the site to which he moved his store and the post office. The top two floors were the living quarters for his wife and three daughters. As of November 2006, the structure remains standing having experienced many transitions, most recently being home to a small cafe.

Alice Lanen attended the area's public schools and graduated from Groveland High School, class of 1910. Of George Duffy's education, nothing is known. His brother Patrick operated a grocery store in nearby Haverhill, and a picture of George as a teenager, working behind the counter, exists. Another picture shows him in a World War 1 United States Army uniform when he served for about two years, much of that in France as a member of an engineering (railway building) detachment.

**George Washington Duffy, author's father,
in United States Army, circa 1918.**

After the war, he returned to South Groveland, but as to what he did for a living there is no record. My birth certificate shows him to be a chauffeur. There is a possibility he was a police officer in Boston, and I know we resided for a time in the Dorchester section of that city.

Nevertheless, I was born in Haverhill on May 12, 1922, as were Eleanor (November 17, 1923), Robert (October 28, 1924), and Richard (May 12, 1927). By the time Natalie (June 28, 1929) came along, we were living in Newburyport, Massachusetts, where our father had found employment as a butcher in one of the many meat markets dotting the downtown shopping section. Mothers, for the most part in those days, were homemakers, and with five of us spread over a seven years span, ours must have had her hands full. We all attended the Immaculate Conception Parish elementary school, and that pinpoints the date of our move to Newburyport at 1929 because I was in the second grade, having begun school at St. James in Haverhill at age five.

Author, at an early age and mother circa Summer 1922.

Author's mother with five children, circa 1934. Richard is standing,
Author is at left, then Eleanor, Natalie, and Robert.

Author at time of graduation from Newburyport High School, 1939.

On Monday, October 16, 1939, I and thirty other seventeen and eighteen year old youths gathered at the Main Gate of the Charlestown Navy Yard in Boston, and were marched, suitcases in hand, to the *Nantucket*. One passing workman offered what at the time was a curious comment. "You'll be sorry," he said. In our suitcases, we all carried a prescribed number of items from handkerchiefs to pajamas. The latter went home on our first liberty; pajamas, we were told, were worn only by upperclassmen. This was probably the least of the restrictions and indignities imposed upon us in the "goldfish bowl" life we were to live for the next year. It is not the purpose of this narration to go into details of our daily existence aboard the ship in that winter of 1939-40. Nothing of my personal experiences remains in writing. As we went home three out of every four weekends, there was no need for correspondence. Of note are the facts that the first classmen graduated in early April, with governor Leverett Saltonstall presiding over the ceremony, and a new class came aboard. Concerning the summer cruises, however, we were required to maintain a daily journal. This, I did and will present it herewith.

First of all, the *Nantucket* was commanded by Captain Clarence Arthur Abele, United States Navy (Retired), a graduate of the United States Naval Academy, class of 1898. He was also the superintendent of the Massachusetts Nautical School (MNS). The other officers in the ship (all graduates of the school with their class years in parenthesis) were Executive Officer Robert M. Gray, (1912);

Chief Engineer Erwin R. Kelley (1909); Navigator John W. Thompson (1912); Watch Officer Richard T. Rounds (1926); Watch Officer James T. Hodgson (1934); First Assistant Engineer John R. Hickey (1934). In addition, carrying the title surgeon was J. W. Mooney, MD, a nongraduate. Prior to departure, the first, second, and third classmen were divided into two divisions and granted two weeks of liberty each. My division returned on sailing day.

By way of explanation, what I have done with the original journal is to present it *verbatim*, warts and all, errors in grammar and spelling, as written, and presented in italics. Comments and explanations are inserted, using standard typeface, immediately following the subject journal entry.

CHAPTER TWO

1940 Cruise (Part I)

May

11 Saturday—Returned aboard at 0740. Preparing ship for sea all morning. Sailed from Pier 1, Charlestown Navy Yard at 1430. Received salutes from most of the ships in the harbor. Arrived off Boston Lightship at 1700. Swinging ship and calibrating compass until 1900. Lifeboat crew took compass adjuster on board the AB 64. Strong wind decreasing during evening, temperatures dropping.

12 Sunday—My 18th birthday! Ship's position approximately 5 miles SE of Thacher's Island off Cape Ann. Steaming at an average of 5 knots on various courses, waiting for daybreak. Marblehead Light, Baker's Island Light, and Thacher's Island Light all visible. Full ahead at 0800, coming down Eastern Point. Arrived at Gloucester breakwater at 0945. Dropped anchor at 1000. Church services on board at 1100. Starboard watch liberty.

Nantucket **at anchor, Gloucester harbor, May 1940.**

The cadet body was divided into two watches, port and starboard. At sea we stood alternate four-hour watches, except for the time between 1600 (4 PM) and 2000 (8 PM) when the watches were 1600 to 1800 (6 PM) and 1800 to 2000. This resulted in an equitable sharing of the night watches. One night, for example, the port watch would have the 0000 to 0400. The next night it would be the starboard watch's turn. Shore leave (liberty) was also taken on alternate days. I was in the port watch for this cruise.

13 Monday—Reveille at 0500!! Drills all morning, including sail drills. Went sailing in one of the whaleboats during afternoon. Liberty at 1630. Nothing much here other than fishing fleet and that smells. Liberty expired at 2000 on dock. Temperature in 50s with light easterly wind.

Lighthouse –
10 pound Island
Gloucester Harbor.

Author's work.

In the cutters, the oarsmen sat in pairs along the centerline, whereas in the whaleboats each man sat a full boat's width away from the side where the blade met the water. The cutters were steered by conventional rudders and tillers, the whaleboats by steering oars. Both whaleboats were the lifesaving boats at sea, rigged to be quickly manned and dropped into the water. The starboard boat doubled as the captain's gig in port. When he used it to go ashore, a standard rudder was shipped. This was fitted with a polished bronze yoke to which lanyards with fancy grips were attached, allowing him to steer in grace and comfort. Also, when he was aboard, a blanket was spread in the "stern sheets" where he sat, white if the uniform of the day was white, navy blue if that was the uniform. These blankets were trimmed on all four sides by four stripes of black or white, in contrasting colors. When coming alongside a pier or returning to the *Nantucket*, in the cutters the order "toss oars" was given by the coxswain. Each oarsman smartly elevated his oar to a vertical position in front of him. The locals and the tourists loved it, and we were the subject of hundreds of snapshots. In the gig, no chance was taken that Capt. Abele might be spattered with water dripping off the oars. Here, they were attached to the boat by lanyards, and at the order "trail oars," we deftly flipped the oars overboard where they docilely snuggled alongside.

14 Tuesday—First complete abandon ship drill. Sail drills following. Third and fourth classes given diphtheria inoculations at noon. Starboard watch liberty at 1630. Temperature and wind—same.

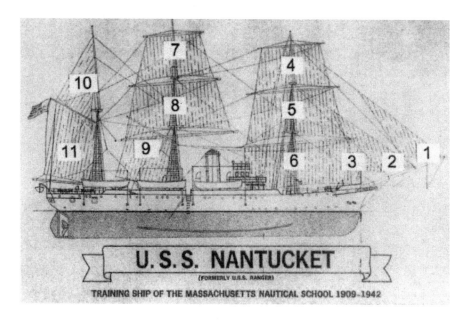

1. **Flying Jib**
2. **Jib**
3. **Fore topmast staysail**
4. **Fore topgallant sail**
5. **Fore topsail**
6. **Fore sail**
7. **Main topgallant sail**

8. **Main topsail**
9. **Trysail**
10. **Mizzen gaff topsail**
11. **Spanker**

15 Wednesday—Regular quarters and drills at 0915. Sailing in a whaleboat with Mr. Thompson in forenoon. Liberty at 1630. Strong southeasterly breeze.

Quarters was the word for the morning formation when the day's work and other assignments were meted out.

16 Thursday—Scraping and holystoning spar deck all morning. Thick fog lifted at about 0700. Still holystoning. On detail in cutter's crew for remainder of day—five of crew in sick bay.

**Cadets holystoning the quarterdeck. Author is standing at left.
Man in center is fourth classman Israel Narkin and
the man at right is his classmate, Robert Pyatt.**

The teak weather deck took quite a beating during the winter months and really didn't get a good cleaning. The holystoning technique called for sand, water, and firebricks. The lower class cadets—third and fourth classmen who were selected—got down on their knees and, using the wet sand as an abrasive, vigorously scrubbed away with the fire bricks. It was a tedious, backbreaking process, but it did the job.

17 Friday—Preparing for sea in morning. Howell and I stowed chain as we weighed anchor at 1100. Sighted a destroyer, most likely American. Holystoning. Sighted a Belgian freighter off Boston at 1500. She either did not see us or did not wish to answer our signals. Completely blanketed by fog until 1800 when Cape Cod was sighted. Passed buoy PH2 east of Provincetown. Fog and rain.

The anchor chains were stowed in small compartments known as chain lockers. As the chain was hauled in by the steam-powered windlass, it dropped into the locker where two cadets armed with long-handled hooks would flake it out in layers.

18 Saturday—United Fruit steamer Maravee passed at 0300. At least two-thirds of the cadets are seasick this morning. The gun deck is a mess, with an attempt being made at a field day. Sea-water is pouring in through the hawseholes.—is very sick. I'm spreading Mess 6 for him. Tanker (unknown) passed close by at 1300. They signaled "Pleasant voyage". Visibility good, temperature rising. Course WSW.

The gun deck was the accommodation deck where we lived when off watch. When originally built for the navy, guns, firing through square openings in the hull, were mounted here. The openings, called gun ports, could be closed and made watertight. Eventually, they were permanently sealed.

Hawseholes are the holes in the hull through which the anchor chains ran. Generally, at sea they were plugged. Why they weren't in this instance is not understandable.

Lower classmen brought the food from the galley to the dining tables.—was assigned to number 6 table, but as he could not perform his duties, one of his classmates had to volunteer in his place.

19 Sunday—We are now on the edge of the Gulf Stream. The sea is smooth and the temperature is 80°. Light fog in morning, weather otherwise ideal. Spread headsails, trysail, and spanker at 1900. Flying jib ripped immediately upon being set. Steaming under three boilers. Average speed 8.5 knots.

20 Monday—Nearing Chesapeake Lightship. Sighted passenger vessel at 0700. Thick fog began setting in at 1100. Several ships are sighted as fog lifts. Furled sail at noon. Chesapeake Lightship was finally sighted at 1245. In the vicinity is the aircraft carrier

Ranger and several destroyers. Fog settled heavily at 1300. Engine was stopped. Finally proceeding up Chesapeake Bay in late afternoon. Saw the Cape Charles streamlined ferry. Dropped anchor off Potomac River at 2130.

21 Tuesday—Port watch on deck at 0300. Weighed anchor at 0600. Moving up Potomac, a very wide river at this point. As we get further up, we can make out large mansions and plantations on the banks. A little river traffic, mainly tugs and tows. Passed Mt. Vernon at 1700. I played Taps while eight cadet guards with fixed bayonets stood at attention. Washington monument could be seen in the distance. Tied up at the Washington Navy Yard at 1830. Directly astern of us is the President's yacht, Potomac, followed by the Maritime Commission's American Seaman. This is the Anacostia River, very narrow, dirty, and possessing a bad stench. The Navy Yard is mainly an experimental station. On the dock right aside of us is the Deep Sea Diving School and next to that is the model testing basin. As far as ships go, though, this could be called a Government Yacht Club. I can't see a single fighting ship. Quite a few cadets sleeping on deck. Rain about 3 AM.

22 Wednesday—Whites are uniform here. Today is Maritime Day—dress ship. Army and Navy airfields across the river from us; the planes are flying low overhead all day. The United States Navy band has been practicing on the drill field. There is no work at all to be done on board, but we still don't get early liberty. Liberty at last at 1330. This is a great city, there is really too much to see. Liberty expired at 2200. Temperature 90°, light rain during evening.

23 Thursday—Life in port certainly is great. Turn-to after reveille and before quarters—the remainder of the day is to our selves. Race boat crew raced a crew from the American Seaman. The seamen in their own boat won by a slight margin. Starboard watch liberty. Temperature still in 80s. Light rain in evening.

24 Friday—Regular port routine. Sideboys standing by all morning. Captain is having a party on board sometime this afternoon. Port watch liberty at 1330. Weather warm with slight rain at various times. American Seaman sailed.

When important visitors came aboard, it was the custom to station four cadets on deck at the gangway access. They stood in pairs and saluted as the guests passed between them. On departure, the same courtesy was followed. These cadets were commonly known as sideboys.

25 Saturday—Field day in morning. U.S. submarine Sea Dragon (SS 194) arrived. Starboard watch liberty. Weather overcast with light showers.

**USS *Seadragon* (SS 194) arriving at Washington Navy Yard,
May 25, 1940.**

Author in Washington, D.C., May 1940.

Field days generally were held on Saturdays or following taking on coal. It was a general cleanup of the ship, with brass polishing, taking up slack lines, and coiling others, essentially preparing for Sunday's captain's inspection.

26 Sunday—Catholic church party at 0530. Captain's inspection at 0930. Port watch liberty party left ship at 1030. Very warm, still overcast. Potomac and Cuyahoga sailed at 2250.

27 Monday—Regular morning turn-to and quarters. Guards and sideboys are standing by. The Potomac, carrying President Roosevelt is expected back in yard this noon. Potomac docked at 1150. Sideboys and guards on Nantucket quarter deck and cadets in the waist. The ship, carrying the President came up the Anacostia, swung around us and docked. Starboard watch liberty. Weather overcast, raining at dusk.

As I was the bugler, I was in perfect position to see Roosevelt seated in the fantail of the yacht. I gave the usual signal for attention and then sounded three flourishes.

28 Tuesday—Left Washington Navy Yard at 0808. A little difficulty experienced in getting away. The yard tug Choptank was assisting us, taking a stern line. I don't exactly remember, but I think we were 1/3 astern, with the tug going ahead when the hawser, a new one, parted. This left us away from the dock in the very narrow channel. The ship was shuttled back and forth, finally getting away. Steaming under three boilers. Ceremonies held again as we passed Mt. Vernon. A fine day, the best since we were last at sea. Dropped anchor in Chesapeake Bay at 2130.

As bugler, my station was on the bridge wing if it was necessary to render honors to a passing warship. I recall the incident with the hawser, and could see it coming. Before snapping, the rope actually began to smoke, and then popped.

29 Wednesday—0000-0400 orderly with Christophers O.O.W. Weighed anchor at 0600. Moving down Chesapeake Bay during morning. Arrived off Pt. Comfort at 1130. Dropped anchor in Hampton Roads at 1215. Weighed anchor at 1330. Moving in to Naval Operating Base. Finally docked at about 1500. In here are the battleships New York, Texas, and Arkansas, the tanker Platte, cruiser Wichita, and the cargo carrier Yukon, several other supply ships, and about a dozen destroyers. Port watch liberty at 1700 in dress whites. The city of Norfolk is about 8 miles from the base.

The USS *Arkansas* (BB 33), USS *New York* (BB 34), and USS *Texas* (BB 35) were old vessels, having been commissioned between 1914 and 1915. The USS *Platte*

(AO 24) and the USS *Wichita* (CA 45) were brand new, with commissioning dates in 1939. The USS *Yukon* (AF 9) was also an old-timer, going back to 1921.

Upperclass deckmen were detailed as cadet officers of the watch (OOW) around the clock. Assigned with each OOW was an assistant, usually an upperclassman whose title was quartermaster (QM), and an underclassman who, with the title of orderly, was the OOW's gofer.

30 Tuesday—Raining most of day. Starboard watch liberty at 1000. I went aboard the battleship New York in the afternoon. Arkansas sailed at 1100, Texas and New York at 1500. Prepared ship for coaling during evening.

31 Wednesday—Coaling ship all morning. Knock off for coffee at 0930. Took on a deck load of about 40 tons. Cleaned up ship in afternoon. Port watch liberty at 1745. Returned at 2210, 10 minutes late. Met two officers from the British freighter Tri-Worlace and, as a result, missed the trolley.

The hard life in the *Nantucket* came as a surprise, I am sure, to most of us. There was nothing, however, more unanticipated than the terrible ordeal of coaling ship. Soft coal was burned in the four Scotch boilers, and it arrived in bulk by barge or rail car, seventy to a hundred tons of it. Storage compartments adjacent to the fire room were called bunkers. Above the bunkers, circular bronze plates fitted to the gun deck and the spar deck accommodated portable cast iron pipes of the same diameter as the plates. The coal was dropped down these pipes to the bunkers.

The process began by pairing up third and fourth classmen according to height. Upperclassmen with shovels filled canvas bags with seventy or eighty pounds of coal which each pair of underclassmen swung between them. The queue of struggling cadets lurched up the gangway, thence to the open holes where the bags were deftly flipped and their contents, for the most part, delivered. Then it was back down the other gangway for the next bag. Upperclassmen, manning brooms, tried to keep the decks clean, but the fine, dusty black stuff spread throughout the ship. Eventually, as the level of coal rose in the bunkers, cadets were dropped in to direct the incoming "black diamonds" into the corners. It was no place for the claustrophobic. When the bunkers were chock-a-block full, the canvas bags were filled and stowed on deck, along with whatever number of burlap bags that were needed to hold the last sweepings. At the end, we were black from head to toe. First, though, the ship had to be washed down. On one occasion I recall we sailed as soon as the last bag had come aboard. I took my place on the bridge, bugle in hand. As luck would have it, we met an incoming destroyer, and I would have to blow the call to attention. Suddenly, Captain Abele, looking to see if I was at my post, was aghast at my appearance. He turned to whoever was the officer of the watch and snapped, "Get him out of sight!"

I probably earned a few demerits for that ten-minute tardiness, which would have to be worked off doing extra duty on weekends.

June

1 Saturday—Prepared ship for sea after quarters. Sailed at 1100. Bad current, some difficulty in getting out. No unusual occurrences. Passed Chesapeake lightship at 1600. All plain sail set at 1630—engine uncoupled.

The propeller shaft had a mechanical coupling device located about 25 feet forward of the propeller. When we set sails and shut down the engine this coupling was opened allowing the propeller to rotate freely and reduce drag.

2 Sunday—Captain's inspection at 1000. Commissioner Queen accompanying. Church service on quarter deck at 1100. Speed about 1.5 knots. Becalmed at noon. Several whales and many porpoises being seen. Furled all sail, port watch on deck, at 1425. All furled at 1530. Steaming under two boilers. Sea calm, weather clear.

Commissioner Queen was Walter K. Queen, one of the three commissioners appointed by the governor to oversee the school's affairs. I have no record of where he joined us, but it was probably in Washington.

3 Monday—Quarters at 0915 followed by studies for all classes. Man overboard and fire drills. The sea is extremely smooth, yet there are still some cases of seasickness. All plain sail set at 1700. Starboard watch on deck. Took in spanker and trysail at 1900. Fog early this morning, light rain in evening. Temperature about 85°. Course 115° p.s.c. (per standard compass). 0800 position, 36° 01' 00" N, 69° 32' 00" W.

4 Tuesday—Port watch on deck furling all sail at 0430. Put practically entire deck load of coal into bunkers. Quarters at 0915, followed by collision and man overboard drills. Headsails, trysail, and spanker set. Studies at 1000. 0800 position, 35° 50' 00" N, 68° 13' 00" W.

The *Nantucket* carried a large (estimated fifteen-by-fifteen-feet) piece of canvas fitted with ropes and chains called a "collision mat." If the ship's hull became broached, the scheme was to lower this mat over the damaged area and at least stanch the inward flow of water. In retrospect it was rather silly, but we practiced, practiced, practiced.

5 Wednesday—Proceeding under two boilers with headsails, trysail, and spanker set. Quarters at 0915 followed by abandon ship and man overboard drills. Both watches set all sail. Uncoupled at 1015. Lookout sighted a passenger vessel, presumably of Canadian National Line, out of Bermuda. We are now in the (-) 4 time zone. Scrub hammocks in afternoon. Weather clear, getting warmer. 1000 position, 35° 20.9' N, 66° 24.9 W.

6 Thursday—Sighted a cruiser, presumably British, running without lights, at 0430. She was very difficult to make out, but I guess we got a good looking over from her. Quarters at 0915 followed by fire drill. Carrying all plain sail except flying jib and fore topmast staysail. Studies at 1000. Weather clear and warm, sea choppy. Light rain in morning. 0800 position, 34° 30' 30" N, 63° 57' 30" W.

7 Friday—Quarters at 0915, followed by collision drill. Still sailing, average speed 6.5 knots. 0800 position, 33° 31' 30" N, 62° 22' 00" W.

8 Saturday—Field day all morning. I'm on new detail as lookout. Sighted a ship, most likely on South African run, headed north at 1240. Remainder of day to ourselves. Took in topgallant sails, trysail, and spanker at 2000. 1200 position, 32° 28' 30" N, 57° 13' 30" W.

All the fixed tasks in the ship were called "details." Lookouts, helmsmen, lifeboat crew, coal passers, mess cooks, sweepers, and so on, were detailed on a weekly basis. This, in particular, accounted for the frequency of drills in order to acquaint each cadet with every job.

9 Sunday—Captain's inspection at 1000. Church service at 1100. All sail set again. Nothing doing all day. 1200 position, 28° 42' N, 54° 40' W.

10 Monday—Furled all sail at 0915. No quarters. Studies at 1000. Today is the day the Maritime Commission is supposed to take us over. 0800 position, 27° 28' 30" N, 52° 45' W.

11 Tuesday—Steaming under two boilers, speed 5.5 knots. Man overboard drill at 0900, quarters following. Sea calm, temperature 90°. Studies at 1000. We have been at sea 10 days and out of Boston 1 month. 1200 position 25° 22' 30" N, 53° 41' 30" W.

12 Wednesday—Another hot day. Our latitude being the same as the sun's declination, we are able to see the sun directly overhead at noon. Quarters at 0915, with abandon ship and man overboard drills. Air bedding. Studies at 1000. 1200 position, 23° 27' 30" N, 54° 51' 00" W.

13 Thursday—Fore topsail set at 0700. Headsails, trysail, and spanker still set. Quarters at 0915, followed by fire and man overboard drills. Studies as usual. Carman and I hove the lead (sand bag) during third period. We are still waiting for the trade winds. It doesn't look as though we will get to St. Thomas as scheduled. Course 251° at 1700. We are at least pointed towards the islands. Furled all sail except fore topsail at 2300. 1200 position, 21° 19' N, 56° 15' W.

CHAPTER THREE

Meet Konrad Hoppe

On April 20, 1917, in the city of Magdeburg, Germany, a son was born to Wilhelm and Elizabeth (Seehaus) Hoppe. In later years all Germany would celebrate this day as it was also Adolf Hitler's birth date! Herr Hoppe was a high school teacher of mathematics and physics. Frau Hoppe, before her marriage, also taught school. Languages—French, Italian, and English—were her specialties. In addition to Konrad, there were two younger children, Marianna, born on January 12, 1919, and Hans, born on January 20, 1922. Music occupied an important place in the Hoppe household. Konrad was a cellist, Marianna played the piano, and Hans, the violin. Their parents were their instructors.

During one summer in his early teens, Konrad spent six weeks in Great Britain. The first three weeks were devoted to bicycle touring. For the second half of the visit, he was hosted by an English family, which included a boy of his age. Konrad found the British people to be "quite friendly and open." His companions were also the guests of other families and frequent tennis tournaments were conducted between the German and British youths. Apparently, the English youngsters were most often the winners. Konrad says the British fed the Germans too much food, putting them off their game. The result of this six week sojourn was in Konrad's words, "I came to learn perfect English."

In 1933 Konrad, probably against the wishes of his father who never joined the Nazi party, became a member of the party-sponsored Hitler Jugend. Originally formed in 1922, and then banned a year later, this youth group was resurrected in 1926, but its growth was slow. At the end of 1932, it had just under 108,000 members, compared to over 7,500,000 in 1939. Konrad quickly rose to be the leader of a twenty-member cell. With the innocence of fifteen years, he embraced the Nazi propaganda. "It taught us good things," he said. "The comradeship was very good for us young men." After about two years in the organization, he was approached by a *Kriegsmarine* recruiter. His school record showed him "skipping" the eleventh grade by being promoted directly from the tenth to twelfth, and his proven leadership qualities in the   made him a prime naval officer prospect. Following a comprehensive examination in Berlin encompassing teaching ability, manual dexterity, and physical coordination, on April 4, 1935, not yet into his eighteenth year, Konrad Hoppe was selected to join crew 35. (Note that the Kriegsmarine designates a class by the year in which it is formed, not the year in which it graduates, as is the case in the United States.)

Crew 35, numbering 450 officer candidates, was taken to a newly constructed naval training station at Stralsund, a small town on the Baltic Sea in northeast Germany. Three months of basic training was accomplished here. Next came vessel assignments, during which Hoppe spent six months away from Stralsund in the old (1902-built) 28 cm-gunned (eleven inch) battleship *Schlesian*. Upon return to Stralsund, he spent two months' classroom time in the cruiser *Emden* studying artillery, torpedoes, and radio communications. At this juncture, the surviving members of crew 35 received their commissions as *Fähnrich zur See* (midshipman), and moved to Marineschule (naval academy) Mürwik at Flensburg near the Danish border on the east coast of the Jutland peninsula. This establishment was dubbed the Red Castle. Accommodations there were a step upward, with only five men to a room compared to the open barracks of Stralsund. Frequent liberty excursions took the midshipmen into Denmark where the locals shouted, "Guard your daughters!" upon the appearance of the young Germans. Considerable leisure time was also devoted to small boat sailing. In all, crew 35 spent twelve months at Mürwik.

Next came another stretch of sea duty. Hoppe was detailed to the training cruiser *Königsburg* at Kiel, from whence a six month cruise, including calls at several Norwegian ports, was made. Upon return to Kiel, he received his career assignment, and was sent back to Stralsund to a new naval aviation school. Hermann Wilhelm Göring had formulated a decree whereby all aircraft and their pilots were to be members of the *Luftwaffe*. Thus, this school was devoted to the training of flying officers to command torpedo, bombing, and reconaissance aircraft. A number of crew 35 were detached from the *Kriegsmarine* and transferred to the *Luftwaffe* for pilot training elsewhere. The pilots of the naval aircraft were non-commissioned *Luftwaffe* petty officers. Coincidental with his assignment to Stralsund, Hoppe was promoted to *Oberfähnrich zur See* (sublieutenant). Twelve months were spent in the flying officer curriculum. Finally, in late summer of 1938, his training completed, and promoted to *Leutnant zur See* (junior lieutenant), he went on active duty. His first posting was to Naval Air Group 106 (twin-engine *Heinkel* 115s). These were reconnaissance aircraft based on the island of Norderney in the North Sea off the northwest coast of Germany. In addition to his flying duties, he served as Adjutant to the Group's commander. This led to flying lessons, as the commander owned a "small but elegant plane with red leather seats."

Konrad's life on Norderney bordered on the idyllic. He says he "spent the most lucky time of my life there, from August 1938 up to the beginning of the war. In those peaceful months nobody, especially in the German navy, ever believed a war was threatening. We enjoyed life with all might. In summertime we flirted with the pretty female bathing guests who, in a holiday mood, were easy to conquer. In wintertime we cultivated our comradeship during hours and hours of throwing dice and drinking a lot. But even then we need not miss the contact to the other sex as there were many pretty girls working at the many children's homes, always ready for a flirt or more. When the loneliness of the island made me too depressive I could get the commander's plane to make weekend trips to one of my girl friends in my home town of Magdeburg, or to Köln, or anywhere else, just for the fun of it."

In 1995, Hoppe returned to Norderney, and found almost nothing to remind him of his prewar days. Instead of a small, primitive ferry, which made the trip to the island once or twice a day, he saw huge vessels carrying hundreds of vehicles and thousands of people. Many of what he called "ugly" hotels had changed the "cozy" island into a crowded city. There was no trace of the old air base, except the name of a small street, *Alter Horst* (old base). "Even the small bar named *Onkel Emil* [Uncle Emil]," he laments, "where we used to take a last drink before returning to our quarters, has disappeared."

In April of 1939, Konrad had once again earned a promotion in rank, this time to *Oberleutnant zur See* (senior lieutenant). When the war broke out in September, little of note occurred on Norderney. Later on, in the course of a routine scouting mission over the North Sea, a British destroyer opened fire on Hoppe's aircraft, but no hits were made and the aircraft returned safely to base. In December, he received orders to report to Hamburg to join ship 21, the *Widder*.

In the course of World War II, Germany utilized its navy mainly not to fight other warships, but to sever the sea-lanes supplying Great Britain. To do so, three main forces were constituted. First, there were the submarines. According to uboat. net, a total of 859 U-boats made about five thousand patrols accounting for the loss of 2,779 Allied vessels. The average bag was 3.2 per boat. The second group was composed of the traditional surface ships: battleships, pocket battleships, and heavy cruisers. These well-known names, considering their firepower, did poorly in their quest for merchant ships, particularly convoys. Look at the record: battleship *Gneisenau*—ten ships sunk; battleship *Scharnhorst*—ten ships sunk; pocket battleship *Deutschland*—two ships sunk; pocket battleship *Graf*

Spee—nine ships sunk; pocket battleship *Scheer*—sixteen ships sunk; and heavy cruiser *Hipper*—ten ships sunk. Only fifty-seven unlucky merchant vessels, one as small as 560 tons, for an average of just 9.5 kills per big gun warship.

The *Widder*, to which Hoppe was posted, was a *Hilfskreuzer* (auxiliary cruiser), one of nine so classified vessels making up the third force to operate against the Allies' supply lines. Of these nine raiders, an anonymous author has written, "They sank a cruiser, an armed merchant cruiser, so gallantly fought two other armed merchant cruisers that the latter were forced to break off the engagements, and by direct attack or mine laying captured or destroyed 890,000 tons of Allied shipping. They created a nuisance, diversion, and destruction out of all proportion to their capabilities and numbers." Basically, these were converted merchant vessels, but reconstructed so their outward appearance was not changed. They would disguise themselves as a Greek, or a Russian, or a Spaniard, or a Jap, and even in one instance, early in the war, as British. Their concealed armament was formidable. All carried six 15 cm (5.9-inch) cannons, and most added a 10.5 cm (4-inch) high angle gun for antiaircraft and star shell use. Five were fitted with six torpedo tubes, three had four, and one with only two tubes. In addition, as many as a half dozen 2 cm and 3.7 cm rapid fire, antipersonnel guns were mounted at the bow, stern, and on the bridge wings. Operating all over the world in waters they had probably traversed in earlier life, these nine renamed freighters rang up the following figures:

	ships sunk	ships captured
Atlantis	19	3
Komet	5	1
Kormoran	10	1
Michel	17	0
Orion	9	1
Orion with *Komet*	2	0
Pinguin	16	16
Stier	4	0
Thor	18	4
Widder	9	1
	109	27

It was intended that the *Widder* would break out of Europe in the first weeks of 1940 when the long, dark nights and winter weather could keep her hidden from British eyes. Such was not the case as delays in the shipyard had a deterrent effect on crew training, and it was not until early May when she left Kiel.

The *Widder* carried a single twin-float seaplane, a *Heinkel He 144*, jocularly called a "one and a halver." This appellation came about because although it was a biplane, the lower wingspread was twenty feet, compared to the upper wingspread of forty feet six inches. Its engine was a six-cylinder, rotary, air-cooled BMW 321 covered by a cowling. Cooling was accomplished by means of a ten bladed fan mounted on the propeller shaft. Strangely, the hub of this fan was an iron casting and very early in the *Widder*'s voyage, returning from a scouting flight, the pilot made a hard landing which caused the hub to fracture. As there was no spare engine on board nor foundry facility to manufacture a replacement part, the aircraft was out of commission. Konrad, who had flown few hours since leaving Norderny was effectively grounded and didn't make another flight for many months.

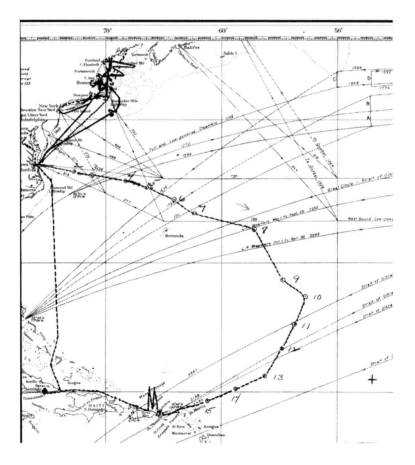

***Nantucket's* track, summer 1940. + is position of sinking of empty tanker *British Petrol* by *Widder*.**

The *Widder*'s first kill occurred on June 13, thirty-nine days out of Kiel. In latitude 20° 10′ N, longitude 46° 56′ W, in broad daylight, shortly before noon, the empty tanker *British Petrol* was intercepted and sunk by gunfire. Incredibly, the school ship *Nantucket*'s noon position that day was 21° 19′ N, 56° 15′ W, just 540 miles away. Had we been, perchance, on reciprocal courses, we would have been only twenty-four hours apart! In fact, on the eleventh, our noon position was 240 miles from the northwest corner of the *Widder*'s prescribed operating area. Commissioner Queen and Captain Abele never realized how close to the war we were!

S.S. *King John* sinking following attack by *Widder*.
July 13, 1940.

CHAPTER FOUR

1940 Cruise (Part II)

Second classman Clarence A. Chapman, heaving the lead.
Third classman Edward R. Donohoe, tending line.
Executive Officer Robert M. Gray, MNS '12 on bridge wing.
First and Second Classmen wore their white hats on the back of their heads.
Third classmen had theirs cocked over the right eye, and Fourth classmen
wore theirs "squared", i.e. level above the eyebrows.

Before I interrupted this narrative to introduce Konrad Hoppe, I had mentioned how on June 13, Carman and I were heaving the lead. Going in and coming out of ports, it was the practice to determine the depth of water by what was known as sounding. This involved throwing a seven-pound lead weight, attached to a line marked at two, three, five, seven, ten, thirteen, fifteen, seventeen, and twenty fathoms from a platform extension of the navigating bridge. It was a two-man operation. One heaved the lead, the other tended the line. The leadsman, grasping a toggle inserted just above the two-fathom mark, would swing the weight back and forth, gaining momentum until he could make two 360° swings. Then at the bottom of the second swing, he would release the line and the lead flew forward. As the ship's motion overran the lead, he would take up the slack, and when the line was in a vertical state, pump it up and down, sounding the bottom and reading the depth by the marks on the line. It was tricky. On the high seas, where we learned the technique of the 360° swings and the up-and-down motion as the line became vertical, a seven-pound lead could be a lethal weapon, so the neophyte practitioners used a bag of sand.

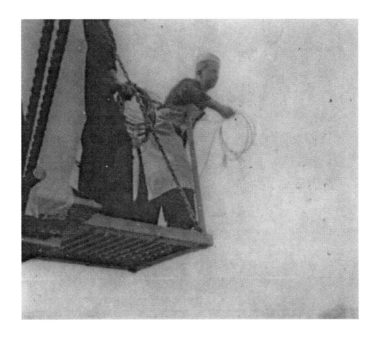

Second classman Edward W. Emerson heaving the lead.

14 Friday—Fore topsail and spanker now set. Speed at 1100-7 knots. Quarters at 0915 and lecture by Dr. Mooney. Studies as usual. Still trying to find trade winds. 1200 position, 20° 14' 38" N, 58° 41' 00" W.

The *Nantucket* in the trade winds, bound for St. Thomas.
Note speck of white just above topsail yard. That is the lookout's white cap.

15 Saturday—All sail except fore topmast staysail and trysail set at 0700. Topmast and topgallant stun'sails set at 0830. Field day in morning. The procedure for the afternoon started thusly—the t'gants, fore sail, spanker, and headsails were taken in, stopping the ship. Motor sailer was lowered away at 1315. On board were Comm. Queen, Mr. Rounds, Mr. Kelley, Doctor Mooney, and several cadets for the purpose of taking pictures of ship. All sail was then set. Then the motor sailer got into difficulty and we had to stop again. After all sail was set again and the photos taken, it was necessary to stop again in order to take the motor sailer back aboard. In all, this operation took about two hours. Weather clear, temperature 90° 1200 position, 19° 25' 20" N, 61° 30' 00" W.

One of the pictures taken that day.

16 Sunday—Sombrero (Island) light, 18° 36' N, 63° 26' W., was sighted at 0300. Passed abeam of the island at approximately 0700. The light is on a small coral reef and is a British possession. St. Thomas is 95 miles from here. Captain's inspection at 1000. Church service at 1100. Sighted first of Virgin Islands at 1140. Port watch furled all sail at 1800. Arrived off St. Thomas some time during night. Drifting around waiting for daybreak.

17 Monday—Under way at 0600. Took pilot aboard at 0630, anchoring 15 minutes later. Several quick rain showers during morning. In here are the Danish tankers Scandia and Christianholm and the Primo of Oslo. This appears to be a fine harbor, well sheltered with high mountains on three sides. There is a good dock at the West India Co. coaling station. A large amount of bauxite is handled by this concern. We are in the rainy season here, this accounts for the showers during the day.

18 Tuesday—General field day this morning. The Captain is having a party this afternoon. Port watch liberty at 1330. The town is rather small with some good looking buildings in the center, but only shacks in the outskirts. There are half a dozen churches plus the U. S. Customs House and Post Office, several hotels, and Fort Christian built by the Danes. Liberty expires as usual at 2000 on the dock.

19 Wednesday—Turn-to after reveille, nothing much doing all morning. Relieved Marcus in gig's crew, and went sailing with Capt. Abele, Comm. Queen, and Mr. Kelley. We all went swimming at one of the beaches on the east entrance to the harbor. Prepared ship for coaling during evening.

20 Thursday—Reveille at 0445. Moved to West India dock after breakfast, taking aboard about 100 tons of coal. Left dock and anchored out again. Weighed anchor and sailed at 1500. U.S.S. Upshur (DD 193) entered harbor. Course 017° p.s.c. Set all sail except fore topmast staysail and spanker, uncoupled at 1830. Met S.S. Sea Thrush headed South at 2030. Some signaling was done but they were poor.

The 1920 commissioned *Upshur* was one of the American four-stackers that would be given to the British a few months later in exchange for long term leases of British territory for use as military bases. She became HMS *Clare*.

In my prior description of coaling ship, I mentioned being on the bridge, black with coal dust, as we met an incoming destroyer. That incident occurred this day.

21 Friday—Field day all morning. This was the regular post-coaling field day. Scrubbed clothes all afternoon. Still sailing, average speed 4.5 knots. Course up until 1430—017° p.s.c. Wearing ship, course changed to 207° p.s.c.

22 Saturday—Rifle practice on poop deck for third class during morning. Mr. Queen and Capt. Abele supervising. Wearing ship at 1845. Weather clear and warm. From noon to 2000 we went 17 miles.

23 Sunday—Captain's inspection at 1000. Church service immediately following. Wind is picking up, doing 4.7 knots at 1400. Regular Sunday holiday. No work, nothing to do.

24 Monday—Sighted San Juan light at 0250. Took in topgallants and foresail. Furled all sail at approximately 0600. Dropped anchor in San Juan harbor at 0900. This is quite a naval base. Destroyer Div. 64 is anchored here and the tender Dixie (AD 14). The Army and Navy air stations are also very active. Port watch liberty at 1330. The city is very large, 150,000 population. Spanish is the common language, but English is understood. It is rather hot, the temperature at noon was 100°. Liberty up at 2000. Note: Under sail all but 6 hours out of St. Thomas.

The *Dixie* was a modern destroyer tender, having joined the fleet just two months prior to our meeting her in San Juan. Her first duty station was to be Pearl Harbor.

25 Tuesday—Regular port routine. Sideboys standing by all morning. Captain and Commander of Dixie came aboard. Large Navy seaplanes are taking off right near us. Nothing doing during remainder of day,

26 Wednesday—Destroyer Div. 64 sailed. Hull being painted all morning. Port watch liberty at 1315. There are four ships of the Bull-Insular Line in here. Our cutters are sailing on their regular trips.

27 Thursday—Rain during early morning. U.S.S. Dixie sailed at 0600. No quarters. Rifle practice on quarterdeck. In gig's crew during afternoon, relieving Rogers. Sailed on the one lone trip. Comm. Queen sailed for the States on the Porto Rico liner Boranquen [sic]. Rain squalls during evening. Starboard watch liberty party got soaked. Temperature still 90° to 100°.

Correct spelling of liner's name is *Borinquen.*

**View looking aft from lookout post on fore topsail yard.
Note cadets in formation on both sides of quarterdeck.**

28 Friday—Sailed from San Juan at 0900. Hoisted the jib to get headed down the harbor. Set all sail at 1000. Uncoupled, doing 5 knots at 1100—a little over 7 during the afternoon. Set main catchall for first time this summer. Turn-to, cleaning up boats and oars. Kerosene seems to take off most of the sludge, but the paint will have to be scraped off and the boats repainted. Course 292° p.s.c.

San Juan must have been filthy!

29 Saturday—Headed up the coast of Hispaniola, land in sight all day. Field day in morning. Rifle class for third class in afternoon. Rain during evening. Temperature 75°.

30 Sunday—Course 270° p.s.c., still in sight of Hispaniola. Captain's inspection at 1000. Church service at 1045. Nothing doing all day. Weather ideal.

July

1 Monday—Quarters at 0915, followed by fire and collision drills. Studies at 1000. Cuba sighted during morning. Furled sail at 1600. Surprise man overboard drill following. Everyone really thought some one had gone over the side. An airplane carrier and a destroyer were seen during the early afternoon.

When underway, there existed the strong possibility of someone falling overboard. Thus, a cadet was always "detailed" to stand watch at the stern. If a person went into the water, this cadet was to call out the alarm and throw a life ring to the swimmer. In addition, hanging on the rail, was a cylindrical buoy which, in the event of a surprise drill, would depict the victim. During the hustle and bustle of getting the sails in, Captain Abele or one of the officers casually sauntered aft and flipped the buoy. It was a "real life" situation with everyone on deck involved in the furling operations, when suddenly the lookout shouted "man overboard." No wonder we thought it was an actual emergency.

2 Tuesday—Heavy rain during the night. Dropped anchor in Guantanamo Bay at 0615. There are three destroyers and a tug here at present. There doesn't appear to be much ashore at all. Liberty for second and fourth classes at 1400. Liberty expired at 1630!! Temperature is up near 100° again.

3 Wednesday—Reveille as usual at 0515. First and third classes shifted into undress whites, neckerchiefs, etc. Left ship at 0645 in marine motor launches. Split up into three groups on range—one on firing line, one in butts, and third group standing by. Each cadet had 10 practice shots—prone, then 10 prone for record, 10 sitting, and 10 rapid fire—prone. Maximum for 30 shots was 150. Yours truly made the outstanding

(?) score of 35 prone, 39 sitting, and 13 rapid fire for a total of 87!!! The aircraft carrier WASP and destroyer U.S.S. Morris (DD 417) anchored in the afternoon. Very, very hot.

The Quincy, Massachusetts built *Wasp* (CV 7), commissioned in April, was in Boston when we sailed on May 11. On September 16, 1942, engaged in the Battle of the Solomon Islands, she was torpedoed by the Japanese submarine I-19. United States forces later delivered a coup de grace. The *Morris* was also newly built, commissioned in March. A Sims class, she survived the war, earning fifteen battle stars.

4 Thursday—Dress ship for holiday. Liberty for first and third classes at 1330. Using motor sailer. There is nothing ashore but a glorified Navy Yard. The Marine-Navy baseball team beat M.N.S. 24 to 4. Van Gemert and Winslow sailed to second and fourth places in the sailboat regatta, to win first place. Liberty expired at 1730. Machinist Logan celebrated the 4th by falling off the Marine dock! An epidemic of diarrhea is beginning to hit the entire ship's company. Several rain showers during the morning. U.S.S. Dixie anchored in morning. Now here are the Dixie, Wasp, and destroyers 187, 195, 257, 416, 417, 419.

The *Dixie* appeared to be taking its time to get into the Pacific. The first three destroyers, in order, were the USS *Dahlgren*, USS *Welborn C. Wood*, and USS *Welles*. All ancient four-stackers, the *Wood* and the *Welles* were destined to fly the Royal Navy's white ensign. *Wood* was renamed HMS *Chesterfield*. The *Welles* became HMS *Cameron* and was badly damaged in December 1940 in an air raid on a British port. Henceforth, she was used as an experimental damage-control hulk. The 416 was the USS *Walke*, built at the Charlestown Navy Yard and commissioned in 1940. She was sunk by Japanese naval gunfire off Guadacanal on November 15, 1942. DD 417 is mentioned earlier. The last of the six was USS *Wainwright* (DD 419), commissioned a month after the *Morris* and which was awarded five battle stars.

5 Friday—Second and fourth classes on the rifle range. There are very few unaffected by the dissentary [sic] epidemic. Not much turn-to, only a few able to work. Our southern cruise is to be terminated, and unless present orders are rescinded, we go North from here. Personally, I am very disappointed. This has been a very hot day. The thermometer on the main mast has quit!!

My disappointment was incurred by the cancellation of port calls at La Guayra, Venezuela; Cristobal, Panama Canal Zone; St. Petersburg, Florida; and Havana, Cuba.

6 Saturday—Field day all morning. Nothing doing all day. Swimming party in afternoon and movie party at night. I did not bother to go to either. Practically everyone is feeling low, the epidemic still rolls on. If we had more sleep, better food, and a lot finer living conditions, this would never happen. A good deal more water, also. Now the question is, where do we go from here? This has been the usual day, hot and dry.

This may have been the first cruise the *Nantucket* made to the tropics. Historically, the training cruises had been to Northern Europe one year and to the Mediterranean the next. The summer heat of the Caribbean raised havoc on board, as can be seen. The entire supply of fresh potatoes, as another example, rotted out.

7 Sunday—Reveille at 0545—a little more sleep. Catholic church party at 0830. Returned to ship at 1000. Captain's inspection at 1015. Whaleboat and two cutters out sailing. Just before this, a small sailboat with two Cuban kids in it, overturned about a half-mile up the river. I was in the cutter sent out to the rescue, but a boat from the 257 reached them first. The kids had a load of bread—it was floating in the water. The temperature on the mainmast at noon was 114°.

8 Monday—Two cases of heat prostration in the last 24 hours. Salt tablets are being provided for the use of every one. Two cutters and whaleboat out sailing. Sideboys standing by all morning. Destroyer U.S.S. Upshur (DD 193) entered harbor at 0700. We received orders at noon to proceed to Norfolk. Sailed at 1800. Head winds all along the coast, yards braced up to lessen wind resistance.

9 Tuesday—Course approximately NE through Windward Passage, with Cuba close at hand. Sighted several ships including United Fruit steamer Platana, flying Panamanian flag and bound for Cristobal. All fore and aft sails set at noon. Passing close to islands in the Bahama group during night.

10 Wednesday—In sight of various islands during day. A great many ships are using this lane, probably the busiest in the world at present. All cadets air bedding. Quarters at 0915 followed by abandon ship and man overboard drills. Studies at 1015. Scrub hammocks in afternoon. San Salvador Light sighted during evening. Headsails hauled down at 2200 to allow two approaching ships to see our lights.

11 Thursday—Quarters at 0915 followed by fire and man overboard drills. Studies at 1000. Still sighting quite a number of ships. Speed is 6 knots. Course 295° p.s.c. Temperature dropping. Weather clear.

View looking forward from lookout post on fore topsail yard.
Note safety netting on jib boom commonly referred to as "Cadet catchers."

12 Friday—Quarters at 0915 with collision and man overboard drills. Studies as usual at 1000. Turn-to in afternoon. Shades of Guantanamo! The temperature is up to 100°. The sun is beating down on the black skin of the ship.

13 Saturday—Topsails set at 0700. Field day in morning. Rest of day to ourselves except for extra duty men. Canteen as usual in afternoon. Topsails furled at 1800.

14 Sunday—Overcast, rain all morning. Heavy sea breaking over bow at times. Oilskins are uniform. All day, since midnight, all that we have done is set the headsails, haul down the headsails, set all fore and aft sails, change the tack, haul down all sails, set the flying jib, etc. etc. etc. etc. etc. This is the first bad day we've had since Norfolk. Sighted the U.S.S. Wasp and destroyer escort headed north at 1600. Blinker contact made.

15 Monday—Quarters at 0915 with fire and man overboard drills. Classes at 1000. We are nearing Norfolk. We might get in tonight. There are quite a few ships being sighted, mainly tankers. Land is in sight all afternoon. The life rings on the bridge wings have been repainted to M.N.S. Nantucket. Rather cool in morning. Temperature rising rapidly through day. Received word by radio that we are to anchor in Hampton Roads instead of docking at the Operating Base as we expected. Finally dropped anchor at about 1930. Very cool, jackets are necessary. Motor sailer lowered and trip made immediately.

When we left Boston in early May, the *Nantucket* was the USS *Nantucket* on loan to the State of Massachusetts. On June 10, after we left Norfolk, I wrote, "Today is the day that the Maritime Commission is supposed to take us over." Apparently they did, but it took until July 15 to change the lettering on the life rings to *MNS*. And that is probably why we didn't go in to the Operating Base; the *Nantucket* was no longer a naval vessel.

16 Tuesday—Early breakfast. Lighter alongside with coal. Coal ship all morning, field day in afternoon. Took a deck load in both waists. No liberty. No one wanted it anyway. In at the Operating Base are the Wasp, Helena, St. Louis, Nitro, and William Ward Burrows. Clear day, temperatures in upper 80s.

The USS *Helena* (CL 50) was another new ship. Her commissioning took place in September, just before my class entered nautical school. She survived the Japanese attack on Pearl Harbor, but was lost in an engagement off New Georgia on July 6, 1943. Commissioned in May 1939, the USS *St. Louis* (CL 49) was also at Pearl Harbor. She survived the war and received eleven battle stars. USS *Nitro* (AE 2) was a dedicated ammunition and explosives carrier built in 1921. She also finished out the war. In February 1940, the U.S. Navy acquired the *Santa Rita*, built in 1929 in Denmark, from the Grace Steamship Company. In short order, she was converted from a pure freighter to a combination passenger/cargo vessel and became the USS *William Ward Burrows* (AP 6).

17 Wednesday—Field day all morning. Port watch liberty at 1330 in dress blues. Liberty expires on dock at 2000. Slight rain showers in afternoon. A great supply of fresh stores is being taken on board. U.S.S. Tuscaloosa docked at Base.

The *Tuscaloosa* (CA 37) was a bit older than the *Helena* and the *St. Louis*, having been commissioned in 1934. She made it through the war, picking up seven battle stars.

18 Thursday—Quarters at 0915. Third and fourth classes tying knots on foc's'l remainder of morning. Starboard watch liberty at 1330. Still more stores coming aboard. U.S.S. Wasp sailed at 0700, U.S.S. Helena at 1530. Destroyers 190, 191, 194, 197 arrived and 417 sailed. Weather clear, temperature 90°.

The USS *Satterlee* (DD 190) was transferred to Great Britain the following October and became HMS *Belmont*. She was lost with all hands in January 1942 after being torpedoed by the U-82. The USS *Mason* (DD 191) also went to the Royal Navy where she was renamed HMS *Broadwater*. Her career ended in October 1941 at the hands of the U-101. Next, the USS *Hunt* (DD 194), as the HMS *Broadway*, managed to live out the war as did the USS *Branch* (DD 197) under the name HMS *Beverley*.

19 Friday—Regular morning turn-to. Prepared ship for sea after 0815 muster. Weighed anchor at 1130. Sailed for Portland, Maine. Passed U.S.S. Wasp anchored near Chesapeake Lightship at approximately 1500. Esso tanker S.B. Hunt passed astern of us at 1645. Weather clear, sea calm. All fore and aft sails set.

The 1919-built Esso tanker *S. B. Hunt* was torpedoed, while in convoy, early in the morning of July 7, 1943, by the U-185 in a position about 125 miles east of Fortaleza, Brazil. She did not sink, and there were no casualties suffered by her crew and Naval Armed Guard. The convoy continued on to Trinidad where emergency repairs were made, allowing the vessel to later proceed to Galveston, Texas, for full repairs. She returned to service in January 1944 and a year later at Pearl Harbor was transferred to the United States Navy, renamed USS *Flambeau* (IX 192), and utilized as a Mobil Floating Fuel Storage Ship.

20 Saturday—Passed S.S. President Hayes bound for Cristobal out of Boston at 0800. Blinker contact made. Field day all morning. Remainder of day to ourselves. Fore and aft sails hauled down at 0645 when a floating life ring was sighted. Starboard watch crew in boat. The ring had been cut, removing identification marks. All that was left—S.S.—IA N—K. A short while later another was seen. The name could not be made out. S. S. Eureka (?), flying Panamanian flag, crossed our bow at 1700. Temperature moderate, visibility low.

21 Sunday—Sighted a tanker "not under command" at 0600. We had just set all fore and aft sails and hauled them down as we changed course. She was the Norwegian tanker Alar with Risor as her home port. In reply to a query they said they were cleaning tanks. She had the stack marking P&D and was very high out of the water, I am now a coal passer relieving Savage, who is in sick bay, I'm in the 0800–1200 watch. Captain's inspection and church services in morning as usual. Thick fog set in at 1900. Fog horn blowing most of night. Slight rain.

Coincidentally, this vessel had been at Hoosac Pier during the previous winter when the author made this sketch.

Regarding the *Alar*, she had declared herself as "not under command" and unable to navigate, by displaying "in a vertical line one over the other, not less than six feet apart, where they can best be seen, two black balls or shapes, each two feet in diameter."

In the hierarchy of the engine room, the coal passer was at the bottom of the pyramid. As the title indicates his main job was to deliver coal from the bunkers to the firemen. In the class-oriented *Nantucket*, coal passers were underclassmen, and firemen were upperclassmen. Woe to the coal passer who didn't anticipate the firemen's slightest whims.

22 Monday—Quarters at 0915 followed by fire and man overboard drills. Studies at 1000. Turn-to and studies in afternoon. Fishing trawler crossed our bow at 1630. Fog set in again during night. Sea very calm—flat as a mirror.

23 Tuesday—Quarters at 0915 followed by collision and man overboard drill. Studies at 1000. "Scuttlebutt" has it that we are lost, but we could hear a foghorn supposed to be Portland Lightship at 1600. Surprise "man overboard" drill at 1600 but we weren't going fast enough to leave the buoy very far astern. Stopped at 1630. Fog drifting in at various times. Speed at 2100, .5 knot, at 2300, stopped.

Dragger off New England coast. Summer 1940.

24 Wednesday—Still off Portland in thick fog. No quarters. Finally headed in at 1145. Dropped anchor in Portland harbor at 1330. Port watch liberty at 1530. Several merchant ships here—Japanese, Greek, American, also a Coast Guard cutter. Fog all day. Liberty expired at 2000 on dock.

25 Thursday—Regular morning turn-to. Quite a few special liberties, also party at hardware company. Starboard watch liberty at 1330. Temperature in upper 80s.

A number of parents made their way up to Portland and asked that their sons be granted extra days off, thus the "special liberties". The "hardware company" was a ship chandlery whose owner was interested in the creation of a nautical school in the state.

26 Friday—Very thick fog set in during early morning. Light rain. Port watch liberty at 1100. Most of us wore topcoats, but ashore the sun was shining and a heat wave was hitting its peak—95°. U.S.S. Blakely (DD 150) and U.S.S. Biddle (DD 151) entered port in morning. Liberty expired, as usual, at 2000 on dock.

These two four-stackers had almost duplicate service histories. Both were commissioned in 1919, decommissioned in 1922, and then brought back into service in 1939. Both lasted out the war in varying capacities before being again decommissioned in 1945. The *Blakely*, though, was torpedoed by U-156 on May 25, 1942, off Martinique, losing six men and about sixty feet of her bow. She was repaired and returned to service.

Saturday 27—Regular morning turn-to and quarters. Sailed for Greenport, Long Island at 1100. Sea calm, sun shining, with less than fair visibility. General knock-off in afternoon. Temperature dropping during evening.

Sunday 28—Very thick fog in morning, forcing us to stop at 0600. Dropped port anchor until fog lifted sufficiently at 0700. Position close by Pollock Rip Lightship. Passed Stone Horse Lightship at 0800, Handkerchief Shoal at 0845, Cross Rip at 1000. Dropping down Vineyard Sound at noon. This water is a yachtsman's paradise. There are a great many yachts and motorboats cruising around. Met collier Eastern Crown at 1215. Passed Vineyard Lightship at 1420. Dropped anchor at approximately midnight.

29 Monday—Reveille at 0515, both watches on deck. Up anchor at 0600. Preparing ship for port—placing gangways, taking stores out of boats, etc. Dropped anchor at 0715 in Greenport harbor. Two coast guard patrol boats here—both sailed at 0800. This is nothing but a summer resort—millions of sail boats, motor boats, and even a seaplane. Starboard watch liberty at 1330 in dress whites. Liberty up as usual at 2000 on dock. Ship's side painted during afternoon. Weather clear, temperature in upper 80s.

30 Tuesday—Regular port routine, quarters at 0915. Studies. Seamanship examination. I scraped fore topmast with Ball and Frisch. Liberty at 1330. Nothing much doing in the village. We are getting the ship ready for Boston. Temperature about 90°.

31 Wednesday—Loosed all sail except spanker at 0815. Furled sail again at 1100. I was on the foretopgallant, fore, and foretopmast staysail. Relieved Curtin in cutter for afternoon, as Town team took M.N.S. 14 to 5. Starboard watch liberty. Weather clear, light breezes.

Bob Curtin was the pitcher on the baseball team.

August

1 Thursday—Examination for fourth class. Third class turned-to painting on fo'c's'l. Port watch liberty at 1330. About the only thing to do is go to a movie. Liberty up at 2000 on dock as usual. Very cool in morning, good breeze in afternoon.

2 Friday—Prepared ship for sea during morning. Quarters at 0915. Weighed anchor at 1100. Fifteen minutes later Cadet Kean, second class engineer, dove over the starboard side in an attempt to swim ashore to Shelter Island. Port watch lifeboat crew, McCollom, cox.; Melzar; Coffey; Carman; Doell; Smith; and I in gig. Mr. Gray also climbing in. We picked Kean up, very tired, but only about 75 yards from shore. Back to the ship. Kean dressed and we took him ashore for good. No one knows exactly the cause for his action!! Our "lost" mail has finally arrived. I have three postmarked July 1, 2, and 7. Fore and aft sails spread for a couple of hours at 1800. Course is approximately SE between Block Island and Montauk Point. Met a Pocohontas collier out of Newport, R. I. bound for Norfolk, Va.

I was in the chains, heaving the lead when Kean went over the side, and I quickly called to Mr. Gray, who was standing on the bridge wing. The details of exactly what happened next have faded from my memory, but I do know that I was assigned to the lifeboat and had to scramble out of my perch, onto the bridge, and scoot down the deck to where the boat was already being lowered. We managed to get between Kean and the shore, and Gray persuaded Kean to come aboard. It turned out Kean had received a telegram that morning telling him his mother was quite ill, and requesting he ask the Captain to allow him to come home. As we were due in Boston on Monday, the request was denied. Most of the cadets, particularly his classmates, knew what he was doing because enough money was raised to help him buy a shirt and trousers and a pair of shoes and to pay for his train tickets, as all he was wearing were swimming trunks. Also, it was not by chance no cadets were on the after deck when he dove. If Cadet Kean was punished for his attempt, I have no idea. He did, though, graduate with his class in April 1941, in spite of my prognostication that we were taking him ashore for good. Also, I wonder at this late date about the absence of the quarterdeck man-overboard lookout.

3 Saturday—Regular field day all morning. Several fishing trawlers in sight. This water is full of sharks. We could see them very plainly as they slowly swam along near the surface. Passed Nantucket Shoals Lightship at 1215. Large schools of mackerel are being seen.

4 Sunday—Moving up coast of Cape Cod. Left land astern in morning, sighted Cape Ann about noon. Captain's inspection at 1000, followed by church service at 1100. Sailed around Cape Ann down into Lanesville, then headed for the Isles of Shoals. Tuna fleet out. Passed Newburyport at about 1600. Turned around and headed south at 1700. Cruised off Boston Lightship all night.

When we passed the mouth of the Merrimack River, several Newburyport-based motor yachts in the area, their owners recognizing the *Nantucket* and knowing I was on board, approached us to within hailing distance asking for me. Captain Abele and the officers on the bridge were amused.

Launching the port whaleboat.
Man tending the forward fall is Able Seaman Wilcox.

5 Monday—About two miles south of Boston Lightship at 0600. Engine stopped until 0800. Man overboard drill at 0930. Moving through The Narrows up into harbor. A great many merchant vessels here—one of the most active weeks in recent shipping years. U.S.S. Wasp at Army Base. A cruiser and several of the new two-stack destroyers in Navy Yard. We finally docked at 1115. Starboard watch liberty, 1330-2200. Preparing ship for coaling all afternoon.

6 Tuesday—Started coaling at 0600. All coal aboard by 1000. Took on deck load of 100 bags. Liberty at 1530. About 40 cadets who have been considered to live at a distance have liberty until 2200 Thursday. Home at 1700.

7 Wednesday—At home.

8 Thursday—Left at 1930, aboard at 2040.

Those travel times are amazing! Overall, it was a good thirty-five mile trip. I'd catch the elevated train, City Square to Sullivan Square, and then a trackless trolley to Malden. There I stuck out my thumb, and inevitably the first car or truck to come along would pick me up. Frequently, they were going on Route 1 past Newburyport, so I had a non-stop ride. Returning was equally as delightful. Many drivers went out of their way to deposit me at the Navy Yard gate, which begs the question, how come we had our old berth in Charlestown Navy Yard now that we were not the USS *Nantucket?*

9 Friday—On regular port routine. Prepared ship for sea in morning. Sailed from Pier 1 for Boothbay Harbor, Maine at 1545. Passed twin lights on Thacher's Island at 2030.

10 Saturday—Regular field day started on deck but it was decided to go right in. Cadet Leo Ranen, first class, suffering from appendicitis was removed from ship near The Cuckolds Light by a picket boat from Damariscove Island station. Dropped anchor at 1000. Starboard watch liberty at 1330, expired at 2000 on dock, except for first and second classmen invited to a dance until 2400. This port is just another summer resort with the usual fleet of yachts and sailboats.

11 Sunday—No Captain's inspection. Catholic church party at 0730, Protestant church party at 1015. Nothing doing for rest of morning. Port watch liberty at 1330. Back aboard at 2000.

12 Monday—Regular morning turn-to. First classmen taking lifeboat examination. Cadet Eaton, second class, taken to hospital for observation and possible appendectomy. Van Gemert, then Ranen, now Eaton??? Fog setting in again. Prepared ship for sea during afternoon. Weighed anchor and sailed for New Bedford, Mass. At 1800, braced yards around, heading into a stiff wind. Rather cool at night.

13 Tuesday—Quarters at 0915. Fire, collision, and man overboard drills following. Studies at 1000. The sea is rather choppy, yet the man overboard drill was one of the best this summer. Studies in afternoon. Cape Cod in sight during late afternoon.

14 Wednesday—Passed Pollock Rip Lightship at midnight, Stone Horse half an hour later. Suddenly turned about and cruised between the two lightships. Fog settling in thickly. Anchored at 0120. Collier Berkshire also anchored nearby. Fog began to lift at 0730. Weighed anchor and proceeded. Left Pollock Rip at 0800, passed Stone Horse at 0845, Handkerchief at 0915, Cross Rip at 1100, Vineyard at 1510. Air bedding in morning. Quarters at 0915 with abandon ship and man overboard drills. Set all fore and aft sails at 1000; hauled down at 1530. Tied up at Homer's Wharf at 1830. Had the usual trouble—almost split the dock this time. Also in here are the Mystic collier James L. Richards, Morgan freighter El Almirante, and the schooner Thomas H. Lawrence.

Three-masted schooner off New England coast. Summer 1940.

Collier was a common term in those days, used to describe a vessel dedicated to the coal trade. A number of shipping companies offered ships to carry coal from the Hampton Roads estuary to dozens of ports all along the New England coast. As there was no highway system as we know it today, the sea ports and the railways were integral parts of the distribution system.

Also, I was beginning to look at Capt. Abele as being a bit less than godlike.

15 Thursday—Word was received this morning that Cadet Leo Ranen, First class, had died in Boothbay, Maine last night. Catholic church party at 0630, returned at 0800. Quarters at 0915, followed by fire drill. Studies at 0945. Guards and sideboys standing by. Starboard watch liberty 1330-2200. Knock-off all afternoon.

16 Friday—Reveille at 0600! Quarters at 0915, followed by collision drill. Studies at 1000. The new Master-at-Arms came aboard this morning. Port watch liberty at 1330. Returned aboard at 2145.

17 Saturday—Field day as usual in morning. U.S.C.G.C. Anemone tied up at end of dock at 0900. Captain's inspection at 0945. Starboard watch liberty at 1130. Visitors aboard all afternoon.

18 Sunday—Catholic church party at 0830. Port watch liberty at 0945. I have liberty until 0800 on Monday.

19 Monday—Returned aboard at 0800. Coaling ship and usual field day all morning. Not too much coal. Ship prepared for sea, but bad weather is holding us up. Light rain with fog most of morning. Studies during afternoon. Word passed at 1430 to prepare for sea. U.S.C.G.C. Anemone moved forward to allow us to clear her stern. At 1530, starboard watch shift (uniforms) *to go ashore. Now, no one knows when we will sail.*

20 Tuesday—Reveille at 0500. Still dark and cold. Rain during night. Prepared ship for sea and sailed for East Lamoine, Maine at about 0600. One of the paid seamen and two cadets had gone on to the dock to handle lines and the whaleboat was prepared to return to the dock, but then everyone on the bridge forgot about the three men and headed out to sea. Finally it was discovered. but it was a good row away. The three back aboard safely and we're off again. The freighter Glenbank of Glasgow passed us about 0900, headed for New York. After making the turn at Hen and Chickens Lightship, the fore and main topsails were loosed, then word was passed that F. P. Melzar, Jr., C.O. was stricken with appendicitis. Topsails furled and we headed up into Vineyard Sound. A surfboat from Cuttyhunk Coast Guard Station took him off to Martha's Vineyard. All fore and aft sails set at 1100. Studies and turn-to in afternoon. Took in all sail at 1900. Set again at 2130. Working on sails all night. Very cold, sea choppy.

Third classman John J. Howell, Jr. takes a break.

21 Wednesday—Quarters at 0915 followed by fire drill. Studies at 1000. Position at noon, east of Salem, Mass. Yards braced up sharp, no sail set. Sea choppy. Scrub hammocks in afternoon. Wind died down in afternoon. We will have to move right along if exams are to be held tomorrow. Cold at night. Using fore and aft sails when practicable.

22 Thursday—Land in sight at daybreak. Taking stores out of boats, putzing, etc. Preparing to drop anchor. Finally dropped anchor at 1015. Exam schedule has been pushed ahead one day. Putting up awnings and general turn-to in afternoon. This is a very sheltered anchorage between Mt. Desert Island and East Lamoine. There isn't much of a town here, though. Boats out sailing in afternoon.

Putz was a brand name for a brass polish that past generations of cadets had rendered into a verb.

23 Friday—Regular morning turn-to. Third class seamanship examination during morning. First, second, and fourth class exams in afternoon. Boats out sailing—good breeze. Third class deck and engine cutter crews out for practice before dinner. Mail received.

24 Saturday—Field day all morning. Port watch liberty at 1330, uniform undress blues, neckerchiefs, and leggings. Orders were to stay in immediate vicinity and above all not to go to Bar Harbor or Ellsworth. But there is nothing in this vicinity except a general store and that is almost sold out. Most of the fellows took the chance and went to Ellsworth, nine miles away. The countryside is covered with blueberries and blackberries. Liberty up as usual at 2000. Very windy and temperature down to 45°.

25 Sunday—Regular morning turn-to. Captain's inspection at 1000 followed by church service on quarterdeck. Temperature still in 40s. Dress blues were uniform for inspection. Strong winds during early part of the day, dying out in evening.

26 Monday—Regular turn-to. Final examinations at 0900. Navigation for deck cadets, electricity for engineers, and signaling for fourth class. Temperature higher, light breezes. All boats, except motor sailer, out. Result of race: Wood, cox., 1st; Dickie, cox., 2nd; Smith, cox., 3rd; Christophers, cox., D.N.F. About a two hour race. At colors, Wood, O.O.W. had the dinghy hoisted. About a dozen of us on the boat falls, ran up the deck and brought the boat up fast, and stove a hole in it at the waterline. Everyone got quite a laugh out of it, except Wood, who stood us all on a seam for about an hour.

27 Tuesday—Regular turn-to. Loosed all sail after 0815 muster. Signaling exam for third class in morning, navigation in afternoon. First and second class first aid exam in morning. I did some typewriting for Mr. Rounds instead of taking the signaling exam. Furled all sail before supper. Very good job—and quickly done. Received a 4.8 in seamanship final. Not much wind, temperature higher. Twenty seven days to Boston!

Third classman Edwin A. Schmidt catches up on his sleep.

28 Wednesday—Studies in morning for first and second classes. Fourth class navigation exam in afternoon. I relieved Shuttleworth as Quartermaster for the 1200-1600 watch. Much warmer all day. 82° in sun at 1530.!!! Examinations just about finished up. Turn-to, painting fore and main fife rails. Mr. Connors, new watch officer, has duty today.

Apparently, Mr. Gray, the Executive Officer, resigned from the school. Mr. Thompson took his place and Mr. Rounds moved into his slot. That left an Officer of the Deck spot open.

29 Thursday—Fog in morning, bell on fo'c's'l being rung. Turn-to for lower classes, studies for upper. I took my signaling exam. Fog cleared after noon, all boats except one cutter out sailing. Crew in whaleboat digging clams.

30 Friday—Foggy again until 0900, Quarters at 0915. Prepared ship for sea. Mess cooks and strikers painting on gun deck all day. Sailed for Glen Cove, Long Island, at 1100. Used spanker to swing ship around, Quite noticeable swells in Frenchman's

Bay. Running into moderate breezes coming on the port bow. Visibility fair, possibility of fog again. New details go into effect at 2000. I am 1200 to 1600 Orderly. Rain during early evening, continuing through night. Set all fore and aft sails at 1630. All lines and gear were laid out on the port tack when the wind shifted over to starboard. Then it was discovered that the steering gear was jammed. Joe Foley had hung his dungarees on the steering cable running through the engineers' washroom. Double wheel on the quarter-deck was used until the problem could be cleared.

The *Nantucket's* engine's piston rods were located to the left and right of the narrow space delineated by the safety rails. When steaming, a cadet usually an underclassman, would be detailed to ease into this space on his hands and knees, carrying a long-spouted oil can. He then would attempt to lubricate the joints in the two-piece, flailing, back-acting rods.

31 Saturday—Raining at intervals during 0000-0400 watch. Damp and cold. Fog set in at 0100. All sail taken in. This is the kind of a night when the deckmen wish they were engineers. Fog whistle blowing. Field day in morning. Rain stopped and fog lifted at 1430. Position at 1600, approximately 50 miles east of Gloucester, course 242° p.s.c. Weather reports state a hurricane is moving northward and may hit New England. All weekend leave at New London, Conn. submarine base has been cancelled, according to news reports.

September

1 Sunday—0000-0400 as Orderly on bridge. Very soupy fog, horn being sounded. Position in vicinity of Race Point. No lights can be seen and only an occasional fog signal may be heard. Anchored near Provincetown at 0500. Fog began to clear and anchor weighed at 0814. Heading for canal. Visibility improving. Took pilot aboard and entered Cape Cod Canal at 1259. Made passage in 47 minutes. Strong wind making up. Anchored off Wings Neck at 1445 to wait until storm danger has passed. SE storm warnings flying. Regular sea watches on deck. Also in vicinity are colliers Jonancy (PSCo.), Sewall's Point (Mystic), and Eastern Point (Sprague).

2 Monday—On bridge 0000-0400. Beginning to rain, wind velocity increasing. Raining hard at 0300, wind force 7. Starboard anchor out with 45 fathoms of chain in about 4 fathoms of water. The hurricane center will pass out to sea before it reaches here. Storm died down by 0700. Sea still rough. Sky clear. Quarters at 0915. Today is Labor Day—no turn-to. Will get underway at 1030. Proceeding for Glen Cove under three boilers. Met destroyer 414 at 1045. Passed Hen and Chickens Lightship at 1229. Met City of Atlanta at 1230. All fore and aft sails except flying jib set at 1430. Point Judith Light abeam at 1520. Fog set in again at 1700. Engine stopped at 1800.

Destroyer 414 was the new USS *Russell* built by the Newport News Shipbuilding and Dry Dock Company and commissioned in September 1939. She was awarded an amazing sixteen battle stars in World War II.

Tuesday 3—Dropped anchor in Glen Cove harbor at 0700. Field day all morning. There is quite an argument going on about special liberty requests. Twenty-four lower classmen have put in for specials. The whole argument was ended though when it was announced that liberty for the port watch would commence at 1330 and end at 0900 Thursday.

4 Wednesday—On liberty. Stayed at St. Nicholas rectory in Jamaica. Went to LaGuardia Airport, World's Fair, and to the city.

The assistant pastor at St. Nicholas church, Rev. Stephen Frederick Lanen, was a relative. His father, Frederick Edward Lanen, and my mother, Alice Lanen Duffy, were first cousins. He was twenty years older than me, and I never felt comfortable in his company. I imagine he really did not approve of my choice of a career.

5 Thursday—Took 0559 train out of Jamaica. Returned aboard at 0915. Port detail as Orderly with McCollom, O.O.W. and Chapman, QM. Coxswain of spare liberty cutter at 1330.

6 Friday—You don't get much sleep standing four on and four off. Nothing much doing all day. Mayor Sherwood of Glen Cove aboard during morning. The "old man" had guards and sideboys present to render honors. But I sounded the bugle call for attention to the port side when it should have been attention to starboard, and Smith, R. S. couldn't get a sound out of the bosun's pipe—just a lot of wind.

7 Saturday—Attempt made at getting a field day started, but there was hardly anyone around to work. At 0815 muster, after the cutter crew, etc. had fallen out, there were 5 men left. Starboard watch returned at 0915. Field day going at 1000. No liberty until bright work has been done and decks cleaned. Engineers liberty at 1330, deck men at 1430. I am restricted. Baseball game ashore. M.N.S. lost 6 to 0. In gig crew for two trips, relieving Buckwalter. Liberty is up at 2200 on dock.

I must have received demerits for some infraction causing me to be restricted to the ship.

8 Sunday—Captain's inspection at 1000. Uniform—dress blues. Church services immediately following. Sea Scout Ship 12 came out in their whaleboat, challenging a race. Regular race boat crew, Christophers, cox., barely won by about ½ length. Starboard watch liberty, but only 1330 to 2000. Awnings taken in, all boats hoisted where possible, ship prepared for sea.

9 Monday—Weighed anchor at 0630 and sailed for Fall River, Mass. Heading East through Sound. Quarters at 0915 followed by man overboard drill. Buoy overboard on port side, but the bridge says "starboard side." Crew, already in starboard boat, have to shift to port lifeboat. Cates, cox., did a fine job in the smooth sea. Studies at 1000. Mr. Connors took class for first time. Two weeks from today, we are due in Boston. There's a lot of work to be done before then, though. Turn-to in afternoon.

10 Tuesday—Position at 0043, two and one half miles SE of Point Judith. Engine stopped most of time. Fog set in at 0230. Fog very thick during forenoon. Quarters at 0915 with collision and abandon ship drills. Studies at 1000. Full speed ahead at 1330. Passed Brenton Reef Lightship at 1440. Anchored off Conanicut Island near Newport. R.I. at 1535. Regular sea watches on deck.

11 Wednesday—Underway at 0630. Anchored 400 yards off City Pier, Fall River at 0915. Liberty for port watch, 1330 to 0900 Friday.

13 Friday—Returned aboard on 0900 cutter. Painting and tarring already started. Fore and mizzen rigging about done. Painting fo'c's'l quarters all day. Quite a few visitors aboard. Starboard watch liberty at 1330 until 2000 on Sunday. Still on orderly duty with McCollom, O.O.W.

This is the engine room end of the *Nantucket's* engine room telegraph system.

14 Saturday—Field day as usual all morning—rather hard with only a few men. Visitors aboard all afternoon. Sea Scouts from S.S.S. Dewey assisted with their cutter. Weather clear and warm. Cadet F. P. Genova is newest addition to appendicitis victims. He was taken to the Union Hospital in Fall River at 2000 last evening.

15 Sunday—Thick fog set in at 0230, finally lifting at about 0830. Captain's inspection at 1000, followed by church services on quarter-deck. Catholic Church party request not granted. Visitors aboard again. The city had a cop at the dock to hold back the crowd, but he had to send for a couple of cadets to go in and help. Starboard watch returned from liberty at 2000. Threat of another hurricane coming up the coast.

16 Monday—Hurricane approaching New England. Sailing postponed for possibly a day. General turn-to. Finally weighed anchor at 1630 and sailed for Cataumet, Mass. under three boilers. Uneventful trip. Anchored at 2345 about three miles from Cataumet.

17 Tuesday—Underway at 0645. Dropped anchor 15 minutes later. It's quite a trip in to the town (hamlet might better describe it, but it's still bigger than E. Lemoine). Continued painting on both decks.

18 Wednesday—Reveille at 0530. Regular morning turn-to. Chipping and painting all day. Everyone is turned-to for one of the few times this summer. There is still a h—of a lot of "quacking". Less than five days now. I'm not even trying to keep clean and almost all my gear can stand up and walk around by itself.

19 Thursday—Reveille at 0515. Painting all day. Just about finished now. Mail to us here is addressed to North Falmouth and postmarked Cataumet. Quite a lot of talk going on—someone stole a watch and money from four different lockers last night. The engineers have been pulling a lot of that night school stuff lately, but there's apt to be a little difficulty if it happens to certain persons tonight.

Although hazing was forbidden, it had a long history at MNS. The first and second classmen were the perpetrators, the third and fourth classmen the victims. During the 1939 cruise it was particularly vicious, so much so that when the *Nantucket* returned to the United States from northern Europe, she put into New London, CT, where a formal hearing was held. Several of the first class narrowly escaped suspension and the withholding of their diplomas. The new first and second classes were put on notice and reminded of the hazing ban, so when I and my classmates reported aboard, we escaped the physical harassment endured by so many before us. Oh, there was hazing, but it was not physical nor abusive. It does appear from this journal entry that a few of the engineers were up to some late night hijinks before we reached Boston, but apparently they were talked out of it, or my class, which would become second class in a matter of days, threatened retaliation.

20 Friday—Squaring up on the painting during morning. Shift hammocks at 1315 muster. Port watch liberty at 1430. Motor sailer towed cutter ashore. No. Falmouth is closed up for the winter, so Falmouth was the only place to go to, and there wasn't much there either. It was something to do, anyhow.

21 Saturday—Regular field day all morning. Entire poop and quarter-deck holystoned. Starboard watch liberty at 1330, expires at 2000 on dock. Strong wind and rough sea all day. Raining at 2000.

22 Sunday—Captain's inspection in dress blues at 1000, followed by church services. Prepare for sea at 1330. All set except for motor sailer. Sailing scheduled for 1700.

Swedish freighter at Hoosac Pier, Charlestown, Winter, 1939-40.

That ends my journal for the 1940 cruise, which terminated the next day when we docked at our regular berth at Pier 1 in the Charlestown Navy Yard. Many years later, I obtained a transcript of my marks earned in the two years in the school. At the end of the first six months, I scored 4.05 in the final exams for a ranking of eighth in the class, and 4.14 in average marks for the term, placing me in third position overall. For the sea term described above, my final exam score was 4.95 for second place, and my term average was 4.46 and sixth place.

CHAPTER FIVE

The *Widder*'s End

At the same time the *Nantucket* was finishing her summer's cruise, Konrad Hoppe in the *Widder* was also experiencing the final days of that vessel's voyage. On September 20. still in the central Atlantic, she was refueled by a *Kriegsmarine* tanker. In the next two weeks, no potential victims were sighted, so in early October the *Widder*'s commander, Hellmuth von Ruckteschell, notified the *Seekriegsleitung* (SKL) he was terminating the voyage, and they headed for Brest, which was reached on September 30. Her engines were shot. Breakdowns were commonplace. Even her ammunition was degrading and was jettisoned.

It had been a successful sojourn. Including the previously mentioned *British Petrol*, the tally was nine vessels sunk and one captured, for a total of 58,644 tons. They flew the flags of Britain, Holland, Greece, and Finland. The majority of the actions were mere blips on the screen of history, but several are noteworthy. According to Konrad, the raider's operating area originally was delineated by latitudes 18° 00' N and 24° 00' N, and longitudes 46° 00' W and 50° 00' W. Her second victim, on June 26, was the Norwegian motor tanker *Krossfonn* (9,323 tons) sailing in ballast from Casablanca to Fort de France, Martinique. She was captured, without incident, at latitude 21° 59' N and longitude 44° 45' W, about sixty-five miles east of the above operating area. It does appear von Ruckteschell eventually utilized a much greater portion of the Atlantic than originally designated. Back to the *Krossfonn*, her captain and chief engineer were taken prisoner aboard the *Widder*, and a German prize crew was assigned to supervise the Norwegian crew who dutifully brought their ship to Lorient in northwest France. The Norwegians were eventually repatriated to their homeland, and the *Krossfonn* became the *Spichern*, a *Kriegsmarine* supply vessel.

Forty days after the *Krossfonn* capture, during which time the British freighters *Davisian* (6,433 tons) and *King John* (5,228 tons) were disposed of, a second Norwegian tanker, the *Beaulieu* (6,114 tons) was "shot to pieces." Her master, chief officer, and two crewmen were killed. The two surviving deck officers took charge of the tanker's two lifeboats and eluded a boat from the *Widder* carrying a demolition crew. Their caution was needless because von Ruckteschell had decided to take no prisoners. Fortunately, five days later the British tanker *Cymbaline* came along, picked up the twenty-eight occupants of the two boats and took them to Gibraltar.

The *Widder*'s seventh victim was a once-in-a-wartime encounter—the *Killoran*, a full-rigged, three-masted barque. Flying the Finnish flag, she was a neutral. That did not faze von Ruckteschell one bit. He found an excuse to sink her. Someone in the *Widder* owned a movie camera and captured for posterity (the author possesses a video copy) a brief footage of the grand old lady, heaving to with most of her sails set, then plunging to the bottom when the demolition charges detonated. That occurred on August 10. Eleven days later, in what was becoming his classic routine, von Ruckteschell slowly followed a converging course that, after dark, would place the *Widder* dead ahead of the British freighter *Anglo-Saxon* (5,596 tons). Reversing course, he came down on the unsuspecting victim and literally "blew it out of the water." Only seven crew members managed to survive in an eighteen-foot wooden boat. Seventy-two days later, only two were living when they rode up onto a beach at Eleuthera in the Bahamas. Following the delivery of the *Beaulieu*'s lucky men to Gibraltar and the discharge of her cargo, the *Cymbaline* (6,317 tons) sailed for the Caribbean. Unbelievably, on September 2, the *Widder*'s lookouts sighted her and that night attacked. The result was an added twenty-six men in the prison quarters, seven lost, and the *Cymbaline*'s master and two crew spending fourteen days in a lifeboat before being rescued.

In due course, the *Widder*'s crew was paid off and disbanded. All had leave for Christmas. The ship itself was finished as a *Hilfskreuzer*. She was stripped of her armament and converted to a repair ship under her original Hamburg-America name *Neumark*. In that capacity she served the battleship *Tirpitz* during its 1942-1944 operations in and out of the northern Norwegian fjords until that vessel was destroyed by British aerial bombs on November 12, 1944.

CHAPTER SIX

1941 Cruise

May

I was now a first classman, charged with multiple leadership tasks. First of all, I was a top captain, sat at the head of my mess table, and was served first. When setting sail, I was in charge of the fore topmast and topgallant halyards. The foresail, the largest sail in the ship, was mine for both loosing and furling. In the event of having to abandon ship, I was to tend the forward falls at number 2 cutter. If a fire occurred, I was the nozzleman for number 5 hose.

MASSACHUSETTS NAUTICAL SCHOOL

SCHOOLSHIP NANTUCKET

2 April, 1941.

Reposing trust and confidence in the loyalty, subordination, obedience, and ability of

G.W. DUFFY,
I do hereby appoint him
CADET COXSWAIN, C.P.O.

All cadets under his command are enjoined to render him loyal and prompt obedience in the execution of his duties.

C.A.Abele, Captain,
Over   Superintendent.

The *Nantucket*, as a rule, underwent dry-docking and routine maintenance and repairs at the navy yard prior to its annual training cruise. Due to "defense work in progress in the yard," the work this year was awarded to a private concern on Staten Island, New York.

2 Friday—Left Pier 1, Charlestown Navy Yard at 0900 bound for Staten Island. Raining hard, temperature 42°. It's not going to be any fun out there. There are only 39 cadets on board, 20 deck and 19 engineer. Everyone is on detail, some have two details. I'm helmsman. Kind of tricky at first, but great once one gets the knack of it. Standing the 1000-1200 and 2000-2200. We are doing over 9 knots. That helps warm us up. Mr. Connors said he didn't think it was ever this cold in May! Well, there is nothing like an open bridge.

As the first class consisted of twenty-six cadets, and I believe we all made the trip to Brewer's, I'm curious now why only thirteen second classmen came along. Also, because the school's curriculum was being lengthened to three years, there was no incoming class, and the full complement of cadets for this cruise would be eighty-five. Connors, who graduated in 1932, had been sailing in tankers where the wheelhouses were enclosed and heated!

3 Saturday—Standing 0400-0600 on the wheel. It really is breezy up there now. Quite a swell running—its quite a job to stay "right on." We're moving 2° every time the swell hits us. It looks as though it's going to be a good day. The sun is shining for the first time in quite a while (it seems). In sight of N.Y.C. shortly before noon. Stood 1200-1400 on the wheel going through Ambrose Channel. Four ex-coast guard cutters of the Lake class anchored in the lower harbor with the British white ensign flying. Also a British cruiser taking ammunition aboard at Bayonne. Tug Alice Moran assisted docking at Brewer's, Mariner's Harbor.

M/T *Circe Shell* at Mariners Harbor.

May 4-15—Mariner's Harbor. This is rather a small yard—five being the largest number of ships in at a time. Since we have been here, the McKeesport and Wichita of American Pioneer Line have been in, as well as the Circe Shell and British Valour and the seized Italian freighter San Leonardo. On Thursday night, the bosun, Harry Brenner, and a gang boarded the Italian and returned with just about everything that was moveable, including 8 life rings, two chain falls, and a pelorus!

It takes about an hour to reach Manhattan from here by way of the South Ferry. Liberty, as usual every other night, from 1630 to 2300 and all day on weekends. There has been a lot of work done on board with over half a hundred workmen here at a time. The chart house has been rebuilt, new deck forward of the anchor windlass on the gun deck, bilge pumps overhauled, jib boom backstays, etc. renewed, new main t'gallant yard, repairs to dinghy and gig and davits, etc. Some things like the pumps hadn't been touched since the ship was built. I'm on detail as Officer of the Watch, with Coffey as Orderly. We are certainly not getting any sleep. Everyone in the city thinks we are English—the Paramount Theatre lets us in free! We were supposed to leave on the 12th, but it has been postponed to the 14th.

The British tanker *Circe Shell* was sunk by the German U-161 on February 21, 1942 in a position about 40 miles NW of Port of Spain, Trinidad. *Wichita* was sunk by U-516 on September 19, 1942 about 200 miles ENE of Port of Spain. There were no survivors. Austin L. Dougherty, MNS 1942, was the *Wichita's* third officer. It is possible he was with us in the shipyard. *McKeesport* was sunk by the U-258 on April 29, 1943 while in convoy ONS.5 in a position 61° N, 34° W.

14 Wednesday—Left Brewer's at 1800, proceeding out the Kill. Very warm evening, though rather breezy. Steaming on three boilers. Quite a few ships in Ambrose, including Sea Train New York and Leif, a small Norwegian flying the A. H. Bull house flag.

The *Sea Train New York* was a unique vessel in that she was fitted with railway tracks. Rail cars could be hoisted on and off with special cranes. Because of gauge differences in other countries, this was purely a domestic service.

15 Thursday—Field day all day—from the bridge right down to the gun deck and from 0400 to 1700. Entered Cape Cod Canal at 1830 with a strong head current. Passed the motor barge Luzitania and met the United States destroyer 431 and the Eastern freighter Norwalk. Proceeded up the coast.

The 431 was the new (commissioned in 1940) USS *Plunkett*. She survived World War II, earning five battle stars.

In Cape Cod canal, May 15, 1941. Cadets taking a break from scrubbing various canvas items shown drying on lines and on deck.

16 Friday—Underway at 0500, anchoring in Dorchester Bay near Castle Island at 0712. Using the motor sailer as the running boat. Still another general turn-to. Liberty party ashore at 1330 until 0900 on Saturday. Remainder of cadet body on dock waiting to join ship.

17 Saturday—No turn-to. Captain's inspection at 1030. I am in the motor sailer, relieving Carman in morning. Larry Brandt, seaman, left this morning to take a job as a rigger in Brooklyn, N.Y. Very choppy in bay with heavy rain during early evening.

18 Sunday—Liberty for port watch at 1000. Very windy and somewhat cool. Went home. Rode with O'Malley family.

Roger O'Malley was a second classman who lived in Gloucester. So his parents detoured to Newburyport before heading home to Cape Ann. Typical.

19 Monday—Liberty party on dock at 0800. Fire, collision, and abandon ship drills during morning. Also sail stations. T'gallants and trysail bent on. Field day on gun deck in afternoon. Starboard watch liberty 1630 to 2000.

I certainly didn't take the chance on thumbing a ride if I had to be on the dock at 0800, so I probably took the first train out of Newburyport to North Station in Boston. After that it was the El to City Point.

20 Tuesday—Drills during morning. Prepare ship for sea. Left Dorchester Bay at 1500 for Provincetown, Mass. Out the North channel to the Lightship. Provincetown in sight before dusk. Cruising around Bay.

21 Wednesday—Anchored off Provincetown at 0700. Using dinghy as running boat. Fire, collision, and sail drills in morning. Sail drills again after noon meal. Rigged second cutter and went sailing with Mr. Hodgson. Fine day for sailing. Curtin and Coffey went sailing in dinghy. Strong wind—they tried to jibe—the cutter picked them up about 500 yards from the ship. They were O.K., except that Coffey had my jacket on!

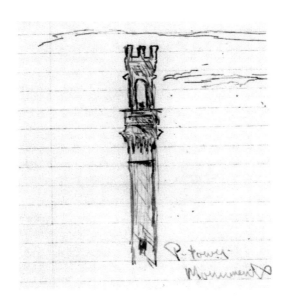

Provincetown Monument.

Jibing is similar to wearing, as previously described. The helmsman turns away from the wind. In a small boat this maneuver must be carefully handled, otherwise the result is a capsize.

22 Thursday—Regular port routine. Quarters at 0915. Fire, collision, and abandon ship drills. Then sail drill. We thought that would be all, but in the afternoon we went up again. And it was hot! The young men don't know their lines. They let go the wrong ones, and don't haul on the right ones. Turn-to after that. Rifle practice on bridge after supper. Five rounds for the "crow" men, then others after that. Weighed anchor at 2105, bound for Boston. Steaming on two boilers.

I was being a bit harsh on the "young men." The running rigging on the *Nantucket* consisted of well over one hundred halyards, sheets, tacks, vangs, topping lifts, clew lines, etc., not to mention numerous boat falls, mooring lines, and stunsail gear.

The arms insignia for the cadet petty officers contained an eagle with its wings outspread. The bird was commonly referred to as a crow.

23 Friday—At daybreak, swinging ship for deviation off Boston Lightship. Proceeded in through "The Narrows", anchoring near Castle Island at 1027. Liberty for port watch, 1400-2000. Very hot ashore. Rain showers during evening.

24 Saturday—Field day in morning. Preparing for sea. I worked with Mr. Hodgson on steering cables. Weighed anchor at 1440 in a driving thunderstorm. Rather uncomfortable. Out through "The Narrows." Met the U.S.S. Plunkett. Quite a swell outside—everyone is waiting for the first seasick victim. Set fore and aft sails at 1639, with exception of flying jib.

25 Sunday—All fore and aft sails set. Speed dropping down though. Captain's inspection at 1000. Church service at 1100. Ship is tossing around quite a bit. The engine revs are down so far, that we are not even making steerageway. Between 1400 and 1500, we made 1.2 miles!!! It's very cold and it's a problem to keep warm. Took in all sail during early PM. About 2/3 of the young men are seasick and then they got anti-typhoid shots, to top it off. They are a tough looking outfit.

Under classmen were referred to and addressed as "young men."

26 Monday—Changed course at 0645 to 303° True. We are making hardly any headway at all. F. Spollett, 2/c engineer, is pretty sick and I believe an attempt will be made to put him ashore. Quarters at 0915 with fire and collision drill. Studies following, as usual. Coast Guard patrol boat Argo alongside at 1800. Life boat crew with Mr. Hodgson, coxswain, took Spollett to the Argo. Rather a heavy sea and the Argo really rolled. We are approximately 100 miles south of Newport, R.I.

27 Tuesday—Regular routine. Quarters and fire and collision drills. Studies. Course is 285° True, direct for Sandy Hook. The Captain is evidently trying to get in close to shore and get rid of this head wind. At noon we were 125 miles due east of Barnegat Light, N.J. Course changed at 1600 to 250° True. No one knows just where we are bound for and the engineers are sweeping out the bunkers. Set headsails at 0845 and furled at 1530. Port watch has the screw watch tonight.

"Screw watch." That was the much-hated midnight to 0400.

28 Wednesday—Regular routine. Quarters at 0915. Abandon ship and man overboard drills. Course is now 217° True for Winter Quarter Lightship. Scrubbed hammocks in afternoon. Passed through the largest school of porpoises that I have seen—at least 35 or 40. More than a dozen under the forefoot at one time. Passed Winter Quarter Lightship at 1930. Did some star sights at twilight—not too good.

29 Thursday—Off Cape Henry at 0700. Clocks set back during the night to Eastern Standard Time. Tug with coal lighter on hand as we anchored off Naval Operating Base, Norfolk, Va. Commenced coaling at 1030. Knock off for dinner (1 hour), and 20 minutes at 1500. Frank Massey, M.N.S. '40, aboard the U.S.S. Prairie (AD 15), paid a visit during afternoon. Fresh water boat alongside at 1600. Knock-off and wash. We started to use the water as fast as the boat could put it in the tank. Millions of fresh water for all! 1900. Very strong wind, almost a gale, came down from the North. Caused a bit of concern for over an hour. Men aloft to lash down fore topgallant sail. Motor sailer back from trip thoroughly wet down. Had to rig guess warp and almost lost O'Malley overboard. Spray flying over bow and coming up from bow of lighter. Extra lines on lighter. Any of us who did any work got wet in the process.

Massey graduated in April, 1940, thus was a first classman during my six months as a fourth classman. He was quite fortunate to have drawn an assignment to the *Prairie*, less than a year old.

30 Friday—Memorial Day. We will certainly remember it. Reveille at 0530 and coffee. Commenced coaling at 0600. Knock off for 3/4 hour at breakfast time. It is certainly a better day for coaling than yesterday. It is cool and overcast with light showers early in the day. Carrying a deck load. Built up coal bags, full, to form enclosures in both waists and filled the spaces with loose coal. Navy tug took lighter away at 1100. All the meals have been cafeteria style. Weighed anchor at 1328, bound for Portsmouth, N.H. Proceeded out Hampton Roads. Clear of "restricted channel" at 1600. I am Officer of the Watch. Bill Ball is Quartermaster, and G. A. Davis 3/c, Orderly. Standing 2000 to 2400 watch with Mr. Connors. No standing around. Got to be "On the ball" every second. You learn your stuff, though. The O.O.W. also makes the clock rounds every half hour.

The OOW carried a clock fitted with a paper dial which rotated in conjunction with the hour hand. Throughout the ship were keys to be inserted, registering on the paper the fact that the OOW had visited that site on his rounds of inspection.

31 Saturday. Field day. I have the 0800 to 1200 bridge watch. Weather clear with an excellent horizon. Fooling around with navigation most of watch. Knock off after field day. Canteen at 1500. Met a Norwegian whaling ship, Southbound at 1630. On the bridge for the 1800-2000. The weather has become overcast rather suddenly and it looks as if there may be rain.

**Nantucket at sea under sail, looking aft on main deck.
Note drinking fountains in center, commonly known as the scuttlebutt.**

June

1 Sunday—Raining hard as we took over the 0400 to 0800. Clocks are being moved ahead 20 minutes each watch to change to Eastern Daylight Savings Time. Met S.S. City of Birmingham south of Block Island, heading for N. Y. C. Since we left Norfolk we have been averaging a little better than 8 knots, steaming on three boilers. It begins to look as though we might make Portsmouth on schedule! Inspection on gun deck because of weather, Mr. Thompson inspecting. About 1330, 10 miles E x S of Block Island, in poor visibility, a small cabin cruiser carrying two men and two women was sighted. They asked for directions, saying they had left Providence for Newport and had gone by Newport, right to sea. Luckily, they hit Block Island, refueled, but then headed out in the wrong direction. We took them as far as Negro Ledge off New Bedford after giving them some hot tea and sandwiches. Anchored off Wing's Neck, at the West entrance to the Cape Cod Canal, at 2100.

The *City of Birmingham*, carrying 263 passengers, 113 crew, and 5 U. S. Naval gunners, was torpedoed on June 30, 1942 by the U-202 about 250 miles east of Cape Hatteras. She was bound from Norfolk, Virginia to Bermuda and was being escorted by the USS *Stansbury* (DD 180). Lost were 2 passengers and 7 crew.

2 Monday—On the bridge 0000-0400 with Mr. Hodgson, Ball, and Davis. Making clock rounds every half hour and taking 12-15 minutes for each round. Underway at 0615. Field day in A.M. 1200-1600 on bridge. Abeam Thacher's Island at 1600. Surprise "man overboard" drill at 1615, Stevenson coxswain. Dropped anchor at 1945 off Kittery Point, across from Fort Constitution. U.S.S. Trout (SS 202) 250 yards upstream. Using motor sailer as running boat.

The *Trout* was sunk with all hands on its eleventh war patrol by a Japanese warship in the East China Sea on February 29, 1944.

3 Thursday. Stood 0400-0800, a bit cool. Quarters at 0915 with fire and provide all boats drills. Lowered 2nd and 3rd cutters, gig, and whaleboat for rowing drills. I coxswained the 2nd cutter. Mr. Hodgson in charge overall. All sail was loosed at reveille and furled at 1100. The Trout sailed during rowing drill. The U.S.S. Triton (SS 201) sailed in afternoon. Starboard watch liberty 1300-2000.

The *Triton* was equally as unlucky as the *Trout*. She was lost with all hands on her sixth patrol on or about March 15, 1943.

4 Wednesday to 6 Friday—We are anchored in Pepperell's Cove, about 60 fathoms of chain out. This is claimed to be the deepest harbor on the Atlantic coast. Not much traffic, however. There is a bad current and quite a few narrow turns. Weather is very changeable, temperature is low. NE storm warnings were hoisted Wednesday. Rain and cold all day Thursday.

Actually, Portsmouth lies on the south bank of the Piscataqua River, and we were anchored on the Kittery, Maine side. From the Cove, the river extended a mile and a half in a westerly direction before angling off to the west-northwest. This mile-and-a-half stretch is shown on an 1866 United States Coast Survey chart to have center channel depths from fifty-seven to seventy-five feet at mean low water.

7 Saturday—Weighed anchor, bound for Fort Pond Bay (Montauk), L.I., N.Y. at 1015. Proceeding to sea. Quite a bad swell and—is seasick again or as per usual. Course is outside Provincetown and through Vineyard Sound.

8 Sunday—On the bridge 0400-0800. Strong head wind and current. It seems that whatever way we head, we still get a head wind!! Captain's inspection at 1000, passing Vineyard Lightship. Met collier James Elwood Jones at 1050, bound for the canal. Church services at 1100. Anchored at 1900 in Fort Pond Bay, Montauk, L. I. Whaleboat being used as running boat. This isn't much of a place—a dozen fishing boats and the tail end of the Long Island Rail Road, plus a handful of automobiles.

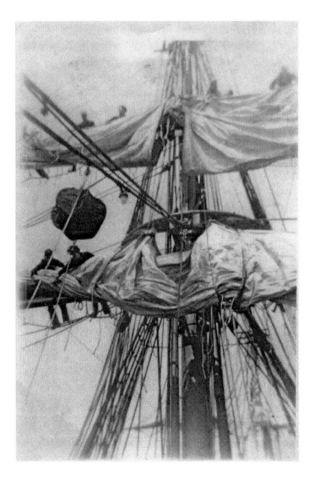

Nantucket **at anchor in Fort Pond Bay, Montuak, Long island,
New York. Cadets furling fore topsail (upper sail) and foresail (lower sail).
Author at far left on foresail yard.**

9 Monday—Three months from today and its "Goodbye Nantucket". Quarters at 0915. Studies following. Rifle drill on deck from 1315 to 1400. Boats out sailing. I took 2nd cutter, racing 3rd cutter (Mr. Connors), and gig (McLean). We finished third. It has been a very good day with excellent visibility and a fresh breeze.

10 Tuesday—Regular routine. Quarters and collision drill. Studies. Boats out sailing in afternoon. Prepare for sea during evening. Rifle drill on deck after dinner.

11 Wednesday—Underway at 0600. Steaming on two boilers into Long Island Sound. Set all sail except flying jib and t'gants at 0845 on port tack, headed up towards Point Judith. Studies at 1000. Sighted seven submarines, identifying two—163 and 164. Wearing ship at 1130, course back down Sound. Submarine off Fisher's Island practicing diving. Topgallants set at noon. Not much wind, though. Scrub hammocks in P.M. Furled all sail at 1500. Anchored in Fort Pond Bay at 1700.

Watching submarines in Long Island Sound. Captain Abele on bridge wing. First classman John J. Howell, Jr. at steering wheel.

SS 163 was the USS *Barracuda* commissioned in October 1924, and the SS 164 was the USS *Bass* commissioned a few days under one year later. Both boats experienced numerous problems and were laid up in the early 30s. Although they returned to service in 1940 or 1941, neither compiled any war record and were decommissioned in early 1945.

12 Thursday—Underway at 0705. Proceeding on same course as yesterday. Quarters at 0915. Starboard watch crew over with Stevenson, cox. Port watch crew over right after. Howell is on wheel, so I went in the boat. DiCori was coxswain. Our time was about two minutes better. Set all sail except flying jib and fore topmast staysail at 1005—uncoupled. Studies. Submarine diving off our starboard bow at noon. Furled all sail at 1315. It took us just about an hour on the fore sail! Headed back for Montauk. Anchored at 1515. Rain showers during late evening.

13 Friday—General field day all day. Painting done in gun deck. Occasional rain during morning. We are preparing for some sort of an inspection at Newport. S.S. Robin Moor has been sunk recently, reputedly by a Nazi sub. Quite a bit of comment has been aroused.

The *Robin Moor* was the second United States merchant vessel sunk in World War II. In November 1940, the MS *City of Rayville* struck a German-laid mine in Bass Strait, between the Australian mainland and the island of Tasmania. One crew member was lost. The *Robin Moor* was bound from New York to Capetown carrying general cargo and eight passengers when she was stopped by the U-69. This incident occurred on May 21 in 6° 10′ N, 25° 40′ W. Because the *Robin Moor* was carrying cargo consigned to interests in countries that were at war with Germany, the submarine commander gave the crew and passengers thirty minutes to abandon ship. He then sank the freighter with a torpedo and shelling by his deck gun. Three of the *Robin Moor's* lifeboats were sighted by a Capetown-bound ship on June 2 and their occupants rescued. The fourth boat was not found until June 8 by a Brazilian steamer and its people taken to Recife. None of the *Robin Moor* crew or passengers were lost.

14 Saturday—Underway shortly after 0600, bound for Newport, R.I. Rather foggy outside and the old man didn't know whether or not to leave. Steaming on three boilers. Anchored off Goat Island Naval Base at 1200. U.S.S. New York (BB 34), U.S.S. Prairie (AD 15), and quite a few destroyers in here. Starboard watch liberty at 1400 until 0900 tomorrow. Its still quite foggy. Mr. Wells and Mr. Reynolds, machinists; Seaman Wilcox; "Sarge" MacLellan, Master at Arms; all left today at their own request. Intermittent fog all day. During clear spaces we are signaling to various ships. Can make out another battleship and a cruiser.

With the defense industry heating up, jobs at much better pay than what could be earned at Massachusetts Nautical School were becoming available, thus the departure of these men and the aforementioned Brandt.

15 Sunday—Starboard watch returned at 0900. Liberty for us at 1030. Raining all morning with fog. Weather cleared up in afternoon. There is not much to do in this place. Stevens, DiCori, and I returned at 1900 in a motor launch from the U.S.S. Melville (AD 2).

16 Monday—Still damp and foggy. Naval examining board in charge of Capt. Copeland inspected ship and cadets at 0945. Held fire, collision, abandon ship, and sail drills. Man overboard drill after dinner. All sails furled. Liberty for starboard watch, 1630 to 2100.

Howard G. Copeland was a 1906 graduate of MNS. During the sail drills, I was standing near the examining board, and as the cadets began to go aloft, one of the board members asked Capt. Copeland what they were doing. "Working up an appetite for prunes" was the former cadet's reply.

17 Tuesday—This is "Bunker Hill Day" in Massachusetts, a state holiday, but we have quarters as usual and loosed all sail. Studies, Furled all sail at 1120. All furled in 26 minutes. It is a good day for a change. Port watch overnight, 1330 to 0900 tomorrow. I went ashore at 1500 and returned at 2200. I have never seen so many uniforms in one place. Everyone is wondering who we are, but no one ever thinks that we may be merchant mariners.

Sailing at Newport. Boat to left is one of the whaleboats and foreground boat is one of the cutters as evidence by the rowlock in the gunwale.

**Sailing at Newport. Coxswain is First Classman James J. Coffey.
Cadet to right is Fourth Classman Francis L. Lucas.**

Those overnight liberties were great for the guys who lived in the Fall River and New Bedford areas, but Newburyport was a long trip, so I just set my own hours, going and coming as I pleased.

18 Wednesday—Liberty party back. Parthenais 1 hour late; Carman, Bailly, and L'Esperance 3 hours late; Light about 5. Quarters and studies. Starboard watch liberty at 1300. Fog set in during late afternoon until 2100.

Light and Carman lived in Springfield, and Parthenais was from Lawrence. Apparently, they and the others went home for the night and had problems returning. How many demerits they earned for their transgressions was not immediately noted.

19 Thursday—No milk for breakfast yesterday and then none today—and we are in an American port! So, the entire cadet corps refused to go on deck for 0815 muster and turn-to. Mr. Rounds came down and found everyone still sitting at the mess tables. He raised quite a fuss (naturally). We went up on deck and Capt. Abele, very worried, and far different than his usual self, had a little bit to say. "The only punishment will be mass punishment and if this sort of thing happens again, I shall have to recommend the rescinding of your reserve appointments. That's all." Mr. Thompson later said,

"Granted that you have a grievance and I believe you have. However, you went at this thing the wrong way." Studies at 1000. Sailing at 1045. Port watch liberty at 1300. Mast at noon. I had 5 men on report for a total of 70 demerits.

When a cadet did something wrong—and there was a published Index of Offenses Against Discipline containing twenty-six class A and forty-six class B categories—he was "put on report." Each day, Monday through Friday, the captain held court in a position amidships near the main mast. This was commonly called "captain's mast." The cadet on report had the charges against him read, the captain decided if he was guilty or not, and if guilty, the punishment in the form of demerits awarded. These demerits had to be "worked off," one hour per demerit during the cadet's off duty time. In the abovementioned mast I had written reports on five men. At a guess, the five cadets who came aboard late on Wednesday were under my jurisdiction, and it was my duty, therefore, to put them on report for violating the class B (3) offense of being "absent without leave or after leave has expired."

20 Friday—Weighed anchor, bound for Boston, not Norfolk as originally scheduled. It is a very hot day. Entered Cape Cod Canal at noon. Met S.S. Robin Adair at entrance. Refraction on horizon today is the worst I have seen. Barges and ships are seen double, the second image being inverted. We sighted the U. S. Army Transport Kent and had quite a time making it out. We finally dropped anchor in Dorchester Bay at the usual anchorage at 1955.

That USAT *Kent* was another old clunker, built in 1918 for Grace Lines as the *Santa Teresa*. About the time we saw her, she had become the USS *Kent* (AP 28). In 1943 she was back in the army, converted to the United States Army hospital ship *Ernest Hinds*. She survived the war.

21 Saturday—I am coxswain of the running boat, using the motor sailer. Captain's inspection at 1000 following which uniform was changed to whites. Starboard watch liberty at 1130. It is hot as hell, both ashore and on board.

About this time, President Roosevelt sent a message to Congress concerning the sinking of the *Robin Moor*. He said, "This is a warning that the United States may use the high seas of the world only with Nazi consent. Were we to yield on this we would inevitably submit to world domination at the hands of the present leaders of the German Reich. We are not yielding," he declared, "and we do not propose to."

22 Sunday—Liberty for port watch at 1000 in dress whites. It is still pretty hot. Light thunder storms in evening.

23 Monday—Liberty party back at 0815. Raining intermittently all morning. Our whites are a mess. Running boat trips all day. It finally cleared up around suppertime. Starboard watch liberty 1600-2000.

24 Tuesday—Regular port routine. Quarters and studies. Prepared for sea. Weighed anchor at 1745 for Rockport, Mass. Outside near The Graves, the reversing rams in the engine room went haywire. Out of control signal hoisted. Running slow ahead to Eastward.

25 Wednesday—I certainly was surprised when I came on deck this morning and found us in President Roads! Because of the damage in the engine room we returned to Boston, anchoring as usual in Dorchester Bay at 0900. Quarters and studies in morning.

First classman George B. Stevenson, seated on pin rail with bugle box at his back, offers a number on his harmonica.

27 June to 7 July—Dorchester Bay. Liberties are from 1630 to 2000. On Friday, the 27th, whites were uniform. The liberty party consisted of 12 men! The running boat trips are very wet, but one dries out on the return trip. There is one advantage to this anchorage—we can see all the traffic in and out of Boston.

The motor sailer crew generally consisted of four cadets: a first or second class deck cadet as coxswain, a first or second class engine cadet as motorman, and two underclass cadets as bow and stern men. Communications between the coxswain and the motorman, even though they were within arms' lengths of each other, were accomplished by means of bell signals in a system utilized by tugboats and small vessels lacking engine room telegraphs. It was quite simple: Boat stopped. To go slow ahead, ring one bell. For full ahead, ring a jingle. To stop, ring two bells slightly separated. Boat stopped. To go slow astern, ring two bells in quick succession. To go full astern, ring a jingle. To stop, ring one bell.

For a memory jogger, we would rattle off, "A bell, a jingle, a bell, a bell, two bells, a jingle, a bell." Also to be remembered were full ahead to full astern, ring four bells, and slow ahead to full astern, ring three bells. It gave our dockings and undockings a very professional touch!

8 July—Weighed anchor at 1230, bound for Provincetown, Mass. We are scheduled to take four days, so we certainly aren't going direct. Man overboard drill off Graves Light, Stevens, coxswain. U. S. Navy minesweepers in practice maneuvers off shore. Began to set all sail at 1330. Finally uncoupled. Running under all plain sail except flying jib. Furled t'gants at 1900. Position at 2400, 30 miles east of Cape Ann. Foggy and damp all night.

9 Wednesday—Fog has cleared and it has appearances of turning into a good day. Wearing ship shortly after 0800. Quarters at 0915 with collision drill. Headed south. Set topgallant sails at 0940. I am the 0800-1200 "Boatswain's Mate" and what a workout one gets on all this sail work.

10 Thursday—Still under sail. Set topgallants in morning. Quarters at 0915. Fire drill and then man overboard with all sail set. Backed around main yards to stop ship. Wore ship after boat is hoisted. Headed north again. Studies both in morning and afternoon. Breeze died down early in afternoon and then about supper time it picked up great. We really heeled over—the right way to sail.

11 Friday—Still under sail. Everyone is wondering just when we will get in. We have been in port so much lately that we miss it all at sea. Another man overboard drill at quarters. Finally furled sail and steamed up at 1900. Laying-to off Provincetown at midnight.

12 Saturday—Dropped anchor in harbor at 0600. Using cutter and gig for running boats. S.S. Steel Pier in and out.

The *Steel Pier* was an excursion boat which left Boston every morning, laid over in Provincetown for four or five hours, and then returned to Boston.

14 Monday—Quarters at 0915, prepare ship for sea, and studies. Weighed anchor at 1100, leaving for Rockland, Maine. Fog for a short time early in afternoon. Uncoupled shortly before 1600. Setting all sail except flying jib. Speed through the night 0.0! We did drift a bit, however.

15 Tuesday—"Steam up" at daybreak. Furled all sail. There is still practically no wind and the sea is flat. Slight breeze sprung up at 0830. Both watches on deck, loosing all sail except flying jib. Quarters and air bedding. Studies both morning and afternoon.

16 Wednesday—Wearing ship at 0830. Quarters, fire, and collision drills. These sails are getting to be a very definite pain in the neck. The "old man" has got everybody pretty sore at him. He jumps and yells and makes a big fuss over the smallest things. All sail furled at 1500—total time, 23 minutes. Proceeded under steam. Man overboard drill, Hutchinson, coxswain. While we were drifting under canvas, we rolled very slightly. As soon as the ship got under way, though, it was hard to keep our footing.

17 Thursday—Yesterday everyone thought that sailing was, for the time being, out of the question. But that crazy fool down aft decided he'd sail today. The engine was stopped and uncoupled, men sent aloft to loose, and then, for some unknown reason, were called back down. The jib, fore topmast staysail, and spanker were set and we just drifted. Fog closed in shortly after noon. Took in sails at 1430. So, when the ship was ready, weather wouldn't permit our movement. All the time since P-town, when the sun was shining, we drifted. Now they want to go someplace, we have fog. I'm glad I have only 54 days left. Anchored at 2128, although the fog was lifting at intervals. Used port anchor, walking it out to 15 fathoms and then letting it go from there. Regular sea watches on deck.

18 Friday—Fog bound. Can't see a thing. Began to weigh anchor at 0830. There were 60 fathoms out. Heaved 'round to 30, then the fog dropped down. Quarters and studies. At noon it looks as though we are stuck for a good while. Finally got underway at about 1345, though its very foggy. Lookouts posted aloft and on jib boom. You can't see more than a ship's length ahead. Anchored at 1630 after coming up through 22 foggy miles without seeing ¼ of the buoys.

18 July to 21 July—Rockland, Me.

22 Tuesday—Weighed anchor at 1100. Set jib to swing bow around. Steaming out into Penobscot Bay. Passing trial-run buoys, marked with numbers from upriver and painted white with black diamonds. A very good day, cool in the Bay, tho it is probably a "scorcher" inshore. Wooden mine sweepers are built at Rockland. One of them was on the trial range as we left. Met the S.S. William J. Salman in Two Bush Channel. Studies in afternoon. Everyone expected a man overboard drill during the 1600-1800 watch, but the "old man" crossed us up and tossed the buoy at about 1830. Carman, Coxswain.

The SS *William J. Salman*, 2,618 gross tons, was torpedoed and sunk on May 18, 1942, by the U-125 at 20° 08′ N, 83° 46′ W. This position is about 125 miles south of Cape Frances on the Isla de la Juventud in the Caribbean. Of her crew of twenty-eight, six, including her master, were lost.

23 Wednesday—Set all sail during the 0400-0800 watch. Uncoupled. Course about NW. We are probably going to sail for a day and a half, then steam down to Martha's Vineyard. Quarters as usual. Collision and provide all boats drills. Studies. Air bedding. Scrub hammocks. I worked harder on mine today than I ever have, yet I was using a salt water soogee, lye, and fresh water solution. Sighted the Swedish bark Abraham Rydberg bound for Portland out of Boston. It was a rare sight. She was running before the wind—we were close-hauled on the port tack. The Rydberg is painted white, and with her white sails, presented a very nice picture. Our position at the time was about 10 miles NE of Cape Ann. Wore ship at 1630, both watches on deck. Now on starboard tack.

24 Thursday—Still under all sail. Wore ship during 0400-0800 watch. Quarters and fire drill. Both watches wore ship again. Studies at 1000. Furled all sail, with both watches on deck at 1300. Man overboard drill at 1620. Burns, coxswain. I went as Rated Man. Shortly after this, the steering engine went on the "blink"; hand steering resorted to. It took quite a while to get the thing straightened up again. Highland Light in sight at 2100.

Although Burns was the coxswain, and normally the coxswain was in command of the boat, for some reason, I as "cadet coxswain, CPO" was assigned the command.

25 Friday—Passed Cross Rip Light Vessel shortly after daybreak. Ship was suddenly stopped by Chief Kelley—a bearing or something burned out. The port anchor was dropped at 0645. Anchor aweigh again at 0730. Whites are uniform on deck after 0800. Dropped anchor in the harbor of Vineyard Haven at 1015. Rigged out boat booms, dropped gangways, lowered dinghy and 1st cutter. Motor sailer lowered later in day. Painted hull all afternoon. Field day on gun deck. Very hot. Starboard watch liberty 1630-2000. Rain started at 2000 as the liberty party was returning.

For some reason, there are no entries for 26 Saturday through 28 Monday. The journal is intact, and its page numbers consecutive, but I have no clue as to what happened. On the 29th, we are still at Vineyard Haven, so we'll take it from there.

29 Tuesday—Rain started at 2000 last night as the liberty party was returning. The sea was very choppy with a high wind. At 0030, the wind was very strong. The motor sailer, tied up to the port boom with a "guess warp", and a stern line to the ship, tossed around and parted the "guess warp". While the Captain and Mr. Hodgson with 20 cadets finally got the boat tied up astern, the ship began to drag anchor. The yards were braced 'round, but this did no good. The starboard anchor was dropped, and we held, after dragging about 350 yards to within 100 yards of the breakwater. At that we had less than 20 feet of water. In the morning we attempted to go back to the original anchorage, but the engineers had steam in only one boiler and the anchor cables had picked up a full round turn. The port watch had been turned out at 0400 and stayed on deck until 0800. It was funny, there we were with the motor sailer threatening to go adrift, the ship almost aground and there was the "old man" yelling about having his square ports closed! We weighed anchor at 1130, bound for Boston.

30 Wednesday—Regular sea routine. Quarters, with collision drill. Very poor day—overcast and damp. Engine uncoupled at 0130, fore and aft sails set. Set all plain sail during 0400-0800 watch. Furled topgallants at noon, also flying jib. Appears as if it might rain—breeze springing up. Rain during latter part of day.

31 Thursday—Still overcast. Starboard watch wearing ship at 0400. We worked right through the whole 0400-0800. Still under sail, running before wind, 15 miles Southeast of Cape Ann, with all headsails, both topsails, foresail, and spanker set. Prepared for quarters. First call had gone and the bugler was ready to sound muster, when "Man overboard!" We were doing four or five knots, and it's quite a trick to get this ship stopped without being caught aback. The main topsail was braced up, staysail hauled down, and spanker clewed up. Carman was coxswain, and his crew really had to row. Quarters followed, but the port watch set the spanker. At 0920 a sailing vessel was sighted, heading North. She turned out to be a topsail schooner, three-masted—a very nice sight. Studies later. Starboard watch on deck at 1245 commenced furling sail. The canvas was wet, but we did a good job, particularly good on the heavy foresail. Kept the jib and spanker set until 1500. Steam up, and headed in at 1530. Very foggy. Stopped, off Boston Lightship at 1700. Several small vessels in vicinity. Underway shortly after 2000, moved into harbor, anchoring off Deer Island Light. Several tankers nearby, and the Swedish ship Vingaren. We were right in the middle of the channel.

August

1 Friday—Weighed anchor at 0600, going into Dorchester Bay, dropping the hook at 0703. Field day, all day long.

2 Saturday through 6 Wednesday, at anchor.

7 Thursday—Weighed anchor at 1145. Bound for Portland, Me. H.M.S. Lady Nelson passed as we left anchorage. Mine sweepers operating in Inner harbor. I am helmsman out through North Channel. Studies as usual. Man overboard drill at 1500, Malcolm Light, coxswain. Set all sail immediately afterwards.

8 Friday—Position at 0600, 8.5 miles SE of Cape Ann Light. Still under sail, but making very little headway. It's a fine, clear day. Quarters as per usual, with collision and provide all boats drill. Studies. I was 1000-1200 helmsman. Our course was set at 029° p.s.c. and for most of the watch we had no headway and the compass heading went up as far as 065°—almost 40° off course. Hauled down jib and staysail in order to bring her about. Studies in afternoon. Passed S.S. Pan Maine out of Bucksport at 2130.

9 Saturday—I was 0400-0600 helmsman and it was COLD. Field day all morning. Still under sail. 1200-1400 helmsman. All cadets turned-to painting, etc. in afternoon. Saturday P.M. has always been a day off, but somebody screwed up the detail. I supervised painting in the "eyes". 1800-2000 helmsman.

10 Sunday—Passed S.S. Yarmouth bound SW at 0300. I was 0200-0400 helmsman. Very good breeze during morning. T'gants and flying jib not set and we were really spanking along. Captain's inspection at 1000. Church services at 1045. And we really have the afternoon off. Starboard watch on deck set t'gants at 1410. Breeze died down later, and t'gallants were furled after supper. Very fine horizon for star sights after sunset. Everyone out with his sextant, but I have the 2000-2200 wheel watch.

11 Monday—Standing 0400-0600 wheel watch. A very bright moon makes almost daylight around the deck. Wearing ship at 0615, headed approximately NE. Set t'gallants. Quarters at 0915, with fire drill. Then the "old man" tossed over the life ring. We had quite a time getting the main yards braced around with jigger tackles and everything else fouling. Ball was coxswain. Studies at 1000. Sloop Nomad out of Boston came up close by. Coast Guard patrol plane circled around. Two destroyers sighted at 1030 came up close at 1230. They were on simulated firing practice. Wearing ship 1230 to 1315. I was on wheel. Studies in afternoon. Furled t'gants after supper. There is quite a breeze springing up and it looks like rain.

12 Tuesday—Stood 0200-0400 wheel watch. If this is Summer in the North Atlantic, I'll hate to see Winter in the North Atlantic—it really was cold. Raining at daybreak. Starboard watch wearing ship. Oilskins uniform. Quarters for watch below at 0915. Both watches on deck at 0930 to furl sail. The rain had stopped, but the canvas was very wet and furling was like trying to bend boards. Steam up and full ahead at 1030, headed for Portland. A very heavy swell running. One wave broke right over the quarter-deck, wetting down Mr. Hodgson and the entire Third class. Studies in afternoon. Artificial respiration instruction for upper classes. Furled fore and aft sails at 1730. Then at about 2100 when we were only 4 miles from the Portland Lightship the "old man" decided not to go in. So we steamed around, maintaining position all night.

13 Wednesday—Proceeding in at 0600, dropping anchor at 0830. Several destroyers, a naval tanker, and the Prairie are in. The harbor has changed quite a bit in the year. The Bath-Todd shipyard is just about the biggest improvement.

14 Thursday through 17 Sunday. At anchor off Portland's Eastern Promenade.

18 Monday—Underway at 1100, U.S.C.G. S.S. Oceanographer going out just ahead of us. Met two destroyers shortly after dinner. Studies as usual. Man overboard drill with Shershun, coxswain. The sun was shining on the water right in line with the buoy so quite a length of time was spent in finding it. Ship being swung for deviations, first classmen on all three compasses. Swinging ship again at 1630 with Mr. Rounds observing all three compasses. Setting all sail at 1700. Got the fore topsail yard up "2 blocks." Curtin, Hutchinson, Burns, and I were fore-handing and Olsen belaying, when the halyard got away from us. A couple of fellows came close to being hurt when they were snapped up the deck. I burned both of my hands trying to hang on and Olsen burned one finger and the back of his legs. My right fingers are pretty sore and the skin is off two of them. Turned in to sick bay for the night. I guess the sails were finally set.

The routine for setting the fore topsail was this: Cadets went aloft to cast off the gaskets holding the furled sails on top of the yard arm. Then the clews (corners) of the loosed sail were hauled out to the ends of the fore sail yard. There was a double (two-sheaved) block on the topsail yard and another on the topmast. The halyard ran between these and then to a fairlead block on deck. A number of cadets would grasp the halyard and run down the deck, hoisting the yard into position, essentially bringing the blocks together, thus the term "2 blocks." At that point, several cadets would grab the halyard above the fairlead (fore-handing), the order would be given for the cadets at the end of the halyard to let go, and another cadet (in this case Olson) would quickly fasten the loose line around its belaying pin. In this instance, we couldn't hold the halyard and the yard crashed down. The halyard came snaking up the deck, whipping at the cadets' legs. I made too much of an effort to hold on and paid for it. My left hand was not badly injured, and that is what I used to make this and the following days' entries. Actually, I was, and still am, ambidextrous. Throughout my elementary and high school years I wrote with my right hand, and drew with my left.

19 Tuesday—The bosun has rigged stoppers on the halyards. I'm on the binnacle list for the day. Quarters at 0915, with collision drill. Wearing ship immediately afterwards. Starting to rain. Sea is starting to roughen up and—is sea-sick! We filled out our license applications during studies. Furled t'gants in afternoon, main topsail and spanker after supper. Jib ripped out. A miserable day, oilskins are uniform.

A stopper was a length of line attached to a ring fastened in the deck, close to the fairlead. When the yard was 2-blocked, the stopper would be hitched around the halyard, holding it while the slack portion was belayed. Curiously, we used stoppers on the mooring lines which were much less dangerous than the halyards.

"Cadets who are too sick to perform duty of any kind shall be placed on the 'Sick List,' and those who are incapacitated in a lesser degree (can go to studies or perform light duties) shall be placed on the 'Binnacle List' by the Surgeon" (Regulations 1935).

20 Wednesday—Fog has set in, but the sea is very calm. Main topsail and spanker set during 0400-0800. Quarters as usual, with provide all boats drill. Studies at 1000. Scrubbed hammocks during afternoon. Fog lifted. Blue sky. Land in sight at 1800. Believe it is Mt. Desert Island. All sail is set except flying jib—speed about 4 knots. Scuttlebutt is that we are going in in the morning. I'm mail orderly on new port detail. —is joyously announcing the sighting of land—he ought to carry a bag of it round his neck. Wearing ship at 1930, heading up along coast. Furled t'gants.

21 Thursday—Changed course during the night, headed about West. T'gants set at 0700. Visibility rather poor and we can no longer make out any land. The engineers haven't started to steam up yet, so no one knows when we will go in. Quarters at 0915 with fire drill. Studies. We are making hardly any headway, with all sails set, just drifting to the SW. Studies as usual after dinner. Wearing ship around to the E. I am still sleeping through the whole night. Get my hammock at 1900 and turn in within an hour. Get lowered at 0645.

22 Friday—Commencing to furl sail at 0700. Steam up in the fire room. Underway at 0800. Port watch furled t'gants and clewed up other sails. Starboard watch furling at 0800. We are definitely going in this time. Quarters at 0915, man overboard drill with Shershun, coxswain. Cleaning up ship, straightening out lines and sails, rigging gangway. Land in sight at 1100 on both sides. Moving up East side of Mt. Desert Island, past Bar Harbor. Anchored at 1430 near the old coaling station. Exactly one year to the day since we anchored here last year and the place hasn't changed one bit. Coast Guard picket boat circled us just before we anchored. Had several photographers on board. Lowered the dinghy and 2nd cutter. Motor sailer evidently will not be used.

Journal entries after accident.
Top is left-handed (temporary) and lower two are normal (right-handed).

23 Saturday through 28 Thursday, laid at anchor while final examinations were administered, and ship was prepared for arrival in Boston scheduled for September 3. I was designated as mail orderly for this port, which entailed a nine-mile bicycle trip into Ellsworth. On one of my trips, I was stopped by a lady who resided in East Lemoine who wanted to take my picture. I complied and asked her to send a print to my mother. She did so, and interestingly the two ladies struck up a correspondence which continued for years. Also, by the time we left East Lemoine, my right hand was sufficiently healed as my journal entries indicate.

Author as mail orderly, East Lamoine, Maine, August 1941.

29 Friday—Underway at 1630. Very good visibility. Very cold wind springing up as soon as we get out of Frenchman's Bay.

30 Saturday—Laying-to off Saddleback Ledge Light from midnight to 0400. Moving up Penobscot Bay. Anchored at 1015 off Castine (population 500). Mail trip as soon as I am ready.

31 Sunday and 1 (September) Monday. Laid at anchor.

The reason for this brief visit was to acquaint the populace with a nautical school. The state of Maine was planning to establish such a school in Castine, utilizing a closed-down teachers' college. Among other activities taking place over the weekend was a baseball game between the town team and the MNS team. I recall the diamond, in excellent condition, was located on the college grounds. In addition, the ship was open to visitors, and the motor sailer received a good workout.

2 Tuesday—Reveille as usual at 0515. Preparing for sea. Hoisted motor sailer and cutter. Anchor aweigh at 0630 and we're headed for Boston! Quarters at 0915 with fire, collision, and provide all boats drills. Commenced field day immediately afterwards. Proceeding down W. Penobscot Bay. Camden and Rockland in sight. Fore and aft sails set. Quite a strong breeze, a lot of spray flying. Continued field day all afternoon. Several destroyers sighted. This apparently is our last night at sea.

3 Wednesday—Boston was in sight when I came up for the 0400 to 0800. We anchored off Castle Island at 0615. The distance from Castine to the anchorage was 175 miles and the time elapsed 23 hours and 45 minutes, pretty good for the old "Nancy". Preparing for Commisioners' inspection. Then the Commission isn't coming aboard, so the "old man" decides to kedge the ship, since we are in only 22 feet of water. We had dropped the hook inside of a Finnish freighter, so we had to move up around her bow. Used the motor sailer. It was intended to drop the kedge anchor from the motor sailer but she managed to tow the ship to the designated spot, astern of an anchored barge. Then a tug came along and took the barge away, so up anchor again. We finally got set at 1130. Now, they aren't going to let the First class off today and what an argument that has caused.

We averaged 7.3 knots for that run down from Castine!

The kedging process involved the motor sailer carrying a small anchor attached to a mooring hawser. The motor sailer would move to the proposed anchorage, drop the anchor, and the ship would haul in the hawser, effectively moving to the new position. This may have to be repeated, depending on the distance to the new anchorage.

The *Nantucket* docked at North End Park, across the Charles River from the Charlestown Navy Yard on September 4, and the first classmen were finished. When the final academic rankings were released, I was to be "Graduated with Distinction," ranking third in the class with a 4.31 average on a scale of 5.0. The graduation ceremony was scheduled for the twenty-third. In the interval, we all had one major obstacle to overcome—the Bureau of Marine Inspection and Navigation's licensing examination. To my knowledge, no one had any difficulty. I completed the tests in less than three days and was duly granted the lofty license of "Third Mate, Steam and Motor Vessels, Any Tons, Oceans," which would be officially presented at graduation. In the meantime, I bought a small steamer trunk and packed what I thought I'd need when I found a job. Graduation took place as scheduled at 1100 on Tuesday, the twenty-third, in Boston's Faneuil Hall. One of the Boston newspapers editorialized,

Nautical School Graduates

The Massachusetts Nautical School in awarding diplomas to twenty-four graduates this week was not dealing with quantity in students but rather quality.

Fifteen qualified for third mate's berths and eleven were given "tickets" as third assistant engineers. Their training at the Nautical School fitted them for these assignments by the United States Bureau of Marine Inspection and Navigation. Each graduate has a job waiting for him.

These graduates are now members of an alumnus that is American to the core and active in the duties of citizenship. Loyalty to county, state and school is ingrained in every living graduate.

Massachusetts has every reason to be proud of Nautical School men for they accept and live up to a high code of honor wherever they are and whatever they are doing.

Editorial from unkown Boston newspaper.

**The author upon graduating from the Massachusetts Nautical School,
September 23, 1941.**

If the jobs were there, we had to go out and find them. During the summer, I had busied myself writing letters to a number of select steamship companies in New York City. These were companies whose ships I had seen in Boston, and thus, I felt some familiarity with them. I received several replies inviting me to visit their offices after graduation. This activity came to the attention of Captain Abele who one day sent for me. In so many words, he told me I would be making a mistake to take a job as an officer. I should start as a quartermaster or a cadet officer, he said, and gain shipboard experience before taking on the responsibilities of a watch officer. Frankly, I didn't agree with him, but passively accepted his advice.

CHAPTER SEVEN

The *American Leader*

Within days, I was off to make my fortune, fittingly traveling to New York via the overnight boat from Boston. Fortunately, I had a cousin, Richard Griffin, living and working in the city, and he graciously allowed me to move into his apartment. This saved me the expense of a hotel room and also gave me a telephone number to go with my job applications. By October 1, the prospect of being hired was such that I asked my mother to send my trunk.

On the third I wrote,

> *I'm still looking for the trunk. It is going to be very close. I mean, Alcoa called me yesterday and now I'm trying to get in touch with the Port Captain. Their ship, the Alcoa Pathfinder, is sailing at noon and the only reason that they would call me is to report for duty. So I have to call back in 15 minutes. Now if they still want me that trunk has just got to be here.*

> *I have applications in with six or seven companies and every one of them will have a vacancy inside of two weeks. Any choice I make is going to be difficult. One line, running to Africa is paying $260 a month. Well, I am going to call Alcoa and see what they have to say.*

> *No luck there. The ship is sailing in an hour so even if the trunk got here I wouldn't have been able to make it. At 11 o'clock I'm to call U. S. Lines and at two o'clock ring up A. H. Bull. Then sometime today or tomorrow I have to get in touch with Robin Lines. The whole idea is to keep my name in front of them all the time. I can expect calls from Bull, Alcoa, American Export, American South African, Robin Line, and the United Licensed Officers Assoc.*

Following were paragraphs concerning money, the World Series, and correspondence with other family members. My final sentence was "U. S. Lines just told me that they are putting me on a ship at Baltimore. Love. George."

Ten days after graduating from the nautical school and not six months past my nineteenth birthday, I had an officer's position in a ship! Also, good fortune struck as Railway Express came through with the trunk, and I was able to reroute it to Baltimore.

American Leader in Chesapeake Bay, September 1941, shortly before author joined her crew. Photo courtesy of Mariners Museum, Newport News, Virginia.

She was the *American Leader*, a brand new diesel-powered vessel completed in June in Richmond, California, and had made a trip to the Far East before returning to several ports of discharge on the East Coast. Because of a few mechanical glitches encountered on her maiden voyage, she was in a ship repair yard under the terms of the builder's guarantee having the problems rectified. That was great for me as it provided several days to become acquainted with my new home and fellow officers. As the company provided relief officers for the night watches in port, I stood no watch and worked from 0800 to 1700 with an hour off for lunch. The regular captain, Haakon A. Pedersen, had gone home to Brooklyn, New York, and relief captain Harald Milde was in command. The chief officer was Bernard Backston, an affable, pleasant gentleman. The second officer, who stood the 0400 to 0800 and the 1600 to 2000 bridge watches when the ship was underway, was a man named Campbell, who I didn't get to know very well because he left the ship when we arrived in New York. Mike Biondic, the third officer, had the 0000 to 0400 and the 1200 to 1600 watches. Filling out the watch schedule, I was on the bridge from 0800 to 1200 and 2000 to 2400.

In 1936, the United States Maritime Commission embarked on a massive shipbuilding program intended to revive the country's merchant marine. Four classes of dry cargo vessels were designed and designated according to their length as C-1, C-2, C-3, and C-4. The *American Leader* at 417' 9" was of the C-1 class. Her other particulars were

beam ....60'
gross tonnage 6,750
loaded displacement tonnage 12,875
deadweight tonnage 8,975
cargo capacity (tons) 7,262
speed ....15 knots
cruising range ....12,000 miles
shaft horsepower 4,000
crew 49
passengers 8

We left the shipyard on Wednesday, the eighth, moving to the Canton Piers to commence loading cargo for Manila, Shanghai, and Hong Kong. What a trip this was to be! I was on top of the world! The next day, we shifted to Sparrow's Point to take on railway tracks, and sailed that evening for Philadelphia. There, we picked up a large quantity of canned goods. By afternoon on Saturday, the eleventh, we were headed down the Delaware River on the way to New York.

There are experiences in life which remain indelibly imprinted in our memories, and my 8:00-12:00 watch that evening is one of mine. We were running up the New Jersey coast from the Winter Quarter lightship to the Ambrose lightship at the entrance to New York harbor. Night had fallen, and I could see the lights of other ships seemingly all around me. And the captain had left me alone on the bridge! I must have made a good impression on him during the week I had been aboard. So, I gathered my wits, calmed down, and figured I'd just let everyone avoid me. The exception would be any ship crossing in front of me from the right, which, by rule, I had to keep clear of. All the traffic, however, was moving parallel to the coast, and I never came close to anyone during the four-hour watch. But I'll never forget it! From then on, watch standing was a piece of cake.

Something else that had a lasting impression on me was my new lifestyle. For two years I had lived in an old ship under conditions acceptable to a naval enlisted man of the late nineteenth century. I had slept in a hammock, suffered the loss of any privacy whatsoever, and, for the first of those years, my daily existence was dictated by the demands of the upperclassmen. "Young man! Young man! Do this! Do that!" Suddenly, it was "Mr. Duffy." Ten days from "raggedy arse" cadet to Mr. Duffy. What a transition! I had my own private cabin, with a shower and toilet shared only with another officer in the adjacent cabin. A bedroom steward made up my bunk every morning, and performed whatever housekeeping as was required. My meals, ordered off a typed multiple-choice menu, were served by a white-jacketed steward. Almost unbelievable!

We spent the week of October 12-18 in New York, and I was thriving. I wrote to my mother,

> *I have my uniform all decorated now. Gold stripes and stars on the sleeve, and a new cap emblem. Pretty snappy. I also bought some shoes, shirts, ties, sox, even handkerchiefs. You see I was paid for the completion of the coastwise trip, approximately $47. My pay right now is $5.366 per day. We have to stay on board during the day but at night a relieving mate comes down and we are free to go until 8:00 in the morning. Last night I went up to see Jan Savitt and his orchestra, tonight I think I'll take in Xaviar Cugat. On Friday Phil Spitalny and his all girl band is in town plus the picture "SGT. YORK" which looks pretty good. I figure I might as well enjoy myself while I'm at it because it's going to be a long trip.*

> *As far as I know we sail Saturday for Newport News to load tobacco products. I don't know if we will stop off at Australia or not this trip. The cargo right now is entirely for Manila, Shanghai, and Hong Kong. And what a collection: bicycles, oatmeal, cocoa, soup, iron rails, gasoline, sewer pipe, stoves, barrels of chemicals, bales of cloth, even a couple of pieces of artillery.*

> *We have a new Second Mate. One of the most unusual fellows I've met. His name is Walter H. Lee and he is Chinese. I had heard of him before when I was on the Nantucket. He is a swell fellow and certainly knows his stuff. He will come in handy in Shanghai!!!*

Also, arrival in New York meant the return of Captain Pedersen, the epitome of a ship master. He was not a big man, but a dignified man. A native of Arendal, Norway, he spoke with a slight accent which added to his aura. Until the outbreak of World War II in Europe, he had commanded one of United States Line's passenger ships in the North Atlantic trade. In the mid-30s, for his actions in rescuing the crew of a foundering fishing boat in the midst of a winter storm,

Photo courtesy of Christopher Lee. Second Officer Walter H. Lee of the M.S. *American Leader* in Third Officer's uniform in a prior ship.

Capt. Haakon A. Pedersen.

he was awarded the company's Distinguished Service Medal. He had a wife and teenaged son and daughter, and I, not too many years older than the son, sometimes felt Captain Pedersen regarded me more as a son than as his 8:00-12:00 watch officer.

Sunday, the nineteenth at 1400 saw us in Newport News commencing the loading of cases of cigarettes and hogsheads of tobacco. Sailing was scheduled for midnight, but for some reason departure was not until 0800 on Monday. I recall the harbor pilot asking Captain Pedersen, "Where are you bound, Captain?"

"Hong Kong, eventually" was the reply.

"We are due thereon December 7, but I don't think we'll make it." On Wednesday, during my evening watch we passed San Salvador Island, the first land sighted by Christopher Columbus in 1492. Earlier, I had begun a letter to my mother to be mailed from the canal zone. In it I reflected some of the captain's pessimism: "We are still pretty much in doubt as to whether or not we will get to the Orient. The last newspaper I saw claimed the navy was sending all American ships in the Pacific back to Honolulu. If they let us get out of San Pedro, I wouldn't mind being laid up in Hawaii for a few weeks."

The Panama Canal transit was an eye-opener. We anchored at Cristobal late one afternoon and were told we would commence the passage the following day at dawn. The first surprise in the morning was a boarding party of a dozen United States Army soldiers, all carrying rifles and pistols, and one toting a portable radio. They took up positions all over the ship. The canal pilot had his own escort, an armed United States Navy man. As we passed through the various sets of locks, we could see manned machine gun posts everywhere—in the control houses, on the piers, on the canal banks, and there were probably many more we couldn't see. Furthermore, the transit was slow. What we expected was eight hours, but in reality it took eleven.

The run up to San Pedro was boring. We were generally in sight of land, though so far off that no particular features could be made out. It was just mile after mile of barren land mass. One situation did offer some relief. Transiting the canal just behind us was as another C-1 class vessel, the *John Lykes*. She was a steamship, and we paced her all the way to San Pedro. At times, she'd be ahead of us, and the next day, perhaps, we would make her out astern. Our chief engineer, a big hearty fellow named W. Chester Dowe, would get out on deck and do everything but paddle to keep us in front. It became the engineer officers' password after each watch: "Where's the *Lykes* steamer now?" We did win, picking up the San Pedro pilot several hours before our competitor, who probably didn't realize he had been in a race.

I remember one other incident of that passage which earned me some brownie points with the captain and the chief officer. It happened on one of my morning watches. Both of them were in the wheelhouse chatting when I spotted an object below the horizon up ahead. With the binoculars I made out the white froth of bow waves, so judged it to be a smallish vessel on the reciprocal course to ours. Soon, I recognized it to be a submarine running on the surface, and called it to the captain's attention. On our 1940 and 1941 training cruises in the *Nantucket*, you will recall we had occasionally seen United States Navy submarines at sea, one day spotting seven, and this was no different in appearance. The captain and Backston politely disagreed with me, but fifteen minutes or so later when she passed at about three miles distance, Captain Pedersen smilingly asked, "Mister, how did you know that?"

The intent of the call at San Pedro was to take on bunkers (fuel oil) and water, but we did open one hatch for the purpose of stowing a number of sacks of mail and publications destined for the Philippines. Also, our cranky diesels required attention, giving us two unexpected days in port, much to the delight of Walter Lee, whose parents lived in nearby Los Angeles. Meanwhile, our agent had informed the captain of the imminent arrival of two passengers. I happened to be out on deck when they arrived—in an official United States Navy vehicle. They were enlisted men, one a radioman, the other a signalman, but in civilian clothes. In my initial conversation with them they seemed surprised to learn we were bound for Manila. The signalman disagreed and said he was *going to Honolulu*. When I recounted this to Walter Lee and Mike Biondic and some of the engineers, all responded with laughter. However, the signalman was correct! On November 6, when we departed San Pedro, Captain Pedersen charted a course for Hawaii. Ordinarily, a vessel bound for Manila from a West Coast port would follow a great circle track across the northern Pacific and come down into Formosa Strait off northwest Luzon. We were to follow a longer route, with a stopover in Honolulu.

Captain Pedersen's "night orders" on the evening of the sixth stated, "The Navy men will be on call at all times and there will be no change in the ship's routine until a later date when we may fall in with warships going in the same way." Captain Pedersen's orders meant nothing less than a transpacific convoy. Yet our arrival at the Honolulu pilot station was somewhat unsettling. When the pilot came aboard he was accompanied by a United States naval officer. I was on the bridge with the captain. One of these gentlemen, inferring that we were unexpected, inquired as to the identity of our Honolulu agent, and our berthing orders. "Mine gott," blurted the captain with his Norwegian accent, directing his words to the lieutenant, "you change my orders so that I come here, and now you don't know what to do with me when I am here! I am bound for Manila and am only stopping here under navy orders, and now the navy doesn't know why!" After a brief discussion, the captain was directed to go to anchor about midway between the entrances to Pearl Harbor and Honolulu. This was November 13.

American Leader's Third Officer Mike Biondic
approaching anchorage off Oahu, November 1941.

S.S. *Cape Fairweather* at anchor off Oahu,
awaiting convoy formation, November 1941.
Note Diamond Head in background.

American Leader at anchor off Oahu. View looking forward
showing deck cargo of gasoline tanks consigned to the
United States Army Air Force in the Philippines.

View looking aft showing additional tanks lashed on deck.

On occasion, during the next few days, a navy launch came alongside and took Captain Pedersen into Honolulu, apparently for some manner of conferences. Because we were not in "a port of loading or discharge," the Captain was not obligated to advance any money to the crew, and we were essentially restricted to the ship as almost no one had funds for the long launch ride. Noonan, the deck cadet, made it once, but to say I was disappointed is a major understatement. On the eighteenth, Captain Pedersen returned quickly from his morning meeting to tell us we would be getting underway at 1330. In the interval since our arriving at the anchorage, three other ships had joined us. The first was our old friend from the canal and the "race" to San Pedro, the *John Lykes*. Then there was another C-1, the American Mail Line's *Cape Fairweather*, and the *Doña Nati*, flying both the American and Filipino flags. As we prepared to get underway, we noticed a cruiser moving down the channel from Pearl Harbor and a large American President Line's passenger ship coming out of Honolulu. These, we soon learned, were the USS *Boise* (CL 47) and the *President Grant*.

U.S.S. *Boise* (CL 47), November 5, 1941,
less than two weeks before escorting convoy from Hawaii.

Our two passengers were now in uniform, and it became apparent that the other four merchantmen carried similar specialists. When formed up, the convoy consisted of the *President Grant* at the center, the *John Lykes* five hundred yards to her port, and the *Cape Fairweather* five hundred yards to her starboard. The *American Leader* trailed the *John Lykes* by five hundred yards, and the *Doña Nati* was five hundred yards astern of the *Cape Fairweather*. We were all still carrying our multicolored stack markings, and our white deck houses and buff masts gleamed in the bright Pacific sunlight. At night it was a different matter. We were blacked out. No visible lights were allowed, and the *Boise* demanded strict compliance. Of our first night, one *Boise* officer wrote, "The merchant ships, like sensible people, didn't want to turn off their lights. The captain about went to pieces trying to get them to. He evidently succeeded, since by 2000, they were all pretty dark except for the *President Grant*."

American Leader' **peace time stack: black with white band bordered by green stripes. AP (American Pioneer Line) symbol in green.**

How did the author know that? Many years later, in the late 50s or early 60s, I was the guest speaker at the Wardroom Club in Boston, an organization of mostly retired United States naval officers. My subject was what you are now reading. I had nothing with which to illustrate my talk other than a current chart of the North Pacific Ocean, No. 1401, printed on October 18, 1941, by the Hydrographic Office of the Navy, on which I had plotted the *American Leader*'s noon positions from southeast of Baja California, three days before arriving at San Pedro to the day after departing from Manila. At the cessation of my presentation, I was approached by a gentleman who informed me he had been an officer in the *Boise* at the time of this transpacific convoy. He stated he had kept a personal journal of the voyage and would loan it to me if I wished. I quickly agreed, and he sent it to me. Photocopying was in those days not an option for me, so I typed a copy which I have used to detail events which will be forthcoming in this narrative. Another source of data are copies of the *Boise*'s bridge log book for the dates November 27-28, 1941, obtained from the National Archives in Washington, D.C.

The convoy's course was westerly (272°) toward a position approximately four hundred miles south of Midway Island, which was reached on the twenty-first. From there, the course was altered a mere 8° to the left to 264°, bringing us on the twenty-fifth to within 60 miles north of Wake Island. Meanwhile on Saturday, November 22, at 0744, the international date line had been crossed in latitude 20° 12′ N, changing our calendars to Sunday, the twenty-third. From our position north of Wake Island, the rhumb line course toward Guam was 254°.

At precisely 2000 hours on November 27, east longitude time, I relieved Walter Lee and took over the bridge of the *American Leader*. Our position was roughly 1,700 miles east of the Philippine Islands in the latitude of San Bernardino Strait and 450 miles south of Marcus Island, a Japanese outpost located 930 miles southeast of Tokyo. Off to port, stretching a thousand miles east to west lay the Japanese-mandated Marshall and Caroline island groups. At noon on the previous day we were within 350 miles of Eniwetok in the northwest Marshalls, and at noon on this day, Truk was 600 miles to the south-southwest. Unknown to anyone in the Western world, Truk had become one of Japan's great naval bases. Japan had seized the Marshalls and the Carolines from Germany in 1914 and retained them as a colonial mandate under the League of Nations. Objections by the United States at the time were denied. All subsequent attempts by the United States to determine Japan's intentions in the area were frustrated. It was believed, however, that contrary to the League of Nations expectations, the Japanese were fortifying certain of the larger islands. Indeed, in October of 1940, two disguised German commerce raiders, the *Orion* and *Komet*, and two blockade runners, the *Regensburg* and *Kulmerland*, reportedly called at Lamotrek in the Carolines and Ailinglapalap in the Marshalls. The *Orion* apparently underwent extensive repairs at Lamotrek.

The watch that warm South Pacific evening began routinely. We were, as I recall, maintaining station without difficulty. The cruiser was just off our port bow, and I was on the port bridge wing where I could best keep an eye on her and the fellow up ahead. As usual, a seaman stood lookout watch on our bow, another was steering, and a third was on standby down in the messroom; that was the watch: one officer and three seamen.

At approximately 2030, the *Boise*'s relative position changed as she appeared to reduce speed. We slowly went past her, and when we were clear she altered course to the right, cutting across our wake. I stepped through the wheelhouse to the starboard bridge wing, watching the maneuver with some curiosity. The cruiser was soon lost to my view in the darkness. I called Captain Pedersen and told him what was happening. He came out of his cabin and joined me. The convoy did not change course or speed.

Aboard the *Boise* it was Thanksgiving Day—Republican Thanksgiving. In some years, the span between December 25 and Thanksgiving Day was less than four weeks, and that was the case in 1941. In order to lengthen the pre-Christmas shopping season, Democratic President Franklin Delano Roosevelt decreed that Thanksgiving be observed on the third Thursday in November. Thus, he celebrated the day on November 20 at Warm Springs, Georgia, whereas the navy, remaining Republican, adhered to the old fourth Thursday. (One wonders, did FDR ever know about this transgression?) In any case, the traditional dinner had been served, and the crew was standing by for a preannounced general quarters (GQ) at 1900. (Ship's time in the *Boise* and the *American Leader* differed by two hours. The reason for this was Captain Pedersen's. It is in no way related to the events at hand.) At 1830, half an hour before they expected it, they did go to GQ. Live ammunition was sent to the turrets, but because everyone thought it was the scheduled drill, no one became concerned. What developed, however, was an unidentified vessel had approached the convoy from the north, first being sighted bearing 005° at 18,000 yards. The *Boise*, as described above, swung away from her five charges and closed to 9,000 yards (four and one-half nautical miles) of the oncoming blacked-out intruder. At this point, according to the Boise officer, "We challenged 'AA,' international for 'who are you?' with blinker lights, 12" searchlight, 24" searchlight, then gave the British-American recognition challenge. No answer to any of this, so we opened our 36" searchlights which, as per usual, were in the water. They came up, were to left, and just as they were coming on, closed shutters. The ship was out of range of the searchlights, so nothing conclusive resulted. After a barrage of smoke, the ship turned tail and skipped across the horizon at about twenty-five knots. When we lost contact, we set Condition II. Thought she was Kinagusa type, 6-8" 50 in three turrets."

From the *American Leader*, the captain and I witnessed the *Boise's* searchlights. After that, nothing interrupted the balance of the watch, although I never saw the *Boise* again that evening. Later, "another ship was sighted on the port bow. GQ again. Estimated range 12000, target angle 300 . . . the radar worked on this run, it was on the blink for the first one," wrote the Boise officer. In the morning when I arose I noted that she was again with us, but no one had any explanation of why she had left us or of the searchlights Captain Pedersen and I had seen.

In recent years, I have obtained from the National Archives in Washington copies of the *Boise's* bridge log book. What is written and signed by the November 27, 1800 to 2000 watch officer and approved and signed by Captain Stephan Boutwell

Robinson, U.S. Navy, varies starkly with my memory and the personal account of the *Boise* officer. Inexplicably, the log states, "1840 Sighted darkened ship, bearing 240° T, estimated range 16,000 yards. Went to general quarters. 1845 Set Material Condition Affirm. 1851 Challenged ship. Received no reply. 1852 Changed speed to 20 knots. 1854 Changed speed to 14 knots. 1900 Changed course to 254° T. 1903 Changed course to 259° T. Strange ship changed course to left and increased speed. 1915 Changed course to 249°. 1923 Lighted off boilers #3 and #4. 1927 Lost contact with strange ship."

So, the *Boise*'s log puts the sighting at 240° T. My chart indicates the convoy's base course was 249° T. Therefore, the strange ship would be a mere 9° off the *Boise*'s port bow. The officer's journal says the strange ship bore 005°, which puts it a full 116° away from the starboard bow. That's abaft the beam, whereas the log has her almost dead ahead.

What is this all about? Captain Pedersen and I saw the *Boise* make a drastic course change. Yet her log shows the course was 249° from 1355 in the afternoon to 1900 in the evening, twenty minutes after the initial sighting. Then she altered course five degrees to the right to 254°, and three minutes later, to 259°. Twelve minutes after that, she returned to the base course of 249°. Impossible! I recall this incident as clearly as if it happened yesterday! And the *Boise* officer's journal concurs. What was Captain Robinson up to?

On the twenty-eighth, the next day, both the *Boise*'s log book and the officer's account report the sighting of another Japanese cruiser. Here is what the officer wrote: "1546 went to GQ with service ammunition. Again for a Japanese cruiser. She bore 072, 23000 yards, target angle 340, when at director. She came in to about 11000 yards, then turned and drew aft with a target angle of about 085. This was an Itago class. We dropped astern of the convoy and watched her drop out of sight. Set Condition II again. The big thrill came as we turned toward each other, closed the range rapidly, then unmasked our battery to starboard and she did the same."

The author has only a vague memory of this matter being discussed in the *American Leader*. One bit of light came in a 2003 letter from one of the *American Leader*'s seamen. He asked for "enlightenment regarding a question that's been nagging me for the past 60 years. Soon after we left Manila—perhaps the following morning—my memory says that two or three ships of Japan's navy, on the horizon aft, followed us." Not a very accurate report, but it does affirm the presence at some time of a Japanese warship on our tail, which, as above, occurred on the twenty-eighth.

There are enormous questions relating to this second incident in the differences between the officer's written record and the *Boise*'s log book. First, he says the intruder was sighted, bearing 072°, twenty-three thousand yards, at 1546. The log book shows the sighting at 1743, almost two hours later, bearing 325°, hull down, which could have been thirty-thousand yards or more. At that juncture, according to her log, the *Boise* changed course to 260°, putting the stranger 65° off her starboard bow. Prior to this course change, the ship mentioned in the officer's journal was practically dead astern. An 11° course change would not perceptibly alter that. So, the *Boise*'s log shows her course to be 260°, where the officer tells how his ship has turned toward the cruiser on a course matching the first sighting—072°.

What on earth really happened that afternoon, and why?

Nothing jibes. The cruiser indicates it sighted a strange ship, so does the officer, but two hours earlier. The cruiser made a small change of course, the officer says it was 180°. The cruiser says the first sighting was at 325°, the officer, 072°. The *American Leader*'s seaman, hazily at best, remembers a cruiser coming in from astern. From the author's point of view, the *Boise*'s log book for this second evening is a fabrication. Remember, I had witnessed the previous evening's incident, and that didn't match the *Boise*'s log. Something was happening to us, or could happen. At least one person has conjectured our transiting of the time zones could have caused confusion between log book and the officer's journal. Probably not, but the *Boise* log for November 27 carries this entry: "0800 Set clocks back one hour to zone (-)10 time." How could anyone foul up that? But they did! It was (+)10!

During the morning of the twenty-ninth, in the *Boise*'s wardroom, consternation reigned. The ship's officers pressed Captain Robinson to break radio silence and report the incidents. He rejected their advice. The senior pilot requested permission to fly one of the scout planes to Guam to deliver the information in person. This was refused. The input of a naval intelligence officer on his way to an assignment in the Philippines, and outranked by Robinson, was disregarded. At 0900 on November 30, Guam was sighted. The convoy skirted its north coast, and no attempt was made to communicate with United States forces based there.

If the facts of these two incidents were initially correctly entered in the *Boise*'s bridge log book, when and why were they altered? Was it after December 8? Why was Robinson so obdurate toward his officers' suggestions? Why, later, with Guam in sight, did he not dispatch one of his scout planes to report the aggressive Japanese behavior of November 27-28? Did he ever make a report when he arrived in Manila? In retrospect, those incidents of November 27-28 occurred more than a week before the Japanese attacks all over the Far East. Did Robinson order the log book changes to cover his own guilt?

On December 4, our six-ship group arrived in Manila Bay. Four mornings later we awoke to learn that we were at war with Japan. Then we understood the implications of our darkened ship passage from Hawaii, the *Boise* escort, and our navy radioman and signalman "passengers." With considerable misgivings, we recalled the unexplained departure of the *Boise* on the night of November 27 and the brazen Itago class cruiser of the following day. Had we accidentally brushed the Pearl Harbor strike force and not realized its intent? Had our convoy been in mortal danger? And if it was the Pearl Harbor strike force, had there been a deliberate failure to report it? We asked each other those questions. Frequently in the ensuing years, when conversation turned to the subject of the attack on Pearl Harbor, I have recounted the story of this Manila convoy. In late 1945, I told it to Russell Owen, a *New York Times* feature writer. He passed my tale along to his Washington office. This was during the immediate postwar Congressional investigation of the disaster. At first, as I recall, there was a denial by the navy of my report of the convoy. In fact, the navy denied convoying any merchant vessels in the Pacific prior to the Pearl Harbor attack. We now know, ten days after the *Boise* and her charges left Hawaii, the USS *Pensacola* (CA 24), escorting four troop ships, two army-chartered cargo vessels, and a Dutch-flagged passenger ship, carrying reinforcements and their supplies, also departed Hawaii, bound for the Philippines. Strictly speaking, this was a military operation, albeit three of the vessels were manned by merchant crews. Of note is that this convoy ran to the south of the *Boise* convoy's route, perhaps by as much as 1,200 miles.

When Owen reported to me the navy's rejection of my report of the convoy, I said I could produce the *American Leader*'s log book (which was in the company's office in New York). In reply, the navy admitted the *Boise* had seen the Japanese cruisers, but, to quote from the Associated Press of December 1945 "Boise was never closer than 1,400 miles to the Japanese task force which struck Hawaii."

That is not the point I wanted to make. Undeniably, the cruisers were there, menacing us, threatening us, just days before Pearl Harbor was attacked. Now, over sixty years later, isn't it still strange, this convoy story? If conditions in the Pacific were such that it was necessary to send five fast merchant ships to Manila in November 1941 under the protective guns of a United States cruiser, how and why was the attack of December 7, 1941, possible?

Was our little convoy destined by Washington to be the bait? Were we intended to be the pigeons for the hawk? Were eyes and ears that should have been defending other approaches concentrating in our direction, waiting for us to get knocked off and become the cause celebré? Someone knew that the *Boise* and the five merchant ships were headed into real trouble, but when the balloon went up, so to say, we, who may have been expected to bear the brunt of the surprise attack, escaped.

At the above-mentioned Congressional investigation, Rear Admiral Royal E. Ingersoll, USN, assistant chief of naval operations on December 7, 1941, testified, "We had, for two months or more, taken steps to get our merchant vessels out of the Far East and out of the other areas in the Pacific where they could be captured by the Japanese." Such contradiction! "Two months or more" translates to the end of September. Our Pearl Harbor to Manila convoy departed November 18! Additionally, the planning for this little convoy had to go back into September when the various companies involved—Lykes, American President, American Mail, and American Pioneer—were accepting cargo bookings for Manila, Shanghai, Hong Kong, and who knows where else, for the ships which eventually comprised the group. The ten enlisted men—a radioman and a signalman for each merchant vessel—were not plucked out of a naval station overnight either. Their assignments to five different ships in a least four different West Coast ports took a fair amount of advance planning. In today's vernacular, were we being hung out to dry?

And we were not the only pigeons.

In early December, 1941, President Roosevelt ordered Admiral Thomas C. Hart, USN, commander in chief, Asiatic Fleet, to charter three small vessels to form a "defensive information patrol" in the West China Sea and the Gulf of Siam. This operation is succinctly reported in *Pearl Harbor! The Verdict of History* by Gordon W. Prange with Donald M. Goldstein and Katherine V. Dillon. The pertinent chapter is entitled "Bait for a Japanese Attack."

Bait for a Japanese attack!

One of these three vessels was the *Lanakai*, a two-mast motorized schooner. Her commander, Lt. Kemp Tolley, USN, became firmly convinced the *Lanakai* had been intended bait for the Japanese. Actually, it is rather preposterous a war could have resulted from the attack by the Japanese on such small vessel or vessels. But was this Pearl Harbor—Manila convoy also bait? Imagine the outcry if the *President Grant*, reportedly carrying women and children and members of religious orders, was attacked and sunk, along with the *Boise, Cape Fairweather, John Lykes, Doña Nati*, and *American Leader*!

President Franklin Delano Roosevelt had, in the fall and early winter of 1941, attempted to incite the American public into taking warlike action against Germany. The earlier-mentioned *Robin Moor* sinking, followed by a U-boat attack on the USS *Greer* (DD 145) on September 4, raised feelings against the Nazi regime. On October 17, barely a year past her commissioning date, the USS *Kearny* (DD 432) was damaged by a torpedo from the U-568. She was part of the escort force for convoy SC-48 (Sydney, Nova Scotia to the UK) which lost eleven vessels between the fifteenth and seventeenth. Eleven of the *Kearny* crew were killed and twenty-two injured by the explosion. The third incident of the escalation of hostilities occurred on October 31, when the old four-stacker USS *Reuben James* (DD 245), in convoy HX-156 (Halifax to the UK) was torpedoed and sunk by the U-552. Her entire complement of officers—seven, including her commander—was lost, as well as ninety-two enlisted men. There were only forty-five survivors. Still, neither side crossed the line with an outright declaration of war.

In the Far East, no such belligerent acts emanated from either side. The Japanese probably had good intelligence regarding American actions, present and future. The United States, on the other hand, by the end of November had completely lost track of what was to be the Pearl Harbor attack force. Intelligence thought it knew where the battleships and carriers were, but Japanese guile had hidden their whereabouts. What then, was the Japanese motivation in sending the two snooping cruisers onto the trail of our little convoy? The Pearl Harbor attack force did not deploy from the Kuriles until December 3, east longitude time, six and five days after the November 27 and 28 incursions. Was it an attempt to draw the United States' attention to the area of the Marshalls and the Carolines? But the *Boise* failed to report the incidents, perhaps to the dismay of the Japanese. And again, what of the discrepancies between the *Boise*'s log book and the officer's journal and the author's personal recollections?

One thing is for sure. Had the attack on Pearl Harbor taken place four days earlier, we all could have been dead pigeons.

CHAPTER EIGHT

December 8 and the Escape

The *American Leader* and her crew were extremely fortunate to escape from Manila. Walter Lee, Mike Biondic, and I, doubly so, for we were almost left behind! I didn't like the city. *It was hot, and there were beggars, and the smell was wicked*, I wrote later. I was standing the 1600 to midnight watch, and the crew all got drunk and the Filipino watchmen were letting the longshoremen pilfer the cargo. One evening, I spotted a sling of cases of canned corn coming up out of number 3 hold. Three or four of them were torn open. I yelled at the winchman to stop hoisting and went down into the hatch and gave the watchman hell. He had been giving me trouble all along, probably because of my youthful appearance, and I wasn't going to allow him to get away with any shenanigans. He apologized and said that he would make the coolies return what they had stolen. I told him I'd see that he was fired in the morning. It wasn't fifteen minutes later when he called to me. "Look," he exclaimed. Down in the hold he had assembled about two-dozen cans of corn! What could I do? The bastard had undoubtedly pilfered a few more cases when I was not looking and used these cans to establish his innocence. There were air raid alarms. Crew members of ships arriving from China spoke of being watched by Jap ships and planes all the way. The U.S. Navy gunboats *Luzon* (PR 7) from Shanghai and *Mindanao* (PR 8) from Hong Kong came in. Our particular minds, conditioned by the transpacific convoy experience, accepted the inevitability of war. At 0500 on December 8, a U.S. Naval officer came running down the pier, hurried up the gangway and told Mike Biondic it had started. He gave orders to blackout the ship. (Although it was 7 December in Hawaii and the United States, the eighth was dawning in the Far East.)

As usual at 0730, I went in to breakfast. Mike was there and told me the news. I believed it, but on the other hand I didn't. It wasn't that I had not expected it, but rather the way that it did come that made me rather skeptical. So Mike said, "Read the morning newspaper." Strangely, I had bought a paper a few minutes earlier from a young Filipino who came aboard every morning, and had tossed it onto my bunk without looking at it.

Surprisingly, the day was very quiet. Nothing at all occurred. About midday I took a walk into the city. Laughing Filipino teenagers stood on the streets, gazing skyward, or staring at the few mobile antiaircraft guns that had been quickly emplaced. One was near the Manila Hotel and another in front of the post office. Machine guns were set up on the roofs of the port area warehouses and buildings covering the Pasig River bridge approaches. I went to a movie theatre and saw *Blood and Sand*. On the second day of the war, at noon, a few Jap planes appeared over the city. I didn't see them because I had decided to take in another movie, *Sergeant York*. (I guess I hadn't seen it in New York as I had intended one evening.) It was nice and cool there, so when the sirens sounded I figured it was just a false alarm and continued watching. Later, while I was walking back to the port area, I stopped in at the cable office and sent a radiogram to the folks in Newburyport, Massachusetts, telling them that I had arrived in Manila.

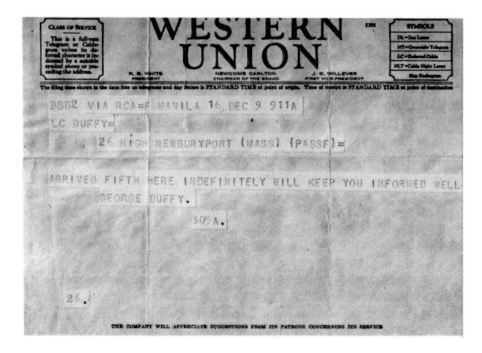

Telegram sent from Manila.

Then I began to see happenings. The postal savings office was mobbed with Filipinos trying to withdraw their money. The banks along the Escolta had people all over them. They had climbed up the walls and were peering through the grill-covered windows; they were pounding on the doors; they filled the streets before them. The curio shops were closed; some proprietors were clearing out their goods. I went to a tailor shop where I attempted to pick up uniform khaki and white jackets and trousers I had ordered—no luck. Walter Lee had asked me to inquire at the post office about parcel post to Hong Kong, which I was told was impossible. Walter had relatives in Hong Kong and was carrying a locker full of gifts for them. When I returned to the ship and attempted to apologize for my failure, he told me not to worry, the Japs were already there! That evening, at about 1800, a number of American P-40s passed overhead, northbound. We did not work cargo during the night because of the blackout, thus my eight hours were quite easy. The air raid sirens sounded four or five times, keeping us jumpy. Out at Corregidor, searchlights were quite active. Small arms fire crackled all around us. (Note: Those P-40s came out of Nichols Field about 10 miles to the south. Earlier in the day, one sources says 0300, another called it predawn, this United States Army Air Corps base had been bombed by the Japanese. I cannot find any account of damage or casualties.)

On the tenth, I believe I did not go ashore in the morning. Merchant vessels had been arriving at the port in substantial numbers, seeking protection and were anchoring in the bay, a mile or so away from the port area. Frankly, we were becoming a little nervous about the future, and those stories about how the United States Navy would easily chase the Japs back to Tokyo came to mind. After lunch, the *American Leader*'s officers were gathered around in the dining room shooting the breeze and not much else. A Manila radio station, every day at 1230, carried a commentator named Don Bell, and we had been tuned into him since arrival. Just as Bell began speaking, George Schabel, the First assistant engineer, bolted out of his room. "Come quick, come quick!" he yelled. George had heard the noise of numerous aircraft, stuck his head out of the porthole in his cabin, and saw them—Japs. We all ran out on deck, and there they were—twenty-seven Japanese bombers moving south over Manila Bay! Behind those were an additional twenty-seven, headed for the Cavite Naval Base. As the first formation passed over the estimated forty to fifty merchant vessels at anchor, the whole bay seemed to lift up in front of us. When the spray and smoke subsided, signal flags were fluttering throughout the fleet, and smoke and flames rose from at least six ships. Soon we could see bomb flashes over at Cavite. A column of black smoke rose from the direction of Nichols Field. An additional thirteen or fifteen bombers followed the earlier two squadrons. All the activity was to the south of the city. The Japs circled and dipped, attacking whatever they wished. After an unchallenged twenty or thirty minutes, they departed. Soon, the smoke over Nichols thinned, and the fires in all but one of the merchant ships came under control. That one, however, apparently took a hit squarely in the forward hold and was slowly sinking. Cavite flamed brightly and a black pall of smoke began to drift toward the city.

When it was all over, no one said much until Bernie Backston, the chief officer, pointed to our cargo booms. There, up in the air over the hatches, swung pallets and slings of canned goods, steel, paint. We had been discharging cargo when the aircraft arrived, and the coolies were so intent in getting off the ship that they hadn't bothered to stop the winches. I remember watching the crew of the *Doña Nati*, our convoy companion, during the attack. She was tied up at the next pier. Her sailors simply grabbed whatever they could, raced down the gangway and out the pier, blankets streaming behind them, clutching suitcases, buckets, or anything else that came to hand. Speaking of the coolies who had been in the *American Leader*'s holds, one of our seamen said, "I never see those guys move so fast in my life. They was just one streak of brown, up the ladder, over the coaming, and down the gangway."

Somewhat later, Mike and Walter and I decided to take a walk into the city. "Look out, Joe! Look out for bomb!" admonished the people we met, and I suppose we were being rather stupid. We did want to look around though. One remarkable sight was the number of pairs of footwear laying about on the streets and sidewalks. The poor Filipinos were literally scared out of their boots and went the way of their forebears, barefooted. The next astounding sight was in the Crow's Nest, the nearest bar to the pier area, where we discovered most of our crew attempting to drink away the jitters. (Captain Pedersen and Chief Officer Backston, rightly assuming the coolies would never return to the ship, had given all of us the afternoon off.) The city seemed rather unperturbed compared to the panic of Monday, the eighth. We wandered around, heard the occasional question, "What's happened to the Army Air Corps?" and looked into a few of the stores remaining open. I remember going into a book shop and finding a young blonde lady at the counter, and when I tried to be friendly she wouldn't respond. Often, over the years, I have wondered as to her fate. With nothing else to do and desiring to cool off, the three of us found a theatre showing something I had not seen, and eventually we were back on board for supper. Cavite blazed all night, and the burning freighter had rolled over.

When the schoolship *Nantucket* was in Washington in May 1940, I reported the arrival at the navy yard on May 25 of the USS *Sea Dragon* [*sic*] (SS 194) and took a photo of the boat. According to the *Dictionary of American Naval Fighting Ships* (DAFNS),

The Seadragon on 23 May 1940, departed New London for the Philippines. With ComSubDiv embarked, she arrived at Cavite on 30 November and commenced training operations as a unit of the Asiatic Fleet. A year later, she prepared for overhaul and by 8 December (7 December east of the International Date Line) she had started her yard period at the Cavite Navy Yard.

Two days later, on 10 December, she and a sister ship Sealion (SS 195), moored together, were caught in an enemy air raid against Cavite. Sealion took a direct hit which demolished that ship and damaged Seadragon. The force of the explosion ripped off part of the latter's bridge. Shrapnel and splinters punctured her tanks and pierced her conning tower, killing one and injuring five. The heat of the explosion scorched her hull and blistered her black paint. Fires and explosions raged along the wharf. A nearby torpedo shop went up in flames (which) reached towards a lighter loaded with torpedoes alongside the Seadragon and Sealion. Submarine Rescue Vessel Pigeon (ASR 6) disregarded the danger and moved in to tow Seadragon out into the channel, whence the submarine continued into Manila Bay under her own power. Temporary repairs were accomplished by the Submarine Tender Canopus (AS 9) and Pigeon, and on the night of 15 December she embarked members of the Asiatic Fleet staff. At midnight 16 December she headed out of Manila Bay. Escorted by destroyer Bulmer (DD 222), Seadragon moved South, via Surigao and Makassar Straits to Soerabaja where she disembarked her passengers, received further repairs, exclusive of a paint job, and prepared for her first war patrol. The Seadragon survived the war, earning eleven battle stars.

The next day, the eleventh, was a continuation of the previous afternoon: no coolies, no cargo work. At noon, the air raid sirens sounded, but nothing appeared. Mike, Walter, and I once more headed for the city and an air-conditioned movie theatre. Whatever we saw has long since been forgotten, but I do remember that I liked it, and they didn't. Afterward we hailed a taxi, but when the driver asked for four pesos, Mike wanted to haul him out and push his face in. At this juncture, Walter decided that we should stop off, before supper on the ship, and have a beer or two at a joint named Legaspi Gardens. He claimed he knew a certain Pauline there and that we ought to meet her. When we found the place, it was closed.

And were we lucky that it was!

As we were near the port area, and the time was approaching five o'clock, there was not much sense looking elsewhere for a cold beer, so we sauntered toward the pier. About then a ship's whistle was heard, blowing incessantly. I believed it to be the *American Leader*. My friends, as usual, disagreed. Imagine our surprise—and dismay—to see as we rounded the corner of the warehouse, our ship prepared to sail. There she was, mooring lines all taken in but for one forward and another aft. The hatches were battened, the cargo booms cradled, and a mobile crane was hooked onto the gangway, ready to pull it away. The old man was bellowing unintelligibly at us from the bridge wing. As soon as we clambered aboard, he ordered the vessel cast off, backed out into the bay, swung about, and headed through the breakwater opening. By then I was on the bridge clad in a blue silk shirt, gray trousers, and white shoes. My only uniform was my cap, which I grabbed out of my room on the way to the wheelhouse. We had a harbor pilot on board, and when we slowed the engines in order to drop him off, he wished us good luck. We told him that he was the one who needed the luck; he was staying, we were going.

I will never know how long Captain Pedersen would have waited for us that afternoon. Certainly not past 1800. Had the *American Leader* gone without us, we would eventually have joined with the thirty-six-man crew of the *Capillo*, sunk later at Corregidor; the fifty-seven crew members left behind by the *President Grant*, which followed the *American Leader* to sea that night; and seventeen deserters from the *Ruth Alexander*. All were picked up when the Japanese occupied Manila, and most were eventually confined in the civilian internee camp at Los Baños.

Walter Lee was busy stabilizing the gyrocompass and getting out the charts for the night's run, so I stood the balance of his 4:00-8:00 watch and on into my regular 8:00-12:00.

> The gyrocompass utilizes the principle of the gyroscope to indicate true north. It consists of an incredibly complicated electrically driven rotor, spinning as fast as 20,000 revolutions per minute, and so suspended that it automatically positions its axis in the direction of the geographical meridian. This permits the reading of the ship's heading, unaffected by any magnetic influence, i.e. "variation" from the earth and "deviation" caused by the vessel itself. (American Practical Navigator, United States Navy, Hydrographic Office. 1943)

Generally, the ship's navigator shuts down the gyrocompass when his vessel is not at sea. About four to six hours before departure from port, he would active the system and this would allow enough time for the gyro to hunt out the meridian. In an emergency such as we had that December 11 evening, the navigator could, by hand, reduce the mechanism's oscillation and produce a true north reading in an hour or so. Thus, I took the bridge while Walter worked in the gyrocompass room.

It was quite dark when we reached the east entrance to the Corregidor minefield, but the moon rose at 2100. There were other vessels ahead of us, and some coming up astern. The captain had been told that a pilot would be available to take us through the channel between the minefields, but no one appeared. In the chaos, there were a few near collisions, and time was a-wasting. On our way into Manila a week earlier, we had made this passage in daylight, and Captain Pedersen, a superb shipmaster, had plotted the positions of the buoys marking the channel. They were not lighted, but he and Bernie Backston managed to find the first pair, and we proceeded in. Then searchlights on Corregidor took over. We were showing our red and green sidelights only, which allowed the soldiers to see us. As we passed one set of buoys, they'd illuminate the next pair and so on. This way, we slowly traversed the dangerous passage. To add to our problems, several destroyers were encountered. These guys persisted in challenging us by blinker light. All they wanted was the ship's name—for what use?—ignorantly disregarding the fact that Captain Pedersen and Bernie and I had much more to do than answer their queries. When I began answering the first destroyer's "What ship?" query with Ameri—, he interrupted with "What ship?" again. I finally had to tell him to stop signaling and read my message, wherein I carefully spelled out "The name of this ship is *American Leader*." I guess the navy signalman figured I couldn't read him and was replying defensively with my nationality. He didn't know that he had a well-trained Massachusetts Nautical School graduate deciphering his dots and dashes, and that's the way I handled the other navy vessels who bothered us later in the passage. It was about midnight when we cleared the south exit from the channel. Mike came to the bridge to relieve me. We could see Cavite, twenty miles away, still burning.

At 0800 the next morning, as usual I went to the bridge to take over the watch. Our course was 180° (south) as we, in Tablas Strait, neared the southern tip of Mindoro Island. On the chartroom table, I found a radio message left there by Captain Pedersen which advised of an attack by Japanese aircraft at daybreak on the town of Batangas. That was not too far away to the north of us. Shortly after nine, the radio operator brought in another message and asked me the location of the town mentioned. He thought it was nearby. I quickly found it on Mindoro about thirty miles from us. The message reported a group of Japanese vessels moving southward. I notified Captain Pedersen, and preparations were made to scuttle and abandon ship. Cases of foodstuffs were placed in the lifeboats, and it looked like the end. Nothing happened, however, and we never saw whoever they were. We continued on to the south into the Sulu Sea, leaving the Island of Panay to port. At one point a U.S. aircraft buzzed us, and what appeared to be a U.S. submarine was sighted on the surface near a small community. Eventually, we transited Basilan Strait at Zamboanga and entered the Celebes Sea. It may be pertinent at this point to remind the reader I had been keeping my own track chart from the West Coast. It is probable Captain Pedersen knew of this and discouraged me from continuing. On the other hand, I ran off my private chart after noon on December 14 when we crossed the equator into the Southern Hemisphere, and I had no replacement.

CHAPTER NINE

Homeward Bound

In retrospect, what an enormous tragedy we had just witnessed. The beginning of the loss of the Philippine Islands! And there we were running to the south, tail between our legs, the Nips nipping at our heels. Not only was the *American Leader* fleeing, but so were the other ships of our convoy and most of the forty to fifty merchantmen which had sought refuge in Manila Bay. It appears that Admiral Thomas C. Hart, commander in chief, United States Asiatic Fleet, had passed the word on the afternoon of the eleventh to all vessels in the Manila area to depart to the southwest although he had no escorts to protect them. A far greater tragedy was the utter disregard for the welfare of the United States citizens and those of other countries living in or around Manila, many of whom could have been carried out of danger by the flotilla of merchant ships at the docks and in Manila Bay. Admittedly, chaos reigned. General Douglas MacArthur and Admiral Hart were not in close communication. It became worse later on when MacArthur neglected to inform Hart of his intention to evacuate Manila on Christmas Day. The Admiral learned of it only by chance two days earlier. Francis B. Sayre, the United States high commissioner to the Philippines, was having little to say. Someone should have ordered the ships held for twenty-four hours or until the women and children could have been rounded up and embarked. Think of the numbers the *President Grant* alone might have taken out! Instead the internment camps of Los Baños, San Tomas, etc., lay waiting.

Through the magic of the Internet, I have now uncovered further information connected to those early days of World War II in the Philippines. Most startling is that on December 8, the Japanese submarine I-124 laid a number of mines at the entrance to Manila Bay. We knew of the mine fields surrounding Corregidor, protecting Manila Bay, but no one in the *American Leader* ever discussed the possibility of the Japanese creating a mine field of their own. On the same day, the United States Navy's submarine S-38 left Cavite to patrol the Verde Island Passage, a strait between Luzon and Mindoro. The *American Leader* would transit this passage on the twelfth. By then, fortunately for us, the S-38 had moved to the western side of Mindoro. On the night of the twelfth, according to Clay Blair, Jr., in his *Silent Victory: The U.S. Submarine War against Japan*, "Wreford Goss (Moon) Chapple, the much loved but not exceptionally bright officer commanding S-38, fired one torpedo at what he believed to be a Japanese ship off the northwest tip of Mindoro and claimed a sinking. However, no Japanese ships were in the area at the time." With the amount of traffic fleeing Manila toward the southwest, it is highly probable Chapple ran across one of them. No records of any sinking at that time and position exist, so it must have been a miss or a premature explosion.

Another oddity concerns the small (1,375 gross tons) Norwegian motor ship *Hydra II*. On December 8, she was bound for Hong Kong in a position one hundred miles east of Varella Light, which is situated on the easternmost coast of what is now Vietnam. On hearing the news of the various attacks all over the Far East, her master opted to run for Iloilo, on Panay Island in the Philippines. The vessel's course took her through Balabac Strait, which had been mined by the Japanese I-123 on December 8, into the Zulu Sea where she met two friendly destroyers whose advice was to make for Manila. Arriving off Manila Bay at 2100 on the twelfth, it was decided to wait and go in at daybreak. As mentioned earlier, there was no pilot available, and the vessel's master may not have been aware of the American mines, never mind those recently laid by the Japanese. At 2140, a tremendous explosion wracked the little ship, and she sank within two minutes. Of her six Norwegian officers, three survived, and of her forty-four Chinese crew only six lived. At Noon the next day, the Swedish motor ship *Colombia*, fleeing Manila, sighted the nine men clinging to the flotsam, rescued them, and carried them all the way to Freemantle, Australia. On January 25, at a hearing in Sydney, the three Norwegians blamed the attack on the Americans, and members of the *Colombia* crew concurred, saying they had seen many American torpedo boats among the islands. The Web site Hyperwar states the S-38 "mistakingly torpedoes and sinks the Norwegian merchantman *Hydra II* west of Cape Calavite, Mindoro, P.I., believing her to be a Japanese auxiliary." Also, John T. Alden in his *U.S. Submarine Attacks During World War II* credits the S-38 with an unsuccessful attack on a Japanese transport December 12 in latitude 12° N, 120° E, which is approximately 175 miles south-southwest from the entrance to Manila Bay. From this writer's standpoint, existing evidence at this late date certainly implicates the American mine field around Corregidor or the mines dropped by the I-124.

Unfortunately, I recall nothing of what I now realize was a most amazing trip through the Macassar Strait, the Flores Sea, the Banda Sea, and the Arafura Sea to Thursday Island off Cape York, the northernmost promontory of Australia. There, we were able to obtain the services of a coast pilot who took us inside the Great Barrier Reef, thence into the Coral Sea and all the way to Sydney, where we safely docked on the morning of Christmas Day. For that remarkable feat of seamanship, United States Lines awarded a second Distinguished Service Medal to Captain Pedersen. His first, gained in December 1938, was for the rescue of the seven-man crew of the foundering Nova Scotia schooner *Fieldwood* "in plunging Winter seas 200 miles Southeast of Halifax." In the early days of World War II, he was also responsible for saving the lives of twenty-nine men from the British freighter *Kafiristan*, which had been torpedoed by the U-54 four hundred miles west of Bishop's Rock. Some memories remain of that long, 1,800-plus mile trip down the Australian east coast. We entered the harbors of Cooktown, Cairns, Townsville, and Mackay, but no one wanted us, nor could they give us any orders or instructions. I have a vivid memory of the vast stretches of the deserted Queensland coast, and the frequent brush and woods fires which the pilot told me were set by lightning. Most of all, I recall sighting Restoration Island, the site of the first landfall made by Captain Bligh and his fellow castaways from the *Bounty*. That held more than a little symbolism for those of us in the *American Leader*, who were also gaining a haven.

As for the other ships in the Pearl Harbor to Manila convoy, the *President Grant* departed Manila with us. Of the fifty-seven crew members left behind, five did not survive their incarceration (see http://www.usmm.org). In February 1944, en route to Milne Bay, New Guinea, from San Francisco, she grounded on Ulna Reef off New Guinea and eventually, in June, was declared a total loss. The *Cape Fairweather* and the *John Lykes* apparently went through the war unscathed. On December 22, the *Boise* operating out of Balik Papan, Borneo, saw both, and there is no further mention of either vessel in any publications relating to World War II which have come to my attention. The *Doña Nati* also escaped from Manila to Australia, where she loaded practically a full cargo of food and ammunition. This she carried to Cebu City in the Philippine Islands, arriving on March 10! The badly needed supplies were transferred to four smaller vessels, only one of which eluded Japanese naval patrols and reached Corregidor. The *Doña Nati* returned safely to Australia, where her master and crew were officially commended by General MacArthur. In April 1964, a wire service newspaper photo showed a vessel named *Doña Nati*, badly damaged in a collision in Japanese waters.

UNITED STATES ARMY FORCES IN AUSTRALIA
OFFICE OF THE COMMANDING GENERAL

Melbourne, S.C.1.
28 March, 1942.

TO the Officers and men of the s.s. "Dona Nati:"

I sincerely welcome you on your return from a Special
Mission which was of outstanding importance to the United
States Army. This service was entered into by you with the
full knowledge of the hazards involved, and with no expecta-
tion of reward. You may have a deep sense of personal
gratification from the knowledge that it was your privilege
to perform a vital service to the United States.

It was your daring and patriotic spirit that brought
about the successful completion of your mission. Your example is an inspiration to all good Americans, and upholds
the highest traditions of the American Merchant Marine.

A copy of this letter will be furnished to each of the
Officers and Men of the crew of the "Dona Nati."

        (signed) Douglas MacArthur

        DOUGLAS MACARTHUR
        General, U.S. Army
        Commanding

        1st. Ind.

Headquarters, Base Section Number 3, Brisbane, Q., March
28, 1942.
TO: Captain RAMON PONS, United States Army Transport
"Dona Nati", Hamilton Dock No. 2, Brisbane, Q.

1. In compliance with the instructions of the Commanding General, United States Army Forces in Australia, I
have the honor to transmit herewith the foregoing document.

        (signed) A. L. Sneed

        A. L. SNEED
        Colonel Air Corps,
        Commanding.

A TRUE COPY:

L. C. OSTRANDER,
Brigadier General, U.S. Army.

Mr. Pedro V. Dawal,
Oiler, on the Special
Mission Trip, Feb.18th
to Mar. 28th, 1942

RAMON PONS
Master, M.S. Dona Nati

As for the *Boise*, her stay in Manila was brief. She anchored in Manila Bay shortly before noon on December 4, and forty-eight hours later was again underway. On December 14 she was in Balik Papan, and on Christmas in Soerabaja in Java. As the Japanese pressed onward, the *Boise* continued southward arriving at Port Darwin, Australia on January 6. For the next two weeks she ran hither and yon—Bali, Java, Flores, Timor—with a lot of drills and GQs, but without any action against the Japanese. On January 21, just before 0800, the *Boise* hit an uncharted underwater ridge which opened a long gash below her starboard boilers and engine room. On February 8, she was in Colombo, out of service. After repairs there and in Bombay, she went to Mare Island, California, for a complete refit, and in June was back at sea, escorting a convoy to New Zealand. During October, covering the reinforcement of marines at Guadacanal, the *Boise* was badly damaged by Japanese shellfire, causing the loss of 107 of her crew. The result was another stateside shipyard stay, this time at the Philadelphia Navy Yard (November 1942 to March 1943). The following five months were spent in the Mediterranean, then she went back to the Pacific where, on the last day of the year, she arrived at Milne Bay. All through 1944 and up to the Japanese surrender, the *Boise* made up for her lack of action in 1941 and early 1942. She received eleven battle stars for her service in World War II.

I still recall our arrival at Sydney on Christmas Day. To our amazement, we tied up in the middle of the morning at the piers just inward of the famed Sydney Harbor Bridge. In spite of it being a holiday, the ship was immediately boarded by our agent and the requisite customs and immigration officers. I remember the immigration fellows remarking, as they scanned the crew list, about the fact

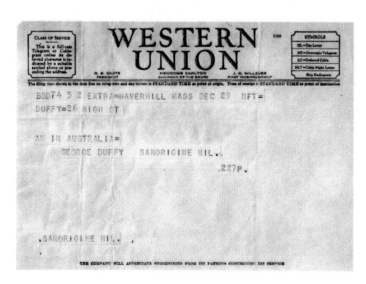

none of the ship's officers, with the exception of Captain Pedersen, showed a wife as next of kin. Of the thirty unlicensed crew, only four were married. The cargo consigned to interests in Shanghai and Hong Kong, and what remained of the cargo destined for Manila, was discharged at Sydney. What happened to it, I have no idea. In February 1951, I received a letter from a Philadelphia law firm asking if I could tell them what became of a shipment of "waste tin plate" loaded at New York for a Hong Kong consignee, some of which was purportedly discharged in Manila! How did I know? We remained in Sydney for seventeen days. The longshoremen, in my mind, worked at a snail's pace without any thoughts of the war. Honestly, those guys would come aboard at 8:00 AM and manage to take an hour to get the tarpaulins and hatch covers off. Then it was everybody down on the quay for a fifteen minute smoko which stretched into half an hour. That's the way it went. Discharge cargo for a while, take a smoko, discharge a bit more, then off for another the smoko, ad infinitum.

When the ship was finally emptied, we sailed for New Caledonia, a French possession a little more than one thousand miles northeast of Sydney to take on about five thousand tons of chromium ore. Before leaving Sydney, though, we picked up a small number of light trucks, command cars, motorcycles, etc., maybe fifty units, for Australian forces on that island.

Discharging Australian Army vehicle at Noumea.

This gave us a day in the capitol city of Nouméa, which was unexpected and delightful. We found ourselves in a French tropical city containing a small naval base and a growing Allied presence. The population was clearly segregated: White French, Asians from French Indo-China, a few Chinese, and the indigenous natives with tremendous bushy heads of dyed red hair, and teeth decayed by betel nut use. The ore was loaded at an anchorage off the small town of Paagoumène at the northwest end of New Caledonia, about two hundred miles from Nouméa. The laborers had the same huge red hairdos!

An amusing incident occurred when we sailed from Sydney, although we knew nothing about it. One of our ordinary seamen was a rather independent character who had, after we docked in Manila in early December, disappeared. It seems this fellow viewed the voyage as a pleasure cruise and decided to tour Luzon. On December 8 he was in Baguio, the summer capital of the Philippines, 150 miles north of Manila. Fortunately, he recognized his serious situation and with a few Filipino acquaintances hired a taxi to take them to Manila. He quickly rejoined the *American Leader* where Captain Pedersen "logged" him for the days he hadn't worked. In Sydney he pulled the same stunt, disappearing again. One day sitting on Lady Jane Beach in the harbor with a local Sheila, he noted a large freighter proceeding to sea. He told the young lady, "That's a C-1 class ship, just like mine." Then seconds later he blurted, "My god, it is my ship." Returning to town, he found the agent's office and learned to his relief we would be back before the end of January. The bad news was the agent wouldn't advance him any money. Why he didn't attempt to find a job is unclear. He did, however, approach the local newspapers offering to write the account of our escape from Manila. The *Australian Women's Weekly* ran the story in its January 24, 1942 issue and paid him a few pounds. It must have been enough to keep him until January 28 when he returned aboard, told his story, and was resigned to the *American Leader*'s articles.

After Paagoumène, we returned to Australia and the port of Newcastle, a short distance north of Sydney, to load a quantity of baled wool. During the passage one night, we encountered bad weather and the ship, in a very tender state with all that weight in the bottom, rolled wildly. The lifeboats, lowered to the boat deck level to provide quick access in the event of torpedoing, were in danger of being swamped. Nevertheless, Captain Pedersen declined to call out the crew to hoist the boats into their chocks because of the risk involved in going out on deck. From Newcastle, we returned to Sydney to finish loading, mostly wool.

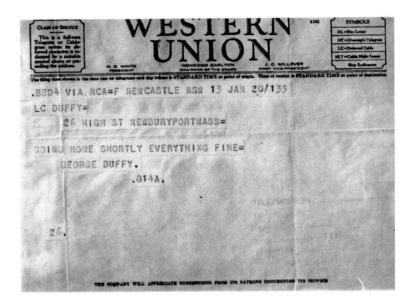

Telegram sent from Newcastle.

In fact, by January 28, when we headed for Boston via the Panama Canal, the five cargo holds were filled to the tops of the hatch coamings.

In all, we spent thirty five days down under, with the majority of the time, perhaps twenty three days, in Sydney. As in Manila, I stood the 1600 to 2400 watch, which gave me plenty of time to explore the city and meet its people. Since, I have been there again in 1979 and 1986, and the memories of all three visits have become overlapped and blurred. Never, however, will I forget the antics of the *American Leader* crew. I mentioned earlier how they, or most of them, had repaired to the crow's nest in Manila after the December 10 bombing. Whatever they imbibed in Sydney brought on a series of violent escapades. Fights, and at least one stabbing, kept the police busy. It spilled over into New Caledonia, where a crewman practically destroyed a bar for which Captain Pedersen had to pay—to be taken out of the fellow's wages. Up at Paagoumène, where the authorities denied shore leave, a charge of cheating at an evening poker game in the crew's messroom resulted in a thrown jar of pickles. It was high and fast, leaving a three-inch gash on the recipient's forehead at the hair line. Bernie Backston and I had a very difficult time stopping the bleeding, cutting the kinky black hair away, and putting in several stitches. One man, who no one dared challenge, was the ship's bosun—the boss sailor.

Bosun Stanley E. Gorski.

His name was Stanley E. Gorski, and he came aboard as an ordinary seaman in San Pedro replacing one of the deserters. As luck would have it, he had sailed with Captain Pedersen in the North Atlantic, and both men were delighted to be together again. During our wait for the convoy in Honolulu, the bosun who had been with us since New York, Joseph Rogers, was hospitalized. Pedersen promoted Stan Gorski to the post. This did not set well with some of the able seamen who thought one of them should have the job. Gorski though, presenting an imposing physique and impressive manner, took control of the deck gang. In port, he was not a member of their drunken orgies, preferring to go ashore as a well-dressed tourist clad in a light tropical suit, silk shirt, fancy necktie, Panama hat, and stylish shoes.

On one of our few evenings in Newcastle he did stop in at a drinking establishment where several of the crew were bellied up to the bar. One of them, an ordinary seaman obviously impaired by alcohol, aimed several disparaging remarks at Gorski, who appeared to ignore the verbal needles. He took off his hat and jacket, casually hanging them on a coat rack. Then without a word, he strode to the bar, grabbed his critic by the shoulder, pulled him around, and with a vicious jab knocked him off the barstool. The poor guy landed flat on his back. Gorski straddled him, dropped to his knees, and tattooed his visage with five or six quick punches. That was it. Gorski stood up, bought a shot of Scotch, put on his hat and jacket and left. His victim never came back to the ship. Probably didn't dare to. I guess he was afraid he'd get tossed overboard. One day, after the ship returned to Sydney, I was headed into the city from the Woolloomooloo docks. I hadn't gone too far when a young couple came diagonally across the street to intercept me. The woman was a stranger, and although the man seemed familiar, I didn't quite recognize him. He knew me because he called me Mr. Duffy. His face was a mess: both eyes were blackened, his cheeks were bruised, his lips puffy, and when he opened his mouth to speak, he didn't have any front teeth! Suddenly it hit me. He was Gorski's punching bag from Newcastle and wanted me to loan him some money he would pay back when he found another ship going to the States. I've often wondered what happened to him, but I didn't contribute to his welfare fund. Examining the *American Leader's* New York payoff sheet dated March 11, 1942, reveals him noted as a deserter with $281.11 in his account. Two other crew members were left behind in Sydney. One, an able seaman, is also shown as a deserter with $370.59 in his wage statement. The other, a mess boy, was technically a deserter with net earnings to date of $70.01. Actually, he was in jail because of the knifing incident wherein he cut the chief steward. He barricaded himself in a cabin which eventually was stormed by the Sydney police. All three forfeited what money was due them.

At that point, I had not reached my twentieth birthday, and these antics came as a revelation. I did not feel threatened by the crew, but soon armed myself with a homemade billy club for the dark hours of my in-port deck patrol. Going back to Newcastle, for example, we weren't working cargo one particular night as the end of my watch neared. It was warm, quiet, and I was enjoying the solitude. Then two of the crew materialized out of the darkness beyond the sheds. In fact, one was chasing the other and, by the evidence of their staggering, both were obviously quite drunk. I waited a few minutes after they traversed the gangway before I went in to see what was happening and found all was quiet. I walked along the passageway and in one cabin discovered the seaman who was being chased sitting on his bunk. He was a big bald-headed man, and blood was streaming from a rather large gash on the top of his skull. I didn't know where the other man was, and as it was he who broke up the barroom in Nouméa, billy club notwithstanding, I wanted no part of him. I scrambled up to Backston's cabin, filled him in, and hurried out onto the quay to telephone for an ambulance. After it arrived, I was chatting with one of the attendants when he informed me he had previously seen the *American Leader* at this same quay a month or so earlier with the same problem. I explained how it couldn't have been us. He checked his log, and sure enough, it was one of the *Leader's* four sister ships! I wonder if on that ship in port they took down the fire axes mounted in various positions throughout the deckhouse, as we did, and locked them up for safety's sake.

The bloodied seaman returned to the ship before we left Australia and is shown on the New York payroll as having earned $640.69, an amount approximately equal to what the other able seamen received. We all signed the payroll indicating receipt of our wages, but his signature is lacking. Strange.

The monthlong homeward voyage was rough on those alcohol-deprived, drying-out characters.

CHAPTER TEN

The Turnaround

As discussed earlier, I discontinued my daily noon position chart when we crossed the Equator on our way from Manila to Sydney. I did, however, create a very small scale replica of the entire voyage. This shows us, upon leaving Sydney on January 28, heading for Cook Strait between the north and south islands of New Zealand. We didn't go directly, but rather in a dogleg fashion. After transiting the strait, the course was set for the vicinity of the Chatham Islands. We passed south of them to latitude 45° south and then ran to the east to longitude 150° west where the course was changed to 070°. That took us to 40° south, 130° west from whence we headed for Balboa. This routing added over 650 miles to the voyage, about two days extra motoring. It was a monotonous passage. No bad weather, but tremendous Pacific swells lifting and lowering us, hour after hour, day after day. We saw nothing, just mile after mile of empty ocean. Of course, we ran blacked out at night, showing no masthead and range lights, and no sidelights.

Reconstructing the Cólon, Canal Zone—Boston leg of our long voyage, we probably arrived at Balboa on February 25 and made the canal transit on the following day. Of interest is the fact we were boarded by a United States naval officer whose only purpose was to question all of our officers as to their naval reserve status, if any. I, being in the United States Naval Reserve, was ordered to report to the navy's district headquarters in New York, which I eventually did. For what reason I never determined, because nothing happened, except in July an envelope containing an honorable discharge was delivered to my Newburyport address.

On board the *American Leader*, we had utterly no knowledge of what the German U-boat force was doing along the eastern seaboard and in the Caribbean. In the five days before we reached Panama, along the general route we would take to Boston, or near it, the following actually took place: February 20. U-432 sank the American freighter *Azalea City*, 125 miles off Ocean City, Maryland. February 21. U-67 sank the Norwegian tanker *Konigsgaard*, 7 miles north of Curacao,

Netherlands Antilles. The U-502 in a position 125 miles west of Curacao, sank the American tanker *J. N. Pew*, bound for Cólon. February 22. U-128 sank the American tanker *Cities Service Empire*, and U-504 sank the American tankers *W. D. Anderson* and *Republic*, all off the Florida beaches. February 23. U-502 sank the Panamanian tanker *Thalia* and damaged the American tanker *Sun* in the vicinity of Aruba, Netherlands Antilles. February 24. U-432 sank the American freighter *Norlavore*, 60 miles off Cape Hatteras. In the same time frame, but further off shore or in the eastern Caribbean, other U-boats sank a total of seventeen vessels.

We received our first check with reality after transiting the canal on February 26 when we were routed north toward Jamaica, then northwest to *Cabo de San Antonio*, the western tip of Cuba, instead of making for the Windward Passage between Cuba and Hispaniola, the most direct line to Boston. The passage would have been a logical area for a U-boat to set up shop. On February 27, using U.S. Navy—provided plots, we began to steer zigzag courses during daylight hours. These called for changing our heading every so many minutes. Without a timer that could be set at the proper intervals, Walter, Mike, and I had a terrible time following the zigzag scheme and in the meanwhile maintaining a sharp lookout and conducting routine navigational duties. Fortunately, we saw no marine traffic and did not have to deal with right of way situations. It is interesting that up ahead of us the Germans were keeping busy. On February 26, while we were in the canal, the U-504 operating on the northern fringes of the Bahamas torpedoed the Dutch tanker *Marmura*. As we blithely continued on our way, the carnage continued: February 27. U-578 torpedoed the American tanker *R. P. Resor*, twelve miles off Manasquan Inlet, New Jersey. U-432 sank the American freighter *Marore* off Cape Hatteras. February 28. U-578 torpedoed the USS *Jacob Jones* (DD 130) off Cape May, New Jersey.

After we rounded Cuba and picked up the Gulf Stream and went past the Florida Keys, we stayed inshore hugging the coast, running along the ten-fathom curve to the vicinity of Cape Hatteras. From there we ran straight toward the entrance to New York. And, other than sport fishermen off the Florida beaches, we still hadn't seen anything. One night on my watch just past Hatteras, we were in a violent rainstorm with visibility reduced to a mile or less. Captain Pedersen was on the bridge with me, as was Bernie Backston. Suddenly, out of the darkness loomed the shape of a southbound empty tanker. In just a few moments she was gone, but not before we witnessed a bright flash on its stern. They had taken a shot at us! With that sort of trigger-happiness, who needed to see other ships? Luckily for us, the U-boats mentioned above had all gone elsewhere when we came along, and there were no sinkings around Cape Hatteras or on the New Jersey coast for the first few days in March when we were proceeding through those waters. To further illustrate how risky it was to be off the eastern seaboard in those days, we went to Boston via New York. A New York harbor pilot came aboard off Sandy Hook and brought us through the East River into Long Island Sound. Without a sound pilot, we proceeded toward Buzzards Bay, where we anchored off the west entrance to the Cape Cod Canal to await a favorable tide and pick up a pilot. Captain Pedersen, who had not been in this area in recent years, was somewhat confused with the appearance of a new lighthouse on Cleveland Ledge, which was not on our charts. Because the *Nantucket*, with me aboard, had been in Buzzards Bay numerous times in 1940 and 1941, I recall attempting to convince him it was indeed a lighthouse structure, not a ship aground. When the pilot boarded, he told Captain Pedersen we were down by the stern. In other words, our draft was more under the rudderpost than under the bow. He wanted it corrected, so Bernie began putting water into the ship's empty forward liquid cargo tank. This was accomplished by jamming the nozzle of a fire hose into the on-deck opening of a sounding tube and starting the engine room fire pump. The fulcrum effect would bring the bow down and the stern up.

We arrived in Boston in the afternoon of March 6, docking at the Mystic piers at the northeast side of the Charlestown Navy Yard where I had spent the two previous winters aboard the schoolship *Nantucket*. Because we would not commence discharging cargo until Monday morning and night relieving officers would be hired, Captain Pedersen and Bernie sent me home to Newburyport for the weekend. I headed for the nearby North Station, but first detoured to the *Nantucket* which, the reader may recall, was moored at the North End Park opposite the other end of the navy yard. I had to go aboard and tell all how I had disregarded Captain Abele's recommendation and taken a job as watch officer. Everyone, cadets and officers alike, was agog at my stories and descriptions of the attack on Manila and Cavite. I nearly missed the train I wanted to take. Aboard the train were several young ladies from Newburyport who were commuting to and from colleges in Boston. I recall my Southern hemisphere sun tan elicited many favorable comments.

They were two busy days. Most of the neighborhood fellows were still around, except for the few who were off at prep school or college. I was appalled at how juvenile they were! Even those who had been a year or two ahead of me in high school seemed to be silly kids, cracking lame jokes. They hadn't the slightest idea of what the war was like, and seemed not a bit to care. By comparison, back at the *American Leader* on Sunday evening, everyone was considerably amused by the appearance of about twenty *Nantucket* cadets who rowed over in the cutter that was always in the water. They wanted to see this wonderful ship I had described on my Friday visit. In particular, Captain Pedersen was impressed with the spontaneity and comradeship of their visit and the respect in which I was held. He spoke of it frequently in the next few days.

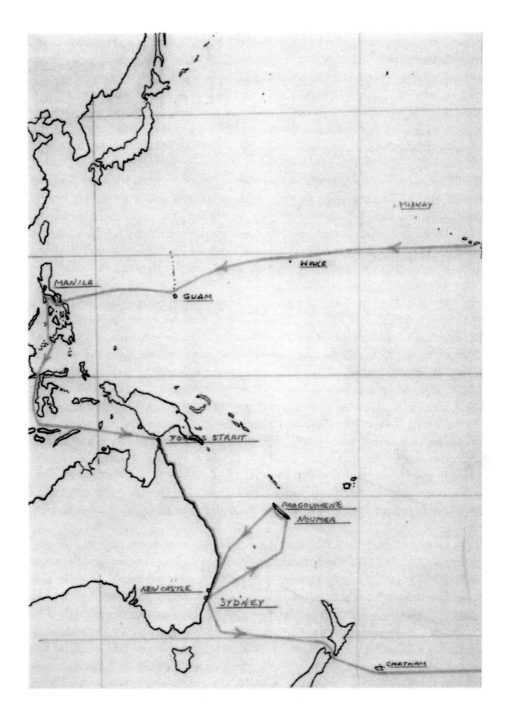

The *American Leader's* voyage.

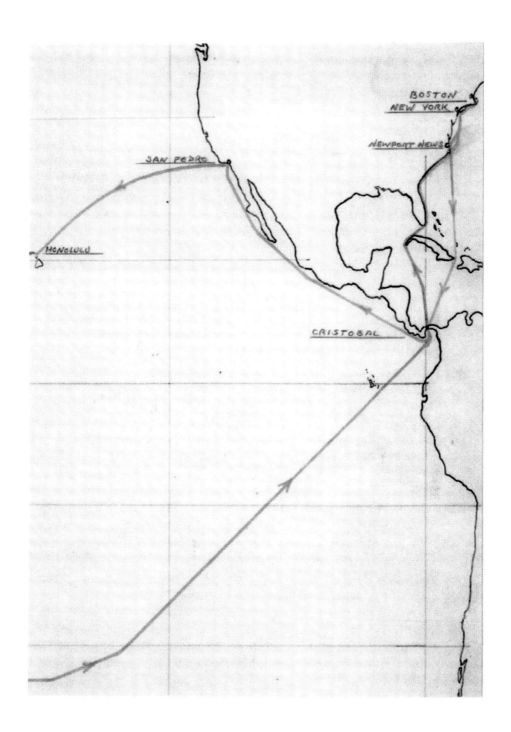

Sometime Monday afternoon disaster struck. The longshoremen, getting down into the lower hold in hatch number 1 found it full of water! No one had remembered the fire pump, presumably until after we had docked in Boston, and the engine room gang shut down the main engines and everything else not needed in port. The pump had pumped and pumped and forced a leak somewhere in the tank. The bales of wool were wet, not soaked, but nevertheless wet. The cargo was discharged with some difficulty and we were able to sail for New York on Tuesday in the early evening. The net result was Bernie Backston lost his job. Captain Pedersen went home, and Walter Lee and I ran the ship, as Mike Biondic decided to leave. Of course, relieving officers took the night watches. Most of the unlicensed crew decided to go elsewhere, although, in one of his last acts, Backston fired the deck crew. There were two exceptions: Stan Gorski went home to Wisconsin, promising to return, and Felix Nordfors, the ship's carpenter and a favorite of Captain Pedersen, stayed.

New York was great! In short order the remainder of the cargo taken on in Australia was discharged, and then we shifted the ship to a railway berth in New Jersey where the chrome ore was unloaded into rail cars. After that it was into a shipyard in Hoboken for conversion to wartime service. Several inches of concrete was poured on the top of the deckhouse. Gun tubs to hold .50 caliber machine guns were placed on the flying bridge wings, and a spacious gun platform was erected on the stern. This would take an ancient four-inch cannon and two .30 caliber Lewis (machine) guns. Life rafts and their frames were installed, two on the after deck, and three on the fore deck. The *American Leader* had a special cargo locker for valuable cargoes located under the deckhouse at the upper 'tween deck level, actually in the engine room space. This was converted into quarters for the Naval Armed Guard. The new crew was slowly coming aboard. Of note is that as soon as I was paid off on March 11, and Mike Biondic left, Captain Pedersen promoted me to Mike's position with a pay increase to $225 per month from $161. My old spot was filled by Alexander Shershun, who had just graduated from the Massachusetts Nautical School. Chester Dowe departed, and George Schabel took over as chief engineer.

Two new cadets were assigned: Gordon Tyne (deck) from Gloucester, Massachusetts, just a short distance from Newburyport, and Joe DiCicco (engine) from nearby Brooklyn. Frank Stallman opted for another voyage and was promoted from third assistant engineer to second assistant. All of this was happening in a rather haphazard manner, and finally we received our armed guard. These were eight young navy men commanded by a newly minted ensign, a good ol' boy from the dinky town of Daphne, Alabama.

Part of *American Leader's* deck crew. From left, Bosun Gorski,
Carpenter Nordfors, Able Seaman Delany, Able Seaman Hiza,
Ordinary Seaman Porchia, Ordinary Seaman Kalloch.

American Leader crew's mess room. From left, Gorski, Marcinkus,
Dickinger, Pride, Harrison, Smith (center), Nordfors (back),
Delany (foreground), Savuca (back), Pekich (foreground).

Time flew quickly, and there was much to be done and much to be taught to our new shipmates. On the other hand, we worked only from 8:00 AM to 5:00 PM and had the entire weekends off. I know I went ashore every night and trekked back and forth to Newburyport almost every weekend. I had plenty of money and wouldn't be spending much in the upcoming months.

It was probably shortly after the end of March before we shifted back to the cargo piers in Manhattan and began loading operations. Initially, the cargo was steel bars and ingots, going down onto the ship's tank tops. This was reasonable, we thought, as we believed we were going to north Russia. In the shipyard, special heating elements had been installed in the mast houses holding the controls and mechanisms for the electric cargo winches. Soon, however, we began seeing crates and barrels marked Abadan, Bandar Shahpour, and Basra arriving in the shed. That meant the Persian Gulf.

About this time an incident occurred which had a lasting impact on me and the state of my well-being throughout the upcoming voyage. I was in the ship's office doing some paper work for Captain Pedersen, who was getting back into the routine, when I heard and noted a stranger in the passageway. He was well dressed, wearing a suit and necktie, had a snappy hat on and was carrying a raincoat. I went out and bluntly asked him, "Who are you?" He declined to identify himself so I told him to get off the ship, to which he replied something to the effect of what would I do if he didn't. I became angry and told him again to get off the ship or I would physically throw him off. He retorted, saying he didn't think I could do it. "If I can't," I replied, "I'll call for help and we'll both do it." At that, he backed off and departed. The following day, Captain Pedersen was again on board and sent Walter Lee to find me. As I entered the Captain's office, to my amazement, the interloper of the previous day was sitting on the settee. He stood up, smiled, and stretched out his right hand. "Hello, George, I'm Bernard Hickey, the new Chief Officer." I shook his hand and turned to Captain Pedersen asking, "Captain, do you know we met yesterday?"

"Yes," he replied, "I have heard about it."

Walter filled me in later. Hickey, he said, was quite impressed with the way I handled myself the previous day and reported the incident to Captain Pedersen. The captain, in turn, according to Walter, said something about my character and ability and added, "It is quite surprising as he is only nineteen years old." Walter then warned me to be careful with Hickey as he appeared to be embarrassed by the knowledge he had been bested by a "junior officer" twelve years younger then he.

**Stan Gorski, Walter Lee, and author
posing on *American Leader's* flying bridge, April 1942.**

Our departure from New York was a stop-and-go drill. I recall being at home in Newburyport on April 11 and 12. When I left that Sunday afternoon my farewell was tinged with the knowledge of the long voyage ahead and the fact it would be many months before I returned. Something occurred in New York, however, and I know I was home again on the eighteenth and nineteenth. That Sunday, it was good-bye all over again, and this time for sure. On Sunday afternoon, April 26, the *American Leader* in a very routine workaday manner backed out of her slip at Pier 59 on New York's west side. There was no fanfare, this was just another vessel easing into the Hudson River. A number of shoreside personnel, last minute sailing details attended to, watched her go. There may have been more than the usual onlookers as Captain Pedersen was a longtime employee of the company, and he was embarking on a lengthy, dangerous trip. I recall seeing Captain S. J. Topping, the marine superintendent, going ashore just before the gangway was taken away.

It was a warm, bright day, and a few puffy fair-weather clouds dotted the brilliant blue sky. The ferries seemed to be crowded with families. The country was at war, but there was no war in New York harbor that afternoon, unless one considered the *American Leader*. Her stack, once black with a broad white band bordered above and below by thinner green bans, was painted gray, as was her once-white deckhouse, buff masts, and black hull. Her armament stood out prominently. Ship watchers could not have missed the nine black-cocooned A-20/DB-7 Havoc attack bombers lashed to her weather deck. We didn't immediately go to sea, anchoring off Staten Island where thirty-odd other deep-laden freighters and tankers were gathered. Captain Pedersen used this opportunity to hold a fire and boat drill. Of note is our fifty-eight man merchant crew and Naval Armed Guard was now supplemented by twelve civilians, eleven of whom were construction managers going to the Persian Gulf. The twelfth man, fortunately, was a medical doctor who took over the duties usually performed by the chief officer. We had set sea watches, so I was on the bridge until 1600 when Walter Lee relieved me. After supper, at about 1930, I turned in to get a few hours of sleep before being called at 2330 for the 0000 to 0400 watch, during which nothing transpired. That would be my routine at sea for this voyage.

CHAPTER ELEVEN

To the Middle East and Asia

In midmorning of Monday the twenty-seventh, when I awoke, we were proceeding down the Jersey coast, the fifth in a line of five ships. A U.S. Navy blimp was escorting us. Someone told me most of the ships at anchor had sailed at short intervals after daybreak, heading off to the east. Our small convoy followed, with the Delaware River entrance our destination, where we would anchor for the night. It was a strange operation. There was no pilot boat on station, the blimp left us, and if a U-boat had come onto the scene, her commander would have found five fat targets milling about in confusion in the growing darkness. Finally, the pilot boat came out and led us to designated anchorages.

At dawn the blimp reappeared and with the pilot boat again leading the procession we proceeded to sea, bound for Chesapeake Bay. There, things were better organized. After spending a day on the Degaussing Range calibrating the ship's defense against magnetic mines, we anchored for the night. At dawn we sailed, but this time alone. The Hampton Roads pilot took a letter to my mother when he disembarked. In it I wrote, "Things look pretty good along the coast and the patrols are far better than when we came up, back in March. Plenty of blimps, bombers, destroyers, etc. But there are quite a few wrecks to be seen." We ran close to shore, following the ten-fathom depth curve all the way to the Florida Keys. In this stretch I saw but one ship, a northbound tanker whose silhouette I discerned against the Miami area shore lights, early in my 0000 to 0400 watch on May 3. She passed inside of us, and may not have been aware of our presence. Earlier, we had several potentially close calls, none of which we were aware. We had left Hampton Roads in the morning of April 30 and I calculate had rounded Cape Lookout at about 2000.

Completely unknown to us was the sinking by the U-402 of the Russian freighter *Ashkhabad* (5,284 tons) in the early morning hours of that day, seventeen miles south-southwest of Cape Lookout. There were many ships out there, and the

German U-boats were finding them. Available records show little action along the Eastern seaboard during the week before our departure from New York. On April 28, however, the day we were proceeding from the Delaware River to Chesapeake Bay, the U-136, in a position roughly thirty miles east of Asbury Park, New Jersey, sank the Dutch freighter *Arundo* (5,163 tons). As we blithely approached Florida and the Caribbean, things began happening all around us, of which we had utterly no knowledge. We passed St. Augustine, Florida, in my midnight to four watch on May 2.

In the morning of the previous day, ten miles southeast of Cape Canaveral, which is ninety-five miles south of St. Augustine, U-109 torpedoed the British motor vessel *La Paz* (6,546 tons) and a Nicaraguan lighter named *Worthen* (555 tons). The *La Paz* was later raised, but we were sailing right into a trap, which, by good chance, was never sprung. On May 3, within a few miles of the position where the *La Paz* and the *Worthen* were hit, the U-564 sank the British freighter *Ocean Venus* (7,714 tons). On May 4, 8, and 9, in a strip of ocean thirty-eight to forty-three miles north of Miami and one mile wide, water we had traversed on May 2, that same U-564 torpedoed three ships: the British tanker *Eclipse* (9,767 tons), the American freighter *Ohioan* (6,078 tons), and the Panamanian motor tanker *Lubrafol* (7,138 tons). Additionally, on May 5, 100 miles north of Miami, she torpedoed the American freighter *Delisle* (3,478 tons). The freighter's master turned the stricken ship toward the beach, where she would eventually ground and be salvaged, although she was lost later in the war. The *Eclipse* survived in a like manner to be raised and presumably returned to service.

At Key West, we parted company with the United States and swung across the Straits of Florida to again skirt *Cabo de San Antonio*. Meanwhile, we had avoided two other German submarines which had gone past the Florida Keys into the Gulf of Mexico. One of these, U-507 had a phenominal streak, getting six ships in five consecutive days. They were the American freighter *Norlindo* (2,686 tons) and the American tanker *Munger T. Ball* (5,104 tons) on May 4. The next day it was the American tanker *Joseph M. Cudahy* (6,950 tons). In fact, all three were sunk with a span of eleven hours in an area north of the Dry Tortugas. On the sixth, moving toward the mouth of the Mississippi, U-507 caught the American freighter *Alcoa Puritan* (6,759 tons), then on the seventh the Honduran *Ontario* (3,099 tons), and on the eighth the Norwegian *Torny* (2,424 tons)! Later successes were accomplished on the twelfth, thirteenth, and sixteenth. The second of the two submarines which had gone into the Gulf of Mexico, the U-506, worked the area west of the Mississippi delta getting two ships on the tenth and twelfth respectively. By those dates, though, the *American Leader* was well out into the Atlantic Ocean.

I recall having Cuba in sight during my afternoon watch of May 3. That portion of Cuba where we made landfall seemed particularly barren and unpopulated, so Ensign Willie Dryer, the commander of the armed guard detachment, decided to have a live firing exercise with the four-inch gun. He may have asked Captain Pedersen's permission, but considering his attitude it is entirely possible he didn't. Certainly the outcome came at a complete surprise to all of us. He had mustered his crew, ordered a few practice loadings and simulated firings. Then, with the gun loaded, ordered it aimed at the beach, and called out "Fire!" I was on watch at the time, keeping a sharp lookout from the flying bridge, and really not paying much attention to the goings on back at the gun, but never imagined he'd actually let a shot go—at a foreign country! Because of the surprise factor, I never saw an impact on the shore, but my wrist watch was a casualty of the muzzle blast. It never ticked again. The situation with Willie and Captain Pedersen was not pleasant at all. Somewhere in his ninety-day training stint he was led to believe he would be in command of the ship to which he'd be assigned. At one point, soon after departing New York, he appeared on the bridge and actually gave an order to Captain Pedersen having something to do with the ship's position relative to the other vessels in our five-ship convoy. And now this! Unbelievable!

After rounding *Cabo de San Antonio*, on May 4, the course was set for Port of Spain, Trinidad. Ahead of us, and of course not known to us, was the U-125. At noon on May 3, in a position sixty miles west of Jamaica, by torpedo and gunfire, it had sunk the Dominican Republic—flagged *San Rafael* (1,973 tons). Twenty-four hours later, still between us and Port of Spain, the U-125 torpedoed the American freighter *Tuscaloosa City* (5,687 tons) eighty-two miles south of Grand Cayman. On the sixth, we had left the German behind as in the identical latitude and longitude of the *Tuscaloosa City*'s loss she sank the American freighter *Green Island* (1,946 tons). Later, in the same general area on May 6 and May 8, respectively, the British freighter *Empire Buffalo* (6,404 tons), and the Canadian motor tanker *Calgarolite* (11,941 tons) went to the bottom as the result of the U-125's torpedoes. We arrived at Port of Spain on the morning of May 9, docked, took on a full load of bunkers, and departed in midafternoon. On sailing, we found ourselves in the company of three small coasters, escorted by a small patrol boat. After about an hour, Captain Pedersen, dissatisfied with the convoy's slow speed, had a signal sent to the escort indicating we were leaving, and they were soon out of sight astern.

The run from Port of Spain to Capetown was uneventful and boring, particularly my midnight to four in the morning watch. There was nothing, simply nothing to be seen. We were blacked out, as were the ships of all warring nations. My watch consisted of the usual two able seamen and an ordinary seaman doing their hour-and-twenty-minute stints of steering, keeping a lookout, and standing by. We did have two extra sets of eyes in the form of the navy gunners, one on duty at the aft gun and another in one of the .50 caliber gun tubs on the flying bridge. One advantage to that watch is it kept me away from Hickey. I generally slept through breakfast and had lunch every day at 1130, before taking over the bridge from Shershun. Hickey wouldn't eat until 1200. In the evening, I had supper at 1700, and Hickey generally wouldn't come in until 1730, when I was gone from the dining saloon. Even during the balance of my afternoon watch, he rarely, unlike the affable Backston, would come onto the bridge and socialize a bit.

We reached Capetown in eighteen days or so and were immediately directed to dock where fresh water was available. As we were not to remain long, the deck and engine watch officers were told not to break watches, but to stand their regular sea watches in port. That suited me fine, so I had supper and changed from my regular khakis to slacks and a shirt and headed off for a quick visit to the city, which, incidentally, was under no black out. At the gangway I was met by Hickey who said he was ordering two officers to be on board at all times and I, therefore, could not leave the ship. That was it. Case closed. Revenge wreaked.

We left Capetown the following day and, unexpectedly were routed well off shore to the south and east. Instead of running up the African coast and through the Mozambique Channel, we passed far to the east of Madagascar. This added hundreds of miles, perhaps fifteen hundred, to our voyage. We were told to do this by the British Admiralty, so there must have been a reason. Long after the war I came across a translation of a German book entitled *Die U-booterfolge der Achsenmächte, 1939-1945*. (Axis Submarine Successes, 1939-1945.) There I learned of the activities of four Japanese submarines, operating in the Mozambique Channel between June 5 and July 9, 1942. In the waters we ordinarily would have traversed from Capetown to Basra, they sank twenty Allied and neutral merchant vessels and damaged one other. I have a letter to my mother, stating we arrived at the head of the Persian Gulf on June 20! So the British guessed right on that one, but it appears twenty-one ships never got the word and were sitting ducks for the Japanese!

Incredibly, shortly before I stopped working in 1991, I was the boarding agent for a Norwegian oil tanker at Portsmouth, New Hampshire. Her chief officer told me his father was in one of those twenty-one ships, the Norwegian-flagged *Wilford*, and her survivors were machine-gunned by their attacker. He was astounded when I informed him it was a Japanese submarine because he had held a lifelong hatred of the Germans for what he thought a German U-boat had done. A postwar account, based on testimony given at a maritime inquiry in Durban on July 28,

1942, by survivors of the *Wilford*, does not mention machine-gunning of survivors. Specifically, however, it does say the *Wilford* was the victim of intense, close range gunfire, which set the vessel ablaze, ultimately causing her to sink. Her master, second officer, and seven Chinese crew members were killed in the action.

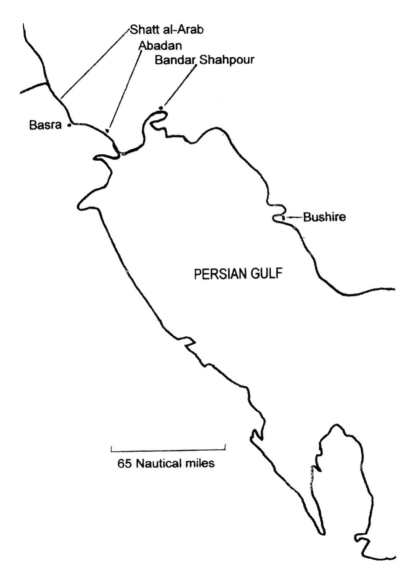

Location of ports in Persian Guld visited by *American Leader* in June and July 1942. We also took bunkers at a solitary pier somewhere on the Western shore near no habitation.

Quite by coincidence, in more recent years I became acquainted with a former Danish merchant seamen, Gunnar Kryger, who had been in the neutral Swedish freighter *Eknaren*, torpedoed by the I-16 on July 1 in the lower reaches of the Mozambique Channel. After his ship sank, he found himself in the ocean, alone, supported only by his life preserver. To his utter delight, an American freighter with a sharp-eyed lookout found him and took him to New York. He obtained employment in the United States merchant marine, ultimately became a United States citizen, and settled in Vermont.

One incident of our voyage around Madagascar occurred one afternoon on my watch. We were two or three days out of Capetown and a brisk wind was blowing from the northwest, carrying with it the strange and distinct odor of Africa. Captain Pedersen came into the wheelhouse at one point, and I called it to his attention. He was not particularly impressed, but I have never forgotten it. I have had similar olfactory experiences when sailing to Bermuda where the sweet smell of the islands' blossoms greets the mariner well before landfall.

The *American Leader* suffered little or no delay in getting up the Shatt al Arab to Abadan. I recall going to anchor in the midst of many other waiting vessels in the morning of the twentieth. Numerous of what were mostly tankers, some with Norwegian flags, were visible, and Captain Pedersen had Shershun, and then me, busy on the Aldis lamp attempting to make contact. My memory is hazy, but I believe the Norwegians ignored us. In any case, we went up the river in the afternoon, anchored again, then in the morning went alongside the discharging berth. The only cargo delivered there were the nine aircraft and their associated crates. Our passengers departed as well. By midnight we were headed downriver for what was a twelve-hour run to a godforsaken place named Bandar Shahpour. I wrote,

> *Bandar Shahpour is on the Khor Musa, which is nothing more than a channel through a vast expanse of mud flats. As far as one can see—North, South, East, or West—is level desert or mud. It is the beginning of the Iran State R. R. and populated by about 2,000 of the dirtiest human beings I've laid eyes on. Outside of a few new buildings erected by the British, the place consists of just mud huts. There are a few white men here who live from one American ship to the next, in order to get some good meals, all our magazines, and what cigarettes can be spared.*

We remained in Bandar Shahpour for a considerable length of time because our next port was to be Abadan again, and we were there on the Fourth of July. Continuing the letter to my mother, dated June 25, but which, I believe, was mailed later in Abadan, I said,

Today marks the end of the second month out of New York, and don't I wish I were back in the U.S.A. where the summers are a bit cool. No kidding, Hades must be only ten miles from here. The temperature at Noon hasn't been below 115° any day yet and by 4 o'clock its up another couple of degrees. Everyone is in a perpetual state of sweat—sleeping, eating, working. And the amount of liquids one can drink is amazing. I think nothing of downing five glasses of water at a time and always have a tall glass of iced tea or cocoa in the refrigerator. I eat but one meal a day, that at supper, and just a little at breakfast.

What I didn't tell her was that Captain Pedersen had set up a cot in the below-water shaft alley and slept in relative comfort there.

Bandar Shahpour was a busy place in those days. Several finger piers, carrying railroad tracks, extended from the shore and our cargo was discharged directly into the rail cars. A number of other vessels were present and we were all attended by a few British and Russian functionaries. One incident I vividly recall was the arrival of a small British passenger ship carrying several hundred British Indian soldiers. They were Dogras, as I recall. Smallish in stature, their commanding officer was a rather tall Englishman. He came aboard the *American Leader*, and I was the first officer he encountered. He wanted to take a bath, he said. I told him he'd have to settle for a shower and directed him to mine. Afterward, he thanked me profusely and returned to his troops. I never obtained his name nor what he and his men were up to in that part of the world. (Author's note: Dogras still serve in the army, but it is the Indian Army since 1947. As fighting soldiers, they saw action in Malaya in 1941 and 1942. After that they fought the Japanese in several battles in Burma from 1943 to the war's end in 1945. So, why the Dogras I saw were in Persia remains a mystery.)

Another person I met was the postmaster, one of the few English-speaking persons in Bandar Shahpour. In fact, we became quite friendly, and I made a daily visit to the one-room post office to chat with him. Just for the kicks, I asked him to send a postcard, with a message written in Farsi, to me at my Newburyport address. He did, and I still have it, with a translation done many years later by a classmate of our daughter Maryellen at Simmons College in Boston.

As I said, we returned to Abadan from Bandar Shahpour, and in my letter described the scenery we passed through going up the Shatt al Arab, which is formed by the confluence of the Tigris and Euphrates Rivers about two hundred miles from the gulf.

It is like going back a thousand years to travel the 30-odd miles up to Abadan. The river cuts through a desolate plain and the only vegetation is within a half mile of the stream. Just solid groves of date palms, enclosed by mud walls. The people dress in long robes and live in clay houses. The chief mode of transportation is by water. You can see their homemade boats—everything from canoes to ten-oared barges and the big sailing dhows. It's almost artificial, you think you're watching a movie. Abadan is a town owned and operated by the Anglo Persian Oil Company and is the largest or at least one of the largest refineries in the world. There are a number of Europeans there, and the place is not too bad, although the native quarter is restricted [author's note: out of bounds] *to crews of ships. (They say a couple of seamen have last been seen going into the quarter alone.) The oil company maintains clubs for the officers and men, complete with movies, books, and magazines. One evening, I saw newsreels of the bombing of Pearl Harbor which I had not seen before.*

From Abadan, we went further upriver to the large city of Basra in Iraq to load cargo for the United States. There were no deep water docks there, thus we had to anchor in the stream. Part of our cargo was Syrian tobacco out of Latakia which, in those days, played a major role in the advertising of Philip Morris cigarettes. We could get ashore here, but the city was a huge disappointment. It was filthy to the extent of small piles of human excrement in the gutters awaiting the next rare rain storm to be washed into the river. At some point, dated July 8, so it probably was in Basra, I wrote to my mother,

> *They tell us here, that Air Mail to the USA takes but 10 days. And for the equivalent of 70 cents, it's pretty good. I've already written one letter from another port in Persia, but I rather doubt it ever gets delivered. There is very little to write about outside of the weather and the Persian Gulf's weather has nothing to recommend. My clothes, my bunk, and as a matter of fact, the whole ship is covered with sand dust. If it isn't so hot that one can't see for the sweat, the sun is blacked out by sandstorms. One or the other, I don't know which is worse. I get hay fever in the States and out in this part of the world, the sand has got me sneezing. Well, as I said a couple of lines back, there is nothing to write about. Everything is going OK and as good as can be expected. About the best we can expect is New York by the first of October—I hope. Love.*

That was delivered in Newburyport on August 5. Strangely, it was an "Air Mail Letter Card," one of those fold-up, one page affairs. It carries a three-cent United States postage stamp, is censored by a U.S. Army Examiner, and the cancellation is dated "JUL 20 1942 AMERICAN BASE FORCES A.P.O. 816." It also carries the rubber stamped note "NOT IN AIR MAIL." Strange. I wish I could remember how I obtained the "Letter Card" and where I mailed it.

From Basra, we went back down the Shatt al Arab, into the Gulf and anchored off the small town of Bushire. Here, as in Basra, barges or lighters delivered the cargo, but as no bumboats made an appearance, there was no way to get ashore, not that anyone wanted to after the smells and sights of Basra.

A funny incident occurred on deck one afternoon. For some reason, I was supervising the operations. (We must not have broken sea watches, and I was standing my usual 12:00 to 4:00.) Hickey wanted to shift some of the previously stowed cargo from one hatch to another: These were bales, maybe the tobacco. Anyway, the longshoremen in the hold would place the bales in rope slings, and the winch operator would hoist them out and drop them on deck. There two men would grab a bale and place it on the head of a third man who then walked along the deck and casually, without looking, dropped it into the next hatch. Of course, one of these bales landed on the head of one of the fellows working in the hatch and knocked him unconscious. I became involved, along with the native foreman, in attempting to resuscitate the victim. The foreman kept yelling "Aspa! Aspa!" at me which I finally figured out to be Aspirin. So I duly went up to the sick bay and returned with a pitcher of water and a bottle of Aspirin. When I went down into the hatch the poor fellow was somewhat recovered, so I had him down about a half-dozen of the pills and gave him the bottle to take home. He probably had suffered a concussion and I have no idea what good those puny little white pills did for him. I laughed at supper time when I recounted what had happened; surely it wasn't funny to the Persian.

From Bushire we headed to Bombay, which was chaotic. Many ships were at anchor there, and launch service was available to those who wished to go ashore. I've forgotten the details, but Eric Kamins, my counterpart engine room watch stander, and I managed to get time off. We found a room at a large hotel near the India Gate and hired a horse-drawn carriage to take in the nighttime sights. The streets were crowded and noisy, PA systems blasted unfamiliar music, the lights were bright, and drunken merchant seamen seemed to be everywhere. In the morning, tea and rolls were delivered to the room, and when I took the lid off the sugar bowl, the brown sugar was roiling—ants! There was no promise of a berth in Bombay for some time, causing us to be sent to a forlorn area in the Gulf of Kutch in the northwest area of the country. The port was named Bedi Bundar and again we anchored off, unloading into barges the steel ingots loaded in New York. From Bedi Bundar, it was a 1,235-mile run down the west coast of India to the port of Colombo in Ceylon (known today as Sri Lanka), where we arrived on or about August 12.

I wrote two short notes to my mother from Colombo. Neither carries a specific date. The first is stamped "PASSED BY U.S. NAVAL CENSOR." Somehow,

I became acquainted with a man named Harvey Renfrew who worked at the United States consulate, and I met several naval officers and enlisted men who were stationed there. Maybe they allowed me the privilege of using their mail service, although the second note doesn't carry the censor's stamp. In the first, I wrote,

> *It is hard to say just how long this will take to reach the United States but I guess I can be pretty sure of your receiving it. Which is more than I expect happened to other mail sent previously through regular postal service. As we have been out four months, we are about fed up with everything. So, once we get started I don't think there'll be much stopping us. New York will sure look great. About the best we can figure on is being on the Atlantic coast around the early part of October.*

Before leaving, I sent a second, equally brief missive.

> *Just a few lines to let you know that everything's O.K. and that this will be the last letter I'll write for the next 7 or 8 weeks. It's really a great feeling to step ashore again after all those liberty-less whistle stops in the Persian Gulf. There are some wonderful hotels here, where the meals leave nothing wanting but a second helping. Speaking of food, how is the tea situation in the States? You know, "Ceylon for good tea." So, I've picked up a few pounds. The Japanese attacked this place back in early April and I guess they were sorry they ever tried it. Everyone has a different story as to the number of planes shot down, etc., but damage was small and the Japs haven't returned, As long as this is the closest we get to them, I'm satisfied. Most of the boys, though, would like to see a "real air raid."*

> *Love.*
> *George.*

No question, Colombo was a delightful, civilized break from what we experienced in the Gulf. We were tied up to a pier, had access to the city as we pleased, and thoroughly enjoyed ourselves. With Captain Pedersen's permission, Stan Gorski contracted with a local painting contractor to paint the entire ship with the deck crew paying the bill. A scheme was devised whereby several men would stay aboard for safety purposes while the others went off to the beaches and who knows where else for bit of rest and recreation, or maybe to just plain get drunk. That, and the knowledge we would soon be heading home, made for a happy ship.

Colombo was clean and bustling. The British Army and Royal Navy were very much in evidence. Manned antiaircraft batteries were positioned in various parks and open areas, with the gunners' tents close at hand. While we were there, a Royal Navy aircraft carrier was moored just a short distance from our pier, and by virtue of the ship's public address system we eavesdropped on the crew's daily routine. One Sunday we witnessed an inspection of sorts. The captain stood on the after end of the flight deck, and apparently every man in the crew, marching in single file, passed by him, snapping off a hand salute. The band of the Royal Marines played just one tune—"Life on the Ocean Waves"—over and over again. Strangely, I never learned the words, but the melody remains in my head, sixty-five years later.

The cargo we had loaded in the Gulf was quite valuable. One consignment consisted of about one hundred well-constructed wooden cases, weighing a total of ten tons, and containing opium! At Colombo, we picked up a substantial percentage of Ceylon's annual rubber production. Liquid latex was pumped into our cargo tanks, barrels of the white, sticky stuff went into the hatches and, at the end, more were lashed on deck. An estimated 2,500,000 bales of sheet rubber filled the cavernous holds. Every one in the crew had amassed a collection of wood carvings, mainly elephants, plus the abovementioned tea. In retrospect, the *American Leader* and its cargo was a very valuable commodity, yet we were sent out of Colombo in a routine manner without any semblance of an escort. While we were in Colombo, we read in the daily papers of German raider activity in the South Atlantic Ocean. Captain Pedersen mentioned this to the Royal Navy personnel who gave him the routing orders for our run to Capetown. "Don't worry about them," was the reply. "They've gone home."

Without the availability of a good navigational chart, I estimate the run to Capetown to be approximately 4,800 miles, which we accomplished in about 15½ days. Again, it was a routine, boring passage, although I had bad scare during one of my midnight to four watches. It was a black night and every star in the sky was sparkling, when on the eastern horizon a bright light appeared. It took me only a second to recognize what it was, the new moon rising, but for that instant I was really shaken. The following night, conditions were the same, and I wasn't going to be surprised. Up it came. A few seconds later, there was a wild yell from the main deck. Willie Grover, one of the oilers, had come up out of the engine room for a bit of fresh air, and suddenly was startled by the bright light on the horizon. "Mate! Mate!" he screamed as he bounded up the ladders, not daring to look back. He came running to the bridge wing where I managed to calm him. Deep down, I think we were all a bit jumpy.

CHAPTER TWELVE

The Raider *Michel*

After the raider *Widder* arrived in Brest on October 31, 1940, she laid at anchor for two weeks while discussions took place concerning her future movements. Von Ruckteschell eventually was called to Berlin to make his voyage report, and three days later when he returned to his command he was sporting the rare decoration of *Das Ritterkreuz des Eisernes Kreuzes* (the Knight's Cross of the Iron Cross). His entire crew was awarded Iron Crosses, First Class to the officers and Second Class to the crew. At this point, the *Widder* crew was disbanded and given their Christmas vacations. Interestingly, the date of the Knight's Cross of the Iron Cross citation was October 31, 1940, coinciding with the *Widder*'s arrival in Brest.

Von Ruckteschell was then presented with yet another award, the command of a partially built vessel laying in a shipyard in German-occupied Gdansk, Poland, which was to be converted into a state of the art commerce raider. He immediately began to assemble a crew, choosing a number of officers and ratings from the *Widder*'s roster, but, because of incompetency or personality clashes, dismissing others. His ultimate officer's list follows:

First Officer *Korvettenkapitän* Wolfgang Erhardt
Navigating Officer *Kapitänleutnant der Reserve* Ludwig Rödel
Radio Officer *Kapitänleutnant* Götz-Frederick Rabenau
First Gunnery Officer *Oberleutant zur See* S. Jacob Schwinn
Adjutant and Second Gunnery Officer *Oberleutnant zur See* Jürgen Herr
Commander *Esau* and First Torpedo Officer *Kapitänleutnant* Malte von Schack
Second Torpedo Officer *Oberleutnant zur See* Willie Schmolling
Flying Officer *Kapitänleutnant* Konrad Hoppe
First Medical Officer *Marine-stabsartz der Reserve* Doktor Friedrich Wilhelm Schröder
Second Medical Officer *Marine-stabsartz der Reserve* Doktor Hans-Christel Pfeiffer
Dentist *Marine-zahnartz* Edmund Scherf
Administration Officer *Kapitänleutnant (V)* Otto Saupe

Supply Officer *Oberleutnant* Ludwig Stadler
Chief Engineer *Korvettenkapitän (Ing)* Fritz Hanstein
Second Engineer *Oberleutnant (Ing) der Reserve* Eric Bethke
Third Engineer *Leutnant (Ing) der Reserve* Gustav Jördens
Prize Officers (all *Oberleutnant zur See der Reserve*) Edgar Behrend
                                                        Carl Cords
                                                        Walter Duborg
                                                        Heinrich Heitmann
                                                        Adolf Wimmel
Meteorologist Dr. Herbert Weise

In early January of 1941, von Ruckteschell's star continued shine as he was promoted to *Fregattenkapitän der Reserve*, and on September 7, his new command was placed in commission and given the name *Michel*. Throughout the ensuing winter, the ship worked in the Baltic, drilling, practicing, maneuvering, until every move became a knee-jerk reality. At the end of January 1942, von Ruckteschell moved his base of operation from Gdansk to Kiel and thence through the Kiel Canal to Cuxhaven at the mouth of the Elbe River. What follows is a narration of the *Michel*'s voyage compiled from information supplied by her surviving crew members. Of most importance are excerpts from an anonymous enlisted man's daily journal, which has been translated to English by Konrad Hoppe. Additional information has been derived from Konrad's own journal, which was kept in a more casual manner.

March 9. 1230 Departure. 1930 Anchored off Helgoland.

March 10. Crew mustered before commander. He explained what is to be done. Additional personnel were on board for the run through the channel. The most important of these were *B-Dienst* radiomen, fluent in the English language, for the purpose of listening to and deciphering the British radio frequencies if an attempt to intercept the *Michel* was made. Also, a temporary quadruple 3.7 cm gun mount was sited on the flying bridge, just for the passage and manned by its own crew.

March 11. 0530 Weighed anchor and proceeded along Dutch coast with an escort of one antiaircraft cruiser, one minesweeper, and a number of torpedo boats. 1800. The convoy entered the Schelde River and anchored for the night.

March 12. 0530 Weighed anchor, but at 0745, the *Michel* ran onto a sand bank off Ostend. The *B-Dienst* operators reported the British were attempting to find the *Michel*. Eventually she freed herself from the sand, but it was decided to return to the anchorage, which was actually off the Dutch town of Vlissingen. Before reaching that point, however, the *Michel* went hard aground and remained there until the following day.

March 13. On board it was believed the British were still hunting and it was possible their reconnaissance aircraft had spotted them. At some time during the day, the *Michel* was refloated. It was then decided to make a night passage, so at 1900 the convoy set sail.

March 14. 0025 The *Michel* came under fire from a British naval force which was estimated to consist of a cruiser, several destroyers, and a number of S-boats. The running battle went on until 0430 when the British made smoke and departed. There were no reports of any damage to the *Michel*, but at 0700 a badly wounded officer from one of her escorts was taken aboard for medical treatment. He died about an hour later. Following the wild melee, the *Michel* crew were told they had sunk one destroyer and two S-boats, and damaged another destroyer and two S-boats. There is no record of the ammunition expended by the *Michel* other than the fact its entire supply of star shells—more than ninety—were fired. 1400 Arrived Le Havre. The crew went to battle stations because of an air raid alarm. 1700 All clear, and crew went to work cleaning the vessel, and taking on stores and ammunition. The body of the dead officer was removed by shore authorities, after which the crew was mustered before the Commander. He told them the final tally of British losses was one destroyer and four S-boats sunk, and another destroyer and two S-boats damaged. (Author's note: In "Royal Navy Vessels Lost at Sea" found at http://www.naval-history.net under "British WWII Losses by Date" shows between March 12 and March 15, 1942 only two casualties and neither of them was in the Channel. On March 12, the 2,312 ton Fleet Air Arm target vessel *St. Briac* was mined off Aberdeen, Scotland. On March 15, HMS *Vortigern*, a World War I vintage destroyer of 1,090 tons, while escorting a coastwise convoy off the Norfolk coast, was torpedoed and sunk by a German E-boat. Interesting!) At 2100 the *Michel* left Le Havre, bound for St. Malo, on a course which took them inside the Channel Islands.

March 15. 0700 Arrived St. Malo. After docking, the crew spent three hours rigging camouflage tarpaulins and were then given three hours rest time which postponed the noon meal until 1400. The official report of the action in the channel reported the *Michel* sank only one S-boat and set three on fire, and one destroyer was heavily damaged and perhaps sank. Also, it was learned Vlissingen had been bombed, as the British thought the *Michel* was still there. The German propaganda machine flourished! There was no shore leave, but von Ruckteschell,

***Michel* in the English Channel, March 1942.**

First Officer Erhardt. Chief Engineer Hanstein, Gunnery Officer Schwinn, Adjutant Herr, and Doctor Schröder, all in civilian garb, did go into the town to do some shopping and sightseeing. According to Konrad Hoppe, von Ruckteschell was particularly interested in seeing Mont Saint-Michel, the abbey situated on a rock in the bay which is only accessible a few hours before and after low tide. Everyone else remained on board and took turns with the bridge binoculars surveying the French girls promenading along a nearby beach, examining the old houses and fortifications, and wistfully scanning signs such as Petit Royale Bar en Hotel where afternoon tea was being served. One crewman likened it to a pirate town. At 1830 the vessel was ready for departure, except that the officers had not returned. A half hour later they did and the *Michel* proceeded to sea on its way to Bordeaux. All personnel were at general quarters and zigzag courses set. Other than sighting a *U-boot*, there was no traffic.

March 16. 0800 Passing Brest. 1230 Passing Lorient.

March 17. 0600 Anchored in the Gironde River. The radio specialists and gunners who had been aboard since Brunsbüttel departed, taking the quad 3.7 cm with them. The entire crew went to work painting the ship a light gray color. Hoppe said, "Light gray is difficult to see at night. The lighter the better," he added.

"At night, a ship on the horizon appears black, so the *Michel* had to be made as light as possible."

March 18. 0900 A tanker came alongside to fill the raider's fuel tanks. Remarkably, this was the *Spichern*, originally the Norwegian *Krossfonn* captured by the *Widder* in June of 1940. Those members of the *Michel*'s crew who had been in the *Widder* in 1940, deemed this incident to be a good omen. 1630 Bunkering operation completed with one thousand tons taken aboard. The ship was deep in the water, displacing fourteen thousand tons.

March 19. Last day for outgoing mail. 1800 Loading fresh provisions.

March 20. 0600 The *Michel*, with escorting minesweepers, departed from the Gironde estuary, sailing in the direction of Bilbao, Spain. At 0930 the crew was mustered on deck at which time von Ruckteschell declared a general amnesty for those who had been serving punishment. At 2100, the minesweepers were dismissed. The *Michel*, blacked out, was alone in the dark night, rolling unexpectedly in the short northwesterly chop of the Atlantic Ocean, illustrating a tenderness that would cause considerable discomfort and problems in the future. The months of drills and planning and anticipation were done with.

Another German raider had broken out and was on the loose.

The next day at 0800 in approximate latitude 45° north the longitude of Cape Finisterre, was crossed and the fact that they were at sea for what promised to be a long voyage was impressed on all hands with the announcement that henceforth fresh water use would be restricted. During the evening twilight a vessel was sighted, and at that moment a shower of sparks flew out of the *Michel*'s stack. To say that von Ruckteschell became angry and disturbed is an understatement.

Two days later, which happened to be von Ruckteschell's fifty-second birthday, the first of many messages concerning the approaching equator crossing appeared on bulletin boards throughout the ship:

0053 hours, 23 March 1942

Underwater telegram to all.

In consequence of an extraordinary meeting of the Parliament in its chambers in the morning of Sunday, 22 March 1942, and later in the afternoon of the same day, the Controller of all seas, His Majesty

Neptune has issued an opinion on the expected crossing of the Equator by the German auxiliary cruiser *Michel* into the occupied territory. For further reports watch this space.

The Underwater News Agency.

The day following, another message appeared, addressed to *Kapitänleutnant* Saupe, who was planning the equator hijinks and was probably the author of these and the other missives from the deep. This one read,

With my *Superheterodyneultradezimmeterwell* hearing machine I have overheard one *Matrose* (sailor) express his opinion that he will not be subjected to any indignities because of your vessel's crossing the Line between the Northern and Southern hemispheres.

Beware!

You enter my Domain in Peril!

Neptunis Rex.

More on this will be subsequently related. Suffice to say, von Ruckteschell had no intent to allow the ceremony to be held on the actual day of crossing. He regarded that area of the Atlantic as being more dangerous than it would be further south, and wanted nothing to distract the crew from the performance of their duties.

March 24. The course was southwesterly; on the twenty-sixth it was 180°—due south. Latitude 35° north was crossed on the twenty-seventh. As the weather became warmer many off-watch crew stretched out in the sun, and straw hats were issued to the deck workers. The lookouts spotted a ship, but von Ruckteschell avoided it, as the *Michel* had not reached its operating area.

March 29. Sunday. The crew was mustered on deck in white uniforms, and the band played martial music. The commander promoted a number of men to higher ranks following which all divisions and departments repaired to their individual quarters and began a shipwide celebration. "There was terrible drunkenness," wrote one presumably abstemious observer. The next day, the *Michel* crossed into the territory of raider *Thor* (Schiff 10). Another ship was seen, but could not be attacked for fear that it was the *Thor*. (What von Ruckteschell did not know was that the other raider was 2,400 miles to the south, and increasing that margin daily, bound for the Indian Ocean. The SKL seemed to do a decent job in arranging meetings between the raiders and their supply ships, but in this case it appears that neither the *Thor* nor the *Michel* knew the other's position.)

April 1. The course was changed to the southeast; the first flying fish came aboard. The next five days saw the *Michel* steadily plodding on toward the equator. With the weather increasingly warm, the band held outside concerts; the meteorologist, Dr. Weise, taught daily mathematics classes.

April 3. Good Friday. No work was performed other than the usual watch standing.

April 5. Easter Sunday. The crew was awakened by recorded popular music instead of the routine military march. Breakfast consisted of real coffee, fresh rolls with apple and cherry jelly. In the morning all hands were mustered in whites, and von Ruckteschell told the story of Christ's death and resurrection. "He always takes the opportunity to expound on Christianity," wrote the young German in his diary. At noon, with the sun almost directly overhead, the heat on board was extreme, causing everyone to perspire profusely. Nevertheless, the galley produced an Easter dinner of epic proportions and rare delicacies: cold soup, turkey, potatoes, real butter, pudding, and ice cream. A leisurely afternoon was spent recuperating from this banquet. Numerous types of tropical sea life attracted attention: Portuguese men-of-war, flying fish, seabirds. The band presented a special program which was attended by almost all of the crew, with whom the commander smilingly socialized. For supper, the cooks again offered turkey accompanied by bacon and eggs, more real butter and coffee, with cake for desert. The night was warm and humid, encouraging many of the crew to cool off, under the Southern Cross and the Milky Way, in the small, boxlike swimming pool set up on number 1 hatch.

April 6. 1200. The course was changed back to the previous 180°, and the equator was crossed at 1400. Sleeping below decks that night was impossible, so everyone stretched his mattress on deck where a wonderful few hours were spent under the stars. This was interrupted before dawn by the raucous clanging of the general alarm bell! A ship, probably a ten-thousand-ton tanker, had been sighted. For some reason, von Ruckteschell declined the opportunity to attack, and an hour later it was back to sleep for most of the crew.

This day, Easter Monday, was also a holiday on board the *Michel*. Dinner was chocolate soup, liver, vegetables, and ice cream. Crew members lounged on deck, sun bathed, and studied. A few of the musicians gave impromptu recitals. The day ended with another wonderful night under the stars, but no chance to sleep below decks because of the heat.

April 9. Another ship was sighted, but again no attack. (How lucky were those ships that were seen and allowed to continue on their journeys! They never knew how close they came to calamity.) The only incident of note during the first few days in the Southern Hemisphere was the discovery of oil leaking into the ocean, apparently from a fuel tank. The ship was stopped and a hard-hat diver was lowered over the side. He found and repaired several defective rivets, before he was quickly hauled out because of the arrival of a large shark. A baited hook was quickly tossed over and taken by the shark, which was so heavy that when the crew attempted to bring it aboard the line parted, and the big fish fell back into the sea and disappeared. The weather changed, bringing at first a brisk cool wind, followed by fog and rain. Under these conditions the *Michel* was approaching its first rendezvous with the supply tanker *Charlotte Schliemann*.

**Supply vessel M.S. *Charlotte Schliemann*
at rendezvous with *Michel*.**

April 13. Before daybreak, weather conditions having bettered, the crew was called to general quarters. One of the lookouts had spotted a light on the horizon. It was soon seen to be only a rising bright star or planet, but an hour later in the half-light before dawn the alarm again sounded. This time it was the *Schliemann*. At 0930, in position 34° south, 23° west, the *Michel's* doctors, dentist, and other technical people went over, and on return the boat brought her Master for a visit with von Ruckteschell. The *Schliemann* had been at anchor in the Canary Islands (owned by neutral Spain) since the outbreak of war in September 1939. She and her crew were in sad shape. Many of the men had developed a variety of medical problems, including venereal diseases, during their thirty-month layover. This vessel, built in Denmark in 1928 for Norwegian owners, was originally named *Sir Karl Knudsen*. Fuel transfer was scheduled for the fourteenth.

Although the *Schliemann* had supplied oil to at least one U-boat on her way to the *Michel* meeting point, the German replenishment technique had not kept pace with that of the United States and Great Britain. Instead of bringing the vessels abeam of each other on a parallel course with the fuel line at right angles, the Germans used a bow to stern arrangement with the tanker in the lead. This made for difficult station keeping and on this first bunkering attempt, after about 500 tons had been transferred—half of what had been planned—the hose snapped and the operation cancelled. It was not that the Germans were ignorant of the parallel method, they simply had not practiced it. (Later in the year it was adopted, as will be described.)

April 15. A strange occurrence took place when prize officer *Oberleutnant* Duborg, Meteorologist Dr. Weise, and Radioman/Meteorologist Wilhelm Osterfeld, plus seventeen sailors were transferred to the *Schliemann*. (One source says that the entire party consisted of sixteen men.) Apparently she was en route Japan and some of these men were to be put ashore for the purpose of establishing a weather reporting station on one of the Kerguelen Islands, away down in the Antarcic Ocean, about 1,700 miles southeast of the southern tip of Madagascar. In addition to the personal possessions, and considerable food, tents, tools, etc., taken with them to the tanker, they were issued several months' supply of beer and *Schnäpse!*

It appears that only Duborg, Weiss, Osterfeld, and perhaps a sailor or two, were destined for the remote islands. Von Ruckteschell was extremely suspicious of the allegiance of the *Schliemann*'s crew and feared that they would, under the proper circumstances, defect to the Allies. Thus, the men he sent over were a reverse armed guard of sorts, not to defend the vessel so much as to prevent its surrender.

April 16. The *Schliemann* was dismissed, with the *Michel* conducting target range-finding drills on her as she departed. In the late afternoon preparations for the long-anticipated equator crossing ceremony began. King Neptune, Queen Thetis, and their entourage, appropriately dressed and painted, gathered in the torpedo room. Interestingly, the queen was arrayed in female attire, put on board in the chance that any women survivors would be taken prisoner from the *Michel*'s victims. One of the side ports was undogged and opened and a pilot ladder was dropped from the weather deck allowing the king and queen and the others to exit the torpedo room and climb over the bulwarks—just as though they were coming out of the sea. What an imagination had Otto Saupe!

The crew, called to muster, stood at attention along with the commander who Neptune irreverently addressed as *"Meine lieber Ruckteschell."* One of the entourage, already drunk, fell off number 2 hatch, injuring himself. Following brief instructions by Neptune regarding the next day's routine, von Ruckteschell invited the group to the officers' salon where they were given the best of liquid refreshments. This came to an end at 1900 when Neptune led his party back to the deck, over the side, through the torpedo room and on to the Chief Yeoman's office for more drinks and final planning for the morrow.

At about this time, someone stole a piglet from the *Schweinstalle*, and one of the medical orderlies anesthetized it. The animal was wrapped in a towel and deposited in the bunk of *Kapitänleutnant* von Schack, who probably, as a division officer, at some time had rubbed someone the wrong way. Von Schack was standing watch on the bridge at the time and when he discovered his visitor, no one knew who or why. This was the first of the *equator torf* shenanigans.

April 17. 1030. Eleven days and 2,000 miles late, the proceedings commenced. Duplicating the previous afternoon's action, King Neptune, Queen Thetis, and their servants came over the bulwarks to be again greeted by the commander, standing before, and included with, the mustered polliwogs—officers and enlisted men alike. The king and queen were more elaborately dressed than before, now being adorned with all manner of sashes and medallions and ribbons. The servants wore only loincloths; their skin was blackened with soot. Those shellbacks not on watch or at the lookout posts, or not involved with the initiation, took up vantage points from which to observe the fun.

To his credit, von Ruckteschell submitted to the ceremonial dunking in the swimming pool, but the shellbacks excused him from crawling through the traditional canvas hose and undergoing the other accompanying indignities. The officers and crew were very proud of their commander, particularly when it was realized that he had volunteered his participation. As a token of their appreciation he was given a ship in a bottle constructed by one of the seamen. The ceremony eventually came to an end when the band played and Queen Thetis danced with von Ruckteschell and several of the senior officers. A sidelight to the day's hilarity was the reaction of one of the officers who had been singled out for special treatment. He managed to escape from his tormentors and raced to his cabin where he locked himself in!

April 18. During the morning the smoke of a steamer was sighted. The *Michel* closed in on the potential victim until the mast-top lookouts could see its masts only. The hull was below the horizon, fifteen or more miles away. At this juncture, von Schack and Flying Officer Konrad Hoppe alternately manned the swivel chair on the after mast and directed the *Michel* onto a converging course, but, with her faster speed, maintaining the distance off to ultimately reach a point dead ahead of the target.

Michel's after mast. Note lookout in swivel chair at mast truck, also lookout in crow's nest at crosstree.

After darkness had fallen, von Ruckteschell ordered general quarters and reversed the *Michel's* course, running down the reciprocal of the enemy's estimated heading. At the expected time of meeting, nothing appeared. The other vessel had possibly begun to zigzag, or simply made a substantial course change. The fact was clear to all on board. "We have lost him!" The binoculars on the *Michel's* bridge wings, reputably able to pick out a ship five to six miles away in the darkness, revealed nothing.

The *Michel* went to full speed and began a search pattern. At 0130 in the morning of the 19th, one of the bridge lookouts picked up the shadow of a ship, and von Ruckteschell ordered the attack. The 15 cm guns quickly scored several hits on the vessel's after section, setting it afire. The *Michel's* radio room reported that the enemy's radio was transmitting a distress signal, so additional salvoes were directed to the bridge area. Although the crew could be seen launching lifeboats, the radio operator continued his activity. At this point, one of the *Michel's* bridge wing 2 cm machine guns was ordered to open fire to persuade him to stop, and that did bring an end to the transmission.

Then, von Ruckteschell, seeing three lifeboats in the water and assuming that the surviving crew had abandoned ship, ordered a boarding party away. These men daringly went alongside the apparently sinking ship and boarded her via the rope ladders and man ropes which her crew had used to escape. The pilothouse, chart room, and master's cabin were quickly searched resulting in the collecting of the ship's British Admiralty merchant vessels codes and routing instructions. In addition, interesting newspapers such as recent copies of the *New York Times* were found. A key member of this boarding party was *Oberleutnant* Carl Cords, one of five former merchant officers whose basic assignment in the *Michel* were as prize officers to take command of any captured Allied vessels and bring them to Germany. Cords, naturally, knew what to look for and where to find it.

This first kill was the British tanker *Patella* (7,468 gross tons), carrying nine thousand tons of diesel oil from Trinidad to Capetown. Three of her crew were lost in the action and sixty were rescued and taken prisoner. Of those, one was Canadian, and twenty-three were English (including a number of British Army gunners). The balance were Chinese. Eight men were severely wounded, two slightly. After being disinfected, those not in the *Michel's* hospital were sent forward to rooms specially constructed for prison use. The *Michel* then moved quickly to the southwest.

Arado 196.

In the days following the *Patella* sinking above average Allied radio activity was noted, but by the twenty-second traffic had returned to normal. On that day, von Ruckteschell, acting on a hunch (which he often did) decided to reverse course and ordered the Arado launched.

When Flying Officer Hoppe was on the second leg of his search pattern, and about sixty miles from the *Michel*, he found a large loaded tanker. Maintaining radio silence, he quickly returned home with his report. A converging course was set until the target's masts were seen on the horizon, then the stalk commenced. In this instance, von Ruckteschell wished to try out his secret weapon, the torpedo boat. So, at 2100, with the unsuspecting tanker about seven miles distant, *Esau* was put into the water. The approach was made, the target located, and both torpedoes fired—but nothing happened. Von Schack brought his boat back to the *Michel* where Konrad Hoppe's sailors hoisted it aboard for the purpose of rearming the torpedo tubes. That accomplished, *Esau* was again launched. This time at about 0200 the following morning the torpedoes ran true.

Launching *Esau*, the motor torpedo boat. Standing at right, gesturing is Konrad Hoppe. Malte von Schack, the boat's commander, is standing in the boat's deck in center.

The result was, to the Germans, spectacular. The tanker, loaded with gasoline, erupted in a great ball of fire estimated to be one hundred meters in height. The *Michel* approached the conflagration, so close that her crew actually saw the fear-crazed victims leaping from the decks into the blazing sea. Because of the tremendous flame, which could have been seen for miles, and after picking up *Esau*, von Ruckteschell departed the scene at full speed.

April 24. Noon. The *Michel* had returned to the general vicinity of this second success, and a lone lifeboat was sighted. Not desiring to alarm the boat's occupants, a neutral flag was hoisted. The *Patella*'s Chinese crew was brought up on deck, lined along the rail to watch the rescue, giving the raider the appearance of a common European merchantman. Indeed the survivors peacefully came on board and said that they were from the Panamanian-flagged *Connecticut* (8,684 gross tons) owned by Texaco of New York, manned by American merchant seamen plus a United States Navy gun crew, bound for Capetown. The Germans soon revealed their true identity and eighteen new prisoners joined the *Patella* men down in the forward quarters. One other American had survived, but later died in the *Michel*'s sick bay. Twenty-four merchant seamen and all eleven of the U. S. Navy Armed Guard detachment were burned to death. Sometime later, SKL congratulated von Ruckteschell, informing him that the *Connecticut* was a very valuable ship.

During the next five or six days little of note occurred, except that the below decks rumor of an arriving supply ship failed to materialize, and the commander performed the marriage ceremony of Seaman Walter Gustick(?) to his fiancée (in Germany). The morale on board the *Michel* was high. Her officers and men were now confident and self-assured. Two successes in four days were the reward of countless drills, constant alertness, and the belief that the job could be done when the time came. She was a happy ship.

April 30. The Arado returning from patrol came down hard on a wave and its engine broke away and fell into the ocean. Fortunately, spares were carried, but, nevertheless, it was decided to put the reserve aircraft into service. The aircrew spent many hours on into the night resolving its problems. Then, at 2330, all hands were called to battle stations. A vessel was in sight. Von Ruckteschell again opted for an attack by *Esau*, and at 0130, Hoppe and his deck gang had the boat in the water. Forty-five minutes later, from what he described as a favorable position, von Schack released his two "eels." Again, he missed or the torpedoes were duds. Neither detonated.

Upon hearing this bad news by radio from the *Esau*, von Ruckteschell, using the material seized from the *Patella*, ordered the proper challenge transmitted by blinker light to the target ship. Also, a copy of the Royal Navy's white ensign was broken out at the gaff. These actions caused the other ship to stop, at which

Torpedo boat *Esau*.

point the *Michel*'s main batteries were ordered to open fire. The first salvo fell considerably short, the blame for which was believed to be a malfunction in the range finder. Meanwhile, the raider's radio room reported that the intended victim had transmitted a distress signal which was acknowledged by a shore station. At this juncture, von Schack, without torpedoes, quite bravely deciding to utilize his speed, attempted a running, close-in attack with his 2 cm machine gun. It jammed. The enemy vessel, by now thoroughly alarmed and agitated, decided to make a run for safety and slowly drew away from the *Michel*, which still had to retrieve *Esau*. This was not accomplished until 0830—in full daylight. At 1000 von Ruckteschell broke off the chase. It was feared aboard the *Michel* that the enemy had been able to obtain a good description and perhaps photos of their ship.

The attacked vessel was the British steamer *Menelaus* (10,300 gross tons), northbound to the United States. Although she appeared to be faster than the *Michel*, some of the raider's officers urged that the pursuit be continued, believing that they could eventually catch her. Von Ruckteschell, however, in an extremely bad mood, ordered the course changed to the south and shut himself in his cabin. As one crewman wrote, "It was a day of misfortune. Very bad!"

**Photo courtesy of The Steamship Historical Society of America, Inc.
The S.S. *Menelaus*, in an unknown United States port,
following her escape from the *Michel*.**

May 1. The *Michel* continued to flee southward. Considerable apprehension prevailed on board as many in the crew thought that certainly the English forces were out looking for them. The high spirits of the days previous were completely deflated. "The mood is (-) 20°," confided the seaman in his journal.

May 3. Sunday. The band conducted its regular concert, and in the afternoon the crew was mustered before the commander. He spoke about the lost battle and said the *Charlotte Schliemann* had been summoned to a rendezvous to serve as a practice target in order to sharpen the *Michel's* techniques. Von Ruckteschell made reference to certain unnamed members of the crew who he believed did not have the will to fight. "We must be clean at heart," he said, "and then we will again have success."

May 6. Wednesday. The *Schliemann* arrived. Since Sunday, the *Michel* and *Esau* had conducted intensive drills against simulated enemy vessels, but heavy weather hampered operations with the tanker. Later in the week conditions became more favorable. During this period, the *Patella* and *Connecticut* prisoners were transferred. However, von Ruckteschell kept eight people on board. Four were

Chinese from the *Patella* who, since their capture had been employed in the *Michel's* laundry room and the Germans, particularly the officers, were most grateful for their services: white uniforms, jackets, trousers, shirts, and wing-tip collars absolutely sparkled. The hand of the ever-resourceful *Kapitänleutnant* Saupe had struck again. The other four were Chief Engineer Bainey and Chief Officer Harris of the *Patella*, and Chief Engineer Galen McCray and Chief Officer Willard M. Carroll of the *Connecticut*. Until the next victim fell to the *Michel*, these gentlemen were hosted for Sunday dinner, including unlimited Scotch whiskey, in von Ruckteschell's private dining room.

Also with the *Schliemann's* arrival came a surprise. Three of the men who had departed with her on April 15 returned. Apparently the SKL had decided to keep the tanker in the South Atlantic for the time being, provisioning and bunkering the *Michel*. Or, perhaps the plans for the weather reporting station in the Kerguelens were cancelled. In any case, Dr. Weise, *Oberleutnant* Duborg, and Radioman/Meteorologist Osterfeld rejoined their old friends.

May 15. The *Schliemann* was once again dismissed. In the course of the next five days, the *Michel's* radio room reported a considerable increase in Allied wireless traffic. Some vessels sounded to be close by. Because the *Menelaus* did see the *Michel*, it was decided to alter the raider's silhouette by adding a second (dummy) smokestack.

May 20. Just after daybreak, masts were sighted. First indications were that it was a warship, but a closer look revealed it to be a merchantman, probably of good size, possibly an armed merchant cruiser, coming from the direction of Capetown. The usual night attack was planned, and, in spite of the impending action, the weekly motion picture was shown throughout the afternoon.

When the *Michel* opened fire on this vessel, her master ordered her engines stopped. In spite of the barrage of incoming fire, an eighteen-year-old able seaman managed to reach the boat deck and switch on the lights. Seeing those happenings, von Ruckteschell silenced his guns. This was the Norwegian *Kattegat* (4,245 gross tons)—in ballast. Her thirty-two man crew, composed of twenty-seven Norwegians, three Brits, and two Danes, having amazingly suffered no casualties, joined Chief Engineer McCray and his friends in the *Michel's* forward prison quarters. As the *Kattegat* was too small to be of any use to Germany, plus the fact that she had no cargo, and had received substantial damage to her hull and deckhouse from the first salvoes, two torpedoes were fired at point black range. When they failed to detonate a demolition party boarded and sent her to the bottom.

May 21. Regardless of the quick success of the previous night, *Korvettenkapitän* Erhardt told the crew that their techniques need to be improved and more drills could be expected. A vignette of the *Kattegat* affair was that one of Saupe's petty officers, who was ordinarily involved in the *Michel's* store—and record-keeping business, went along with the explosive specialists who were to scuttle the Norwegian. While they busied themselves below, this fellow looted the master's living quarters, bringing back to the *Michel* a linen tablecloth, silverware, and a few apples. That evening, someone's birthday was celebrated in the crew's quarters, using the white tablecloth and the purloined utensils from the sunken ship!

May 24. *Pfingstentag* (Pentecost). Fresh bread rolls, honey, and real coffee for breakfast. During the morning the band presented a concert. Dinner was served at noon: duck, asparagus, real butter, and ice cream. The band played again in the afternoon. *Oberleutnant* Schmolling, who was an eager accordionist, but not highly regarded as a musician by some, angered the commander with his jazz renditions. In the evening, the crew partook of bacon and eggs, more fresh bread rolls, and red wine. (It is not clear if all received wine with the meal; perhaps only the officers.) One petty officer, who had access to the wine supply, did secure a bottle which he generously shared with the chief cook. Later, Saupe appeared at the same petty officer's room with another bottle which he and the petty officer split!

May 25. *Zweiter Pfingstentag* (Second Pentecost). A holiday. In the early afternoon a shark was caught. Later the band played a special-requests concert, which brought the commander to the realization that the crew did not care at all for classical music. At supper, the officers hosted the petty officers, some of who were reserve officers, and probably in line for promotion. It was thought the officers used this occasion to teach table manners to the petty officers.

May 26. SKL reported that the raider *Stier* (Schiff 23) had broken out of Europe and was on the way south. Two days later Konrad Hoppe and his pilot *Luftwaffe* Sergeant Emmel received a scare when, while on a routine scouting flight, the Arado's engine failed and they had to get down on the ocean about 45 miles from the *Michel*. Fortunately, Hoppe was able to contact the *Michel* by radio before he lost altitude. This was done on ultra-shortwave using English language code words, so as to not arouse suspicion if a nearby Allied vessel chanced to overhear the transmission. What had happened was in the repair and strengthening of the engine mounts and installing a new engine following the April 30 accident, an oil line was not properly fitted. When the Arado became airborne, the line crimped, shutting off the oil flow. Hoppe and the pilot located the fault, and in the course of about two hours fixed it. After discussing the risks of attempting a takeoff without the *Michel* standing by, Emmel carefully, very carefully, coaxed the Arado into the air. When they were safely back aboard their ship, Hoppe said, "I celebrated, as is the custom of aviators who have survived a bad situation, and was rather drunk when I went to bed." Because of the use of the radio, von Ruckteschell felt it necessary to vacate the area, and proceeded to head further south. Also, this day marked the end of the fresh potato supply, and the cooks went to the dehydrated version until the next supply ship.

Arado 196 being retrieved.

May 30. Southbound, crossing 30° south. A crewman named Stockinger attempted suicide. (There is nothing known of this incident. From a seaman's point of view, it must have been a halfhearted try, maybe more of a cry for attention. If someone on board a ship in the middle of the South Atlantic sincerely wanted to end his life the simple act of dropping off the stern would do it. No mess, no fuss, no questions to answer.)

May 31. The radio room reported much Allied activity and what appeared to be a distress call from an American ship. Von Ruckteschell regarded this with considerable misgiving, believing it could be a trap. However, after several hours of discussion with his officers, he decided to look for the American. The course was changed to 0°T. At 1800 the mast-top lookout sighted a vessel without masts or bridge structure. Judging this to be an aircraft carrier, the *Michel* took evasive action, but continued in a Northerly direction. (This is a good example of the *Michel*'s ability to observe another vessel while remaining hull down with only the lookout and a bit of the mast above the observed vessel's horizon.)

In the morning (June 1), the radio room and code breakers had deduced that the vessel in distress was stopped and drifting. The next day she remained afloat, awaiting assistance. At this time the *Michel* was able to obtain good radio bearings and a course was set directly for her. On the sixth, the derelict's signals were loud and clear, but the *Michel* was nearing the southern boundary of the *Stier*'s operating area, creating a potentially dangerous situation. At 1830 the American freighter was sighted, and *Esau* quickly launched. Thirty minutes later von Schack scored two hits. The American began transmitting "SSSS" in series, indicating a submarine attack, which was exactly what von Ruckteschell desired. By 2230, *Esau* had been retrieved, and the raider departed the scene. The radio room reported the American was radioing they were abandoning ship.

This vessel was the brand new Liberty ship *George Clymer* (7,176 gross tons), built by the Oregon Shipbuilding Corporation of Portland, Oregon, and delivered to the American Mail Line in April. She was bound for the Persian Gulf with a full load of military cargo, including aircraft lashed on the weather deck and hatches. Her propeller shaft had fractured, and the crew were unable to effect repairs. Later the next day, the *Michel*'s radio men heard the *Clymer* transmitting in plain English. The crew had reboarded, the operator stated, and he asked for rescue ships and aircraft to be sent to his position. He was told that there was nothing available. The radio officer asked for instructions and continued to transmit "SSSS," adding he was on battery power and would not be able to operate much longer. (Presumably, the reason for the plain language transmission was the *Clymer*'s master, before abandoning ship the previous evening, had consigned his codebook to the deep.) Uncharacteristically, von Ruckteschell decided to go back and administer the coup de grace. Upon arriving at the *Clymer*'s estimated position at daybreak on the eighth, nothing could be seen. Following several hours of searching, it was presumed the ship had sunk and her crew picked up by a passing steamer. If this is correct, it illustrates a rather muddled line of thought on the part of von Ruckteschell and his officers. Why had the Arado not been launched to find the *Clymer* and/or the ship they believed had rescued her crew? It is possible the weather had deteriorated since the night of the sixth when it was decent enough to allow the launching of *Esau*, but no records from the *Michel* exist to provide an explanation. Why, after running away and then deciding to go back, the lack of aggression? Also, when a ship sinks a tremendous amount of flotsam remains at the scene. The raider's crew saw nothing. One incident provides a clue. While at the *Clymer*'s estimated locale, a small, rather tame, land bird (a canary or parakeet, perhaps) alighted on the *Michel*. It could have been a pet of one of the Americans. At least that is what the Germans thought, convincing themselves that the *Clymer* had indeed sunk.

It is now known, contrary to what the land stations had said about no help being available, the British armed merchant cruiser (AMC) HMS *Alcantara* had been dispatched to the *Liberty*'s assistance. Aided by her Sea Fox, a twin-pontoon biplane, which was catapulted at 0900 and recovered a few minutes before noon, she found the *Clymer* in midafternoon of the seventh. The AMC's bridge log book records the Sea Fox being catapulted again at 1532 and recovered at 1745, presumably for an antisubmarine patrol while the ship was stopped and involved in the rescue operation. The log states, "1714 Embarkation completed." At 1749, a base course of 080° was set and the *Alcantara* moved away at 12.7 knots, zigzagging until 1855. Its bridge log book is silent as to any action taken to scuttle the disabled freighter. The *Clymer*'s position at the time of her breakdown on May 31 is not known, but what is apparent is a drift to the westward, perhaps as much as fifty miles or more per day. That the *Alcantara* was aware of this is proven by the fact that at noon on the seventh, when the Sea Fox returned to the AMC, her observer reported the *Clymer* only about thirty miles, roughly two and one-half steaming hours, away. They had an idea where the *George Clymer* was; the *Michel* seemed not to have a clue. More on that a bit later.

The *Alcantara* continued through the night, until 0100 on the eighth, when the course was reversed to 260°. In her log book, her position at 2000 on the seventh, calculated from earlier star sights, was 14° 42′ S, 18° 04′ W. She ran five hours on 080°, then five hours on the reciprocal course of 260°, but her position at 0600, also based on starsights, was just over thirty miles beyond her 2000 position on the seventh. This indicates an incredible westerly current of three knots! Indeed, plotting the position of the AMC at 1749 when it left the rescue scene and the position of the *Clymer* at 0909 on the eighth, when the *Alcantara* approached her again, shows a drift of fifty-one and a half miles, a little over three and a third knots.

Did von Ruckteschell and his officers know of this phenomenon? Probably not, but there are no hard facts to go on. In what records do exist, there are errors. For example, in a recap of his successes dated January 13, 1943, the *Michel*'s commander gives the position of the *Clymer*'s torpedoing at 1900 on the sixth as 13° 51′ S, 18° 20′ W. The same recap carries a small scale track chart of the *Michel*'s wanderings throughout the South Atlantic. This shows the *Clymer* sinking in approximately 14° 30' S, 18° 10' W. In a Tokyo-originated set of messages to the SKL, dated August 21, 1942, excerpts from the *Michel*'s KTB list her successes to June 25, including the *Clymer*, and give the position of her sinking as 14° 51' S, 18° 20' W. This could be a typographical error.

Incidentally, as these Tokyo originated messages clearly state they are excerpts, it appears as though the KTB or a copy was carried to Japan by the *Doggerbank*. Whatever, it is clear von Ruckteschell returned to the latitude and longitude where he believed the *Clymer* had been sunk, not taking into consideration the westward drift. If the *Alcantara*'s logbook is correct, and there is no reason to believe it is not, the *Clymer*, assuming the three knot drift of the seventh and eighth, thus was torpedoed at about 14° 35' S, 17° 15' W. (Note: The *Doggerbank* met the *Michel* on June 21 and departed on June 27. This will be covered chronologically within this chapter.)

Was there a chance the *Michel* and *Alcantara* could have met at daybreak on the eighth? The answer is yes, but highly improbable due to the *Michel*'s faulty navigational records. We simply don't know where she was, her KTB and any copies never were recovered after the war, and what information is at hand has been created from memory. We do know, from the track chart, she searched for only a short time, then went off to the east, with the *Alcantara*'s chances of intercepting her greatly diminished. Meanwhile on this same day, the AMC from 0909 to 0953 "inspected" the *Clymer*, then resumed her course of 260° until 1400 when she turned around to return to the Liberty ship. Her log shows, "1740. Cutter alongside. 1827 Cutter hoisted." Whatever transpired is not noted. The following day, the ninth, the *Alcantara* did not return to the *Clymer* until 1415 when she opened fire with her 15 cm batteries, continuing intermittently until 1503. No notation appears as to the result of this bombardment. In the morning of the tenth at 0900 the *Alcantara* again closed on the *Clymer* for a visual examination, then went off on a westerly course until 1225. At this point, she reversed course and returned to the Liberty where between 1702 and 1705 she put five more 15 cm rounds into her. On the eleventh, unbelievably, the *Clymer* was still afloat and at 1600, according to the *Alcantara*'s log, something which is not legible to the author was "fired at derelict." *The Official Chronology of the U.S. Navy in World War II* (http://www.ibiblio.org), under the date June 8, 1942, sums up the entire matter: "British armed merchant cruiser HMS *Alcantara* embarks survivors from damaged U.S. freighter *George Clymer*, attempts to scuttle the freighter prove futile and *Alcantara* must leave with American ship still stubbornly afloat."

Years later, Konrad Hoppe mused, "We were very fortunate we did not meet the *Alcantara*. Probably we would have sunk her, but not without serious damage to ourselves." As to his commander's decision to finish off the *Clymer*, Hoppe said, "What an error! What an error! What an error! 'No ships available for help,' the English said, and they sent an armed merchant cruiser! We were very, very lucky!" Unfortunately, far more unlucky were thirteen Allied merchant vessels and their crews which fell prey to the *Michel* in the upcoming months. If only the sighted aircraft carrier had been fitted with radar or optics matching those on the raider. If only her air patrols had caught sight of the German. What if? It was not so close with the *Alcantara*, the chance of detection by her Sea Fox was there, but the pendulum swung again in favor of the *Kriegsmarine*.

June 9 and 10. The *Michel* was on a leisurely (5.7 knots) easterly course between Ascension and St. Helena Islands. Shortly before Noon on the 10th von Ruckteschell guessed there was enemy traffic in the area and changed course to 045°. A bit of excitement occurred that day when fire broke out in a rubbish container on the after deck. It was quickly extinguished, but First Officer Erhardt banned any form of tobacco smoking for three days.

June 11. At 1700 von Ruckteschell's hunch paid off. A ship was sighted. She had a very tall funnel which appeared strange to the Germans, and created some suspicion. Nevertheless, at 1830 the *Michel* crew was at battle stations, opening fire at a range of 1,800 meters (just under one nautical mile). The target quickly began to burn. Von Ruckteschell ordered cease fire, but at this juncture his radio room reported the enemy attempting to transmit a distress signal. The twin 3.7 cm guns were directed to fire on the bridge/wheelhouse area. At the same time a torpedo was sent at the hapless vessel, some of whose crew were seen jumping into the sea. Neither this torpedo or a second, loosed half a minute later, exploded. Finally, torpedo number three struck the stern causing the British *Lylepark* (5,186 gross tons) to disappear below the surface of the South Atlantic.

The *Lylepark* was bound for Capetown and thence probably to the Persian Gulf with a military cargo. Of her forty-five man complement, twenty-one swimmers clambered aboard the *Michel* using rope ladders and cargo nets that had been hung over the side for such purpose. Interestingly, one survivor was a German-speaking Arab. Interrogations revealed the British Admiralty was trying to keep strict control, as far as routing was concerned, of all Allied merchant ships in the South Atlantic. In fact someone revealed another ship could be expected in the same position on the next day. Nothing transpired, however. Several of the *Lylepark*'s crew, namely Captain Charles S. Low, Chief Officer Robert Read, Second Officer Geoffrey Coysh, and a Royal Artillery gunner, Phillip Thomsett, chose to be not taken prisoner and managed to elude the raider. The captain found a life raft and eventually a second one. The two officers managed to right a capsized jolly boat.

How the gunner remained afloat is not known. Captain Low was found on the afternoon of June 14 by a Fairey Swordfish torpedo plane operating off HMS *Archer*, an escort-type aircraft carrier. Thomsett had previously been rescued by the same vessel, and she was actively searching for other survivors when Low was spotted. Read and Coysh sailed for fifteen days until they were sighted and picked up by the British SS *Avila Star* (14,443 tons) bound for Liverpool via Freetown from Buenos Aires with a cargo of refrigerated meat.

In his later written report on the sinking of the *Lylepark* by the *Michel* to the British Casualties Section, Captain Low provides an accurate picture of the *Michel*'s tactics at the very onset of an attack. The author has long propounded the theory that the *Michel* could not use her 15 cm guns and the 10 cm on a target dead ahead. She would have to bear off to a broadside position. Yet accounts by survivors tell of the opening salvoes coming from ahead, and the *Michel*'s KTB carries detailed plots of attacks which began with the raider approaching its targets on a reciprocal course. It seems a bit risky to cross ahead of an oncoming vessel, but von Ruckteschell made it work. According to Captain Low, he was proceeding from his cabin to the navigating bridge, heard two blasts from his ship's whistle, and saw a ship without lights on his port bow, crossing over to starboard. This maneuver did allow four of the *Michel*'s six 15 cm guns and the single 10 cm gun to sight the target. In his report he tells of immediately seeing four or five flashes of gunfire followed by detonations all around him as the whole of the midships accommodations was shattered. A most perceptive observation. He also was able, after leaving the *Lylepark*, to obtain a good look at the *Michel* which was illuminated by the flames of his stricken vessel.

As soon as he was taken aboard the carrier and related the story of the *Lylepark* sinking, he was shown Admiralty intelligence reports dealing with known German raiders. One of these, identified only as Raider H, was, said Captain Low, the ship that sank his ship. The *Archer*'s commanding officer, Commander James Ian Robertson, RN, believed this was of utmost importance and should be made known to London as soon as possible and in the most secure manner available. The following day, therefore, one of the *Archer*'s Swordfish, piloted by Lt. E. Dixon-Child, with observer Sub Lt. P Shaw, and gunner Petty Officer Townson, was sent off to Ascension Island to drop the message at the island's cable and wireless station. No one in the *Archer* knew of the presence on Ascension of a 1,300-man United States Army task force which had on June 12 completed a major landing field. Upon seeing it, Lt. Dixon-Child decided to take advantage of the situation. As he came in he was suddenly subjected to machine gun fire. No damage was inflicted, and the first aircraft ever to land on the island was duly welcomed. The following day, a letter was sent from the offices of J. & J.

Photo courtesy of Hamish Low. Capt. Low awaiting rescue by HMS *Archer*.

Photo courtesy of Hamish Low. Captain Low being assisted to the deck of HMS *Archer*.

Denholm, the *Lylepark*'s owners, to Captain Low's wife in Perth, Scotland. She was informed of the ship's loss and the fact of her husband's survival, but little else. It is now clear, however, that the Admiralty had undeniable evidence of the presence and identity of Raider H in the South Atlantic Ocean.

Tower Hill Memorial, London.

The *Archer* put into Freetown on June 20, and Captain Low was reunited with his officers seven days later. On the 28th, the *Avila Star*, carrying the three, along with twenty-seven other passengers, headed for home. On July 5 tragedy struck again when the German U-201, in a position about 630 miles west of the Portuguese city of Setubal, sank the *Avila Star*. Captain Low survived to spend three more days in the ocean, this time in a lifeboat, before being saved by the Portuguese destroyer *Lima* and taken to Ponta Delgada in the Azores. He remained there in a hospital and a nursing home for seventy days until the *Lima* took him to Lisbon, arriving on September 26. He was flown that evening to Bristol, England, and never went back to sea. Sadly, Chief Officer Read didn't make it. Second Officer Coysh survived but did not go back to sea until after the war. Total lives lost in the *Avila Star* were 84, survivors numbered 112.

HMS *Archer* was originally laid down as the C-3 class diesel-powered freighter *Mormacland* by Sun Shipbuilding of Chester, Pennsylvania, and completed in April 1940. A year later, she was acquired by the United States Navy, converted to an aircraft carrier, and then in November 1941 transferred to the Royal Navy. In appearance this vessel was quite unconventional, having a flight deck covering only 70 length of her length and no island. The navigating bridge was tucked under the forward end of the flight deck. This description certainly coincides with what the *Michel's* mast top lookout saw on May 31.

What the *Archer* and *Alcantara* were up to in the South Atlantic cannot be uncovered. Hopefully, they were looking for whatever had caused the disappearance of the *Patella*, the *Connecticut*, and the *Kattegat*, the aborted attack on the *Menelaus*, and the torpedoing of the *George Clymer*. All of these incidents occurred in a 270,000 square mile rectangle from 14° 25′ S to 28° 07′ S, 12° 27′ W to 18° 04′ W. One source says the *Archer* was returning to the United States to have maintenance and repair work on her four diesel engines. It is possible, because in November she left the States headed to North Africa with a deck load of P-40 fighter aircraft. Another source has her departing Freetown on May 13 for Capetown and transporting bullion back to Freetown. This may be just what she was doing a month later when she found the two *Lylepark* survivors

The *Michel* hunted fruitlessly along a line stretching to the SSW for another nine days. In this period, two occurrences of interest took place. On the thirteenth, in the evening, von Ruckteschell commanded that a shipwide celebration be held to recognize his attainment of sinking or capturing 100,000 tons of enemy shipping. This had been accomplished with 10,000+ tons from his World War I U-boat career, 58,644 by the *Widder*, and the *Michel's* to-date total of 32,759. The band played, but the festivities were probably subdued, at least by comparison with what transpired five days later.

On the eighteenth, in the late afternoon, the crew was mustered before the commander. The uniform was blue shirt, white trousers, white hat, and black shoes. The occasion? The awarding of decorations (Iron Crosses of different classes) approved by the SKL to thirty officers and men. Following supper, the various messes to which these men belonged began celebrating. The libation of choice was a champagne-and-cognac-based fruit punch. Later a crewman would write, "The whole ship is drunk." Indeed. One sailor, armed with a carving knife stolen from the galley became extremely violent and was subdued with great difficulty. The next day, only one entry—"Hangovers"—appears in the crewman's diary.

June 21. 1400 At 28° S, 18° W, about 550 miles northwest of Tristan de Cunha, the *Michel* met the German minelayer *Doggerbank*. This ship was the British-flagged *Speybank* (5,154 gross tons) when on January 31, 1941 it was captured in the Indian Ocean by the raider *Atlantis* (Schiff 16). A few weeks later the German freighter *Tannenfels* broke out of Italian Somaliland and met the *Atlantis* and the *Speybank*. Paul Schneidewind, the *Tannenfels's* Chief Officer was selected to command a prize crew, and departing *Atlantis'* company on March 21, brought the *Speybank* all the way to Bordeaux, arriving on May 12. During the next eight months, *Speybank* became *Doggerbank*, and the prosaic British tramper was given a new life as a minelayer, all the while maintaining its very British Merchant Navy outward appearance.

Eventually, on January 21, 1942, laden with 155 contact-type and 55 acoustic-type mines, plus a large quantity of torpedoes and torpedo mines to be delivered to U-boats, the *Doggerbank* embarked on her perilous voyage. On board, to orchestrate the minelaying operations when their time arrived was *Oberleutnant* Waldemaar Gruetzmacher and thirty handpicked *Kriegsmarine* veterans chosen from various minelaying and minesweeping units.

The merchant crew numbered an astonishing seventy-seven men who, for the most part, considered the voyage to be a *Himmelfahrtskommando* (heaven-bound detachment). Eventually, with the full realization of what was being asked of these civilian sailors, SKL ordered that they be conscripted into the *Kriegsmarine*, although their "uniforms" consisted of nothing more than arm bands reading *Deutsche Wehrmacht* (German Armed Forces). Schneidewind's reserve commission was activated, and he was promoted to *Kapitänleutnant.*

On March 12 and 13, sixty contact mines were laid in the approaches to Capetown, and on the fourteenth, fifteen more off Cape Aghulas, the southernmost point of Africa. From here, the *Doggerbank* disappeared into the Indian Ocean to await further orders. A month later, she was again off Aghulas and on the night of April 16-17 the remaining contact mines were rolled off the stern.

Minelaying produces little or no gratification for the minelayer. He never sees or hears of the results of his dangerous voyages into enemy waters. History, if he lives to read it, is his only reward. For the record, therefore, *Doggerbank's* mines cost the Allies two hundred men killed or wounded, two freighters sunk, two others badly damaged, and *HMS Hecla*, a 14,000 ton destroyer depot ship so badly holed that she barely managed to reach the dockyard at Simonstown. Add to that the value of the lost cargoes, the loss of use of the crippled vessels, and the cost of their repairs. The minesweeping operations went on for months. Ships were delayed, others were sent further to sea. None of this was known to the crews of the two *Kriegsmarine* vessels, the raider *Michel* and the minelayer *Doggerbank*, as they approached each other that June afternoon. Sailors of both ships "manned the rail," and the proper salutes and greetings were passed. The highlight of this meeting was the arrival on board of five bags of mail for the *Michel*. In a nice bit of logistical planning, somewhere in the South Atlantic the *Doggerbank* had met the Yokohama-bound blockade-runner *Dresden*, which left Bordeaux on April 16, carrying mail for both ships.

June 23. The *Charlotte Schliemann* made a scheduled appearance. The *Patella* and *Connecticut* prisoners were then moved from her to the *Doggerbank*. Also transferred were survivors of the British *Gemstone* (4,986 gross tons) and the Panamanian *Stanvac Calcutta* (10,170 gross tons) victims of the raider *Stier* which had taken bunkers from the tanker two weeks earlier. Visiting officers and men from the *Doggerbank* and the *Schliemann* were entertained with band concerts, and, for the first time, a choral group performed. Also, a small number of *Michel's* officers, who had organized a chamber music group, appeared. Konrad Hoppe, the cellist, was "astonished" that their listeners didn't like this music, and even made jokes about it. The usual bunkering operation took place, and on June 26, the *Michel* hosted a farewell party which went on into the night. The next day, both vessels were dismissed. The *Schliemann* moved to its waiting position and the *Doggerbank* headed for Yokohama with her mixed bag of prisoners who faced, at best, an uncertain future. This group consisted of fifty-six men from the *Patella*, eighteen from the *Connecticut*, thirty-two from the *Kattegat*, twenty-one from the *Lylepark*, and a total of sixty-six from the *Gemstone* and the *Stanvac Calcutta*. The *Stier's* commander, *Kapitän zur see* Horst Gerlach, kept the *Gemstone's* Captain Griffiths on board, along with a steward from the *Gemstone* who had been severely wounded. Also remaining on board were two badly wounded men from the *Stanvac Calcutta*. James Muldrow and Saedi Hassan.

In the ensuing two weeks, von Ruckteschell took the *Michel* on a long-ranging S pattern. He first ran eastward, crossing the Greenwich meridian at 2° south on July 4. Late in the day on the fifth, he angled back, steering 284° for three and a half days, then proceeding on a general heading of 035°, which took him between Ascension and St. Helena Islands. On the morning of July 14, in latitude 7° south, he again headed east. During this period, the following were noted:

2 cm cannon on aft mast house.

June 29. Two of the pigs were butchered. Fresh pork for dinner. In the evening a repeat of the June 18 Iron Cross awards celebration was held. Each crew member was issued two bottles of beer, plus a ration of *Schnäpse* and Cognac.

July 1. Small arms practice, with each man firing five shots. In the evening there was another celebration where champagne was served. The seaman who ran amok during the June 18 party, did it again.

July 2. For some unexplained reason, von Ruckteschell appeared on the bridge in civilian clothes.

July 5. Sunday. In the afternoon, the band presented a concert featuring old German classical pieces. Most of the crew, as usual, expressed no interest.

July 8. The crew was mustered before the commander. He told them he was taking the *Michel*, without orders from nor knowledge of the SKL, into the Gulf of Guinea. They would be facing more danger than they had previously experienced, he said, and there was indeed the possibility the *Michel* could be sunk and her crew taken prisoner. In such case, no one should reveal information to the enemy. Konrad Hoppe wrote, "Our hope to find single girls outside the islands (St. Helens and Ascension) hadn't become a reality so we had to go inside."

Attempts were made to alter the ship's appearance so she would resemble a bona fide merchantman. A few of the crew were designated to impersonate merchant seamen if an enemy aircraft came in for a close look. The *Esau* was launched on several occasions for drill purposes, but also to allow the former merchant marine officer/prize captains to observe and critique the disguise.

July 15. A ship was sighted and pursued. At 1800 the attack commenced and for the first time the *Michel* used its main armament, its torpedoes, and the *Esau* in a coordinated assault. Although many hits were scored, the enemy vessel transmitted what were probably distress messages for almost five minutes, but nothing understandable was copied by the *Michel's* radiomen. This was the British *Gloucester Castle* (8,600 gross tons) bound from the UK to Capetown with 139 crew and 12 passengers. When only sixty-one survivors were picked up, including a Mrs. Smith and her ten year old son Graham, a sixteen-year-old girl named Patricia, and another unidentified child, the *Michel* crew was deeply disturbed. Furthermore, the *Michel's* KTB synopsis indicates an additional six women and two children were lost. The *Michel's* men ultimately justified their actions with the observation that the *Gloucester Castle* was traveling without lights. Also, they were very critical of the *Gloucester Castle's* crew for quickly abandoning ship without regard to the passengers, and for not attempting to rescue people who were in the water. "Cowards," they called them.

Mrs. Smith, her son Graham, and Patricia.

Incidentally, a survivor of the *Gloucester Castle*, Quartermaster Frank Chadwick, wrote after the war the total number of persons aboard was 165, and of them only 41 were picked up by the raider—37 crew and 4 passengers. His breakdown of the fatalities is 112 crewmen and 12 passengers. The author is inclined to accept von Ruckteschell's 61 as he surely knew how many castaways his people picked up. Chadwick's 41 could have well been a typographical error or a misunderstanding on the part of whoever transcribed his story.

July 16. 0900. Four ships were in sight, two tankers and two freighters. Initially, von Ruckteschell didn't quite know what to do, but soon opted for a simultaneous attack on the tankers after dark. *Esau* would take one, the *Michel* the other. After the usual preparation and approach, *Esau* fired one torpedo, scoring a hit. The vessel immediately radioed she was under submarine attack. Meanwhile, her gunners saw the torpedo boat and opened fire. Because of the phosphorescence of the sea, the tanker was able to avoid the second torpedo and escape.

The watchstanders in the second tanker, undoubtedly alarmed and distracted did not see the *Michel* closing in. Her United States Naval Armed Guard gunners, however, were all at their stations. When von Ruckteschell ordered, "Open fire," he and his men were surprised to receive two or three five-inch shells in return, none of which hit. This was the first and only time a vessel under attack was able to counter the *Michel*'s fire. Also, it was able to transmit "RRRR RRRR" indicating attack by a surface ship.

After an extraordinary barrage of gunfire, and taking two torpedoes, the *William F. Humphrey* (7,883 gross tons), bound from Capetown to Trinidad in ballast, sank by the stern. Twenty-nine persons, many of whom were severely wounded, were picked up and taken prisoner. One died in the *Michel*'s operating room. Four went down with their ship.

The third assistant engineer in the *Humphrey* was William N. Wallace, Jr., of Wilbraham, Massachusetts. Bill entered the Massachusetts Nautical School six months before me and graduated in April 1941. Thus, we had been together among the one hundred and twenty man cadet/student body for eighteen months. Although Bill was training to be an engineering officer and I was studying seamanship and navigation, we were not unknown to each other. Not too long after the war ended we met at an alumni association affair and discovered our mutual involvement with the *Michel*. Bill has written an account of the sinking of his ship, which I have edited and insert herewith.

———

William N. Wallace, Jr. 1938.
Photo courtesy of William N. Wallace, Jr.

Before I joined the *Humphrey*, I had been in the S.S. *Santa Rita*, a C-2 vessel of the Grace Line. After a trip to Egypt via South Africa we returned to Capetown, docking briefly for routing orders. During the war sailing times were not posted, but several of us went ashore believing we had ample time to spend a few hours sightseeing. While we were gone, the captain received orders to move the ship out to an anchorage. In the process, he received orders from the signal station to proceed to sea and New York. Shortly thereafter, the three of us came back to the pier and saw our ship disappearing over the horizon. As two of us were engineers, we couldn't believe the captain would sail short-handed. Efforts to contact the *Santa Rita* were unsuccessful.

So, we went into the city and found the American Consulate where arrangements were made for board and room. Right after the attack on Pearl Harbor, I made an arrangement with my father whereby I gave him $300 to be held in the event I became stranded someplace in the world. I immediately sent him a cablegram and he remitted the money. Shortly, we two engineers were called to the Consulate and were told two ships, one a fast troop transport and the other a slow, empty tanker, both needing engineers, were in port. We were asked, "Who wants what job?" We hesitated, so the Consul tossed a coin and

I won the right to pick, but I decided to ask him to flip the coin again. "If it comes up heads, I will take the trooper and if tails, I'll take the tanker." It came tails and I went to the *William F. Humphrey*. She was an old, 1921 vintage vessel, built in Quincy, Massachusetts, just outside of Boston. I signed on as Third Assistant Engineer, standing the 8-12 watches, and we sailed for New York the next day, July 7, 1942.

On or about 9:30 PM on the 16th, I and the Oiler, having completed his rounds, and the Fireman/water-tender, having finished cleaning his burners, were standing around the log desk having coffee, when suddenly we heard a horrendous racket and the ship shuddered. This was, of course, the first salvo hitting us. The two crewmen ran up the ladders, leaving me alone on the platform. Shortly thereafter, the general alarm began ringing and the bridge telegraph swung to Full Astern. At about that time, I heard our five-inch gun fire one round. When I had the engine running in reverse, I decided to put on a life jacket. Salvo after salvo hit the ship. Then the lights went out and the engine came to a stop. This told me the steam lines had been shot away. The engine space immediately filled up with steam and became extremely hot. At that time I decided to leave and started up the engine room ladder in the darkness. I had gone about two levels when for some reason I could not go any further. I was trapped on the refrigerator flat. As I wandered around, trying to find my way out, another salvo hit and I received a slight wound in the head. I thought that I was doomed so decided to go over to the side where the next salvo would get me and end it all. Another salvo did hit and I received another minor head wound, but that wasn't enough to do me in. Because the space was filled with steam, now being mixed with ammonia from the refrigeration plant, I was having trouble breathing. My lungs became very painful, and I felt I couldn't take it any longer. I walked back to where the engine room ladder was located and it suddenly dawned on me that I had a flashlight in my back pocket. Using it, I saw why I couldn't get out. Most of the ladder was shot away, with only a few feet of treads remaining. I made a gigantic leap, the ladder held and I got out.

The first thing that I saw on deck was that our five-inch gun was out of action, knocked askew, and was pointing straight up into the air. I also saw that we were being shelled by a large ship, not a submarine, as I thought. We had three pet monkeys on the ship. They had been kept chained up on the after deck, and were jumping up and down, shrieking wildly. There was nothing I could do for them. I then went into my cabin, because I had my $300 there. I grabbed my wallet from my locker and stuck it in my back pocket. Next, from force of habit, I locked my locker and turned around to leave. At this moment a shell burst on the deck above and blew down the overhead (ceiling) of my room. I received another wound in the head that almost knocked me out, and left me partially stunned. As I was utterly exhausted, as well as being injured, my thoughts were to lie down on my bunk, but it was all cut up and covered with junk. So, I went outside and crouched down behind the mooring bitts. For a few minutes I watched the shelling and the machine gunning and watched one shell pick off our smokestack. Another shell shot away the number three lifeboat.

Knowing that the ship was doomed, I jumped overboard and started swimming. When about 100 feet from the ship, I felt something go by me in the water and my first thought was that it was a shark. It was a torpedo, however, and debris from the explosion showered all around me, but I wasn't hit. Immediately afterwards another torpedo went by my feet followed by a second explosion. This time I put my arms over my head for protection, but again wasn't hit. The vessel attacking us came into sight. It looked just like an ordinary freighter. They passed by the stern of the Humphrey and took a "pot shot" at our five-inch gun with one of their heavy guns. The *Humphrey* then settled by the stern and the bow raised up. When in an almost vertical position, it plunged towards the bottom. (Latitude 05° 27' S, Longitude 00° 58' E.)

My throat, nasal passages, vocal cords and lungs were damaged from having inhaled the steam and ammonia gas, so I decided to take a gulp of sea water to relieve the burning sensation. I immediately began to vomit violently, and retched for a considerable length of time. I then noticed the ship that had attacked us was stopped and was in the process of taking some of our crew out of one or two lifeboats. I swam in that direction. Even though my vocal cords were burned, I managed to call out and an officer on the gangway told me to come alongside.

At that time I heard a voice in the other direction asking my identity. I replied, "The Third Assistant." The voice said, "Come over here, we have a raft." Although 800 miles from land, I decided that I would take my chances, rather then become prisoner. Actually, there were three rafts containing ten men. At daybreak, we sighted the two lifeboats and paddled to them. Both were damaged by shrapnel. It was decided to take the better of the two, plus all the survival equipment from the other, and from the rafts, as well. By noon, the leaks were sealed, a sail was rigged, and the course set in an easterly direction. Six days later, after covering an estimated 500 miles, which is a story of its own, our boat was sighted by the Norwegian freighter *Triton*. Three days after that, we were put ashore at Freetown, Sierra Leone.

Author's note: In addition to Wallace, the men in the lifeboat were

1st Cook Benjamin Manaya Alba
2nd Cook Benjamin Trompete Alba
Chief Steward Nicanor Alba
Coxswain Jennings Bennett, USN
Second Officer Fritz Borner
Wiper George Deallaume
Oiler James Evans
Captain Richard Schwarz
S2c Lee Smith, USNR
Radio Officer Gerald Wilson.

It should be noted that Captain Schwarz and Mr. Borner were German-born naturalized United States citizens, and that the Albas, all from the same family, were Filipinos.

Wallace continues,

Before we left the *Triton*, Mr. Borner said it would be nice if the officers and crew of the *Triton* could be rewarded for rescuing and caring for us. He suggested a few cases of beer. I spoke up and said I could lend the money. Everyone was surprised, as I never revealed in the lifeboat I had almost $300 on my person. So I lent money to anyone who wanted it, from Captain Schwarz on down. I was eventually reimbursed when the captain received funds from the New York office.

The first day in Freetown was a busy one. We were examined by a medical missionary and debriefed by the American Consul acting as an intelligence officer. We bought a few clothes, and arrangements for lodging and meals were made. Late in the afternoon, ten of us (the eleventh, the gun captain was badly wounded and was hospitalized) hot and thirsty, spotted a place where we could get a drink. We all had a beer together and then the captain and the second officer left, having further business to take care of. The rest remained, telling stories, and putting down more beers. Ever since the sinking, I couldn't talk above a whisper because of the searing suffered by my vocal cords. Suddenly,

I spoke up and we were all amazed that my voice had returned. Later in life I regretted I didn't remember the name of that beer so that I could recommend it to the New England Journal of Medicine as a cure.

After two weeks in Freetown, our number grown to eighty, the R. M. S. *Aquitania* arrived, carrying German prisoners bound for Boston. Captain Schwarz, Mr. Borner, Mr. Wilson (the radio officer) and I were given private cabins and ate in the First Class dining room. We were allowed to become friendly with some of the prisoners and the captain and Borner undoubtedly impressed them. When we arrived in Boston, it took twenty-four hours to disembark the prisoners while we were detained aboard. When I was allowed ashore, I called my parents who strangely had been notified twice that I was missing in action. I went home for the weekend and on Monday went down to New York and checked into the Marine Hospital. Eventually, I was deemed fit for sea duty and sailed for the duration of the war and, in my case, until retirement.

As for the *Santa Rita*, she didn't make it either, being torpedoed by the U-172 in mid-afternoon on July 9, about 750 miles northeast of Puerto Rico. Crewmen from the submarine actually boarded the sinking freighter and looted her food stores. In addition, 66-year-old Captain Henry Stephenson was taken prisoner. He remained in German custody until being repatriated in a prisoner exchange in January, 1945.

July 17. The *Michel* searched for the tanker hit by *Esau's* torpedo on the previous evening. Eventually, a ship was seen, and preparations were made for the customary night attack. The crew was called to battle stations at 1900. Open fire was ordered at 2000. Three torpedoes were fired, two of which detonated against the target. Before the ship sank (position 05° 14' S, 03° 04' W), a boarding party swept through the chart room, radio room, wheel house, and captain's quarters, reaping a sizeable harvest of routing orders, charts, secret instructions warning of "German raiders carrying two torpedo boats," and merchant-ship signal codebooks *S.P. 2405* and *S.P. 02272*. This was the Norwegian *Aramis* (7,984 gross tons), indeed the "escapee" of the preceding night. A total of twenty-three of her forty-three man crew were taken prisoner, one of whom died in the *Michel's* operating room a few hours later.

After sinking three ships in as many days, the *Michel* crew was quite weary. In addition, these actions took place between latitudes 9° 22' S and 5° 14' S (562 and 314 nautical miles, respectively, below the equator) so the ship was very hot, with living conditions similar to those of April. Von Ruckteschell decided to run at full speed toward the southwest, which he did for three days. On board, the objects of much attention were the English lady, Graham, Patricia, and the unidentified second child. Arrangements were made by Dr. Schröder to provide living accommodations in the hospital, and they were free to visit a nearby open deck area. This was in sight of a space utilized by the younger officers for exercise, resulting in a great deal of posturing and muscle flexing, from which the ladies undoubtedly turned their heads. No one, of course, other than the medical personnel, had any contact with these four people, but stories spread through the ship: "The lady is very anti-German, but that is because she comes from Plymouth which has been destroyed by the *Luftwaffe*." "She believes the reason they are being treated so well is our guilty consciousness resulting from the killing of the other passengers." "Graham says when he grows up he will become a Royal Air Force pilot and bomb Germany."

During this period occurred the famous incident involving the commander, a section of radio specialists, and a popular musical recording. These particular radio men dealt with such mundane, but necessary, matters as the copying and posting of the daily radio news and personal messages to crew members; acting as disk jockeys in the playing of wake-up music in the morning and other music at other times; receiving special broadcasts from Radio Berlin and transmitting them throughout the ship on the public address system; and so on. Probably the most popular recording in their repertoire was a number entitled *Röte Mond* (Ruddy Moon), sung by one Rosita Serrano. It was despised by von Ruckteschell, and it is possible he banned it or at least ordered it to be played only at a certain time. In any case, his patience ran out when once again the radio men spun the disk. Suddenly, there he was at the radio room door. The commander! In midsong, Rosita was silenced as von Ruckteschell snatched the record, marched deliberately down the passageway, out on deck, and gave it one last spin into the South Atlantic Ocean. The next day, daringly inserted in the radio news bulletin was an item stating that a German auxiliary cruiser operating in the South Atlantic had sunk a vessel named *Röte Mond*, and that passenger Rosita Serrano did not survive. A day later there was a rebuttal by von Ruckteschell, but no details exist.

July 23. There was another marriage of a crewman to his fiancée in Germany. This was celebrated with a party: rum and water was served. Sometime later, either this man or the fellow who was married earlier by von Ruckteschell, received a message from his "wife," stating, "We are now divorced!"

July 24. A birthday was celebrated until 0130 the next day.

July 25. Another birthday party. The *Michel* was now moving easterly, heading 100°.

July 26. Under a low, angry looking sky, the Arado went aloft, as it was believed that the *Michel* was on the track of single vessels bound for Capetown. Before being swung over the side, Flying Officer Hoppe discovered a substantial error in the aircraft's magnetic compass, which, upon investigation, appeared to be caused by a large tool bag in the cockpit.

In the afternoon the commander again awarded a number of Iron Crosses—six First Class, and thirty Second Class. The pilot of the Arado, Sergeant Walter Emmel, received the Iron Cross, First Class. The same medal went to the designated battle helmsman. This second fellow had proved to be a very cool and collected seaman who could absolutely be depended upon under sometimes difficult and confusing situations in the heat of action. Of course, he had caught von Ruckteschell's eye, and it was von Ruckteschell who made the decisions as to who would be honored. In this instance the commander reasoned that he would be setting a good example for the lower ratings, showing them they were appreciated. His gesture backfired! Instead, consternation swept through the decks. Every one of the petty officers and the higher-rated seamen believed that they alone had done more to deserve recognition than the lowly wheelsman. Stories were spread saying that this sailor had, back at Kiel, attempted to avoid the voyage altogether by acting strangely and stupidly. Some of his comrades claimed he received more vacation time than they. Others spoke of his crying at night. Hoppe, who had been awarded the Iron Cross, First Class, for his service in the *Widder*, felt there was a possibility of similar unrest among the officers. There was none, as they appeared quite content with the status quo. The party went on through the night. "Much drinking because of these decorations," wrote the crew member. "Very drunk! Very drunk! Totally *bezotten*!" Whether it happened that particular night is not clear, but Mrs. Smith and Patricia reported they see eyes looking at them through the air vent into their room. "There is a bad man at the door," they said.

July 27. The course was changed again to the southwest, and the noontime radio bulletins reported great Allied air raids on Hamburg. The word around the ship was there would be a meeting with the raider *Stier* on the following day. Since breaking out into the Atlantic in late May, this ship had little success: two sinkings for 15,156 tons. *SKL* believed a joint operation with the *Michel* could be of benefit to the *Stier*, her commander, and her personnel. As a result of the *Widder* cruise and his record to date in the *Michel*, von Ruckteschell had a total of seventeen sinkings and one prize to his credit. So the thinking in Berlin was the "old fox" could probably teach his ten year younger counterpart, Horst Gerlach, a few tricks. Indeed he did, and at some risk.

July 28. 0430. The *Stier* should have been in sight, but it was not. Hoppe wrote, "At 0830, after some difficulty we found her and went to battle stations. Against my wishes, the *Esau* was launched. They didn't know anything about this weapon, so when they saw it there was some excitement. No harm resulted, however." The rails were manned and von Ruckteschell ordered the signal "COMMANDER TO COMMANDER, I AM GREETING YOU," be sent by signal lamp. This meeting of two German warships in the South Atlantic warranted celebration. Visits to the other ship were made by commanders, officers, and crewmen. Special food was served, as well as real coffee, good beer, and liberal shots of *Schnäpse*. Hoppe wrote of "visits between ships, and much drinking, an orgy of drinking." Experiences and intelligence accounts were relayed. Almost to a man, the *Michel* people felt they had the better ship, and the better commander. Many of the *Stier's* complement voiced the comment (confidentially, of course) that a transfer to the *Michel* would be most acceptable. One voice in the *Michel* demurred. "Life there is better than here. Her commander is not overbearing, and doesn't take advice from von Ruckteschell." Hoppe commented, saying, "The *Stier's* officers seem young (he was only twenty five), but give a good impression. I found it a problem to interact with such youths of lower rank than mine. They, of course, had to address me as *Kapitänleutnant*, so there was little man to man conversation." He was quite dismayed to learn the *Stier's* scout planes were Arado 213s, which he described as "kites," small aircraft, which are of no use at all. Also, they are folded up and stowed on deck, not out of sight below." Furthermore, he said the Flying Officer was not a commissioned officer, but a lowly petty officer who Gerlach ordered into the air in conditions when he, Hoppe, would not consider flying. All of this, he added, led *Kapitän* Gerlach to moan in excuse for the *Stier's* poor performance, "Without a good aircraft I can do nothing."

**The raider *Stier* from the *Michel* during one of their meetings.
Note lookouts at the mast tops.**

It is interesting to compare the two vessels. In fact, their vital statistics show them to be similar:

	Michel	*Stier*
gross tonnage	4,740	4,778
length	436 feet	408 feet
beam	55 feet	56 feet
draught	24 feet	21 feet
speed	14 knots	16 knots
crew	400 men	324 men

As for armament, the *Michel* was favored. The *Stier* did not (as inferred above) carry a torpedo boat, nor did she have the *Michel's* 10 cm cannon and above-water torpedo tubes. Hoppe felt the *Stier* was improperly laid out for the role as a raider. He wrote, "She is not well designed. We had the experience of the *Widder* cruise, and brought many ideas to the shipyard where the *Bielskoi* was being converted to *Michel*. As a result, we became an efficient man-of-war with economic use of space."

July 31. After two days together, the raiders moved away from each other, but on the next day, at noon, rejoined. This may have had something to do with the impending return of the *Charlotte Schliemann* at the same hour. That evening, after dark, with the three vessels hove to in close proximity, an odd incident occurred. Two sailors from the *Stier*, in a rubber boat, approached the *Michel*, but were detected by her alert lookouts. If this was a simulated attack, it was thwarted, but the *Stier* boys certainly had risked being shot. Undoubtedly this caper was carried out with the knowledge, and perhaps encouragement, of Gerlach. Nothing is known of von Ruckteschell's reaction.

August 2. 0530 Early wake up. The *Stier* departed. 0700 The *Gloucester Castle* prisoners, including the lady and her son, the other boy, and Patricia were transferred to the *Schliemann*. Patricia was very fearful to go down the ladder, but the German sailors managed to calm her and assist her into the boat. Also transferred were the prisoners from the *William F. Humphrey* and the *Aramis*. (Note: In October 1945, the author was repatriated to his home town of Newburyport, Massachusetts. Returning as well to the same small community was Charles E. McAddes, who had been an able seaman in the *Humphrey*. McAddes told in a newspaper interview how he had gone to a ship named *Sir Karl Knutsen* [*sic*].

Bunker operations then commenced, and the *Michel* took aboard about seven hundred tons of diesel fuel. This time, the British/American technique of parallel sailing was utilized. It went very well. In fact, in the afternoon, with the hose connected, both vessels had to turn in order to provide a lee for the safe retrieval of a motor launch by the *Michel*. In spite of the new procedure, the difficult maneuver was successfully carried out. The next day was stormy, and the boat could not then have been hoisted aboard. The two raiders headed northwest, looking for less wind and calmer seas. The tanker tagged along, a hundred or so miles distant. On board the *Michel*, many discussions took place regarding the recurring bad weather. Dr. Weise, the meteorologist, propounded theory after theory, much of which was belittled and denounced by von Ruckteschell. The commander, it was said, was proud to have the knowledge to discuss technical matters with the experts. Perhaps it is better to say that he liked to argue with them. Weise was not an officer, but a civilian described as being a nice, sympathetic, well-meaning gentleman. Von Ruckteschell's attitude puzzled and angered him, to the point where he decided to give his reports to the first officer for transmittal to the commander.

August 8. Ludwig Rödel's forty-fourth birthday. Konrad Hoppe nearly boycotted the party. He felt that he was too old for such matters. "The punch did taste quite good," he admits, but the movie raised his ire. "There is no one film that one can watch without criticism, especially those showing half-naked girls, which are totally without appeal."

August 9. A few minutes after midnight, Hoppe, standing the 0000-0400 watch, was startled by the appearance of the commander. The joint operation with the *Stier* had been a failure. Nothing was seen, under atrocious weather conditions, in four days of searching an area ranging from 20° S to 22° S, 20° W to 24° W, a situation that dictated a change. Von Ruckteschell told Hoppe to instruct his signalman to contact the *Stier* by blinker light, stating he was leaving the area, and the *Stier* should follow him in a northerly direction at full speed. Gerlach replied in the negative. What happened is the *Michel* had just transmitted five radio messages. Even though they were encoded short signals, each of which consisted of no more than ten groups of four letters, and perhaps sent on different frequencies, it was possible the British had managed to obtain radio directional bearings. Von Ruckteschell always acted on his intuition, and at that point felt in danger. He instructed Hoppe to "Tell *Stier* I am going," and rang up full speed on the engine room telegraph. Eventually, Gerlach followed. Then with a show of independence and perhaps some anger, using his slightly superior speed, overtook and passed the *Michel*. At dawn she was not to be seen. It should be noted the *Michel* had been at sea two months longer than had the *Stier* and probably was encumbered by marine growth on her hull.

At noon, First Officer Erhardt, just relieved from his bridge watch, entered the officers' dining room reporting gunfire could be heard. Those present expressed doubt, but then the radio room advised a nearby vessel was transmitting "RRRR RRRR." The *Stier* was in action—and in daylight, no less! Uncharacteristically, but confident that the *Stier* had things under control, von Ruckteschell maintained the course and soon found the *Stier* watching the British-flagged *Dalhousie* (7,072 gross tons) roll over and sink, to be followed by an underwater explosion. Gerlach's two-month drought was broken. Not only did he get a ship, but it was his birthday. Also noted was von Ruckteschell's fortuitous decision to move north in answer to his hunch, thereby putting the *Stier* onto the unlucky *Dalhousie*. Said the *Michel*'s commander, who had not approved of the joint operation in the first place, "Now we can part company, as he has gained confidence." The Germans saluted each other; the *Michel* moved eastward to its designated operating area.

***Dalhousie* from *Michel* (*Two views*).**

***Hsk Stier* watching S.S. *Dalhousie* sink.**

Prior to the *Dalhousie* incident, the *Charlotte Schliemann* had briefly, on August 6, joined the raiders again, and two additional *Michel* crewmen, descibed as "specialists," were transferred for transport to Japan. The *Schliemann* was dismissed, supposedly the final parting, but in actuality to go to a waiting position.

August 10. The SKL reported the *Kriegsmarine* supply tanker *Uckermark* had departed Bordeaux and was headed for a rendezvous with the *Michel*. She was carrying ammunition, torpedoes, lube oil, all the miscellaneous food and supplies required to refill the *Michel*'s storerooms and larders which would have been depleted by five months of consumption when she arrived, and, most importantly, eagerly awaited mail. One commodity not in short supply was alcohol. In the evening, celebrating the good news of the *Uckermark*'s departure, and a birthday, the petty officer recorded in his journal the recipe for the punch that was served. "Seven bottles red wine, three bottles champagne, three bottles cognac, three bottles mineral water, three tins strawberries."

August 12. Dr. Weise had another unfriendly confrontation with von Ruckteschell. The meteorologist had prepared a lecture on the subject of the climate in southern Russia, relative to what the *Wehrmacht* would find there. Many of the officers and petty officers had assembled for this. Dr. Weise had spoken barely three sentences when he was interrupted by the commander, who propounded several questions quite unrelated to weather in Russia. Wrote Konrad Hoppe. "Atrocious! One may ask questions if preparing for an examination, but not if the lecture is explanatory in nature." A heated discussion broke out, and to some of those present, it appeared their commander was attempting to demean Dr. Weise, who was a very competent man in his specialty. Unfortunately, the petty officers were witness to the squabble. Hoppe added, "There was a great deal of drinking born out of frustration with our commander's attitude." Aboard the *Michel*, then in its fifth month at sea, the stress and strain was beginning to take a toll.

On the same day, the raider's radio news bulletin contained quotations from the American press, stating a German raider was operating in the South Atlantic Ocean, and it would soon be caught. (A week later, the *Newburyport Daily News* of previously mentioned Newburyport, Massachusetts, carried the following:

> *A New England Port, August 19, (INS)—Torpedo boats swarming from a German surface raider took part in the sinking of a medium size American merchantman in the South Atlantic, with a probable loss of 16 American seamen, two officers reported today.*
>
> *The officers related that the enemy craft dispatched a fake distress signal, pounced without warning and machine-gunned a lifeboat to accomplish the first known sinking of an American vessel by a surface raider.*
>
> *Both the captain and the second officer, natives of Germany, did not want their names used for fear of reprisals to their families, attributed a cross-fire from three directions to torpedo boats, pointing out they heard motors which could not have been used by larger ships.*
>
> *There were 11 survivors. Approximately 19 crew members were thought to have been taken aboard the raider from a life raft and a boat, both of which were found later. Sixteen men had been killed by machine gun fire on the deck of the merchantman.*

This, of course, was the *William F. Humphrey*.

In its August 31, 1942 edition, *Time* reported a somewhat different version of the action. Under "BATTLE OF THE ATLANTIC, Invitation to Destruction," the magazine reported the following:

> *The U.S. cargo ship's skipper ordered Sparks to relay the S.O.S. Neither the captain, the first officer nor Sparks saw anything suspicious about*

the signal reporting a ship in distress some 30 miles distant in the South Atlantic. Soon night closed down over the unruffled sea and the third officer spotted lights about three miles away. Swiftly the lights grew closer to starboard. At three-quarters of a mile the approaching ship opened fire. Shells from eight-inch guns tore into the cargo vessel, quickly putting its deck guns out of action. Torpedoes from the deck tubes of the attacker plowed through the sea. On the victim's port side, tracer bullets slashed the darkness.

It was a trap, bated with the cynical confidence that a U.S. merchant ship would observe the law of the sea and relay a distress signal, thereby revealing her position. As the lifeboats were lowered, machine-gun fire forced the occupants to leap into the sea and swim for a raft. Later the captain said he was sure the raider had launched at least two motorboats because the attack came from three sides. Within half an hour the cargo ship went down. Out of the darkness the raider loomed closer to the spot. "We slid over the side of our raft and held on," said the second officer. "We heard a voice saying in perfect English: 'Come alongside boys.' After a while someone said in German, 'There's nobody on this one.' Then the raider disappeared. Later we found lifeboats with their oars shipped, indicating that some of the men had accepted the invitation to go alongside and had been taken prisoner aboard the raider."

At least 15 of the crew were killed by gunfire. Some 20 were taken prisoner. The rest, after making 450 miles in five days in a sail-equipped lifeboat, were picked up and taken to an African port. They were the first survivors to confirm the presence of an armed surface raider in the South Atlantic.

August 13. Since leaving the *Stier*, the *Michel* had been headed east, loafing along at a leisurely 9 knots. At daybreak, the course was changed to the southeast, then at sunset, back to the northwest.

August 14. Another of von Ruckteschell's hunches paid off as a ship was sighted and tracked throughout the day. 1930. In position 19° 26' S, 08° 28' W, *Michel* opened fire. The target had already seen the *Michel*, turned away and began transmitting a distress signal. Again, as in the case of the *Gloucester Castle*, everything was brought to bear on the doomed vessel: the main batteries, the rapid fire antipersonnel guns, torpedoes, and *Esau*. Torpedoes from the *Esau* and the *Michel* (one each) found their mark. This was the British *Arabistan* (5,874 gross tons), with 3,000 tons of tobacco, spices, hides, and valuable pelts, bound from Capetown to Trinidad. Of her sixty-man crew (twenty-two British and thirty-eight British Indians) only the chief engineer was found when the *Michel* returned to the scene in the morning.

Nothing of note occurred on the fifteenth or the sixteenth. Talk in the crew's quarters concerned a rumor two Allied cruisers had been dispatched to find the *Michel* and the *Stier*. Also it was said the commander continued to be unhappy with Gerlach and the *Stier* because they were careless with their radio. As an example, von Ruckteschell never replied when SKL called. He sent his messages to Germany at night, on a prearranged frequency and blind (unaddressed).

August 17. 0700 A large vessel of perhaps fourteen thousand tons materialized out of a rainsquall. Because of the possibility it was an armed merchant cruiser, the *Michel* turned away, acting as any God-fearing merchantman would under the circumstances, but kept it under surveillance. In an hour both vessels were hull down to each other, however, the *Michel*'s mast-top officer lookouts soon determined the stranger's course and speed. On board the *Michel*, preparations commenced for a night attack. If the other vessel was an armed merchant cruiser, the surprise element gave the Germans an enormous advantage. During the afternoon, Hoppe and von Schack, key participants in the raider's offense, took a snooze in anticipation of the evening's activity. Awaking, they learned von Ruckteschell had amazingly broken off contact! Apparently, First Officer Erhardt had concluded the vessel, tentatively identified as the former German passenger vessel *Marnox Van St. Alegonde*, now under Dutch registry, was probably carrying troops. If such was the case, and the *Michel* sank her with the resultant heavy loss of life, the Allies' reaction would be the *Michel*'s death sentence. Erhardt, thus, convinced von Ruckteschell to abandon the chase. Hoppe and von Schack could not understand Erhardt's sudden lack of aggression and fighting spirit.

August 18. Air temperature 13°C to 15°C (middle 50s °F), a welcome relief from the tropics. Calm sea. Unlimited visibility. The Arado made a two-hour patrol without seeing anything. During the afternoon, several officers were sitting around the wardroom when von Ruckteschell casually entered. In the ensuing conversation he said he had come to the realization he made a mistake the previous day, and should have carried out the attack.

August 19. The good weather of the eighteenth rapidly changed into a furious storm with the wind reaching Beaufort force 12 (hurricane velocity, more than 75 miles per hour).

August 20. Extremely high seas were encountered, and it was necessary to stop the engine. The *Michel* rolled heavily but took no seas aboard. Storerooms and offices became shambles and the door to one space could not be opened because shelving and furniture had fallen against it. No food could be prepared other than soup. Strange noises were heard everywhere, as the ship was tested to it utmost. The crew curled up in their bunks and hammocks and, trusting the integrity of their ship and thanking its skilled builders, rode out the storm.

August 21. The seas and wind abated as quickly as they had arisen. First officer Erhardt angrily mustered all hands for a tongue-lashing, berating them for their dereliction in failing to secure the various areas in which they worked and blaming them for the severe damage incurred throughout the ship. He created a competition to spur the clean up.

August 22. Because of the expenditure of so many torpedoes, which left the torpedo storeroom empty, work had been underway to convert the space into a reading room for the sailors. It would also serve as a vacation room. The bulkheads were paneled, and the deck covered with parquetry featuring a large Iron Cross. A painting by a talented crew member depicting the *Michel* in the Gironde was prominently displayed, plus others showing some of the raider's successes. The room was fitted out with "nice" furniture, source unknown. It is possible this room was the product of long-range planning, and the materials had been aboard since Kiel. On this day, the room was officially opened with a celebratory party which, according to Hoppe, "lasted too long." The first fourteen men to be assigned to the room "on vacation" were designated. In the wardroom, discussion continued on the subject of the abandoned attack of the seventeenth. The younger officers continued their criticism of their older peers who had overruled them. The radio news bulletin reported the *Uckermark* finally on the high seas, and had shot down an Allied aircraft near the Azores. Earlier, she had to return to Bordeaux twice to undergo repairs to damage suffered during enemy air attacks. The mail was on its way, but still far off. (Note: This was wishful thinking. The *Uckermark* did not break out of the Gironde until September 9.)

August 23. At 1030 in approximately 39° S, 4° W, the *Michel* again joined up with *Charlotte Schliemann* which, in the interval had met and refueled the *Stier* at Gough Island. Gerlach, inexplicably, was on his way home, estimating he would reach the Gironde before the end of November! At that meeting, Seaman 1/c James Muldrow, USN, who had been in the armed guard aboard the *Stanvac Calcutta*, and who was seriously wounded when the *Stier* sank that ship on June 6, was transferred to the tanker. Germany was not to be on his itinerary. He reports seeing Mrs. Smith and Graham, Patricia, and the other youngster living in the *Schliemann's* deck house. (Note: Jimmie Muldrow was killed in an automobile accident in Florida on February 1, 2003.)

The *Michel* and the *Schliemann* remained together for four days during which the *Michel* took on fuel in what had become a smooth, well-practiced routine. Also, the tanker's second officer, who broke a leg during the June rendezvous, rejoined his ship. In the eyes of the regimented, career oriented *Kriegsmarine* officers, this man was a strange personality. He was sixty years old, had been a seaman all his life, and with such a wealth of experience was only a second officer and quite happy with his status. It was observed he was rather lively after six weeks in a cast. The meeting of the two vessels was also commemorated by a craft exhibit in the new reading room where ship models, knot boards, sketches, paintings, poetry, etc. produced during the five months at sea, were proudly displayed by their creators.

August 25. Cleanup of the storm damage continued, and the door to the clothing locker was opened. Many of the crew were suffering from head colds, including the commander and his adjutant, *Oberleutnant* Herr.

August 26. The *Schliemann* was dismissed for the final time, bound for Yokohama via Batavia and Singapore.

During the next five days, von Ruckteschell moved to the southeast, crossing the fortieth parallel for a day or so, then going north to a waiting position in 38° 30′ S. The weather was poor, with low visibility and rough seas. There was grumbling in the wardroom. Finding a ship under such conditions was impossible and polite suggestions that he go further north were offered to the commander. During this period, the band, which had not been heard from for many weeks, began to rehearse, attempting new pieces. Several birthdays were celebrated with the usual parties.

September 1. Steering 100°. In the afternoon a film was shown, a variety show with circus acts. Another birthday was observed in the evening. Erhardt and von Schack attended, regaling the sailors with stories of their youth. This party didn't shut down until 0400 the next morning!

September 2. Otto Saupe was also ill with the head cold that had bothered the other officers. On recovery, he rewarded his petty officer, who had been standing in for him, with a bottle of wine. In the afternoon, the crew was mustered and told one or more of them had stolen certain items (*Schnäpse?*) from the wardroom. It was suspected that a duplicate key had been made. The unknown perpetrator or perpetrators were warned of the dire consequences of this action. It was also announced the supply ship *Tannenfels*, coming from the Far East, would be met on the twentieth. To insure sufficient time for censorship, the deadline for outgoing mail was the fourteenth. All official mail and department reports were to be completed by the same date. This was the first opportunity to send anything home to Germany, so the entire ship's company went to work with zeal.

September 3. At 40° S, course was changed to 180°, due south. Von Ruckteschell had come up with the idea of finding a loose ice floe. He felt that if he got into the ice, the marine growth on the hull could be scraped off. He ran into more heavy weather instead. The Roaring Forties were that indeed, as the *Michel* rolled and pitched.

September 4. The bad weather continued, unabated, but von Ruckteschell pushed southward.

September 5. No work was possible. The vessel suffered some damage resulting in taking on water and the flooding of two storerooms. The commander decided it was quite injudicious to continue pressing on and ordered the course reversed to the north.

September 6. Crossed 40° S.

September 7, 8, 9. Moving in a general northwest direction. The first anniversary of the *Michel*'s commissioning was celebrated on the seventh. A formal recognition of the day was held, with the crew mustering before the commander, followed by the inevitable party. At some point in this time frame another crew member (Denzler?) appeared before the commander to have a marriage ceremony performed.

September 10. At daybreak, Hoppe's bridge watch was startled to see an oncoming ship about five miles distant. This was a rare and feared occurrence, considering that the stranger could be an Allied warship. The general alarm was sounded, the *Michel* turned away, and the smoke maker was activated. It seemed the enemy also changed course, although by not too many degrees. Soon the ships were out of sight of each other, but the *Michel*, at maximum speed was off on an end run. With von Schack and Hoppe alternately manning the after mast's swivel chair, the raider ran parallel to its prey's course. In the early afternoon, a converging track was plotted which would, after dark, put the unseen attacker dead ahead of the oncoming unwary freighter.

CHAPTER THIRTEEN

Bloody September

September found the *American Leader* back in Capetown. We arrived on the sixth and anchored in the roadstead. Unless challenged, no ship at sea identified itself in those bleak days. We flew no flag, the ship's name on each side of the bow and wheelhouse was painted over, as was the name and home port on the stern. Everything was gray and, depending how long had been the voyage, rust-streaked. On this particular day, Eric Kamins, the third assistant engineer, who stood the corresponding 12:00-4:00 watches in the engine room as did I on the bridge, were out on deck watching an unidentified freighter pass by on her way into the docks. It appeared to be a Luckenbach Lines freighter, loaded to her marks. Both of us remarked at the pretty sight of the "stars and stripes" flying at the gaff on her after mast. We were over four months out of New York, and this was the first American ship we had seen. Made us a bit homesick, I recall.

We didn't expect to go into the docks. Captain Pedersen had left the ship upon our arrival at the anchorage, taken ashore by a British naval launch. In the late afternoon, however, the launch returned with instructions for us to go in and tie up astern of the vessel that Eric and I had observed earlier. Ordinarily, when we were performing the docking routine, the captain and Shershun and I were on the bridge; Hickey was forward and Lee aft. Now, with the captain ashore, Hickey took command and went to the bridge. Lee and I took over on the bow and stern, respectively, positions with which we were both unfamiliar. To say that what we did was not much of an exhibition of seamanship may be an understatement. Lee got a line ashore before I did and pulled the bow in, causing the stern to swing out. Eventually, he slacked away, Hickey maneuvered my end in, and I got a hawser onto the dock, promptly heaved away and the bow veered off. Hickey nearly collapsed from the excitement. Captain Pedersen just stood there on the quay in amazement. After a few more seesaws we did get the ship parallel and secured. I didn't even think of asking permission to ride into Capetown that evening. All in all, Hickey and I had not been getting along throughout the trip. He blamed

Eric Kamins, the *American Leader's* Third Assistant Engineer. Christmas 1977.

me for the docking fiasco, so I wouldn't give him the satisfaction of telling me I couldn't go ashore. Instead, I went up ahead to the other ship (she was indeed a Luckenbacher) and swapped news with her skipper and deck officers.

In the morning, we backed out of the dock and went to anchor again in the roadstead. Although Captain Pedersen had his orders, we needed new charts. At about noon, a small boat delivered a package, we weighed anchor, and headed to sea. We had proceeded some distance when I realized that the signal station on Lion Mountain was trying to attract our attention. I replied with our Aldis lamp, and received in plain language the message: "*AMERICAN LEADER* RETURN TO ANCHORAGE," which I repeated to the captain as I acknowledged each word. Back we went. It was almost 1700 when the naval launch pulled alongside, and another package came up on the end of a heaving line. Once again, the carpenter hove in the hook, and once again we were headed home. When I took over the bridge at midnight for my usual watch, we had run south until the Cape of Good Hope light was abeam, and then had gone to a course of 270°, true west. This wasn't exactly in the direction of New York, but in wartime, one quite often travels three sides of a square to avoid the fourth. A strong wind was blowing from the SW with a heavy swell. What, however, had that thirty-odd hours stopover in Capetown cost us?

Our immediate destination remained with Captain Pedersen. The cargo was consigned to New York and Newport News, but as to how we would get to the East coast of the United States—via the Straits of Magellan or Trinidad?—stood as a large question. And if it was south? Most of us had figured on a warm weather trip, but those who had winter gear were counting their blessings. During the day of the eighth, and following on into the ninth, the weather continued to deteriorate. We were burying our bow into the oncoming seas, as well as rolling heavily, endangering the two life boats which had been swung out and lowered to boat deck level, ready for quick use.

American Leader's **port side life boat lowered to deck level.**

On the afternoon of the ninth, the deck crew was called to boat stations. Both boats were taken in and secured in their chocks. On the tenth, the wind had died to nothing, and the sea flattened out appreciably. That morning at dawn, Walter Lee sighted a vessel off to the south of us. She was on a northeasterly course, making considerable smoke, and soon disappeared astern of us. Actually we saw several ships after leaving Capetown, including one rather slow, apparently British freighter, traveling in the same direction, which we quickly overtook and passed. Thus, Walter's indifference to the morning sighting was not questioned. At noon, we had attained a position on our new Capetown-acquired chart, which the British Admiralty had signified as being in "safe waters." To that point, the *American Leader* was being steered manually, with daytime lookouts posted. Here we went over to automatic, gyroscope-controlled steering, and the crew returned to their routine deck work. (Of course, the armed guard stood by at their assigned gun positions, and we went to hand steering during the night watches.) The day rapidly improved, and I soon had a sun-sparkled, bright, glaring horizon in front of me. My basic duty was to keep a sharp lookout, and that's what I did until Walter came up and relieved me at 1600. I do remember the day as though it was yesterday, and how, in spite of my dark glasses and the filters on my binoculars, the sun's glare kept me from seeing anything that may have been more than a few miles dead ahead. We were still steering 270°, and Captain Pedersen had not revealed our next port.

The evening meal was dominated by a discussion concerning Chief Steward Medicis's bet with Second Cook/Baker Albert whereby the steward had said that he alone could turn out a better three meals in one day than could the three cooks together. There was much interest in the wager, but no one picked a favorite. The food had been poor all trip; the Steward was no cook. The sum of $25 rode on the outcome, but I have no idea who was to judge the contest scheduled for the following day. At some point after supper, I went into my room to continue working on a series of letters I wanted ready for mailing when we arrived in the States. This evening I planned to do something for Bob Dickie of Newburyport who was in the navy and had survived the Japanese attack on Pearl Harbor. After seven o'clock, when I had written a few paragraphs, I became quite nervous and irritated. Suddenly, I took the letter, tore it to bits and threw them into the wastebasket. "*Duffy,*" I asked myself, "*what the hell is wrong with you?*" Deciding that a cup of cocoa could help, I went out to the pantry and downed a good, hot mug. There was a blueberry pie in the refrigerator, and thinking it would go great at midnight, put a slice on a saucer and carried it back to my room. With a strange feeling still gripping me, I stripped down to my underwear, snapped out the lights, and crawled into the bunk.

Up on the bridge Walter Lee had just plotted the ship's position, which he had determined from the results of his star sights at twilight. While he was involved in that, Hickey had taken over the bridge. Captain Pedersen was in the meanwhile standing by in the chartroom, as was Joe Cohen, the radio operator, in his "shack." The Captain had completed his regular evening walk on the boat deck and still wore his leather jacket. Lee finished his work and went into the wheelhouse, joining Hickey. The time was approximately 1930. At Capetown, Captain

Pedersen had received instructions regarding the transmitting of position reports during this passage. This evening the first was to be sent, so he took off his cap, put on his eyeglasses, and busied himself with the codebook. Perhaps five or ten minutes later, 1940 at the latest, Lee was standing on the starboard bridge wing, peering into the darkness. There was no moon, and the stars twinkled through an increasing cloud cover. Visibility, therefore, was poor, as little as a mile in the gloom. This was the type of night we liked. We couldn't see anything, and no one should be able to see us.

Suddenly, practically dead ahead, just a few degrees on the starboard bow, the black shape of an oncoming ship materialized. Lee reacted quickly, calling out, "Hard left," to the helmsman. The ship answered to its rudder and began to turn. The lookout on the bow jumped back, grabbed the lanyard on the bell mounted on the foremast, and clanged one quick clap, indicating that he had sighted something to starboard.

Unbelievably, the oncoming vessel was the nondescript, smoke-trailing "steamer" that had come up from the south that morning and headed away to the northeast. She was, in fact, the German navy's *Hilfskreuzer Michel*! Schiff 28! What we most feared—a German raider—had us in its gun sights!

Seconds after Walter Lee shouted "Hard Left," the *Michel* opened fire and came down our starboard side, pounding us point-blank (perhaps 800 yards) with her main batteries, and smaller caliber rapid fire guns. There was no need for range finding nor central control. The gunners aimed and shot at will. We continued on a wide circle to the left as the raider swung under our stern and came up on the port side, continuing its fire. This maneuver had been practiced time and time again with *Esau* as the mock target. Thus the two vessels were in concentric circles, with the attacker on the victim's port quarter, very much in control of the situation. As the KTB covering the *American Leader* incident has never been found, one must rely on accounts of other *Michel* successes to determine how many 360° circles were made before the target stopped and sank. In the case of the *Eugenia Livanos*, she made three, the *Empire March*, one. The *American Leader*, probably made one complete circle before coming to a halt.

The *Leader*, as pointed out previously, was a motorship. In the event of an engine problem, and the main diesel propulsion engines did have a propensity to stall on occasion, there was mounted on the very top deck, abaft the stack, an emergency generator, powered by a small diesel engine supplied with 350 gallons of fuel. The tank containing this oil was hit immediately, and burst into flames. The burning oil spread across the deck and cascaded down the ladders to the decks below.

Meanwhile, the starboard life boat had been destroyed, the deckhouse had taken numerous hits, the ship's compressed air whistle wailed an incessant death dirge, and some of the crew broke out a hose in a futile try to subdue the oil flames. Someone in the engine room, probably Assistant Engineer Marshall Soper, had started the saltwater fire pump.

Meanwhile, the *Michel*, after firing a hundred-odd shells at its prey, remained off the *American Leader*'s port side, her guns momentarily quiet while a torpedo was launched. This penetrated number four hold, aft of the deckhouse, blowing off the steel pontoon-type hatch covers, and causing the vessel to settle by the stern. The raider's main batteries did not go into action again, but the secondary, rapid-fire weapons sporadically swept the *Leader*'s decks, attempting to prevent anyone who could possibly man the four-inch gun or the machine guns from so doing. Although it was obvious from the raider her victim was mortally wounded and was slowly sinking, the gunfire increased in intensity. Flames and sparks billowed skyward creating a beacon visible for miles. Thus, fifteen or twenty minutes after the first torpedo hit, it was necessary to fire a second to hasten the end. This probably exploded in the engine room on the port side, away from the scrambling crew who were abandoning ship from the starboard fore deck.

As recounted earlier, I had routinely turned in at 1930 in order to obtain about four hours sleep before being called for the midnight to 0400 bridge watch. Then, as always, I soon fell into a deep slumber. My room was on the starboard side of the deck house, so when the raider opened fire, there was not much between them and me, just three-eighths of an inch of steel plating. Also, my porthole was probably cracked open to provide some ventilation while I slept. Thus, the first salvoes literally blasted me back to consciousness. My initial reaction was that our gunners were shooting at something, but quickly changed as I felt the explosions around me and saw flashes of light. I put on my trousers and a sweater, and my uniform suit coat. (Captain Pedersen demanded that his deck officers wear uniforms on watch, thus, the coat was always at hand, though I must admit there were nights on the midnight to four when I cheated on him.) A number of articles had been laid out in my cabin ready for the possibility of ship abandonment: my steel helmet, my .38 revolver, a small camera, my kapok-filled life jacket, and a water-proofed packet containing my seaman's papers and a few American dollars. All of these I gathered up, plus the usual flashlight and whistle, and went out. In retrospect, considerable time had passed, because when I looked aft toward the door to the outside deck, Lee's room, which was two away from mine, was already completely afire, with flames roaring out into the passageway.

217

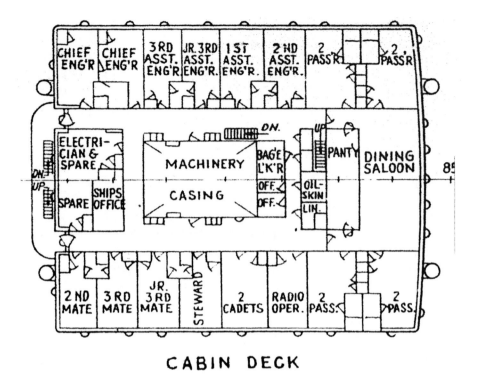

CABIN DECK

American Leader. **Plan of officers' quarters.**

Had I been stunned for some minutes? Then I became aware of someone lying in the passageway. It was Ollie Schneider, the fourth assistant engineer who was to have gone on watch at eight o'clock. His face was chalky-white, and there was much blood on the deck. I think he had lost part of one leg. He was conscious, however, and said to me, "Mate, I'm a goner." Nevertheless, I dragged him toward the outside door, ducking under the flames coming out of Lee's room. When I reached the outside deck, I met several of the crew. I told them to take Schneider down to the main deck, and when the lifeboat was lowered they could put him in. I then attempted to go up to the boat deck, but the ladder was blocked by debris and fire. At about this time, some of the burning oil still flowing from the upper deck dripped on to me setting my life jacket afire. Without any thought as to the consequences of going into the water without it, I untied the jacket and threw it away.

The light from the fires illuminated the entire scene. Number four hatch was blown open—the result of the first torpedo. The housing at the foot of the after mast, which contained the electrical panels for controlling the cargo winches was

218

also blasted apart. Everything was sparking and flashing. It was quite apparent that we were in deep, deep trouble.

At this point, I went down onto the main deck and crossed over to the port side. Why the port side? I don't know, but I did want to get up to the forward part of the vessel where I would be able to see the bridge or perhaps climb up to determine from the captain or the chief officer what was really happening. It was possible, in the *American Leader*, by means of outside passageways, port and starboard, to walk along the main deck without going in to the deckhouse. I hurried along the port passageway, not realizing that our attacker now laid a short distance off and could probably see me. As I gained the fore deck, my way was blocked by the cargo of huge drums of coconut oil loaded in Colombo. There were drums on the starboard side, as well, but on top of those, a catwalk had been constructed to provide access to the forward part of the ship. I knew all of that, but, in my haste, unthinkingly used the port passageway, encountered the drums and attempted to climb up and over them. In the process, I fell into the space between four of them. Fortunately, the steel helmet I was wearing saved me from whacking my head, although I did pick up a few scrapes and bruises. When I pulled myself up and out of that predicament, I decided against going to the bridge and turned my attention to the life rafts. The *American Leader* had five rafts in addition to two life boats. The rafts were simply wooden boxes, each containing four empty fifty-five-gallon drums for flotation. They were mounted on steel frames attached at an angle to the ship's rail and held in place by two wires which came over the top and down to the deck to a pelican hook, a quick release device. A manila line (a painter) temporarily tethered the raft to the ship. Other lines, with knots spaced at suitable intervals (called man ropes) were attached to the rail to be thrown over and serve as means for the crew to safely reach the rafts.

There were three rafts on the forward deck, and when I was clear of the deck cargo I was standing under the solitary port side raft, which I decided to release. I used my flashlight to locate the pelican hook, but when I released it, the raft didn't fall. I flashed the light about to determine the problem, saw nothing, and decided to get out of there, scrambling past the cargo winches to go to the raft directly opposite on the starboard side. Seconds later, the area on the port side where the Germans had seen my light, was deluged with automatic gunfire. It was an absolute Fourth of July fireworks display as the tracers flew over. Fortunately, the two big cargo winches and the mast house protected me. When the firing ceased, I stood up and knocked off the release ring on the pelican hook for this raft and, dammit, it wouldn't fall! Apparently, as the ship was going down by the stern, the rafts' weights were transferred to the side of the frameworks causing enough friction to prevent them from sliding downward. One raft remained, further forward between hatches number 1 and 2. Maintaining a very low profile, I worked my way up along side number 2 hatch and released the hook on this raft. No luck there either. I remembered, however, that the deck crew had been working in this area during my 12:00-4:00 afternoon watch (doing what, I cannot now recall) but I found a few pieces of wood—planks and timbers—against the bulwarks. It was rather bright as flames leapt up from the aft side of the amidship house, illuminating the area. I seized a board, and in desperation pushed and shoved. Ultimately, I prevailed and with a *whoosh* and a splash, the raft went into the ocean. If the man ropes were there, I couldn't find them. Panic? Probably. The vessel was definitely going down by the stern, and I was on the bow, which was rising. Going forward to where the painter was made fast, I grabbed it, swung myself over the side, and, hand over hand, started down. Very soon, I began to be tossed about in the air, as the raft, rising and falling in the sea, alternately slacked and stretched the painter. At one point, I hit the ship. This caused me to decide to let go and fall into the water. It seemed as though I was a long time under. The steel helmet certainly didn't contribute to my buoyancy. As I approached the raft, Blackie Kalloch, one of our seamen, came down the side of the ship. (The man ropes *were* there!)

Ordinary Seaman Karl H. "Blackie" Kalloch and the author in Rockland, Maine, Summer 1978.

I feared that he would let the painter go, so I called to him. Others, by the time I reached the raft, were coming down, so he wasn't about to release it. The second starboard side raft was also now in the water and men were boarding it.

Several problems faced us. On the main deck, starboard side, at number 4 hatch, there were a dozen or so barrels of kerosene or diesel oil. These had been hit, were exploding, and the ignited oil was flowing out the scuppers onto the ocean. This effectively cut off any movement of the rafts in that direction. Furthermore, as the bow continued to rise, the hull created a sort of large sail. We were tucked in the lee, up against what was once the underwater plating, with nothing to grasp. About this time, the second torpedo hit. Fortunately, it was on the port side—away from us—and we experienced only the noise and the partial sight of the column of water that accompanied it. From that point headway was made with the raft. We managed to claw our way around the bow, and the ship moved away from us.

Other memories remain. First, as we drifted around the bow, I was astounded to see many holes in the hull, with tongues of fire spurting out. *We didn't have scuppers there*, I thought to myself, not realizing that these were shell hits which had set the cargo afire. The fire in the deckhouse was now literally sky high, which was of immeasurable aid as we began to hear calls for help and we could direct the swimmers to us. One who we picked up was Pat Trotta of the Stewards Department. Another rescue was almost comical in its dialogue. "Help," we heard.

"Who is it?" someone replied.

"Freddie," came the answer.

"Freddie who?"

"Freddie Potocny!" We hauled him aboard.

That we were able to get over the side and onto the rafts is attributable to the actions of Pat Paris and Frank Stallman. When the first salvo hit the *American Leader*, Pat, fearlessly, went down to the control platform, deep in the ship. He found Frank, who had not left his station. They quickly discussed the probabilities of what was happening. The telephone to the navigating bridge was inoperable, as was the engine room telegraph (ERT), a mechanical device which transmitted engine orders from the bridge to the engine room. When the skylight shattered and it and other debris rained down on them they rang up "stop" on the ERT and shut down both engines. Thus, by the time we on deck decided to go overboard, the vessel was dead in the water, both literally and figuratively. People such as Trotta and Potocny, who had jumped into the ocean, were not left behind in the wake. The successfully launched rafts remained in close proximity. Eventually, after taking a ferocious beating from the 10.5 cm and 15 cm guns, plus the two torpedoes, and the smaller, rapid fire guns, the *American Leader*, with the deck house engulfed in flames, slid noiselessly, stern first into the depths of the South Atlantic Ocean. "There goes our ship," solemnly pronounced one of the castaways. The fire went out. We clung to each other in the darkness. Our position was 34° 24' S, 2° 00' E, about 850 miles west of Capetown.

There were twenty-three of us on an eight-by-ten-foot box, certified to carry only eighteen persons. None of us had seen our attacker. We did not know what hit us. We were aware we had taken two torpedoes and assumed that our assailant was a submarine. Yet there had been that tremendous amount of shellfire and machine gunning. What conversation there was concerned our collective well-being. Most were in good shape, but several appeared to be sick or wounded. The sea constantly broke over us drenching everyone to the skin, and leaving behind globs of congealed coconut oil and diesel fuel. It is highly probable the raft had been hit by bullets and shell fragments, and could well have been sinking under us.

As mentioned earlier, the *Michel's* KTB covering this action did not survive the war. Thus, there is no record of the amount of ammunition expended to destroy our ship and kill our shipmates. It was later insinuated by one of the German crew that she was difficult to sink, and went down very slowly. Another German source said they fired about 150 rounds from the 10.5 cm and the six 15 cm guns. This is not out of line when compared with actual cases. The *Michel's* KTB from October 8, 1942, onward, survived the war and carries detailed reports on the sinking of three vessels, including ammunition consumption, as follows:

	15 cm	10.5 cm	3.7 cm	2 cm
Sawokla	90	15	244	202
Eugenia Livanos	100	11	104	178
Empire March	64	16	149	191

A variety of projectiles were fired by these guns. All were high explosive; the 10.5 cm also used incendiary shells, and, as mentioned in the English Channel battle account, star shells. The forward and after 15 cm guns generally used shells with nose fuses, designed to explode on contact. The forward 15 cm projectiles were fitted with tracers, as were the 3.7 cm and 2 cm bullets. The gun in number 2 hatch and the gun aft of the stack utilized shells with bottom fuses which allowed them to penetrate the target before detonating.

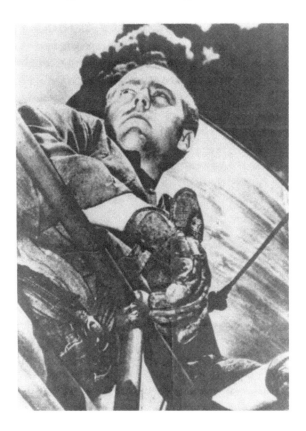

Able Seaman Kenneth J. Pride.

At least an hour, perhaps longer, transpired, and then someone suddenly blurted, "There's a sub!" The dark shape of a vessel emerged out of the night. Submarine or surface ship? No one could tell, but our assumptions being that a submarine had sunk our ship, led us to believe that this oncoming shadow was indeed a submarine. We watched in silence. Each man had his own thoughts, but they held a common thread: this was a Jap, and he'd machine gun us if he saw us. Then, incredibly, a light came on and we could see it was a surface ship. A freighter? The light illuminated the side of the vessel, and, as we watched, four or five figures came out of the water and clambered up nettings which hung from the deck. Encouraged and emboldened by this sight, I decided to reveal our position. Shershun and I were the only officers on the raft, so, technically, I was in command. Fortuitously, my flashlight had survived the dunking, so I blinked "AA AA AA," the common request to commence transmission or attract attention. In a brief time the ship appeared to be coming closer and soon bore down on us. At the last moment, she turned away and from the deck came shouts, unquestionably in German. Then splashes were heard nearby as their heaving lines missed their mark and fell into the sea. Kenneth Pride, one of our able seamen, wanted to swim for the lines, but as we could not see them, I discouraged him. Either we drifted, or the ship moved away, as the gap between us widened. Although the night remained quite dark, I could readily see her details in silhouette.

Suddenly, we received another surprise. A life boat, under oars, with an officer in the stern sheets, materialized. As he neared us, this fellow called out, "How many men do you have?"

"Twenty-three," I replied.

"How many wounded?" To this I responded,

"None seriously."

"Gut," he said, "I will tow you."

After a few minutes of straining at the oars, the line that he had given us parted. He then informed me that he would come alongside and take half of our number. This was accomplished without difficulty, and he headed back to his ship. This man's actions were a superb example of seamanship. Who of the five merchant skippers he was, I have never been able to determine. In 1987 I met two of them, Kpt. Carl Cords and Kpt. Heinrich Heitmann, but then, unfortunately, did not know of their possible involvement with me. Whatever, this man, out on the South Atlantic Ocean in a small boat propelled by half dozen oarsmen, left his ship, found the raft he was looking for, returned to his ship, and then repeated the procedure—without a light being shown.

Between the boat's trips, thus prior to their return to pick up me and the second group, I debated with myself. To go, or not to go? If I remained on the raft, South Africa was about 850 miles away. If I drifted thirty miles a day—and if I was fortunate—I'd make it in a month. I believed that the prevailing winds and current were such that I would easily be carried to the east—and the continent. And I remembered the ships that we had seen along our track out of Capetown. Others probably followed. In the final analysis, though, reason lost out, and the desire for personal comfort took over. I was so wet, so cold, and so miserable. The thoughts of how dry and comfortable a ship could be, swept over me. I recalled the times in the schoolship *Nantucket* when on raw, dank days at sea, we'd sit on the gratings around the smokestack and enjoy the warm air rushing upward from the fire room. I wanted something hot to drink. I wanted off that rocking, tossing, slippery raft. That it could be sinking wasn't any motivation. I wished I hadn't kicked out of my shoes when I hit the water. The fact I was becoming a prisoner of war did penetrate my mental state, so I unbuckled my holster belt and dropped the revolver into the ocean. My abandon-ship packet and camera were gone, having popped out of my uniform jacket pockets. The only items the Germans found on me were a laminated crew list for the number 1 life boat and my flashlight.

When the boat returned for the remaining survivors, I was the last person off the raft. Still wearing my uniform jacket, I half jumped, half stumbled aboard. The first German I met face to face was as astonished as I was benumbed. He was the stroke oarsman, and grasping my sleeve, peered at the gold braid and the star. "*Amerikaner?*" he questioned. They had just gone through a brisk action, and now this rescue, and it was not until the final survivor was plucked from the sea did they, or at least these particular men, know the nationality of the ship they had just sent to the bottom.

On the raider, typical German efficiency swiftly evidenced itself. As soon as I had climbed the net and reached the main deck, two crewmen hauled me upright and quickly, looking for weapons, patted me down. They led me forward to a dimly lit companionway, and I was directed down a ladder to where another German indicated I was to strip and toss my clothes onto a heap deposited by those who had preceded me. Watches, rings, and dog tags went to a box. In an adjacent washroom, using rags, hot seawater, and soap which did not lather, those of us who comprised the last group off the raft turned to the task of cleaning the gunk off each other. When passably clean, we were inspected by one of the ship's doctors whose only real interest, it seemed, was determining if anyone was infected with a venereal disease. Our clothing, we later discovered was headed for a steam disinfecting and a washing. The last step in this assembly-line process was wearing apparel. German uniforms, no less! Rough, burlappy off-white bell-bottom trousers and jumpers of the same material with rating badges still sewed to the sleeves.

Other than the twenty-three of us on the raft and the four or five who we saw going up the raider's side, we had no idea how many had survived. To my particular surprise, when we were led down another ladder into a large compartment, we discovered there were many more. In fact, it appeared to be the entire crew, standing silently in an emotionless, dazed wonderment. I seemed to be floating through a pantomime. Nothing was startling, everything was matter of fact. No one expressed concern or voiced a comment. We, the last group to enter the room, were not welcomed or congratulated. It had been a stunning, shattering experience. The traumatic loss of our ship was compounded by the stark reality of our capture. What merchant seaman ever! ever! had given a second's thought to the possibility of being taken prisoner? After a certain finite point was attained, nothing else made an imprint. We were face to face with the enemy, wearing his uniform, and we hardly comprehended the circumstance. My daze was broken by the appearance of a smartly uniformed officer who stepped up on a bench and calmly surveyed us. "For you the war is over!" he pronounced. Then continuing in surprisingly good English, he added, "You are now on board a German warship. Your treatment will be according to your conduct. If you give trouble, you will be punished. We have had Norwegians here and they were not happy, but it was their fault." With that veiled threat, he hopped off his perch and strode out of the room.

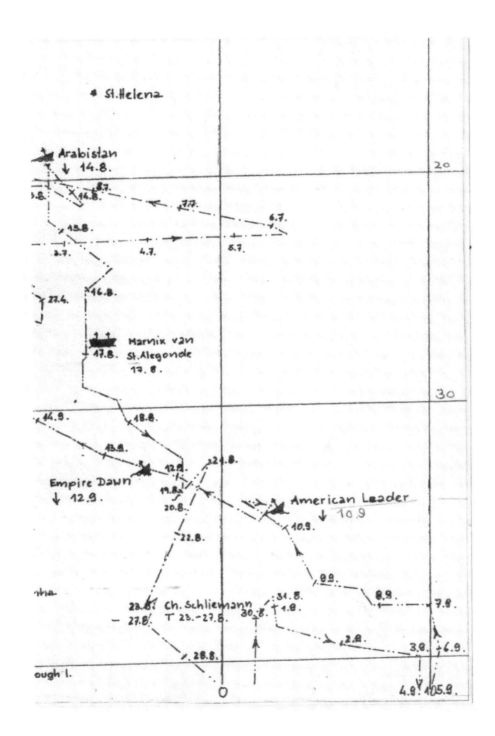

Michel's **track, August 13 to September 14, 1942.**

CHAPTER FOURTEEN

Life in the *Kriegsmarine*

The German crewmen who had been overseeing us were supervised by a burly seaman. He introduced himself in English as Herr Tober, and said that he wanted the officers in a small room which was forward of where we were standing. The remainder of the crew was directed aft to a third room. Mattresses and blankets were available in both places. Beneath us we sensed the pulsating vibration of the engine as the raider proceeded to leave the scene. Our own ship 2,200 fathoms down, our fates precarious, we tried to sleep. Few, if any of us, did. Almost everyone admitted to hallucinations induced by the shock of losing our ship—our home. The explosions, the fires, the black, cold, oily ocean were imprinted upon the subconsciousness of each of us, played and replayed as an endless movie. Eventually, the speakers of the public address system in the rooms brought the martial music of reveille. Tober and his assistants appeared carrying kettles of black, bitter, *ersatz* coffee, loaves of sour, heavy, black bread with a crust that defied one's jaws, and large tins of *Vier Früchte* (four fruits) marmalade, which tasted like turnip, turnip, turnip, and turnip. We—accustomed to as many eggs in the morning as we pleased, cooked any way we wished, with bacon or sausage—simply nibbled at what we didn't realize was the standard German morning meal. Many of my compatriots, I'm sure as I did, thought that the proffered food was a snack accommodatingly provided by our hosts and waited, in disappointment, for breakfast.

The next event was the arrival of an officer who said that he required a crew list. Captain Pedersen referred him to me, which was understandable, as I had been doing the *American Leader*'s paper work throughout our voyage. This officer, who was a doctor, gave me a pad of lined paper and a pencil, and I quickly worked up a roster for him. He told me who he had in his hospital; I checked off the names of all around me, and in the other room, thus learning the number—eleven—and identities of our lost shipmates. They were, alphabetically,

Able Seaman Frans Arvio

Frans Arvio

Messman Alfred S. Bradberry
Engineer Cadet Joseph C. DiCicco
Electrician Charles W. Feeney

Charles Wakefield Feeney, Jr.

Chief Steward Joseph P. Medicis
Carpenter Felix E. Nordfors

Felix E. Nordfors

Seaman 2/c Charles T. Ragland, USN
Chief Engineer George W. Schabel
Junior Third Engineer Oliver O. Schneider

Oliver O. Schneider

Junior Engineer Marshall R. Soper
Deck Cadet Gordon A. Tyne

He then asked me for a physical description of each missing man. Apparently, we were back at the scene of the previous evening's action, and in the floating debris, a body had been found and retrieved. The Germans deemed it imprudent to allow any of us to view the remains, but by process of elimination the doctor and I determined that the body was that of Joseph Carlo DiCicco, the *American Leader*'s seventeen-year-old cadet engineer. The doctor left, and I kept the pad and pencil, the first of many items that stuck to my fingers in the next two months.

A note of interest concerning the raider's return to the site is that had I remained on the raft, instead of giving in to the wet and the cold, my attempt to elude capture would have been for naught. And that is assuming the raft remained afloat all night. Picture the scene: shipwrecked castaway wildly and enthusiastically waving to oncoming freighter, and watching as she stops and puts a large motor boat in the water. The boat approaches the raft and he warily takes note of a machine gun carrying sailor on the forward deck, then, unbelieving, catches sight of the swastika-clutching eagles on the other crew member's caps. Germans! It didn't happen that way, but it could have. Almost as a rule, on the morning following a sinking the *Michel* returned to the scene of the previous night's action. They were essentially a secret operation and did not wish to leave any trace of their presence. Thus, that morning, any of the *American Leader*'s lifeboats and life rafts still afloat were destroyed (after salvaging the chocolate and pemmican, which were delicacies to them). It was on one of the rafts that Joe DiCicco's body was found. Additionally, items such as life rings and lifeboat equipment carrying the ship's name were sought, to be mounted as trophies in the crew's recreation room. Also, this particular morning, the *Michel* crew was astounded to see thousands of bales of rubber, part of the *American Leader*'s cargo, bobbing in the sea.

Before returning to the sinking site, the *Michel*'s lookouts had spotted another ship and attempted to close on her. This vessel saw the *Michel* and changed course. Von Ruckteschell instituted a chase, but after an hour decided to break it off in favor of returning to the position of the *American Leader*'s demise. There, the torpedo boat was launched to pick up whatever flotsam remained. In the early afternoon, with the torpedo boat still in the water, the masts of another ship poked up over the horizon. The boat was retrieved, but with some difficulty, according to Konrad Hoppe. Von Ruckteschell began maneuvering his vessel to get ahead of the target even though his radio room reported a nearby ship using its radio.

At dusk that, evening, Tober escorted Captain Pedersen, Chief Officer Hickey, and First Assistant Engineer Paris out of our quarters and up to the main deck. There, after sundown, in dress uniform, stood *Kapitän zur See der Reserve* Hellmuth von Ruckteschell, several officers, and an honor guard of German seamen. On the rail was the canvas-shrouded body of Cadet DiCicco, covered with an American flag. In a brief bi-lingual ceremony, von Ruckteschell said, as later reported by Captain Pedersen, "If all the people of the world held each other in the same respect as their seamen do, we would not be in this terrible situation on board here tonight." Years later, one of those present, Flying Officer Konrad Hoppe, translated his commander's German remarks into, "The mutual understanding of all seafarers between each other, if also applied between all people in the world, would have spared us the terrible war and all the suffering which followed." Different words. Same message.

Months later, following the sinking of the British freighter *Empire March*, von Ruckteschell conducted another burial service and entered a translation in his KTB of January 3, 1943. It is written,

> *Seamen, before us lies a comrade who, with 22 missing shipmates, became the victim of our bullets. The art of medicine was not able to save him. Now we stand, friend and enemy, in front of his bier, like children who have destroyed a toy—and are sorry. We think: we sailors of this whole earth feel no personal hatred towards each other. We know the sea and its breadth. It is large enough for all the people of this earth. This we know very well. We are through our profession destined to be carriers of peace, to join people together, and to exchange goods, of which this earth has plenty, and to lead people to each other. Otherwise, what do ships exist for? Our*

comrade before us shall remind us of the following: this war demonstrates that the whole world can work to destroy itself, even if it costs millions in gold Pounds. The times before this have demonstrated to you that no nation is willing to give peacefully even one cent to another.

Rather, the human being allows millions of tons of food to be spoiled, surrounds itself with unemployment, and others go hungry. We will promise our dead comrade to examine ourselves, that the blindness may leave us, and that we will try to cease this collective work of destruction which all the people of the earth today set against each other, and to better work towards reconstruction and peace.

Thus, the souls of our dead comrades find a bridge to the Kingdom of the Sun, into which they will enter, and receptive hearts by we who remain here, to whom they send back power and force, will work better than before.

We knew they were after another ship, because in the latter part of the afternoon we had been brought up on deck, ostensibly for fresh air and the opportunity to stretch our legs. Considerable activity was witnessed. Numerous officers peered over the windscreen on the navigating bridge. Many lookouts were aloft, including two in the swivel chairs at the mast trucks. A man who was to relieve one of the latter was seen being assisted in the donning of his leather, full body protective suit. Other crew members busied themselves about the deck house. Why we were allowed to see all of this is an interesting question. Probably they were just "showing off" to give us a lesson as to how we had been under surveillance a day earlier.

Two other interesting surprises were dealt to us that first day. Very soon, we became aware of the presence on board of the four Chinese men who, we correctly assumed, were survivors of an earlier victim. They had the run of the ship, spoke no English, and, in fact, had but one word in their non-Cantonese vocabulary: *Ros*. A common greeting in the German language is, or at least it was in those days, "*Was ist los?*" which translates into "What's happening?" So these poor souls had grasped the last word, their tongues couldn't pronounce the *l*, and they literally ran around the *Michel* greeting everyone, crew and prisoners alike, with *Ros! Ros! Ros!* Next Tober produced three survivors of the *William F. Humphrey*. Two were merchant seamen William W. Hosey, able seaman, and Philip P. McKeever, fireman/watertender. The other was Machinists Mate 2/c James T. Wilkinson, USN. These men, seriously wounded, had been hospitalized, and were unable to accompany their shipmates when the *Michel* transferred them to the *Charlotte Schliemann* during the August 23-26 rendezvous.

After Joe DiCicco's burial, the three witnesses returned to our little room. Tober closed the watertight door with a slam, dogged it, locked it, and turned off the lights. Not a particularly inviting prospect: sealed in, two decks down, an ammunition locker below us, going into action aboard a German warship. Through the keyhole, I saw a German armed with a machine gun stationed outside. We had no way of knowing how many minutes, or even hours, passed, but suddenly the ship's speed increased as the engine's tempo picked up and we heeled over to port, indicating a quick course change. Nothing further happened, and eventually Tober reappeared, wordlessly unlocking and undogging the door so that we had access to the washroom and toilet facility on the deck above. Many years later I questioned Tober about locking us in, with particular interest in who would let us out in an emergency. He didn't have a ready answer, inferring only that "someone" would. I pressed with the knowledge that when the *Michel* was lost she took an unknown number of Norwegians, probably nineteen, with her. These were survivors of the *Höegh Silverdawn* and the *Ferncastle*. Tober acknowledged that, but blamed the raider's officers for not ordering the release of the doomed men.

The intended victim could have been the *Empire Dawn*, a British freighter carrying nothing but rock salt (for ballast) bound from Suez to South America to load bauxite. Her captain, William Athol Scott later told me, "On the eleventh we saw a ship about four miles away. That night I made a large alteration of course in case that ship was an enemy and reported us to submarines in the vicinity. The next day we saw nothing."

Geoffrey Sherring, the *Empire Dawn*'s twenty-year-old second radio officer says, "One of the things we had to do was to alter course very sharply after the sun had gone down. This meant, had we been observed by a submarine, she would expect us to carry on in that same direction and would be disappointed to find we'd buzzed off elsewhere as soon as darkness had fallen. We did this with great care every evening as the sun was going down. As soon as it got nice and dark, we switched course, making allowances for this in our calculations of distance run and everything like that. And then altered back roughly to the course we had set.

"On the night of September 11, we altered course after sundown. What we didn't know was that put our scent off the beady-eyed monster who had been watching us most of the day. He went to the attack, and to his surprise, we were not there. The following morning they sent one of their aircraft up to find out where we were. Shadowing us all day, realizing what we had done, they made arrangements to come in a little bit earlier the next evening—before we made our evasive maneuver. I doubt that it would have been a terribly successful thing to have done anyway, because they would have been aware of it this next time."

Indeed, we in the prison quarters heard the Arado take off the next morning (September 12), but Flying Officer Konrad Hoppe takes no credit for discovering anything that day. Thus, the identity of the vessel that was almost attacked on the night of the 11th is not known. What actually happened on that night as the *Michel* closed in and prepared to attack, the German lookouts sighted yet another vessel. Fearing this second ship was escorting the target and was probably a warship, von Ruckteschell thought he was falling into a trap and abruptly called off the chase.

I still bristle when I recall the ineptness of the Royal Navy's merchant vessel control people in Capetown. For no apparent reason, they held us in port overnight, then let us go, then called us back, then let us go. Additionally, I have since discovered, ALL British merchant ships, when running alone, routinely made a course change after night fall as did the *Empire Dawn*. Capetown didn't advise us in that respect. On the other hand, the masters of the *American Leader* and the *Empire Dawn* had instructions to make scheduled radio contact with shore stations, so there was some commonality. Also, it appears both ships were lulled into false security by being told that after crossing a certain longitude (probably 5° east) we need not post extra lookouts during the day and could relax a bit.

In the evening of the twelfth, Tober again locked us into our prison quarters as the raider prepared for action. The ammunition elevators for the forward 15 cm guns above us clattered and the PA speaker in our room was full of German language chatter. After an interminable silence, there was a whammo, and another, and another. This went on sporadically, and I recall some nervous laughter among us, to which Captain Pedersen objected. "Gentlemen," he said, "men are dying out there. We should respect them."

After being tracked most of the day, the *Empire Dawn* suddenly found itself under fire. Chaos erupted. "The first thing I heard," wrote Geoffrey Sherring,

> was a shout and running footsteps. Somebody said there was a steamer. I thought this was a ship on collision course. Within moments . . . I heard a double bang, and what I was dead sure were two shells going over my head like an express train. As I was on watch, I ran up the motor generator, tentatively tried the big transmitter, and got started with an RRRR call which you repeat three times to signify you are being attacked by a raider. By the time I got my third RRRR out, the current

was already fading, the lights were going dim, and then they went out. I switched over to the battery powered emergency set and attempted the RRRR sequence again. Looking at the emergency set dials, I found that I was getting no outgoing signal. By this time, I realized that there was little point in staying around the wireless room, so I looked for some way of getting out onto the navigating bridge.

Eventually, Sherring made it to the main deck, meeting a group of wounded crew members, and Captain Scott, who was suffering from a serious head wound. Moving toward the stern, which was rising as the ship was then beginning to sink bow first, he came across the badly wounded chief steward and the bosun. Sherring continued,

> I had by this time, only seen the raider once or twice, because I had been looking at things concerning my ship. This ship in the middle distance, lobbing shells into us, was merely an irritation. All the things going through my head related to the belief that no such ship existed. I thought this was some ghastly mistake. All I could say to myself was, "Dammit, I'll give these buggars hell when we get aboard! They must have made the most dreadful mistake." It didn't occur to us to believe or it certainly didn't occur to me to believe, that these were Germans operating three days out of Capetown.

Sherring, the bosun, and the chief steward, went into the ocean and were found by *Esau*, along with twenty-two other survivors of the *Empire Dawn*'s forty-four-man complement. Their experiences upon boarding the *Michel* parallel those of the *American Leader* crew, but with one significant difference. Sometime after the firing ceased there was activity in the stairwell outside our little room. I again positioned myself at the keyhole and espied a British merchant marine officer, in his uniform jacket with its distinctive diamond woven between the stripes, being escorted to the tween deck area where we had congregated two nights earlier. He, apparently, had been taken off the *Empire Dawn* by the *Esau* crew without getting his feet wet and, thus, escaped the hot salt water initiation.

At this juncture there were eight of us in the room: Captain Pedersen, Hickey, Paris, Stallman, Kamins, Shershun, Dryer, and me. Walter Lee was in the *Michel*'s sickbay with a severe shrapnel wound in one knee, and Joe Cohen was being held incommunicado. In the morning, Tober led the surviving *Empire Dawn*'s officers in to join us. They were Third Engineer Jimmie Laverick, Second Officer Roy Neal, Third Radio Officer Leonard Prout, Second Radio Officer Geoffrey Sherring, and Chief Engineer James Young.

Captain Scott's head injury confined him in the *Michel*'s sick bay with Walter Lee. I have no memory of these two men joining us at any time in our cramped little room down at the waterline. In any case, we were in a precarious and unenviable predicament, prisoners of war on board a German *Hilfskreuzer*, which we fully believed would be quickly tracked down and sunk. Our locked-up, lights-out experiences of the two previous nights gave us unmistakable evidence of what would happen if and when an Allied warship came over the horizon.

As mentioned earlier, twenty-five of the *Empire Dawn* crew survived the sinking. Three of them were severely wounded, one passing away that night in the raider's operating room. This was not disclosed to us, nor was the death of a second man on the fourteenth, and a third on the fifteenth. It is not known if any of these fellows were accorded the same ceremonial burial at sea as was given Joe DiCicco and the seaman off the *Empire March* in early 1943. If they were, none of the *Empire Dawn*'s officers were in attendance.

Meanwhile, we, the *American Leader* survivors, began putting together our recollections of the attack and the sinking and the fates of our eleven lost shipmates. The consensus, is as follows:

Able Seaman Arvio: Was in the habit of walking on the after deck every evening from 1930 to 2000 (before his watch). No survivor recalls seeing him at any time during the attack.

Messman Bradberry: On the after deck before the ship sank. Some say that he was seen in the water.

Cadet DiCicco: Was with Chief Engineer Schabel and Third Engineer Kamins at onset of action. His later movements are unknown. Survivors who were picked up by the *Michel* from number four liferaft say that they left a body which was pulled aboard the raider. Others from this raft deny that. In any case, during the following morning, the *Michel*'s torpedo boat found a raft containing a badly disfigured body, which, as recounted previously, was deemed to be that of Cadet DiCicco.

Electrician Engineer Feeney: Went to Emergency Generator Room when attack began and was later on boat deck outside his room. Several people claimed to have seen him in the water. It is doubtful that he was wearing a life preserver, and he may have swam away from the burning oil cascading from the barrels on deck.

Chief Steward Medicis: Severely wounded in or near his cabin. Was carried out by unknown crew members to the starboard boat deck. Supposedly an arm or a leg had been shot off. Captain Pedersen stated that he saw a body on the starboard bridge wing. Why should the Chief Steward have been there? No evidence as to this man's fate or of those preceding him in this narrative exists.

Carpenter Nordfors: Also was on after deck attempting to control fires. Perhaps he and Bradberry went into the sea and did not find a raft.

Seaman 2/c Ragland: Was on watch at the four-inch gun on the stern. He could have been calling the relieving watch, but no one recalls seeing him at any time, so he was probably killed at his station.

Chief Engineer Schabel: Was on after deck with Third Engineer Kamins and Cadet DiCicco during early minutes of the attack. May have been caught later in his room, or been killed on deck. Also, may have gone into the water with Electrician Engineer Feeney before vessel lost its way and came to a stop.

Fourth Engineer Schneider: As recounted, I picked him up outside my cabin and dragged him outside. No one knows what happened to him after that.

Junior Engineer Soper: Was on watch in the engine room. According to Second Assistant Engineer Frank Stallman, went down to the lower flat to start fire pumps. Eventually, left the engine room. Some claim to have seen him in the water.

Cadet Tyne: Was with a group attempting to launch the port lifeboat. At this time he had probably been wounded. When the raider resumed firing he was heard to cry out that he was hit, and he was not seen after that.

Concerning Arvio and Ragland, after the war the *Michel*'s first officer, Wolfgang Erhardt, describing the raider's tactics, said it was routine to simultaneously open fire with the 15 cm and 3.7 cm guns. The larger concentrated their fire on the target's deckhouse attempting to destroy the navigating bridge and radio room. The smaller, mounted on the focsl and poop deck, swept the corresponding positions of the target vessel in order to kill any men stationed there and to prevent others from manning guns which may have been located in those areas. He proudly defended this practice, recounting how the *Michel* had attacked fifteen ships, and only one had managed to get off a retaliatory shot.

We remained in the *Michel* for twenty-seven days which were, other than the two nights' involvements with the *Empire Dawn*, claustrophobic boredom. In the beginning we were brought up to the weather deck each day for a single hour of fresh air and casual exercise. For the final eighteen days, though, that activity was suspended. The *Stier* was in the vicinity. The *Tannenfels* arrived on the twenty-first, the *Uckermark* on the twenty-fifth. Von Ruckteschell, always on guard, gave us no opportunity to catch a glimpse of these vessels in the remote chance that we would be rescued by our own forces and be able to provide descriptions. As seamen, it was no secret to us that other ships were present. From inside our little room the sounds of visiting boats bumping alongside were unmistakable. The PA system revealed bits of information. Strange officers came down to informally "inspect" us. The smell of frying potatoes and onions recently received from the *Tannenfels* or the *Uckermark* told us fresh provisions had come on board. In our naiveté we never imagined the Germans having such a presence in the South Atlantic. These fresh supplies, we conjectured, had come from a neutral South American country, some place with Nazi leanings. In addition to the potatoes and onions, the *Tannenfels* also delivered quantities of cooking oil, rice, dried bananas, canned fish, Japanese beer in 3/4 liter bottles, and many cartons of civilian clothing for Japan. The *Uckermark* brought bunker oil, ammunition, torpedoes, and most important, twenty-two bags of mail some of which was postmarked in late August. Although welcome, the letters carried unpleasant news of bombings and deaths. Konrad Hoppe heard from his family for the first time following the loss of his brother Hans, a medical orderly, on the Russian front. "His sister wrote as usual," he said, "in her very pessimistic mood."

There were few exceptions to our confinement. Once a week, Tober roused us out before dawn and herded us to the open deck where each man was issued a washbasin of fresh water for a full body wash. We had all developed a particularly pungent body odor none of us had ever experienced. The German soap did little to overcome it. On one of those mornings a vessel was seen headed toward us, about three miles off, but too far away to be distinguished as a tanker or a freighter or another raider. The three daily trips to the galley were always via below deck passageways. And that brings me to the most distressing aspect of all. Food. Or better said, lack of it.

Next to the traumatic experience of having our ship sunk from under us, the German food had to be the shocker of the *Kriegsmarine* experience. The black bread to which we had been introduced in our first morning on board was the staple of the diet. Twice a day, morning and evening, it was issued. Tober allowed us to keep a loaf and maybe part of a loaf in our bread box, but carefully monitored the stock. The cooks issued as much as they would to any group of fourteen Germans, but as we ate it rather sparingly, he frequently returned the surplus. Ever since, I have described that bread as "deck sweepings and sawdust." Can you imagine my delight when in 1997, through the good graces of Joseph P.

O'Donnell of Robinsville NJ, the American ex-prisoners of war monthly *Ex-POW Bulletin* printed the following:

> Former prisoners of war of Nazi Germany may be interested in this recipe for WWII Black Bread. This recipe comes from the official record from the Food Providing Ministry, published (Top Secret), Berlin, 24.XI (November 24) 1941, Directors in Ministry Herr Mansfeld and Herr Moritz. It was agreed that the best mixture to make Black Bread was:
>
> 50 % bruised rye grain
> 20 % sliced sugar beets
> 20 % tree flour (sawdust)
> 10 % minced tree leaves and straw

I was close!

Meals were simple, and predictable. In the morning with the black bread and the *ersatz* coffee came the "four-fruits marmalade" or molasses. In the evening, there was a meat paste to be spread on the black bread or a few slices of *Wurst* as the makings of a sandwich, plus tea. The noon meal, the main meal of the day, alternated between (a) *Bohnesuppe* (bean soup) with lentils and chopped *Würstchen* (hot dogs), and (b) *Kartoffeln* (potatoes—in our case, always the dehydrated type), a vegetable (here I ate my first Brussels sprouts), and the inevitable *Wurst* or meat paste. On a few instances canned whale meat was substituted for the latter two delicacies.

The routine was that Tober would yell down the ladder, "*Essen! Essen!*" He'd then tell us what sort of pots or pans were needed. As a rule, I went to the galley for our (the American and British officers) rations. Perhaps at noon, someone would accompany me, otherwise I preferred to go it alone, nosing into the odd alleyway or compartment. I wore my jacket with the stripe-and-a-half and the star on the sleeve, so that when I wandered into a place where I should not have gone, the German sailors gave me a certain respect, turned me around, and eased me out. Of interest is the fact that we ate what the German crew ate. And in the same quantity. I'd stand in the mess line with the Germans and when it came my turn I'd tell the cook *vierzehn Männer* (fourteen men) and he would dollop out my rations. If we were being shortchanged, I never knew it. Other than the dehydrated potatoes, one exception, however, has come to light. Around the middle of our stay in the raider, one of the pigs was slaughtered providing the makings of a fresh supply of *Wurst*. I doubt we shared in this. Had we, I am sure

Tober would have commented on the fact, and the German benevolence toward their captives.

Earlier, I mentioned the fact Joe Cohen was being held incommunicado. This was revealed when I made up the crew list with the doctor on the first morning. Joe was Jewish, and we feared for his well-being. In his position as radio officer he could have had information of value to the Germans. After four or five days he did join us, but made no comments as to what had transpired. Another who was in a precarious position was Eric Kamins, who had been born in Germany. I believe he did not speak German. Nevertheless, he confronted each survivor and earnestly pleaded his case. "Don't tell them about me!" Captain Pedersen, Hickey, Shershun, and I were interrogated, probably by First Officer Erhardt and Navigator Rödel. I never saw either man again. The questions asked of me did not relate to the voyage or the cargo. Instead, they were interested in my training and education, and my watch standing routine. They also probed into my family. What was my father's occupation? How much money did he earn? There were political queries as well. What did I think of Hitler? Mussolini? Roosevelt? Looking back, I feel the two Germans were more curious than anything else. Certainly, none of what I had to say was worth a coded short signal to the SKL.

In the first few days on board the raider, the American and British seamen, oilers, wipers, cooks, bakers, waiters, and bedroom stewards were put to work doing odd jobs for the Germans. Other than the above mentioned exercise hour, the officers were confined to quarters. We had been given the opportunity to go to work, but Captain Pedersen spoke for all with a firm "No." I would have liked to have gotten out and done a little chipping and painting or brass polishing or splicing in return for what intelligence I could garner. Perhaps if I were the only officer to volunteer, I'd have been given something of a supervisory nature. I'll never know.

So, bosun Stan Gorski took over as the prisoners were assigned about the ship performing such tasks as washing paintwork, walloping pots and pans in the galley, and helping the German sailors in their mundane maintenance chores. For three full days and part of a fourth, just before the arrival of the *Tannenfels*, by the process of transferring ballast, the *Michel* was heeled well over, first to starboard then to port, to allow her men to put a coat of paint on the hull. Red lead was applied on those areas that were ordinarily below the waterline, standard light gray on the topsides. This gave her the appearance of a vessel fresh from shipyard, not one six months at sea. A carnival-like atmosphere existed. Martial music blared from the loud speakers. Every available German sailor was dropped over the side on a staging or in a bosun's chair. Others manning inflatable rubber boats tackled hard to reach areas. The prisoners tended the lines on deck and refilled the paint pots.

For us in our little room, the hours and days dragged by. Captain Pedersen, Hickey, Laverick, and Young played cards, usually bridge. I kept busy with two projects. Possessing some talent as a draftsman and artist, I conned Tober into giving me a quantity of paper and a pencil to supplement what I had already purloined from the doctor. With these I produced sketches of the *American Leader* and sold them to the Germans (see page 246). She was a standard C-1 class freighter with nothing of particular note in her appearance that could be of aid or assistance to the enemy. In secret, I was carefully estimating the *Michel*'s features, and translating them into a scale drawing of her. (More on that later.) The other business was the manufacture of rope sole sandals. Out of my earlier experiences as a Boy Scout, Sea Scout, and cadet in the *Nantucket*, had come a high degree of knot tying and associated fancy work capability. Tober obligingly found a length of old Manila rope, scraps of canvas, plus a sailor's palm, needles, wax, and twine. I unlaid the rope, then laboriously broke down each strand to its individual lengths of rope yarn. I then took eight pieces of the yarn and braided them into many yards of flat sennett. This was sewn, flat side to flat side, creating a long oval to form the sole. For the toe strap I used the canvas. What price I put on them, I cannot recall. Probably a few cigarettes (the same currency received for my *American Leader* sketches), which I swapped for clothing or candy. One memory I do have, however, is on departure from the *Michel* my wardrobe consisted of an extra khaki shirt, a necktie, and a pair of British Army boots, over and above the underwear, shirt, sweater, and trousers, and uniform jacket in which I arrived.

An interesting sidelight of the interaction between the *Michel* crew and the prisoners was that von Ruckteschell decreed that his officers, except Otto Saupe, have no contact with us. Yet the combined working parties allowed the American and British seamen, especially Gorski, to administer many subtle, and some not so subtle, messages to the younger unsophisticated *Seemanne*. Arriving on deck in the morning, eyes sweeping the horizon, Stan would announce to all within hearing range, "They're coming! Cruiser boats! Americans! Not one. Two. One comes in close to see who you are, the other stays a few miles out. You shoot at the first one, number two sinks you!" Then there were the blunt comparisons of the multiple choice menus offered on American merchant ships with the black-bread-dominated *Michel* fare. Descriptions of fresh baked muffins and rolls for the morning and afternoon coffee breaks, and the cold cuts and desserts left in the refrigerator for night lunches were met with disbelief, but the seeds were planted. Hints of secret American weapons, such as super powerful depth charges, were dropped. Statements such as "We can build ships faster than you can sink them" certainly gave the youngsters something to think about. But the best psywar trick of all came at the expense of the commander himself—von Ruckteschell. He never knew it, of course, and we were the only beneficiaries, but what a boost to our moral it was.

We knew the names of the ships sunk by the *Michel*. It is unbelievable that, after groups of prisoners had been transferred to the *Charlotte Schliemann* and *Doggerbank*, the vacated prison quarters did not receive a thorough search. In our very first days, notes secreted by the previous occupants came to light. Commencing with the *Patella*, each group of survivors added its ship's name and the date of sinking to numerous slips of paper. In 1989, in Peterborough, New Hampshire, I visited Charles Kelleher who was in the MS *Sawokla*, the *Michel*'s next victim after we had left. When he greeted me at the door, his first words were, "George Duffy! Who would ever have thought, over forty-six years after I found your hidden message in the German raider, you would walk into my kitchen!" In this manner we learned of the *Gloucester Castle*. From the *Patella*'s Chinese came primitive sign-language indications of women and children being aboard. Our British friends from the *Empire Dawn* said the *Gloucester Castle* was a small combination passenger/cargo vessel, and in all probability it was from her sinking the passengers were rescued. Stan Gorski went to work.

Armed with this information, one day on deck he related to Gustav Tober and a few wide-eyed German sailors a most believable tale. Back in Capetown, he told them, the South African government had posted bulletins throughout the city offering a £5,000 reward for information leading to the identity of the German "pirate" captain responsible for the loss of the well-known *Gloucester Castle* and the deaths of so many of her crew and passengers. Swiftly, this news was carried to von Ruckteschell. At once, all prisoners, with the exception of those in sick bay, were assembled below decks in front of the Commander and a few of his officers and crew. *Oberleutnant* Jürgen Herr read, in excellent English, the translation of his captain's deep concern about the price on his head. "Would the Allies put women and children on ammunition trains? Of course not," he added. "So why do they put them on ships traveling blacked out at night?" von Ruckteschell described himself as a gentleman whose father was a clergyman and whose sister was the leader of a religious order in Düsseldorf. He wanted to be able to travel to Great Britain and the United States after the war and not be considered a criminal. The diatribe went on for fully ten minutes.

Of course, there had never been any posters or bulletins. From Gustav Tober all the way to the commander, the Germans swallowed the fiction. Phineas T. Barnum said it best: "There's a sucker born every minute." He would have loved this story.

On September 27, an incident occurred that, had we known of it, would have cheered us immensely. The petty officer who has been quoted in prior pages wrote, "Trouble on the bridge. Something has happened to the *Stier* and *Tannenfels*. There is an officers' conference." Konrad Hoppe says, "I was at that meeting. All we had heard was a message from the *Tannenfels* saying 'Come to this point' and nothing else. I had worked up a special code to be used by us and the *Stier*. We had decided on a special wavelength, but Gerlach failed to use it. I recommended that we not go to the position because we were not told the problem. The Commander agreed. In retrospect, we could have gone, but at the time we assumed the *Stier* and *Tannenfels* were engaged with a warship. Terrible! The provisioning was terminated. All *Uckermark* sailors had to leave. *Tannenfels* had radioed on the 600 metre band, because it was constantly monitored. That is, of course, understandable. The *Stier* was fighting and on fire, and no one there was thinking clearly, and the special frequency was forgotten." The *Michel* never heard another word from either ship.

What happened is that the two German vessels were together, stopped and drifting, with rain falling and visibility two miles or less. Suddenly, a large vessel materialized out of the gloom. The *Stier*'s crew was called to battle stations and the intruder was signaled to stop. Within minutes the *Stier* opened fire with whatever of its 15 cm guns that could be trained on the stranger, which had disregarded the stop order and turned away. This ship soon replied with fire from her own 4-inch gun. The *Stier*, although the faster of the two vessels, was at a disadvantage because five of her six 15 cm guns could not be trained dead ahead. She had to turn away into an almost a broadside posture in order to bring her midship guns to bear, providing a large target. By comparison, the stranger presented a much smaller profile to the raider. In an action lasting barely twenty minutes, both adversaries scored victories: they sank each other! Incredibly, an American Liberty ship, the *Stephen Hopkins*, on its very first voyage, had done the unbelievable. A civilian crew of forty-one and fifteen teenage U.S. Navy gunners had taken on a professional, fully manned German warship and sent it to the bottom. It was not without cost—twenty-seven merchant seamen, ten gunners, and a lone passenger died. The *Stier* lost three men. Everyone else was rescued by the *Tannenfels*, which quickly departed the scene, leaving behind a single life boat and nineteen survivors from the *Stephen Hopkins*. Fifteen of these men reached a small village on the Brazilian shore on October 27, a month to the date of their epic battle.

Little did we know of the effect this mini-sea battle was to have on our fortunes. In the Indian Ocean, on her way from the Far East, the *Tannenfels* had met up with the raider *Thor*. From her she took a hundred-odd merchant seaman survivors of four of the raider's victims: *Olivia* (Dutch), *Herborg* (Norwegian), *Madrono* (Norwegian), and *Indus* (British). According to Konrad Hoppe, the plan was for us to join them and be incarcerated in Europe. Now only the *Uckermark* was available, and she was headed the other way. This was a deferred death sentence for many of the *American Leader* survivors.

Three days later, we were subjected in the morning to a seemingly endless radio broadcast relayed through the ship's public address system. Bands played German marches. Mobs hoarsely screamed "*Sieg Heil! Sieg Heil! Sieg Heil!*" Orators thundered on and on. We had no earplugs, and couldn't shut the thing off. I have since learned this was an appeal for charitable contributions from the German populace for "winter aid" to be given to those poorer citizens facing the coming cold season. Hitler, himself, presided and one of the voices we heard was his. In the midst of the "heiling," and stomping, and trumpet flourishes, Tober stuck his head into our cozy little room. He carefully gazed at each of us to see what we were doing, and when Geoff Sherring caught his eye, Geoff asked him, "*Gustav, was ist das?*" I don't know where Tober could have been all morning to escape this broadcast, but he cocked his head and listened for ten or fifteen seconds. "Ach," he blurted, "dat ees bullsheet!" Four days later we sat through a shorter harangue by, as I later leaned, Hermann Göring, who addressed the German farmers. He told them that they are very important people, and they must be productive.

An activity that broke the boredom to a small extent was the visit each evening by *Kapitänleutnant* Saupe and one of his clerks. We were required to stand and he called the roll. "*Kapitän* Pedersen, Meester Hickey, Meester Doffy, Meester Kamins," and so on. Deeming all hands present, he would then turn to Captain Pedersen and ask, "Do you haf any vishes?" That earned him the sobriquet "Aloysius." Other prisoner groups tagged him simply "Vishes." We had no shaving equipment, so on the second or third night Pedersen pointed that out. The next morning Tober presented us with a razor, a single double-edge blade, a shaving brush, and a small piece of soap. That evening, during his call, Saupe inquired if we had received the material. "*Ja,*" said the Captain, "*danke.*" He then pointed out to Saupe that we had only hot salt water in the washroom, which would not make a satisfactory lather. We needed hot fresh water. The *Leutnant* paused, but then, with a laugh, said, "Ah, *Kapitän*, you are now in the German *Kriegsmarine*. Here you must do vat vee do. In the morning, you take two cups coffee. Vun you trink. Other you shave mit." Amazing, there they were winning the war and shaving with *ersatz* coffee!

Speaking of shaving, a hilarious incident concerning Pat Paris and Engine Maintenanceman Lou Williams occurred about the same time.

Engine Maintainance Lewis P. Williams.

First of all, in the *American Leader* Paris and Williams stood no watches but were day workers, and Paris was Williams's immediate boss. There are a million jobs to do, it seems, in a ship's engine room at sea. It was probably inevitable that friction would develop between them. As I have mentioned, Chief Officer Hickey and I hadn't been getting along from practically the beginning of the voyage, but at sea, because of my 12:00-4:00, watch we saw little of each other. With Paris and Williams, working together eight hours a day, points of view conflicted, tempers rose, and nerves frayed.

On Saupe's visit to the crews' room this particular evening, he asked if any one of the men had barbering experience. Perhaps with visions of a few perks or an extra cigarette, the chance to cut the officers' or the commander's hair recruited several raised hands. Williams, with the unverifiable story of being the son of a licensed barbershop proprietor in Massachusetts, who had assisted his father on busy Saturdays, was chosen. The next day Tober escorted Williams not to officers' country, but to the raider's sick bay where he was handed a straight razor, a piece of soap, a brush, and directed into a washroom. There stood Pat Paris who had asked to be treated for crabs—pubic lice! What a confrontation! Two guys who abhorred each other—one of whom, armed with a piece of delicately sharpened steel, instructed to lather and shave the private parts of the other! It was a standoff. Williams, no way wanted to even touch Paris, nor did Paris desire to allow Williams to threaten his masculinity. What resulted, I honestly do not remember, but I suspect Pat took care of himself. Looking back, I am angered by his stupidity. He must have had those things on the *American Leader* and never cared to rid himself of them. What a callous disregard for his shipmates! I'll bring up this subject again in a later chapter. Incidentally, Williams claimed to have dropped out of the Massachusetts Nautical School before I was admitted. I have never encountered any former cadet who recalls him.

Another tidbit relating to Aloysius and his "Do you haf any vishes?" was Pat Trotta's question about the World Series. At some point in this time frame, the New York Yankees were contesting the St. Louis Cardinals, and Pat asked if the radio operators could determine who had won or who was winning. The next evening, Aloysius reported the radio room had indeed managed to find the game on short wave, but they did not understand what was happening. "The commander vishes your party success," he added. For the record, the Cardinals took the championship in six games.

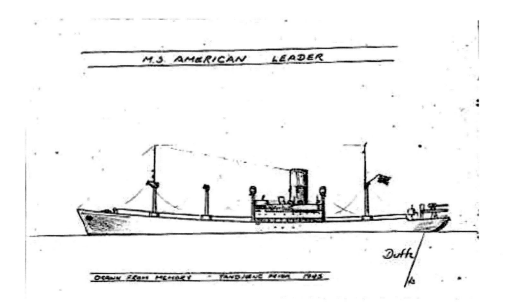

Typical of author's sketches. This done later on Java.

CHAPTER FIFTEEN

A New Host

On Wednesday, October 7, Tober informed us we would be going that day to another ship. When I asked him its name, he simply grinned and said, "It is a very famous ship." We knew that sooner or later this day would arrive, and now we were somewhat apprehensive of the future. Life in the *Michel* hadn't been too difficult. It was quiet and routine, one day pretty much like another. A friendly truce had sprung up between the prisoners and the German crew, particularly the Americans. In fact, Roy Neal, the *Empire Dawn*'s second officer, often remarked that "this would be a pretty bleak existence if you Yanks weren't around to cheer us up." This new ship meant Germany and prison camps, or perhaps abandonment on an uninhabited island. A new set of rules awaited, as did a new German crew. Sometime in the late afternoon, the *William F. Humphrey, American Leader*, and *Empire Dawn* crew members accumulated their few possessions and claimed their respective life jackets. Those who, like me, had come aboard without jackets and had been issued German equipment were asked to return them. When we came out to the *Michel*'s foredeck, a large, very large oil tanker was laying a few hundred yards off. Immediately, we all knew! This was the 584-foot long *Altmark*, the supply ship for the *Panzerschiffe Admiral Graf Spee*.

At the outbreak of war in September 1939, the *Graf Spee* was at sea. The *Altmark* was loading diesel fuel and lubricants at Port Arthur, Texas. The SKL sent the *Graf Spee* into the South Atlantic to disrupt British merchant shipping, and the *Altmark* followed. Between September 30 and December 7, nine vessels fell victim to the German raider, including one small tanker of less than eight hundred tons, and over three hundred crew members were taken prisoner. Remarkably, not a single person was lost from the sunken merchantmen. From time to time, as the two German ships rendezvoused, what prisoners were aboard the *Panzerschiffe* would be ferried over to the *Altmark*. The masters and chief engineers and other officers, however, numbering approximately sixty were retained aboard the *Graf Spee*.

Meanwhile, the Royal Navy was desperately searching, and on December 13, cruisers *Exeter, Ajax,* and *Achilles* found their prey. In the ensuing gunfight, all four warships suffered damage to varying degrees and were forced to break off the engagement. The *Graf Spee* limped into Monevideo, Uruguay where the prisoners were released. When repairs could not be effected in the twenty-four hours allowed under international law, the government of Uruguay added another seventy-two hours. This was not enough and the *Graf Spee*'s commander, *Kapitän zur See* Langsdorff, ordered her scuttled.

When the *Altmark*'s skipper learned of this, he ran far to the south and spent well over a month hiding out beyond 46° south latitude. On January 19, 1940, with all her machinery freshly overhauled, the tanker headed north. By February 13, she had passed the Faroe Islands, heading for the Norwegian coast and the port of Alesund where she arrived on the fifteenth. From there, with local pilots on board, she proceeded through neutral Norway's territorial waters toward Germany. The British Admiralty learned immediately of the *Altmark*'s arrival at Alesund. Fortunately, it had its Fourth Destroyer Flotilla, composed of a light cruiser and five destroyers in the North Sea off southern Norway. This force closed on the coast, intercepted the German who fled into nearby Jossing fjord. HMS *Cossack* followed, came alongside at about a mile and a half into the fjord, and put a forty-five man boarding party onto the then grounded *Altmark*. After a brief skirmish in which seven Germans were killed, 299 British seamen climbed out of the cargo hold to freedom. It had been a particularly difficult imprisonment. The captain of the *Altmark*, Heinrich Dau, was "an ardent adherent of Adolf Hitler and the Nazis." He treated the prisoners as though they were criminals. The food was poor; there were no accommodations, the prisoners simply slept on burlap bags or pieces of carpet; sanitary facilities were buckets and barrels; no one washed; exercise was limited. The survivors' stories were carried in newspaper articles, radio interviews, and movie house newsreels. *Altmark* became a dirty word. She was a "famous ship," without a doubt, and there she was, waiting for us.

The supply operations had been all but completed by the time we came on deck. Jacob's ladders led down to one of the tanker's large motor barges waiting alongside below us. The panorama of German superiority at sea spread before us as we swung over the bulwarks and down to the boat's deck. The Germans made no attempt to hide anything. Both vessels were in full view with no apparent camouflage or fake silhouettes. Lookouts were at the *Michel*'s mast trucks, carefully rotating in the swivel chairs, scanning the horizon. We were not blindfolded or discouraged from looking long and carefully. Except for what we had seen in the dark after our ships had been sunk, no one to this point had experienced a good, standoff look at the *Michel*. I was most interested in completing the sketch I had been working on since I stole the doctor's pad and pencil, and made mental notes of details to be added. The implications were soon in the minds of all. "They ain't gonna put us ashore on any island," growled able seaman Frank Patocka. "They're letting us see too much." As we cast off, another barge carrying two aircraft pontoons in plain sight left the tanker.

Aboard our new ship, an officer and two young sailors greeted us. We were counted and led forward under the foredeck to a trunk hatch with a ladder leading downward. One by one, we descended all the way to the double bottom tank top about forty-five feet down! This was an empty, cavernous, unheated cargo hold, and a death trap if there ever was one! It was lighted, and stacks of thin mattresses and blankets were provided. We didn't know where in the South Atlantic we were, nor where we were going. The *Altmark* was living up to its reputation. Another thing we didn't know was this ship had undergone a name change. For some reason she was now *Uckermark*, and that is what she will be called from here on. After a while, we heard three blasts from the whistle of our tanker, the traditional parting signal between two ships. I have since discovered in my microfilm copy of the *Michel*'s KTB covering October 8, 1942, to March 2, 1943, the entry for October 8, as follows:

> Wind: N-NW 3-7, Sea N-NW 3-5. Swell moderately high out of the NW. The weather has changed today. The barometer is falling and I must shoot a mail sack containing the *Kriegstagebuch* over to the *Uckermark*. 1830 weather: overcast, at times hazy. Rain. Visibility: daytime 4-15 nautical miles, nightime 2-4 nautical miles. Mail transferred. Ship 28 ran in the lee from astern and shot the line over to the *Uckermark*. The ships steered parallel to each other 150 meters apart until the two mail bags were successfully passed. The maneuver went well. It is truly unbelievable that two large ships in a rough sea and a wind force of 6-7 could travel parallel to each other at a distance of 150 meters apart. The principal is that one ship maintains a precise course and speed. Both ships do not attempt to maneuver. Then everything goes well.

So, we had not left the *Michel* as we thought, or the ships had simply parted for the night. In any case, the KTB and any copies, covering March 8, 1942 to October 7, 1942, never survived the war.

On board the *Uckermark*, after we had settled in for our first night on the tank top, the two sailors whose names were Blunk and Kühn lowered the standard evening meal to us, and returned in the morning with breakfast. Of note is the fact that the washrooms and toilets were located on the main deck and organizing traffic up and down that ladder was tricky. Captain Pedersen was enraged at this turn of events and demanded a meeting with the German captain. Surprisingly, things went very well and as a result, we officers, British and American alike, were moved to a fairly decent room with portholes, on the port side of the main deck. Outside the room, near the hatch leading down to the tank top, was another ladder, this one going up to a hatch on the fore deck. This hatch was opened, allowing all prisoners access to the deck, and from then on we were free to come and go as we pleased, from sunrise to sunset, weather permitting. It was a spacious deck, about one hundred feet long, providing a welcome space for leisurely, circuitous walks. One interesting incident occurred that first full day. Running from this deck to the amidships house was a catwalk, and someone, presumably the officer who greeted us the previous day, had posted a man with a machine gun at the deck house end. When the German captain noted the armed sailor, he quickly ordered him withdrawn. The bridge watch, he apparently decided, could keep a proper eye on us. No Heinrich Dau was our new warden!

On either that first day, or the next, an incident occurred that had us laughing until we had tears in our eyes. The fellows down on the tank top had found a couple of brooms and busied themselves cleaning the area. They actually accumulated enough rubbish to fill two or three buckets. One of our crew, who it was I have forgotten, came up and asked Kühn, who happened to be in the vicinity, for a pail and a shovel. Kühn asked why. The reply was, "We got a lot of crap down there."

Kühn didn't understand and queried "Crap?"

"Yeh, you know, *Scheisse*" was the reply, illustrated with two hands depicting a pile of something. Kühn was out of there like a cannon ball. Minutes later he reappeared with the prison officer, the ship's doctor, and an orderly. He had interpreted the conversation to be a request to clean up a heap of human excrement! Truthfully, the more we saw of Kühn and Blunk, the more hopeless they became.

The above noted meeting between Captain Pedersen and Kapitän von Zed evolved into regular afternoon conferences. Both had conversational ability in the other's language, so things went smoothly, complete with a taste of *Schnäpse* and a discussion of world news as it was picked up by the ship's radio operators. It is interesting to note that the *Empire Dawn*'s Captain Scott did not accompany Captain Pedersen to those afternoon chitchats. It was probably Scott's choice as he frequently propounded, "A good German is a dead German."

We never learned our host's name. It began with a z, which in the German language is *Zed*. Behind his back, the crew called him *Kapitän von Zed*. Early on, he divulged to Captain Pedersen the information that he, in World War I, was a prisoner of war in New Zeeland, held in a camp with the famous raider commander Count Felix von Luckner. At some time in the 1960s, poring through a stack of paperbacks in a book store, I found *Count Luckner, The Sea Devil* by Lowell Thomas, the print reporter, radio newscaster, motion picture documentarian, and late in his career, a TV commentator. In telling the von Luckner story, Thomas described an attempt by the count to organize an escape. He chose nine men to go with him, one of whom was a merchant marine cadet by the name of von Zatorski who was to become "our" *Kapitän von Zed*. Notwithstanding the danger to which the fifty-six unlicensed crew members, sleeping on the tank top, were exposed, von Zatorski, as I will now call him, knew what we were experiencing and did what he could to ameliorate our situation. Once a week we were each issued a bottle of Beck's beer. He asked his crew to give us whatever they could spare, such as checker and chess sets, books, magazines, and playing cards. This led to an amazing set of circumstances which would not culminate until 1991, precisely forty-nine years, to the date, from my first full day in the *Uckermark*. This will be related in the final chapter of this book.

We had been transferred at 38° 44′ S latitude, 21° 44″ W longitude, approximately 440 miles west of Tristan da Cunha Island. We ran to the southeast for about 1,650 miles, then easterly for probably 1,800 miles. As we had the run of the vessel's fore deck, it was quite easy to estimate the course. At noon, the navigator and watch officer, joined occasionally by the captain, would obtain sextant altitudes of the sun in order to determine their precise latitude. At that point, the sun would bear exactly north, so we had only to determine its relative bearing from the ship to come up with a good idea of the course being steered. Just a glance at a shadow crossing a deck seam would suffice. I'll discuss further aspects of navigation a bit later. In those times, German ships rounding the southern tip of Africa went down to latitude 45° south or more, depending on the ice shelf and the sighting of any bergs. I have no way of knowing what the *Uckermark*'s track was, but the *Michel*, following us by two weeks or so, according to its KTB, settled on between 48° 35′ and 48° 58′ after having gone as far south as 52° 51′. She ran along the pack ice and sighted icebergs. In the *Uckermark*, we did not see any of that, so it is probably safe to say we went to 45° S, putting us a good 600 miles south of Cape Agulhas, the southernmost tip of Africa.

Later, the *Michel* in December (westbound) ran as far south as 45° 14′ and in January (eastbound) went to 45° 40′. The weather for the eastbound leg in latitude 45° S was not too bad, and we spent many hours on deck. There were some stretches of fog where a seaman would be posted on the bow to maintain a sharp lookout. These fellows generally were clad in their foul weather oilskins: jacket, trousers, and a sou'wester hat. One foggy day, the lookout took off his hat and placed it on a small hatch behind him. As this hatch was near our walking route, I casually snatched the hat and quickly ducked below to hide it. It was a great souvenir, with a swastika stenciled on one of the earflaps. Another series of thefts occurred because of our concern over the probable lack of notification by the Germans to anyone, the Red Cross in particular, of our situation. When we received our weekly beer ration, Blunk and Kühn counted out the bottles and later returned for the empties. Several of us, trying to be helpful, would manage to mess up the numbers, so the boxes would be dumped and the count restarted. Invariably, after two or three recounts the young Germans became frustrated, tossed the empties into the boxes and went back to their quarters. In the confusion we'd get away with a couple of empties every time.

**War-time beer bottle label from *Uckermark* (top)
and post-war (1980s) version.**

What we did, later in the Indian Ocean, was to put "To Whom It May Concern" notes in the bottles and drop them overboard. We had previously conned Blunk and Kühn into providing candles for our room and the cargo hold where the unlicensed crews slept. There were a number of coat hangars in our room, which were divested of the dowels ordinarily fitted as pants holders. These became stoppers and flag sticks for the bottles. Melted wax from the candles sealed the necks. Finally, hand towels, imprinted *Kriegsmarine*, were tied to the end of the dowel outside the bottle. Dropping the bottles overboard was deferred until we had gotten well up in the Indian Ocean, and was, of course, a nighttime operation. Every evening when the hatch to the upper deck was dogged down, so were the portholes in the room. Moreover, these portholes were fitted with deadlight (blackout) lids. The dogs had hexagonal nuts, instead of handles, and required a huge Allen wrench to screw and unscrew them. One evening, either Blunk or Kühn closed everything up, put the wrench down, and hung around to talk. When it was time to leave, he had forgotten all about the wrench, which one of us had secreted.

For about a week, a bottle a night went into the sea. In time, when our supply of bottles for the creation of the floating distress messages was depleted, we had an alternative—the cans containing our occasional morning molasses. These certainly were not as flamboyant as the Kriegsmarine flagged bottles, but every one tossed into the Indian Ocean boosted our morale. To my knowledge not one of those bottles or cans was ever picked up. If the Germans' knew of our efforts, they made no attempt to stop us, although they eventually began opening the molasses cans for us and kept the lids.

In September 1987, at a dinner in Bremerhaven, Germany, I met the *Uckermark*'s first officer, Friedrich W. Bruns. In the course of our conversation, I told him about our above activities, and about a *Mütze*, a small, black cap with an embroidered bill I had also stolen. Bruns picked up a napkin, measured the circumference of my head, and when I returned home, waiting for me in the post office was a box containing a brand new *Prinz Heinrich Mütze!* What a nice gesture!

After probably reaching 40° east longitude, the *Uckermark*'s course was changed toward the northeast. It was spring in the Southern Hemisphere, the days were becoming longer, the temperature rose, and we began spending more and more time on deck. The albatrosses which had accompanied us on the passage from the South Atlantic to the Indian Ocean had been left behind. I don't know who hatched the idea of attempting to do a bit of navigating, but we had a pretty good pool of talent: two captains, a chief officer, two second officers, and two third officers, the latter both well-schooled recent graduates of the Massachusetts

Nautical School. In one of the books loaned to us by the German crew, a map of the world and a compass rose were found. I drew up a ninety-degree arc on paper, and everyone collaborated in creating an acceptable table of the sun's declination. When the German navigators came out for their noon sun sights, we measured the shadow on deck of a small stick. This gave us a triangle. The angle of the hypotenuse was the altitude of the sun. Applying the declination produced our latitude. We could only guess at our longitude by judging the time difference between the ship's apparent noon and noon Berlin time as heard later over the ship's loudspeakers. Plotting the daily latitudes and the course being steered gave us a decent estimate of the mileage we had covered each day. Our activity did not go unnoticed by the Germans. At their daily meetings, von Zatorski laughingly would ask Captain Pedersen, "How many miles do your officers say we traveled yesterday?"

All this confirmed our fears. We were bound for the Japanese-occupied Dutch East Indies or Singapore and then probably on to Japan. Blunk and Kühn joked about "short-legged" Japanese women. The cartons of civilian clothing labeled "for Japan" received by the *Michel* from the *Tannenfels* in September had been in turn handed over to the *Uckermark* and were just that—brown woolen suits (and to our eyes, not particularly stylish). Although Japan was weeks away, each member of the crew had been issued his. Blunk and Kühn proudly strutted in one evening, showing off their new acquisitions. For several days before we made landfall, every one, crew and prisoners alike, were administered antimalarial pills (Atabrine?), which came in bottles clearly marked "On His Majesty's Service." We wondered by what route they had come to the *Uckermark*. Other than that hint of a possibility we would be put ashore at a tropical port, we all felt the Japanese home islands was our destination. Then Captain Pedersen disclosed von Zatorski had offered him asylum. He could remain in the *Uckermark* and return to Germany from whence he maybe, just maybe, be repatriated to his home town of Arendal, Norway. That meant we were going at the first port, while he stayed. Captain Pedersen told us his answer was "No. I will remain with my men."

CHAPTER SIXTEEN

The Indoctrination

November 4, 1942. Passed through Soenda Strait in morning, anchored at 5:00 PM in harbor of Batavia Java 58 days at sea out of Capetown.

We had been underway for twenty-eight days, sailing about 8,400 miles at an average speed of 12.5 knots. During the passage through the strait, a large German battle flag was spread on deck. No aircraft appeared. Von Zatorski probably was concerned with the possibility of an American submarine guarding the strait and, humanely allowed us, as usual, on deck. He did not, however, zigzag. Eventually, approaching the city, we were ordered below and the blackout lids on the portholes in the officers' room were dogged down. The next day confinement continued. The portholes were opened for ventilation providing a glimpse of the surroundings. Some aircraft activity was observed, but little marine traffic, except for the *Uckermark*'s tenders which were shuttling to and from a rather nondescript German freighter. Many years later I learned that she was the *Weserland*, departing Bordeaux on September 9, the same date as did the *Uckermark* leave La Pallice. They did not travel together because the next day the *Weserland* was attacked by a Royal Air Force (RAF) Catalina flying boat. With a single, lucky shot the German gunners knocked out the aircraft. It crashed into the sea killing all but two of her crew, who were rescued and taken prisoner. One of these fellows, Henry Long, was badly injured to the extent that the *Weserland*'s doctor had to amputate a leg. At some point while the two ships were at anchor. Long and his crewmate were carried over to join us. I have no further recollection of these two, and have never located Henry Long, but isn't it a strange coincidence they were shot down on the same day we were sunk.

Blockade runner M.S. *Weserland* shown pre-war as *Ermland*.

November 6, 1942. Inspected by Jap health officials after lunch. 3:00 PM, left tanker under Jap guard. Taken to Tandjoeng Priok Prison Camp. Held "incommunicado."

My postwar research has uncovered this October 28 radio message from von Ruckteschell to the *Uckermark*:

> *FT an Uckermark Nr 31 Uhrzeitgruppe 1749/28 v. 28.10*
>
> 1. *Gefangene nicht in Batavia, sondern erst Yokohama abgeben.*
> 2. *In Batavia Schneider und Stengel ausschiffen. Werden entgegen ursprüglicher Absicht S-28 zugeführt. Sollen in Batavia auf RAMSES übersteigen.*
>
> *HVR*

Number 1 translates to "Prisoners not in Batavia, but only in Yokohama handed over." We fully believed we were going ashore in Java. Von Ruckteschell told von Zatorski to take us to Yokohama, and someone changed the rules! Why were we not to be landed in Batavia? That we were was future bad news for many of the *American Leader* crew as the reader will in time learn.

Number 2 is an order relating to two former *Michel* crew who were transferred to the *Uckermark* at the same time as we were. Disciplinary problems? They were to be landed at Batavia to join the blockade runner *Ramses*, which on October 23 had departed Kobe, Japan, bound for Europe. In any event, the connection was not made, as the *Ramses*, on November 28 in the Indian Ocean, was intercepted by HMAS *Adelaide* and HNMS *Jacob van Heemskerck*. The captain of the *Ramses* immediately ordered his crew to abandon ship. Scuttling charges were set off before Allied boarding parties had any opportunity to prevent such action. The two cruisers picked up seventy-eight Germans and ten Norwegians. The latter were survivors of the *Aust* (three) and the *Kattegat* (seven) making the perilous trip to France, thence to be repatriated to Norway. The *Aust* was a victim of the *Thor* in the South Atlantic on April 3. The destruction of the *Kattegat* by the *Michel* was recounted earlier. The Norwegians made a collective bet, and won, ultimately reaching Australia!

The seventy-four of us, carrying our meager belongings, were put on board a flat-decked, motorized catamaran. Unbelievably, white men were handing over white men to the feared yellow men of the Far East. We headed toward the wharves. Several Jap soldiers carrying rifles with fixed bayonets stood silent guard. Ahead of us, the tropic sun shone on the palm trees, occasionally reflecting a flash of light which we imagined came from a slashing *katana*.

Awaiting trucks carried us a short distance to a prisoner of war compound consisting of a dozen or so varied buildings inhabited by what appeared to be British soldiers. Our immediate destination was an isolated shack consisting of nothing more than a roof, a dirt floor, and palm leaf matting for the sides, surrounded by a flimsy barbed wire fence. We were given straw mats to sleep on, a Japanese issue army blanket, an aluminum pot to eat out of, bamboo slivers to eat with, chop stick style, and a tin cup. Interestingly, the Jap guards, only one of whom was with us at a given time, caused no problems. They were curious about us, particularly the American contingent. Outside the fence, though, the resident prisoners, perhaps for our education, took a beating. All Japanese had to be saluted; a prisoner without a hat was required to stop and bow. Failure to do either triggered a scream, "*Kiotske!*" (attention), followed by a stream of unintelligible Japanese, punctuated with a round house slap to the face. The guards made a game out of it, positioning themselves where they could not readily be seen, then pouncing on the unsuspecting victims.

November 12. Guard withdrawn and outside conversation allowed. Remain confined to sub-camp.

We were a sensation! Everyone could see that we were newly captured, and the conversations were lengthy. There were no Americans in the camp, but the *Empire*

Dawn crew was heartily welcomed by their countrymen. Also in the camp were a number of Australians.

November 13. Shifted to sub-camp No. 6. Allowed all camp privileges except working parties.

This was Camp 6 at Tandjoeng Priok, the second building we occupied. I slept in the porch-like area at the left, shared with Frank Stallman. Two other *American Leader* officers used the similar-sized inner room. A long bulkhead ran down the center line, separating us from a similar porch and room on the other side. The lean-to in the center covered our showering facility.

This compound was situated east of the cargo piers and was, before the war, home to the dockworkers and their families. As a prison camp it was basically a transient camp, the stopping point for prisoners being sent by ship to such places as Burma, Ambon, and the Japanese home islands. Each building, as was the case in our first "barracks," had a confining barbed wire fence with a single gate, which was closed at night. During the day we could roam at will. The entire compound was enclosed by an eight-foot-high, many-stranded barbed wire barrier, patrolled throughout the night by Japanese foot soldiers.

This 1979 view is from the area of the main gate of the Tandjeong Priok prisoner of war camp, looking north to the Java Sea.

This 1979 view is from the location of the main gate of the Tandjoeng Priok camp. These buildings occupy what was in 1942-3 the soccer field.

November 24. First working parties out.

What is meant here is the first working parties, including any of the former German prisoners. Also on this date I wrote the following essay:

> Tandjoeng Priok, Java
> Netherlands East Indies.

For the past 2½ months, I have been making various attempts at writing, but always end up by throwing the notes away. Now that we are settled, I think I'll be able to keep more or less a week-by-week account here and serve the purpose of a diary and a long letter at the same time.

Frank Stallman, the Second Engineer, remarked today that if we're not relieved pretty quick, a lot of the boys are going to find it hard to leave this "fair island". Naturally, I'm getting out at the first opportunity, but look at what I had to eat today—a cup of coffee as soon as I got up, then a hard-boiled egg, tea, rice with palm sugar syrup—for breakfast. For dinner, an onion omelet, rice, vegetables, and more palm sugar. Later in the afternoon, the First Engineer, Pat Paris, and I made a pot of coffee and roasted up a pan of peanuts. It isn't suppertime, yet, but I guess that's a good idea of the food situation from our angle. Don't think, though, that every POW eats that well. The staple, and at one time only, food is rice, three times a day. In addition are vegetables at noon and evening, tea morning and evening, white bread in the evening, a spoonful of sugar at breakfast.

I think Pat gets credit for our fare. He could talk the King of England out of his crown. Walter Lee salvaged some money, so that's a big help, too. The first offer of an exchange on US dollars was 65¢ local currency. With eggs 4¢ apiece, the dollar wasn't worth much. The rate finally went up to 1.65 which wasn't too bad. The boys just came in with a big hand of bananas. There are four of us in together—Paris, Lee, Stallman, yours truly—and doing rather well, thank you.

If ever any of you could see me now, I'd never live it down. I'm wearing a German officer's cap, German sailor pants cut down to shorts, and a massive pair of hob-nailed British Army boots. My hair is cut Japanese Army style—completely off. And since September 10, I have raised a moustache and a goatee which are, strange to say, red. In addition, I have put on a little weight and acquired a gradual tan.

About the only thing which bothers me here, is the realization of the time I'm wasting. Books are scarce—extremely so—and the paper and pencil situation is just as bad. One gets up here at 7:30 AM, has breakfast at 8:00 and then there is absolutely nothing to do until lunch at 1:00 PM. Supper is at 6:00 PM and then lights out at 10:00 PM.

A Dutchman interned here has organized several classes in French. Two English officers and I have a 1-hour session, twice a week. So, if we're unfortunate enough to be here any length of time, I ought to be able to do pretty well. It is surprising, how much high school French I have remembered. And, personally, my German is not bad, either.

This camp is located about 8 miles from the large city of Batavia, and is within sight of the harbor and the docks. Our population is just over 3,600 men. Included are British Army, Indian Army, Royal Navy, Royal Air Force, Australian Army, Australian Air Force, Royal Dutch Army, Navy, and Air Corps, and ourselves—the American and British Merchant Marine and the U. S. Navy. Not everyone was captured on Java, as our case plainly illustrates. There are officers from a Punjab regiment taken on Borneo; all the Aussies came from Timor; the R.A.F. lads (a medical unit) were originally stationed in Malaya, twenty miles from Singapore.

The gang that put up the best fight is the Australian outfit, the 2/40th Infantry Battalion. Seventeen hundred of them in four days' battle counted for almost 2,000 Nips and lost, themselves, forty men. As far as we know, five hundred of them are still fighting on Timor.

December 5. A Dutch soldier escaped. Spent 2 hours in the morning, lining up and being counted by the Nips.

December 10. Three months ago today we were sunk and a year ago the Leader was in Manila during the first Jap air raid. Stan Gorski, our bosun, says that from now on he is going to stay in bed on the 10ths of the months. There have been several practice air raids since our internment here. The Nips have a variety of sirens and whistles, blowing a variety of signals and with probably just as many meanings. When the English officers asked what was what in regard to the signals, the Nips wouldn't tell—"War secrets." So now if a siren sounds, we just say. "Air raid, I hope!" A rather odd position, isn't it?

The Author's Japanese "dog-tag". This was made out of a scrap of plexi-glass from a wrecked aircraft found near the dock area, and the clasp was a bit of aluminum from the same source.

The Japanese allowed the prison camps, at least those I was in, to be organized on a military basis. Each compound had its commander and he had a full staff of officers to assist him. Each subcamp had someone in charge and an assistant. There were officers looking after the food and the cookhouses, payroll officers, and sanitary officers, many of them doing what they had done before capture. In Tandjoeng Priok, the senior officer was a British colonel, so the whole place was run British Army style, right down to the parade commands, bugle calls, and ribald sing-alongs. I still recall two of the latter:

> Bless 'em all, bless 'em all
> The long and the short and the tall
> Bless all the sergeants and double-o-ones,
> Bless all the corporals and their blinking sons,
> 'cos we're saying goodbye to them all
> As back to their billets they crawl
> You'll get no promotion this side of the ocean
> So cheer up, my lads, bless 'em all.

> Kiss me good night, Sergeant Major
> Tuck me in me little wooden bed.
> We all love you, Sergeant Major,
> When we hear you bawling, 'Show a leg!'
> Don't forget to wake me in the morning
> And bring me round a nice hot cup o' tea
> Kiss me good night, Sergeant Major,
> Sergeant Major, be a mother to me.

CHAPTER SEVENTEEN

The Fate of the *Uckermark*

On November 30, our erstwhile German friends in the *Uckermark* ran into big trouble. Following our transfer to the Japanese, she ran up to Singapore and loaded a cargo of *Benzin* (gasoline) to be transported to Yokohama where she arrived on November 24. When the gasoline had been pumped into shore tanks, the vessel was moved to a lay berth to await orders. Also in Yokohama was the raider *Thor* (Schiff 10), which had completed a very successful 268-day voyage out of Germany, sinking or capturing ten ships of 55,587 total tons. This included the taking of the British passenger vessel *Nankin* (7,131 tons) with 185 passengers and 180 crew members on board. German blockade runners carried most of the crew and all the passengers to Japan, while a prize crew oversaw the *Nankin*'s (renamed *Lüthen*) trip to Japan.

Early in the afternoon of November 30, at 1346, to be precise, the *Thor* was tied up alongside the *Uckermark*. The *Lüthen* was across the slip at the adjacent pier. A party of 35 Chinese laborers had been engaged to clean the *Uckermark*'s cargo tanks, although it is possible they were chipping rust preparatory to painting the tanker. Regardless, a spark was struck and the fume-filled tanks exploded with a roar heard miles away. The *Thor* was also destroyed, as was the *Lüthen*, and an unknown Japanese freighter. Casualty figures vary. The *Uckermark* suffered between forty-four and fifty-three killed and twenty-two severely burned. The *Thor* lost thirteen men. Of course, the thirty-five Chinese fellows were blasted to eternity, plus possibly hundreds of Japanese in the shore facility.

On March 3, 1943, an unknown number of injured survivors of the *Uckermark* and *Thor* were being carried home to Germany in the previously mentioned *Speybank/Doggerbank*. She was mistakenly torpedoed in the mid-Atlantic by the U-43. There was only one survivor of 365 souls on board.

Also in Yokohama on the thirtieth, but not affected by the explosion, was the *Charlotte Schliemann*. Her radio officer, Alfred Moser, considered the incident to be an act of sabotage—by Russia. He said he had seen many Russian civilians in Yokohama. Their country was not at war with Japan, he pointed out, and they were free to roam at will throughout the city. Germany and Russia, though, were involved in massive land battles against each other in the Caucasus and at Stalingrad, and it would be quite logical, wrote Moser, for the local Russians to orchestrate this strike at the *Kriegsmarine*. An interesting theory.

I don't know when I heard of this incident, but it was well after the end of the war. In 1947, I was chief officer in a Liberty ship taking on a load of grain in Philadelphia and saw what I believed to be the *Uckermark* at the navy yard. Many years later, I learned the United States Navy, under the terms of Germany's surrender, took custody of a sister ship to the *Uckermark* named *Dithmarschen*. She was renamed *Conecuh* (IX 301) later to be reclassified as AOR 110 and used as an experimental multirole replenishment vessel.

CHAPTER EIGHTEEN

The Telegram

While all these events were taking place, there was no cause for alarm amongst the next of kin of the *American Leader*'s crew. Most families had received a few pieces of mail during the late summer. A letter from me, post marked June 25 at Bandar Shahpour was delivered in July, and in late August my mother received a note written earlier in the month from Colombo. In the latter letter, I wrote to say she should not expect to hear from me for another seven or eight weeks. By early November, thirteen weeks having elapsed, there was probably some rising concern about my well-being. Then on November 5 it came, a Western Union telegram. Instead of the hoped for joyful news announcing my return to the United States, it coldly stated I was "MISSING IN ACTION IN THE PERFORMANCE OF HIS DUTY AND IN THE SERVICE OF HIS COUNTRY." What a devastating moment that must have been. So utterly impersonal.

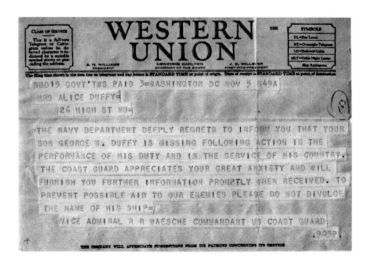

The Missing in Action Telegram.

265

The *American Leader* was due to arrive at the port of Punta Arenas in the Strait of Magellan on September 22. Forty-four days later, the telegrams went out. Forty days after that, the Maritime War Emergency Board in Washington issued an order declaring the crew presumptively dead as of September 22. On December 19 the payment of $5,000 war risk life insurance to each of our beneficiaries was approved. Ultimately, our estimated wages were computed, based on the ship's loss on September 22. In Massachusetts, my mother had to petition the Essex County Probate Court to be named the administratrix of my estate to which my wages and the value of my personal effects would be paid.

The *Newburyport Daily News*. Thursday, November 5, 1942.

NEWBURYPORT YOUTH MISSING

Native Of Haverhill Was On Merchant Ship

NEWBURYPORT—George W. Duffy, Jr., age 20, a native of Haverhill, is missing in action in the performance of duty and in the service of his country, according to word received today by his parents, Mr. and Mrs. George W. Duffy, 26 High street, this city, from Adm. Russell R. Waesche, commandant of the U. S. Coast Guard.

Duffy resided in Haverhill for many years before moving to this city with his parents.

Duffy was a third officer in a merchant ship that lately has been in far eastern wars. He is a nephew if State Detective Richard J. Griffin, Haverhill.

The young man was graduated from Newburyport High school, class of 1939, and from the Massachusetts Nautical school, class of 1941. He was 19 years old when he took his first voyage as a fourth officer on the same ship that he was on at the time he was reported missing.

On the day the war with Japan started, Duffy was aboard ship in Manilla. Three days after the Pearl Harbor incident, the Cavite naval base, where he was located, was bombed, but Duffy's ship escaped damage. The ship left harbor on Dec. 11 for Australia and was unescorted.

Since then, Duffy has been to many ports. His family received a letter, dated last June, from Iran, and letters dated in August, came from Ceylon. In recent letters, he had written that he expected to be home soon.

GEORGE DUFFY'S NAME ON OFFICIAL CASUALTY LIST

The names of Third Mate George William Duffy, Jr., 26 High street, this city; Capt. Paul Buck, Merrimacport, and Cadet Gordon Ambrose Tyne of Gloucester appear among the 31 New England names in the list of 317 on the latest casualty list of the merchant marine covering the period from October 22 to November 21.

Total casualties in the merchant marine now are 2901, including 463 dead and 2438 missing, in the period from September 27, 1941, to November 21, 1942. The figures include only the casualties resulting directly from enemy action.

Undated newspaper accounts, probably from the *Haverhill Gazette* (left) and *Newburyport Daily News.*

317 More Casualties on Merchantmen

31 from N. E. on Month's List

WASHINGTON, Dec. 4 (AP)—The Navy today announced a merchant marine casualty list of 317 names, including 31 New Englanders, for the period from Oct. 22, 1942, to Nov. 21, 1942.

This brought total merchant marine casualties to 2901, or 463 dead and 2438 missing, in the period from Sept. 27, 1941, to Nov. 21, 1942, the announcement said.

The figures include only the casualties resulting directly from enemy action. Names of personnel on United States merchant vessels overdue or presumed lost are considered casualties of enemy action. The list does not include names of the wounded or American citizens sailing on foreign flag vessels.

New England casualties and their next-of-kin:

Massashusetts
DEAD

LOWE, HERBERT EDWARD, messman; mother, Mrs. William Hopkinson, 142 Calghorn street, Fitchburg.

STEPHENSON, FRANCIS LES-

(Continued from First Page)

LIE, oiler; wife, Mrs. Doris L. Stephenson, 35 Maple street, Kingston.

MISSING

ANDERSON, MORRIS ANDREW, P. O. messman; aunt, Mrs. Anna Nelson, 2 Atherton street, Roxbury.

BOUCHER, FRED SIMON, able seaman; wife, Mrs. Artemes Boucher, 75 Thorndyke street, Arlington.

BUCK, PAUL, master; wife, Mrs. Gertrude Buck, Merrimacport.

DUFFY, GEORGE WILLIAM, third mate; mother, Mrs. Alice Duffy, 26 High street, Newburyport.

FLYNN, FRANCIS GIRARD, ordinary seaman; mother, Mrs. Lucy Flynn, 43 Harvard street, Dorchester.

FLYNN, JOSEPH PATRICK, able seaman; brother, Bernard Flynn, 288 Broadway, Fall River.

HERRON, DONALD BROOKS, ordinary seaman; father, Fred W. Herron, 20 West avenue, Salem.

JOHNSON, JAMES, third mate; son, Clarence Johnson, 32 East Main street, Ayer.

MADDEN, ROBERT EDWARD, junior third mate; father, John F. Madden, 19 Bowman street, Dorchester.

MARCINKIS, ANTHONY JOSEPH, wiper; mother, Mrs. Elizabeth Marcinkis, 165 Baker steret, Gardner.

PHELPS, ALLYN DAVENPORT, boatswain; father, Fred Phelps, 150 Lowell street, Somerville.

PRESCOTT, ROGER WOLCOT, able seaman; aunt, Mrs. E. Varney, 48 Chestnut street, Haverhill.

SAWISKUS, CHARLES ANTHONY, oiler; father, Anthony Sawiskus, 308 Dorchester street, South Boston.

Merchant Marine casualty list, probably carried in *The Boston Post*, December 4, 1942. Other than the author and Tony Marcinkus, none of the listed seaman survivied the war.

I hereby certify that on __December 15__, 19 **42**,

the Maritime War Emergency Board found that the

__MV AMERICAN LEADER__ was lost through enemy action

on or about __September 22__, 19 **42**, and that the

member or the members of her crew listed below was or were on

board the said vessel at the time she was lost and has or have

been missing ever since; and that the Board thereupon duly entered

an order declaring the said member or members of the crew presump-

tively dead in accordance with its applicable decisions.

Erich Nielsen
Secretary

NAME   RATING

George Wm. Duffy   3rd Officer

Presumptive death certificate issued by the Maritime War Emergency Board on December 15, 1942, and Legal Notice published in the *Newburyport Daily News* on January 20, 27, February 1, 1943.

CHAPTER NINETEEN

Settling In

December 15. All "ex-German" American prisoners mustered at guardhouse, given paper and pencil and allowed to write home with about 100 words limit.

December 17. Mr. Hickey, the Chief Officer, went to the hospital today, down with malaria. He is the first victim since our arrival. There will, no doubt, be more. Also today, I shaved for the first time since our capture. It is surprising, the change that a few whiskers will make. Pat Paris said that I looked entirely like a new person. Others wanted to know if I thought I was going somewhere. Well, coming events cast their shadows.

At some juncture, we were issued mosquito nets as an antimalarial measure. I know that we had them four months later. The hospital referred to was hardly that, being more of an isolation shack.

December 22. Received my first pay in captivity. (See January 17 entry below.) Enough to buy 2½ eggs or 2 razor blades or 2 cups of peanuts.

December 27. Entire camp allowed to write. Using special postcards and required to use three Nip-composed sentences.

This card was received by my mother in Newburyport, Massachusetts, on September 6, just over eight months in transit.

271

1943

January 1. 500-odd Australian troops preparing to leave. Indications that entire camp will soon be evacuated.

January 4. 530 A.I.F. left camp.

AIF—Australian Infantry Force.

January 5. Let's hope that this year doesn't end up like the last. Christmas was celebrated (and I do mean celebrated) in quite a manner, notwithstanding the circumstances. To kind of go through the day, there were church services in the morning, and at 10:30 a semi-athletic meet. I was on the committee for this affair which included three-legged races, obstacle race, potato race, sack race, etc. It really went over big. A long standing custom in the British Army is that the officers serve dinner to the men on Christmas Day. This was followed here, and since there are English soldiers in this sub-camp, a few of the fellows, including Captain Pedersen did the honors. Another custom is that the officers get a ducking in the wash trough. This was joyfully executed with the exclusion of no one. So, the American Merchant Marine officers were formally annexed to the British Army. Or maybe informally.

Serving dinner to the troops by the officers may have been a British Army custom, but I don't know about that wash trough business.

January 6. 750 Hollanders arrived.

January 10. 200 more Holland troops. These came from Malang, the previous arrivals from Tchilijap.

These Hollanders caused a severe sanitary problem. Toilet paper was not used in the Dutch army, instead each soldier carried a bottle of water with which to wash himself after a bowel movement. Generally the latrines were located over a canal or a creek or a drainage ditch which carried away the fecal matter and the water. Here at Tandjoeng Priok, outhouselike structures were utilized with half barrels collecting the waste. These half barrels were trundled out of the camp every day and dumped into the nearby harbor. These Dutchmen with their water bottles quickly caused the receptacles to overflow. The result was not at all pretty nor acceptable. The next two journal entries tell what happened.

January 14. Dutch troops which arrived on the 6th, left camp. All former German prisoners received anti-dysentary [sic] inoculations.

January 15. Dutch troops which arrived on 10th left camp. Much more of this British Army life and it will be hard to identify me as a "Yank". The latest episode occurred a week ago. Each sub-camp boasts of a soccer team entered in the camp league. Camp 6, my present home, had no goalkeeper. So, in I went. I, who had never seen the game played 'til I came to Java. The field, this particular evening, was a sea of mud. Fortunately, one doesn't roll around as much in this game as in American football. But, at the finish, every man was black from head to foot. We were beaten 5-0, tho I'm not boasting when I say I played a good game. The spectators gave me a good hand all the way, and, as Hickey said, "You were in there fighting—that makes a difference." So now I am permanently attached to the team.

Other sports were played in this camp, although not as organized as the soccer league. The Australians gave us a few demonstrations of Australian-rules football and the Americans put together two tag football teams. Also, the Americans managed to scrounge a bat and ball from the Japs to show our British and Australian friends what baseball is all about. I remember taking part in few pickup basketball games, but that didn't garner much interest at all.

January 17. Almost all remaining Dutch troops (approximately 700) left camp. It is raining this afternoon, and it has been raining since about 10 PM yesterday. This morning, as on other recent mornings, a Jap came in for roll call, but didn't bother to count us. Trivial event? Yes, maybe. But yesterday at this time we were planning an escape for last night. At eight o'clock there was a bright moon and a cloudless sky, and "boom went the apple cart." Two hours later, too late for our purposes, the rains came. By the time we would have been missed and a search started—oh well, there's no use talking about it.

As soon as we were released from our solitary confinement in November, the *American Leader* crew was befriended by the Australians of the 2/40th Battalion. They took us under their wings, so to speak, advising us, warning us, taking us to school on the facts of life under the Japanese Army. Also, several of their officers, namely Captains Russell Piggott and Jack Frost were sizing us up as possible recruits for an escape.

In the early days of their imprisonment on Timor, an attempt to return to Australia almost worked. The plan there was to steal a Japanese aircraft for the 350-mile flight (at a minimum). With everyone in place, ready to eliminate the Jap sentries, the officer who said he could fly the plane was unable to start the engines. The desire to get out burned within these Aussies, and when they were moved to Java they continued to explore the options. Actually, there was only one: steal a boat and sail to India or Australia. Problem was, of the group committed to the scheme, no one really knew how to sail or navigate. Thus, when the Germans deposited us on Java, the prisoners' prayers were answered, and soon Hickey, Gorski, and I were brought into their confidence. The only other non-Australian involved was a tremendous bear of a man named Hans ten Houten who had represented Holland in the single-scull rowing in the 1936 Olympics. Hans spoke the local Malayan dialect. Our group consisted of ten men: Piggott and Frost, we three Americans, ten Houten, and four other officers who names have faded from memory.

Rosi and Hans Ten Houten at home in Holland, in the late 1980's.

The plan was to commandeer a prau, a single-mast, lateen rigged sailboat, many of which were moored in what the Dutch called Visschershaven, located immediately to the east of the camp. In retrospect, it was a foolhardy, stupid thing that we were doing. Everyone in the camp knew that something was in the works. We purchased supplies, packed them into a number of ten-gallon tins, and made them watertight. Then I, masquerading as a Dutch officer, led Gorski and ten Houten pulling a two wheeled wagon full of debris covering a tin or two of our goodies past the guardhouse and out to the camp dump. I had picked up enough Malayan to explain our phony mission to the sentry. From the dump we detoured to a shallow sandy beach where the Dutch had built a small concrete pillbox to protect a gun emplacement. There we deposited our valuable cargo,

Stan and Hans loaded the cart with sand, and we returned to camp to repeat the process until everything was taken out. In the meantime, the tall, barbed wire fence had been carefully cut, a night reconnaissance established a route to the beach, and the Jap sentries' rounds timed and recorded. Our big problem was the inability to keep the project secret *and* a Japanese promulgation stating if one man escaped, ten would be executed. I never knew what occurred, but we did not go that night. Piggott and Frost blamed the weather, and that is what I wrote. In the next few days, Stan and Hans and I retrieved our cache of supplies. My suspicion is that the British colonel put a stop to the business, because never again was escaping discussed. An interesting footnote is during one of our visits to the gun emplacement an officer/prisoner who was supervising a work party of prisoners at the other end of the beach came down and casually asked why we were excavating sand. He may have been the whistle blower.

Since New Years there has been a good deal of POW movement, which leads us to believe that perhaps a new home is waiting for us. On the 4th, 530 Australians were sent away. Since then better than 1500 Dutch troops have arrived and then left a few days later. Now, outside of the Dutch troops unable to travel, the camp consists of about 1800 British, 450 Aussies, and our contingent of 50 Americans. Back away here I was complaining of the time being wasted. Please cancel. Next week, I appear in a short play, a comedy, appearing three nights. I am taking charge of an art project, which the Nip commandant is sponsoring, and also doing whatever paperwork that concerns the "Navy" as we're commonly called. The pay situation, simple though it is, has us right behind the 8-ball. The idea is this—all officers receive a flat rate of 10 local dollars (guldens) per month. Warrant officers and all other ranks are paid per day working. Soldiers get 10¢ per day. According to the Nip commandant, the U.S. and British have made no arrangement with Nippon for the care of merchant service prisoners.

This was so much hogwash. As I wrote above, the Japanese allowed the camps to be run on an internal basis. They did not know we were merchant marine officers. If the limey colonels had said we were "navy" we would have been navy. The Japanese occupying Java had no way of learning of any U.S./British diplomatic arrangements. This was simply a case of our own people discriminating against us.

The only way we have of receiving any money is to work and ALL RANKS SHALL RECEIVE THE SAME RATE—10¢ per day. Yet our 90-day wonder Navy officer gets 10 guldens per month. It really burns us up. Well, under that state of affairs I refuse to do any work of the nature that other officers perform for fl 10. [Although the unit of Dutch currency is called a gulden, it is shown as fl (floren) in connection with numerals.] *And I absolutely refuse to go to work with the soldiers and the seamen. The only persons taking officer duties are the radio operators and the chief stewards, and two of the Empire Dawn's engineers—and they're not worth considering. And poor Shershun. After a hitch on a destroyer while in the Naval Reserve and two years on the Nantucket he goes right back to where he started and goes out with the gang. Imagine that! Holding a Third Mate's ticket and marching in the ranks with a radio operator or steward in charge! Someone said that in a place like this one loses his pride. Baloney! This is where you should keep your pride, your self-esteem. Fly it in the breeze; let your own men know you are still an officer. Let everyone know you're still an American. (I've already had one fight with an Englishman, and he came off second best.) And when I get out of here, I'm going to be the better man because of the place.*

That fight was hardly a brawl, but it was physical confrontation. The fellow in charge of the *Empire Dawn's* gun crew was an artilleryman with the rank of bombardier, the equivalent of corporal in the U.S. Army. He was a burly Londoner and a bully to boot, making life miserable for anyone with a lesser rank. One day, in the chow line, he, for some unknown reason, gave me a push or a shove. I responded with profanity, causing him to take a swing at me. Fortunately, for me, as he probably outweighed me by fifty-pounds, and unfortunately, for him, he missed. I charged him and put my teeth into his shoulder, where he had a tattooed butterfly. End of altercation. I drew blood, in fact I almost took a wing off the butterfly. Sometime later, I happened to be near him when he was asked what happened to his tattoo. He said, "A rat 'et it." To which I replied, "Careful, 'guns,'" and he walked away.

January 28. 20-odd Americans arrived from Bicycle Camp in Batavia. Considerable P. O. W. movement.

Officially known as the Dutch Tenth Battalion Barracks, it was commonly referred to as Bicycle because its troops were bicycle mounted. In prison camp lingo it was usually referred to as Cycle Camp. One of the newcomers was a U.S. naval officer who had survived the sinking of the USS *Houston* (CA 30) in Soenda Strait on the night of February 28-March 1. As mentioned earlier, we had a daily roll call by the Japanese. This was done on an individual camp basis. In Camp 6 we lined up in two groups: (a) officers separated from (b) enlisted men and unlicensed merchant seamen. Captain Pedersen delegated me to take the officer count and Stan Gorski was in charge of the other group. When this naval officer—he was only an ensign—came on scene, he took over from Gorski at roll call and, seeing our officer group standing apart sent Coxswain Fox of our gun crew to tell us we were to fall in with that group. I asked Fox who gave that order, and he said, "The new ensign."

"Well," I said, "you tell the new ensign that he can go f—himself." When that message was passed, the infuriated ensign came storming up to me. "Are you Mr. Duffy?"

"Yes," I replied, purposely omitting the "sir."

"Do I understand correctly what you told Coxswain Fox to tell me?"

"If Fox said I told you to go f—yourself, that is correct," I replied. The guy nearly went apoplectic. He was going to take me to the nearest American consulate. He was going to have me court-martialed. He was going to see that I went to jail. At this point, the Jap who was to count us appeared at the gate. I screamed "*Kyotski!*" and the Ensign scuttled back to the soldiers and sailors, and the *American Leader* crew who had already come to attention. End of discussion. I won that skirmish, but it was the portent of more serious clashes to come.

February 1. More Americans in. Total now 90.

February 2. Kind of neglecting this thing lately. There have been quite a number of prisoners passing through here all during January. All the remaining "Yanks" are here now, and we're in a game of our own. There are survivors of the cruiser Houston, soldiers of the 131st Field Artillery, a couple of Marines also off the Houston, and us, totaling 90 men and representing every branch of the United States forces. What a relief to get rid of those "Limeys."

I guess I forgot the United States Coast Guard!

February 4. Last evening 10 more Americans arrived, including an Air Force Lieutenant and a negro cook off the SS Ruth Alexander. That ship came into Manila a day or so after the war started and was sunk early in January by bombers in Makassar Strait. That makes 100 Americans and one "Yank in the R.A.F."

February 9. 350 Welsh A-A plus some recently arrived Dutch and R.A.F. left camp. Ack-ack regiment interrogated as to supply of heavy clothing. Perhaps Nippon? More P.O.W. expected. Everyone confident of early release, but "ice cream" is pretty poor.

"A-A" and "ack-ack" indicate anti-aircraft, and "ice cream" was camp jargon for news.

Author's work.

St. George's Chapel located within the Tandjoeng Priok camp. This was built by British soldiers during the summer of 1942. It was not very large, perhaps 6 to 8 feet wide and 12 feet deep. The back wall contained two stained glass windows which survived the war and are now displayed at a Christian church in Jakarta.

Services were conducted *al fresco* with the clergyman presiding from the pulpit at the right.

A Japanese propaganda photograph taken at the time of the chapel's completion shows a small organ near the pulpit, but the author has no recollection of its presence during his time in the camp.

CHAPTER TWENTY

The Good News

In the previous chapter, I made an entry on December 15 concerning the writing of letters to home. There were fifty of us, and we were greeted in fluent American English by a young Japanese fellow in bright colored civilian clothes. He told us he was from Los Angeles and had been caught in Japan at the outbreak of the war. He said that he was authorized to allow us to write brief letters for future broadcast. There were a few rules and regulations, mainly concerning the length, including the address and signature. Because I did not have the foresight to make a copy of what I wrote, the exact words have been lost. Reading what listeners transcribed, the letter addressed to my mother read approximately as follows:

> *I have not been wounded and am in the best of health. Japs treat us all right. Regret to say Charles Feeney is not with us. Please be assured that I will be home safe and sound when the war is over and please don't worry. Notify U. S. Lines.*

> *Your loving son,*
> *George.*

Feeney's mother owned property in Maine and spent time there every year, passing en route by automobile through Newburyport. One day in the fall of 1941, she stopped for lunch and bought a copy of the *Newburyport Daily News* which, coincidentally, carried a story about me and the *American Leader*. Subsequently, she contacted my mother. I was aware of their acquaintanceship and felt obligated to disclose the bad news. Because I was not specific, Mrs. Feeney continued to believe for many years that Charlie was alive.

This particular letter was not broadcast from Tokyo until April 23, 1943, the fourth of fourteen that day. Shortwave listeners from coast to coast heard it, scribbling down or taping the almost unintelligible Japanese announcer's words. One, Fred Bender, of Oberlin, Pennsylvania, wrote, "To Kin of George William Duffy. Dear friend. This evening (April 23) at 7:30 PM EWT, I heard the War Prisoner program from JLG4, Tokyo, Japan, on 15.105kc." He then quoted what he heard of my letter. The next day, a Friday, he sent his letter, air mail/special delivery, with a note on the outside of the envelope: "Please make every effort to contact party. Radio message from American war prisoner in Japan. If wrong address Postmaster for Newburyport, Mass. please open." He had been able to decipher my mother's name and address, so his letter was not delayed, and the Newburyport Post Office delivered it on Sunday morning, no less! All the more fitting, it was Easter Sunday—Resurrection Day—and I was alive.

The word spread quickly. My sister Eleanor said that the telephone would ring as soon as it was hung up from the previous call. William B. Coltin, a reporter for the *Newburyport Daily News*, who was also the Newburyport correspondent for the large Boston newspapers was notified. He phoned them and the leading Boston radio stations which broadcast the unexpected news on their late evening programs. Monday's mail brought four additional missives from war prisoner listeners, and that afternoon the *Daily News* featured Coltin's detailed account of Sunday's stupendous happening.

In all, within a few days thirty-one people (excluding government sources) contacted my mother. Maybe more than that, but thirty one postcards and letters have survived, including a letter from the San Diego, California Police Department to the chief of police, Newberry Port [*sic*], Mass., quoting the Japanese announcer and asking that the information be forwarded to my mother.

Who were those dedicated people? Their letters and cards give little or no clues. The majority lived on the West Coast: California (fifteen), Washington (three), Oregon (two).

There were two from New York, and one each from Colorado, Maine, Minnesota, Missouri, Nebraska, New Mexico, Pennsylvania, Texas, and an unknown location. In later years I thought they probably had family members who were missing in action or known to be prisoners, but only three identified themselves as being in those categories. Mrs. Chloe Benge, of Hillsboro, Oregon, mentioned she had a son missing in the Philippines. Ellen Lacey, of St. Joseph, Missouri, was listening, hoping to hear word of a nephew also in the Philippines.

BURYPORT DAI

AND NEWBURYPORT HE

NEWBURYPORT, MASS. MONDAY, APRIL 26, 1943

FORCES GAIN

AFTER BLAZING SHIP WAS SUNK TO AVOID BLAST

Scuttled in the shallow waters of the New Jersey mud flats, between Jersey City and Bayonne, is the large cargo vessel loaded with explosives which burned fiercely for three hours in the middle of New York harbor. When the fireboats and the Coast Guard were unable to control the flames, the blazing ship was taken in tow by the tug boats whose crews ignored personal danger to draw her away from the pier. As the flames spread firefighters opened the ship's sea cocks to scut- tle her. Official U. S. Navy photo.

MISS BEATRICE E. SHEA BRIDE OF JOHN J. BURKE

Easter was the wedding day of Miss Beatrice E. Shea, daughter of Mr. and Mrs. Cornelius P. Shea of his city, and John J. Burke, son of and Mrs. Martin Burke, 84 High

GEORGE W. DUFFY, JR., MISSING FOR MONTHS, A PRISONER OF JAPS

The *Newburyport Daily News*, Monday, April 26, 1943.

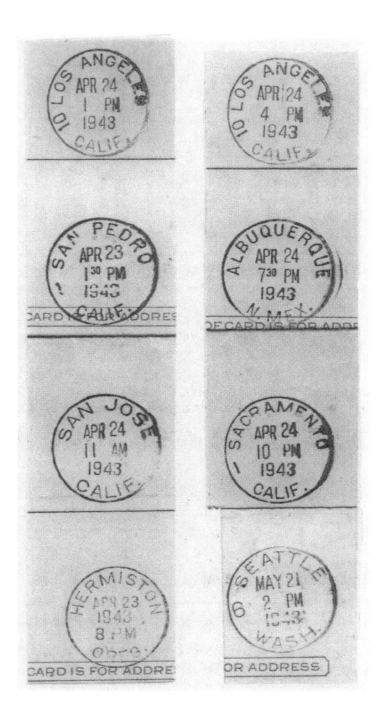

Samples of postmarks on post cards and letters from listeners who had heard author's radio messages sent from Japanese broadcasting stations.

Typical of the post cards received by author's mother from listeners to Japanese radio station.

Author's collection.

283

The third person was acting on behalf of a friend whose son had been captured in the Java Sea and who was contributing postage money. After the war, when I had returned home, my mother wrote to all those listeners, telling them the good news. Ellen Lacey replied. Her nephew didn't make it, having been lost in October 1944 in the sinking of a Japanese prison ship by an American submarine.

To the consternation of the United States government, hundreds of such "ex-officio intelligence agents" and thousands of anxious families grew into a nationwide web of information collectors and distributors. According to one shortwave listener, the volatile radio personage Walter Winchell reported the FBI was investigating persons who were relaying prisoner-of-war messages to their families on the suspicion they were spies. Instead of assisting the distressed next-of-kin, the government was making things difficult. The United States Navy heard my April 23 letter as did the aforementioned thirty one volunteers. At their own expense the citizens mailed my message the following morning. The navy finally got around to it on July 1!

One lady played it a bit dangerously when she wrote, "All the boys broadcasting yesterday seemed to have been on the same ship, although the announcer did not say so. Will you let me know what ship it was and when it was sunk so I can let other families know how old the messages are? They often ask and it is very seldom that I get any sort of clue."

Months earlier the "Missing in Action" Western Union telegrams sent to our next-of-kin ended with the words, "PREVENT POSSIBLE AID TO OUR ENEMIES. PLEASE DO NOT DIVULGE THE NAME OF HIS SHIP." On May 9, the *New York Times* headlined "Crew Thought Lost, Is Held by Japanese," listing eighteen of us from whom messages had been received. Notably, the name *American Leader* was not mentioned. That news article apparently evolved out of a letter to United States Lines from one Margaret Black of New Mexico, telling the company of her interception on April 23 of fourteen radio messages from *American Leader* crewmen. Another perceptive civilian had beaten the military intelligence at its own game.

Meanwhile, the protesting United States government diddled and dawdled. It was not until May 19 that the War Department, Army Service Forces, Office of the Provost Marshal General, Washington, in a letter signed by Howard F. Breese, Colonel, CMP, chief, Information Bureau, passed the content of my letter along to my mother. On June 7, R. H. Farinholt, Lt (T), USCGR, chief, Merchant Marine Personnel Records and Welfare Section, wrote to her stating that his office was "in receipt of an official report from the Prisoner of War Information Bureau,

CREW, THOUGHT LOST, IS HELD BY JAPANESE

At Least 18 Survived Sinking —Safe in Java, Tokyo Says

Eighteen members of the crew of a United States Lines vessel, officially presumed lost for several months, have survived the sinking of their ship and are "alive and well" in a Japanese prison camp in Java, Dutch East Indies, according to short-wave broadcasts from Tokyo received in this country and relayed to the families of the seamen, the United States Lines reported yesterday. One message said the ship had been sunk "with loss of life very small," indicating there is hope for word of other survivors among the forty-eight crew members.

Those reported as sending messages included Captain Haakon A. Pedersen of Brooklyn, master of the ship, who only a few weeks ago had received posthumously the United States Lines' Distinguished Service Medal; Executive Officer Bernard J. Hickey of Bloomfield, N. J.; Second Officer Walter H. Lee of Los Angeles, Third Officer George W .Duffy of Newburyport. Mass.; Junior Third Officer Alexander Shersun of Somerville, Mass.

Also Frank E. Stallman, second assistant engineer, San Francisco; Joseph Cohen, radio operator, New York; Eric O. Kamins, third assistant engineer, Hoboken, N. J.; Stanley E. Goiski, boatswain, Racine, Wis.; Alex A. McKinnon, oiler, Jamestown, N. Y.; William A. Grover, oiler, Alampse, Col.

Also Herman R. Dentzler, oiler, Grosse Point, Mich.; Sidney M. Albert, second cook and baker, Pisgah Forest, N. C.; Ensign W. H. Dryer, Daphne, Ala.; Michael J. Zombeck, third cook, Yonkers, N. Y.; Moody C. Harrison, able seaman, New York; Harold A. Hoag, messman, Guilford College, N. C., and Carl H. Kalloch, seaman, Rockland, Me.

The news of the survival of some of the *American Leader* crew attracted the attention of the New York Times. This article appeared in their Sunday, May 9, 1943 edition.

through the International Red Cross (that I was) interned in the Prisoner of War Camp, Java." The purpose of this letter was to correct the "Missing in Action" telegram of November 5, 1942. No mention of the civilian radio listeners. The Public Relations Office of something called Navy Number 128, c/o Fleet Post Office, San Francisco, received the April 23 broadcast, but how is not clear. In any case, John A. Giles, Lt. (JG), USNR, on July 1 (to repeat), more than two months after the lady and gentlemen monitors had passed along my letter, finally fired off the navy's notification!

Later in the war, a radio officer in an American merchant vessel in a Far East port, quite by accident, stumbled onto a Japanese radio station broadcasting messages from American prisoners of war. In light of the above 1943 experiences, his report is very interesting. "I, too, was in the World War II Merchant Marine, writes James E. Long,

> serving as the Chief Radio Officer aboard the SS *Mary Bickerdyke*. I served on her continuously (six round trip voyages) from September 1943 to June 1946. During the fourth voyage we went to the Philippines and made several short trips between Manila, Tacloban, and Cebu City. One morning, while docked in Manila discharging cargo, I had some catch-up work to perform in the radio shack. As you know when winches were in operation the procedure was to lower the radio antenna to the deck so as not to have it snapped and broken by the booms on the winches. At that time, 500kc (now KHertz) was the International distress frequency as well as the calling/replying frequency for ships via Morse code. For some reason I began tuning the receiver below 500kc to the 100kc-300kc range, which were the aeronautical beacon frequencies that aircraft homed in on for navigational purposes. To my utter amazement I heard a female voice reading in English short letters from American POWs to loved ones at home. I listened for about ten minutes until she signed off. During the next two to three days I went to the radio shack and copied POW's names, short messages, and addresses to stateside families. I had reasoned that because of the frequency used, no one in the States could have received the messages. I then went to the Post Office and bought about thirty penny postcards and transcribed my notes to the cards and mailed them through the Post Office to the States.

> About three weeks later we departed, destination San Francisco. Since I had sailed out of and into San Francisco on previous voyages I had noted on return trips that when the pilot boat met us off the Farallon Islands,

usually one Navy and one Coast Guard officer and a petty officer would come aboard. However, this time there were three or four Navy officers and one Coast Guard officer and the pilot who came aboard from the pilot boat. About fifteen minutes later, the Third Mate informed me that the Captain wanted to see me, pronto. I went to his quarters and met the Navy officers who were from Naval Intelligence. They quizzed me for about thirty minutes, took notes, and then told me to cease and desist in my efforts to inform families of the status of POWs' situations. Their rationale was that I had been privy to knowledge that neither the Navy or the families had access to. Further, my cards, in some cases, were the first inkling of what had happened to loved ones. The tenor of the quizzing was somewhat confrontational and I took the advice and didn't continue my informational campaign."

Amazing! Long thought he was being a good Samaritan, and the navy, apparently without any consideration for the morale of the prisoners' families, threatened to shoot the messenger. How much of this went on during the war, one can simply wonder, but certainly there was a pattern. Why didn't they learn?

Back to the listeners who heard my message, one thing is for certain. These were well-organized, highly motivated, intelligent individuals who sat in front of their shortwave sets for as long as four sessions per day, copying as many as fifteen messages in a ten-minute period. For the most part their postcards and messages were handwritten. A mere five of the thirty-one sent to my mother were typewritten. And were those people efficient! Only a few of the thirty-one does not carry an April 24 postmark! In review, it is astounding some were ever delivered. Newburyport was frequently misspelled as "Newberry Port," and one envelope from Seattle, Washington, bearing the cancellation "Boston & Albany R.P.O.," was addressed to "New Brunswickport." High Street was "Eye Street" on one, "Hi Street" on another.

Today, over half a century later, if one errs in a single digit of an address or zip code, the post office promptly stamps it "Return to the Sender." A few writers commented on the similarity of our words. Wrote one woman, "Most messages are the same, as 'I am all right and being treated fine.'" She didn't realize the young Jap may have coached us to use such terms. Private Herbert D. Hochfield, after quoting me, said, "I hope that I have been of some help to you. Wish I could do more. Won't you write to me about George and weather [sic] this broadcast is a lie or not?" With the mailing of fourteen messages from *American Leader* survivors on April 24, 1943, Irving Bender had forwarded a total of 680 messages. Mr. and Mrs. C. J. Harrison of Seattle, numbered mine as the 245th they had relayed, and for Ray Messer (?) of South Portland, Maine, it was his 163rd. There was no mention of number in the covering letter from Sanford Low of 222 West Seventy-seventh Street, New York NY, but years after the war I learned he had listened to, copied, and mailed the prodigious quantity of 10,379 war prisoner broadcasts! At three cents per letter, a considerable expenditure for those days.

A final comment on those listeners is, when the card and letters carrying my April 23 message came in, everyone believed, because a Tokyo station was involved, we were in Japan. Everyone except Fred Sinclair of West Sacramento, California, and the previously mentioned Ellen Lacey. Sinclair succinctly deduced, "From some of the messages on same broadcast, I'm led to believe he is somewhere in Java, Dutch East Indies. Of course, that is only my guess." Ms. Lacey didn't guess. She addressed her card, "Mrs. Alice M. Duffy, mother of sailor age 20 George William Duffy, Prisoner in Java." Wonder how she figured it out?

CHAPTER TWENTY-ONE

The *Michel*—Again

February 10. Five months ago tonight we were sunk and this afternoon the raider, Schiff 28, came into the harbor, docking at Pier 1. Flying call letters D X E X.

Overall, the intervening months had not been kind to the raider. From September 12, the date of the *Empire Dawn* sinking, until November 29 when the American motor ship *Sawokla* was sent to the bottom, only one or possibly two potential victims were sighted. Because of the impending arrival of numerous long range U-boats in South African waters, von Ruckteschell was ordered to transfer his operations into the Indian Ocean. The run from the South Atlantic was strange, almost disorganized. After dismissing the *Uckermark* on October 8, the *Michel* motored slowly westward to *Punkt Pauke* (Point Kettledrum) at latitude 38° S, longitude 29° W, where she spent three days in the vain hope the *Stier* and the *Tannenfels* would appear. They didn't, so on the fifteenth course was set to the south for a day, then southeast for another, and back to the south for about a day and a half. According to Konrad Hoppe, it was feared the extensive amount of German radio traffic generated by the *Stier*'s "disappearance" could have been monitored by the British who might have then been searching for the *Michel*. It was prudent, thus, to run and hide.

Upon leaving *Punkt Pauke*, von Ruckteschell signalled SKL informing them of his failure to meet the two ships. The SKL replied with the startling disclosure that the *Tannenfels* had reported taking the crew of the *Stier* on board. Further information follows, they said. This news was announced to the *Michel* crew and the Commander declared a one-day holiday in the spirit of comradeship with their fellow sailors. In his KTB he stated, "The task for the *Tannenfels* is not light." On the seventeenth, almost as an afterthought, the SKL notified the *Michel* of the *Tannenfels*'s latitude on the fifteenth—15° N—at least 3,300 miles away.

At noon on the eighteenth the *Michel* headed southeasterly for two days, easterly for two more, and back to the southeast where on the twenty-fifth, the ship reached 52° 51' S. She ran east on that parallel until noon on the twenty-sixth when the course was changed to 050°, approximately northeast. All the while, the engine was being operated economically, with the chart showing the best day's run of only two hundred miles. At noon on the twenty-eighth, the course was changed to 090° (east) and that was maintained until November 3. The chart of that period carries the notation *laufend Eisberge passiert* (running along ice bergs), which is a clue to the 8-knot average speed. Enormous bergs were in sight close by in daylight, thus requiring the vessel to heave to and shut down the engine during the darkest portion of the night.

Then there was the question of the crew's morale. Because of the cold ocean water, the temperature in the ship's living quarters plummeted, and considerable condensation formed, making life most uncomfortable. The apparent loss of the *Stier* was deeply troubling, made all the more by the absence of any information as to just what happened to her. It was feared she fell victim to a warship and that would mean a substantial loss of life to her crew, many of whom the *Michel*'s crew had become acquainted with during the vessels' meetings. "The mood in the ship was not good," remembered Konrad Hoppe. So, feeling relatively safe with the ice berg barrier to the south, von Ruckteschell dictated an 8-day festival in which everyone engaged in the production of stage shows, pantomimes, sing-alongs, etc. The entire complement, officers and men alike, except the Commander, participated. Several rather risqué female impersonations received howls of laughter and indecent shouts. "Very dangerous," commented Hoppe many years later. The beer "ran like a river."

After eight fun-filled days, on November 3 the *Michel* crossed the 40° east meridian and resumed business as usual. She headed northeast for two days, east for three, then generally north-northeast for eight more days. At some point in this stretch of time, Konrad and his commander, having watched the weekly movie, became embroiled in a serious argument. The film included what Konrad felt was a realistic seduction scene which displeased and offended von Ruckteschell who placed the blame for such trash on the government in general and in particular on the propagandist (Paul) Joseph Goebbels. They were too lax and lenient, offered von Ruckteschell. Konrad rebutted, saying the bureaucrats shouldn't be faulted, as they cannot be watching everything. The discussion became heated to the point where von Ruckteschell actually fired his flying officer. A homeward-bound blockade runner, the *Rhakotis*, was scheduled to meet the *Michel* in midmonth, and plans had already been made to send a number of people, including the five prize crew officers, back to Europe in her. Konrad's name was added to the list. After almost a year together in the *Widder* and at least a year and a half in the *Michel*, a senseless argument over an inane subject destroyed the relationship. Eventually, First Officer Erhardt and Doctor Schröder convinced their commander to relent and cancel the dismissal, which he did. After almost eight months at sea, von Ruckteschell was showing increasing signs of the toll the voyage was extracting from him.

On November 11 SKL reported a few details of the *Stier*'s loss to the *Michel*. The type and name of the enemy ship had not been ascertained, they said, but she had been armed with four or five guns, one probably 15 cm and the others 10 cm or 12 cm. Two days later, the raider stopped at 31° S, 65° E to await the arrival of the tanker *Brake*, which showed up the next day. To the disappointment of all, she carried no mail, even though she had come out from France, but did replenish the *Michel*'s storerooms and refrigerator with six tons of potatoes, three tons of fresh meat and an unspecified amount of beer. Six hundred and seventy five cubic meters of bunker oil was taken on.

Tanker *Brake* approaching *Michel*.

The two ships stood together until 1500 on the seventeenth, when the *Brake* departed, headed for Kobe, Japan. The *Michel* remained at the rendezvous location, and on the following day the *Rhakotis* appeared. She had no stores in spite of having recently called at Singapore, Balik Papan, and Batavia, where supplies, particularly fruit and vegetables, were abundant. In a sense this was more of a social encounter, although, as mentioned earlier, some of the no longer needed *Michel*'s crew were transferred. Also sent over to the *Rhakotis* were numerous official reports and a copy of von Ruckteschell's KTB. An interesting facet of this midocean encounter was the presence on board the blockade runner of twenty-two Norwegians and a Swede—survivors of the *Kattegat, Aust, Herborg,* and *Madrono*—being repatriated to their homelands. The latter three vessels were victims of the raider *Thor* and of them only the *Aust* had been sunk. When von Ruckteschell learned of these Scandinavians he became enraged. His KTB for the day contains more than a page of his comments such as "They know our attack strategy. They know our meeting points. They are a dangerous gang to be again sent to sea. They know the arrival and departure routes in and out of Japan. They possess the prisoner mentality. This is regretfully out of order." Aboard *Rhakotis,* the *Kattegat*'s former captain, said he and nine of his crew were dismayed to see the *Michel.* "Each horrible act came so close to us again. We stood there speechless, remembering that pitch black night when she sent her shots into us without pity, as well as the time spent in the dark cell beneath the booming guns."

The *Rhakotis* and the *Michel* parted company the following day, November 19. Twenty-three days later, the *Rhakotis*, having rounded Africa and in a position close to the equator, sighted a lifeboat carrying three persons. Upon rescuing the three it was learned they were from the British *City of Cairo,* torpedoed and sunk on November 6-thirty-six days earlier. Originally, fifty-four crew members and passengers were in the boat, including the *City of Cairo*'s chief officer and a master of a previously sunk British vessel who was being repatriated. Of the three survivors, one was a young female passenger named Diana Jarman. The others were Quartermaster Angus MacDonald and Third Steward Jack Edmead. Sadly, Diana died on board the *Rhakotis.* The British knew the *Rhakotis* was on its way to Europe and were actively searching for it. On January 1, 1943, the blockade runner was nearing the Spanish coast in the vicinity of Cape Finisterre when she was spotted by RAF aircraft which vectored HMS *Scylla* to her position. Scuttling charges were rigged, but never detonated as the cruiser's guns raked the defenseless German. The *Scylla,* it is reported, rescued and took prisoner some of the crew, but another report states eighty survivors including most if not all of the Norwegian merchant seamen and the Swede were picked up by two Spanish fishing boats. Once ashore in neutral Spain they gladly underwent debriefing by Allied intelligence agents, allowing the fates of many missing ships and their crews to become known. Now it is revealed that MacDonald was rescued by the U-410, which was escorting the *Rhakotis*, and spent the remainder of the war as a prisoner. Edmead managed to get into one of the *Rhakotis'* lifeboats which made it to Coruna, Spain, on January 3. It is assumed he was ultimately released to British authorities, but he may have been interned by the Spanish government.

As soon as *Rhakotis* was out of sight, von Ruckteschell took steps to alter his ship's silhouette. The smoke stack was shortened and made thinner, and a pair of cowl ventilators between the stack and the wheelhouse removed. Then it was off to the chase with Konrad Hoppe spearheading the effort. From November 21 to November 28, he made a total of fifteen reconnaissance flights. On November 21, 23, 26, 27, and 28, he went up, generally at about 0900, and again around 1500. On the twenty-fifth, he took off an hour earlier in the morning and added a third flight at 1105. He flew various patterns: diamond, square, trapezoidal. For the most part, he was aloft between two and a half to three hours, although on four occasions he was gone more than three hours with the longest extending to three hours and thirty-three minutes. Unfortunately, for the *Michel* and Konrad, in particular, they were all for naught. Other than two ships seen on the twenty-third nothing was spotted in all those miles of searching. These two ships may have been the same vessel. Early in his morning flight he sighted a ship on a southwesterly course, about forty miles from the *Michel*. He returned, landed, made his report, and resumed his patrol. However, von Ruckteschell declined to mount an attack on this unsuspecting freighter. The moon had been full the previous night. On this night there would be only a small window of darkness in which to close in on the enemy. Calling himself an "old fox" in his KTB, von Ruckteschell apparently decided to trail the ship at a distance until more auspicious circumstances presented themselves. But then Konrad returned with another sighting of a ship with a suspicious high poop deck structure. This caused the commander to believe his Flying Officer was confused, at the same time, though, he couldn't imagine what the high structure on the poop deck could be so decided to leave this ship alone. Throughout this period of high air activity, the *Michel* remained within 27° 53' S and 29° 38' S and 56° 24' E and 57° 24' E, an area 105 miles north to south and roughly 52 miles east to west. In fact, between noon on November 23 and noon on November 28, only 179 miles were logged. (See page 297 for flight plans numbers 30 and 31.)

On the latter day, perhaps acting on one of his hunches, von Ruckteschell motored at half speed to the west. The next day, with wind and sea conditions being unfavorable, no flights were made. In the afternoon, the weather improved and at 1630, with the *Michel* on a northerly heading (350°), masts were sighted dead ahead. It was soon determined the vessel was on a southwesterly course, putting the raider in a perfect intercept position. This was the American motor ship *Sawokla*, a 402-foot-long, 5,984-gross-ton freighter built at Tampa, Florida, in 1920. At the outbreak of hostilities in 1941, she was being operated by American Export Lines. On June 17, 1942, fully laden with a cargo of foodstuffs and war materials, the old vessel sailed from Staten Island in New York harbor, bound for the Persian Gulf. Her voyage was a duplicate of the *American Leader*'s: down the coast to Norfolk, thence Port of Spain, Capetown, and up through the Indian Ocean. In due course, she safely arrived, and then underwent a monthlong delay because of congestion in the various gulf ports. Subsequent ports of call were Colombo, Calcutta—to load 6,000 tons of jute for the United States—and then a return to Colombo from where she departed in the late afternoon of November 19, 1942, homebound via Capetown. In addition to her regular crew which numbered forty-one, she had on board thirteen U. S. Naval Armed Guard personnel, and five passengers, for a total of fifty-nine—all males. Four of the passengers were merchant seamen who, for one reason or another, probably medical, had been separated from other ships. Two of the armed guard sailors came aboard in Colombo. They had, on September 22, been aboard the SS *Paul Luckenbach*, torpedoed by the Japanese submarine I-29 in a position 850 miles west of Cochin, India. All forty-four crew members and seventeen armed guard in four lifeboats sailed 21 to 26 days to reach the Indian coast.

On November 29, the *Sawokla* had covered somewhat over half of her proposed voyage across the Indian Ocean. When Second Officer Dennis Roland finished up his 4:00-8:00 watch at 2000 that evening, he roughly noted his position: 28° S, 54° E, 440 miles ESE of Fort Dauphin at the southeastern tip of Madagascar. The night was black, the sea rough, and the wind at force 4 to 5. Junior Third Officer Stan Willner, making his first sea voyage as an officer, relieved him. After making his logbook entries and leaving the bridge, Roland visited briefly with the chief steward and then the Chief Officer Elmer Saar, who was suffering from glaucoma and had to remain in total darkness. While in the latter's cabin, they heard the lookout on the focsl head sound one bell, indicating something sighted to starboard. At that point, Lt. (JG) L. L. George, the armed guard officer, poked his head through the door curtains, asked if they had heard "that," and suggested he and Roland go on deck for a look-see. Roland deferred, saying that he was tired, needed some rest, and went to his cabin.

He had just entered the room and hung his cap on its hook when the ship was suddenly jarred and the air was filled with a haze. "She shuddered," wrote Roland later, "as if she had run over an obstacle and then continued onward. My personal thoughts were *Well, we're in trouble.* I glanced at my bunk, which looked mighty inviting, and told myself that I may not sleep in it again. I put on my 'tin' helmet and went out into the passageway." When Dennis Roland left his room for the last time, he found many of the *Sawokla*'s crew congregating in the passageways of the living quarters. There was no hysteria, no rushing about, no shouting; nothing that one would imagine it to be aboard a ship in its death throes. More curiosity than fear was exhibited. "What's up?" "Is it a sub?" "Can you make anything out?" "What should we do?" Acrid fumes began permeating the area, followed by whiffs of ammonia, indicating that the refrigeration flat had been hit. Roland told the men that he didn't know any more than they, but suggested remaining inside until the firing subsided, thus giving them a chance to go over the side. They moved from port to starboard, peering furtively out the doors, seeing the angry sea, the flash of heavy guns, and the fiery paths of tracer bullets. Shortly, the lights went out, but the emergency circuits came on, which, with the illumination from the fires that seemed to be burning everywhere, allowed the men to move about. "I then decided to try to get to the bridge via the inside stairway," wrote Roland. "Young Stanley Willner was up there, in his first position as an officer, having been promoted from cadet. We had been together a great deal, as my cabin was sort of a club where we had a tremendous supply of sweets, plus a bottle for making sodas with plenty of cartridges and various flavors. In attempting to reach the bridge, I was unable to get more than halfway because of the debris which blocked my progress. I did get into the Captain's quarters, but that room was burning in several places. I shouted for him and young Stanley, but to no avail. It was a most futile effort on my part as I could barely hear myself above the din."

Roland then went back down to the passageway which was becoming flooded. Walking was difficult due to the developing starboard list. The overall picture was of great destruction, broken lines, gaping holes, fire and smoke everywhere. "Now I began to realize our position," he continued. He once again attempted, unsuccessfully, to get to the bridge as everything was burning furiously. Returning to the passageway, he noted a rapidly developing starboard list and told the men around him, now numbering only six, it was time to abandon ship. They all went up to the port side of the boat deck where the number 2 and number 4 lifeboats, since departing Colombo, had been swung out and lowered to the deck level. The number 4 boat was in two pieces, each suspended from its respective davit and swinging wildly. Roland ordered the gripe on number 2 boat released and the boat lowered. When they thought the boat was in the water, the group went down the rope ladder and man ropes only to find the falls had jammed, leaving the boat several feet above the sea. With great difficulty, the falls, which were manila rope, were cut allowing the boat to become water borne—they thought. Roland, attempting to find the boat's drain plug and cap it, instead felt a gaping hole through which the ocean was rushing, quickly filling the boat. Air tanks, designed to keep it buoyant in such a predicament, their strappings apparently shot away, popped out and the boat promptly sank. The seven swimmers had only two wooden oars and their life vests to keep them together and afloat. The *Sawokla* rolled over and disappeared beneath the surface of the Indian Ocean. The entire sequence, according to the *Michel's Kriegstagebuch*, from the opening of fire to this point, took only twenty minutes!

As was the case with earlier crews, Roland and his mates thought their attacker was Japanese and did not try to attract its attention as it slowly disappeared from their sight. Eventually, though, they were seen and the raider bore down on them. This time, thinking it was a passing ship, they all shouted, "Help!" in unison and were answered, though they didn't understand the language. The vessel was maneuvered so they were on the weather side, where two Jacob's ladders were hung and the seven men climbed to the raider's deck. In total thirty-five survivors were rescued and made prisoners of war. *Esau*, the motor torpedo boat, picked up twenty of them. At noon, the following day, again at the scene of the previous night's action, four more survivors were found on a primitive float, according to the KTB, after spending sixteen hours in the water. Two of the *Sawokla*'s crew were German-born. One of them had been in the prewar years in the German merchant marine. The other, a man named Otto Dickmann, emigrated from Germany in 1923 and had become an American citizen. In his KTB, von Ruckteschell entered that information followed by the word *Kommunist?*! It is not known to whom he referred.

For the next six days, the *Michel* meandered around the Indian Ocean logging days' runs of 62, 121, 126, 138, 77, and 143 nautical miles. Konrad Hoppe went up on the 1st, twice on the third, and once more on the fourth, flights numbered 25 to 28. Returning to the *Michel* on December 1, the occasion of his twenty-fifth flight, Konrad Hoppe was awarded a commemorative plaque by his commander.

**Sgt. Walter Emmel, pilot of the Arado 196,
with Flying Officer Konrad Hoppe, on the occasion of their
25th scouting flight on December 1, 1942.**

Bad weather prohibited flights on the 5th, and probably contributed to the low day's mileage of only 77 miles. Between noon on the fifth and noon on the sixth, the raider covered 143 miles on a course of 095°, then turned and ran to the westward (268°) at full speed, covering 320 miles in twenty-four hours. Another von Ruckteschell hunch? Absolutely, because at 1400 a ship materialized out of the rain about ten miles off. The watch officer soon determined she was headed northeast (045°), which was later refined to 057°, and the chase was on. *Zufall* (chance), entered the commander in the KTB. At 2000, the *Michel* now eighteen miles dead ahead of her unsuspecting prey, stopped and put *Esau* in the water, then slowly ran down the doomed freighter's reciprocal course—237°. The first salvo was fired at 2144 and the fully loaded Greek-flagged *Eugenie Livanos* sank at 2235. It had been a wild melee, with the wounded motor ship making almost three complete four to five mile circles and nearly ramming the *Michel* before succumbing. "That was my mistake," wrote von Ruckteschell in his KTB of the near collision. The *Livanos* carried a crew of thirty-one. Of them, nineteen survived, including her captain, and at daybreak were found in a lifeboat and taken prisoner.

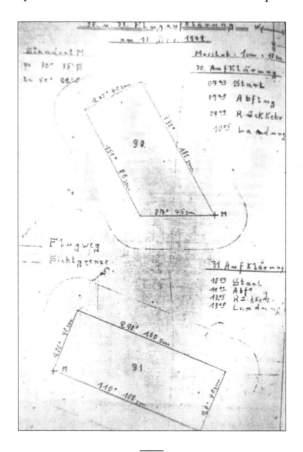

On December 13, von Ruckteschell called it quits and headed for the South Atlantic and home. On the 18th, the *Michel* reached latitude 44° 35′ south, ran to the west, pretty much on the forty-fifth parallel, and by the twenty-sixth was in the South Atlantic on a northwesterly course. Two days later, von Ruckteschell presided over another medal award ceremony. At this time, three *Oberleutnante zur See*—Jürgen Herr, Adolf Wimmel, and Carl Cordes—and twelve enlisted men were presented with the Iron Cross, Class 1. An additional fifty enlisted men received Iron Crosses, Class 2. At the same time, each member of the crew received a remembrance gift in the form of a small (4x4.5-inch) shield-shaped wooden plaque, with a painted metal casting showing the ship's name, an anchor, and the date.

**A replica, now in author's possession of von Ruckteschell's 1942
Christmas gift to each *Michel* crew member.**

On this day also, the commander made the following entry in his KTB: *"Die Gevangenen hatten sich auch eine Weinachtsbaum gemacht, erhielten dasselbe Essen und Naschwerk wie die Bezatzung und etwas mehr Bier als souch. Betrunken ist am diesen Abend, soviel ich weiss, keiner der Bezatzung gewesen."* Roughly translated, he said the prisoners had made their own Christmas tree, and were given the same food and delectables as the crew. He added, as far as he knew, there was no drunkeness by his men. In light of what transpired following the first round of Iron Cross presentations, it is quite probable von Ruckteschell had no idea of what went on below decks.

Many years later, the *Sawokla*'s second officer, Dennis Roland, wrote the following to this author:

As Christmas drew nigh, the Germans wanted us to have a tree so they produced lots of new canvas and showed us what to do. We shredded many a yard. Then a tapered pole, some five feet in length and four inches in diameter at the base was produced. The shredded canvas was pierced with stiff wires and the wires stuck into the tapered pole and trimmed accordingly. The whole tree was then taken away to the paint shop for final touches, so that when it was returned to us several days later we took a great deal of interest in it. It was now transformed into a beautiful green tree with tapered boughs and stiff pine needles. It had a base and all it now needed were the colored balls and some tinsel. Actually, we made several such trees for the various messes aboard ship. The men then collected the silver from cigarette packs and various ornaments were borrowed. The Germans gave us tiny Christmas candles, which we fitted to the tree and lit on Christmas Day. A few days before the 25th, I was called to the German Lieutenant's room. I was escorted by an orderly, who knocked on the door of the officer's quarters. Upon receiving a reply, I was let in first. The Lieutenant stood up and saluted me in the orthodox manner and told me to make myself comfortable. He then spoke to the orderly who then left, returning with a couple of cold bottles of Beck's beer. After the beer and a cigarette, we got down to business. The Lieutenant asked me how we intended to celebrate Christmas. "Well," I said, "we came aboard practically naked and there is really nothing we can do. We haven't any supplies of any kind." He then asked me if I wanted the loan of a phonograph, to which I said "Yes." I remained with him for about an hour, had a few more beers, and we both got a bit tight. We discussed world politics, and I found him to be a rabid Nazi, but still, I liked him.

Christmas Day rolled around and we were still in the cold Latitudes. Steam was turned on in our quarters. The Lieutenant said we were all to dine together, so the officers moved their tables and benches into the crew's quarters, which was much larger and could easily accommodate all of us. We had an idea what was in store for us, as the men were busy the previous few days preparing Christmas bags with lots of delicacies. The day before Christmas, several cases of Beck's beer were brought below and locked away. Christmas morning, we had a treat in the way of cakes, strawberries, and cherries—and goodly portions, too. Then the tables were moved, our tree was set up, and candles prepared for lighting. We managed to get a blackboard and chalk and "A Merry Christmas to All" was written out in script. Then we were issued five bottles of beer apiece, a better than average dinner, and then our Christmas bag. Before mentioning the contents, I want to say we were presented with two bottles of cognac out of which we were able to get three or four shots each. The Lieutenant came down while the tree was still lit, with which he was pleased. We all stood and toasted his health and ours. He presented us with two packs of unused playing cards and four harmonicas. After he made a pleasant speech, I thanked him, we shook hands, and he departed, highly pleased. German sailors came to pay their respects throughout the day. Some of the prisoners, especially the Greeks, cried a bit as they thought of home and loved ones.

As for our Christmas bags, each held the following: a two pound loaf of white bread containing nuts and raisins; a small bag of nuts and raisins; about two dozen walnuts; a couple of handfuls of assorted nuts; a half-pound can of Italian peaches; a pack of twenty-five cigarettes of the better grade; a one pound bar of Dutch milk chocolate; about a dozen erzatz chocolate balls which were really a miracle as they were made from coal tar products and compared favorable with the genuine Dutch chocolate; and last, but not least, a bottle of good German hair tonic which had won several gold medals at various expositions. There were those among us who wanted to put everything into their stomachs at once. Others ate sparingly and saved for lean days. There was a terrific traffic in exchanging one item for another, especially chocolate for alcohol. As usual, someone sampled the hair tonic and there was renewed trading. Some got drunk, and many thought they were drunk. All in all, I had, personally, one of the best Christmas Days I could recall, and it had to be as a prisoner aboard an enemy raider. This went on for three consecutive days—extra food and everyone very friendly. We were allowed access to those in the hospital and we loaned them the Christmas tree and the phonograph.

At noon on Christmas Day, the *Michel's* position was 44° 49' S, 05° 50' E, 810 miles southwest of Cape of Good Hope light. For the first time in many days, the sky was cloudless although the temperature was 5.5°C (42°F) and the wind was light. At 1015, the entire crew, except for the bridge and engine room watches and the lookouts, mustered in overcoats on the fore deck. The course was temporarily changed from 270° to provide a lee and von Ruckteschell delivered his Christmas address. The KTB does not disclose what he said. Before dismissing the attending officers and crew, First Officer Erhardt approached his commander and requested permission to say a few words. Instead of addressing the crew members, he turned toward von Ruckteschell and read the body of the following radio message, which had been received the previous day:

FT am "Schiff 28" Nr. 43 Uhrzeitgruppe 1036/24 v. 24.12 Für Kommandant: In dankbarer Würdigung Ihres heldenhaften Einzatzes im Kamp für die Zukunft unseres Volkes verleihe ich Ihnen als 158. Soldaten der deutschen Wehrmacht das Eichenlaub zum Ritterkreuz des Eisernen Kreuzes.

Adolf Hitler.

Roughly translated, Hitler's message said, "In grateful acknowledgement of your valiant mission in the battle for the future of our people, I bestow on you, the 158th soldier of the German armed forces to receive it, the Knights Cross of the Iron Cross with Oak Leaves."

This was a rare distinction. Only 890 such awards were made throughout Germany's participation in World War II. Two other raider captains were so decorated: Ernst-Felix Krüder (*Pinguin*), posthumously, November 15, 1941, and Bernhard Rogge (*Atlantis*), December 31, 1941. Otto Kähler, who commanded the *Thor* on her first voyage, received the Oak Leaves on September 15, 1944, but that was for his actions as a *Konteradmiral* in the position of *Seekommandant*, Festung (Fortress), Brest, France.

First officer Erhardt affixing his commander's *Eichenlaub zum Ritterkreuz de Eiseren Kreuzes.*

Later in the early evening, the course was changed to 315°, and the *Michel* was really headed home. In the five days after Christmas over 1,400 miles were logged. On the twenty-eighth, the course was changed to 0°—true north. Then a strange set of circumstances occurred. The ship's noon position on December 30 was 25° 58′ south, 8° 58′ west. Twenty-four hours later it was at 25° 42′ south, 9° 15′ west. They had covered only 23 miles! The opening entry in the KTB for the thirty-first is "Ship lies stopped," and then von Ruckteschell goes on to describe how, in the nicest weather, his crew and the prisoners painted the ship. The prisoners, in bosun's chairs, did the deckhouse and the smokestack, and the German crew was over the sides. *"Wo sind da die Feindseligkeiten?"* he asked. (Where is the hostility?) The initial entry for January 1 was also "Ship lies stopped" but at 1110 it was "Course 045°, half speed", then "2100 stopped." On January 2, the first entry was again "Ship lies stopped."

The problem was Konrad's aircraft. Although the engine was running smoothly, fuel consumption had increased 25 percent and it was nearing the one-hundred-hour pit stop. Additionally, the struts on one of the floats needed replacing. If everything went by plan, Konrad estimated the seaplane would be ready for service in the morning of January 1. Things didn't go as intended, and it was not until the morning of the second when the Arado was deemed flyable. Unbelievably, this delay would deliver another victim to the *Hilfskreuzer*. At 0838 Konrad took off. His first leg was twenty-eight miles to the south, then eighty miles to the southeast, followed by forty miles northeast. The last leg, to the northwest for ninety miles, would bring him back to the *Michel*, which had been moving northeast at nine knots for a planned rendezvous at 1044. At 1010, the raider's foremast lookout sighted the topmasts of an oncoming ship, broad on the starboard bow. This was cause of much concern on the *Michel's* navigating bridge as it was quickly calculated they would be within six miles of the stranger when Konrad was due to arrive thirty-four minutes hence. Von Ruckteschell immediately made a course change from 045° to 300°, keeping the intruder hull down, and attempted to notify Konrad by radio. No reply was received and it was assumed, because the Arado's altitude was only 330 feet, the ultra-shortwave radio transmitter could not reach him. In fact Konrad did receive the warning, but his acknowledgement was not received by his assigned operator in the raider. Twenty minutes after the raider's sighting, the enemy ship came into Konrad's view, and he assumed her lookouts saw him. So, he changed course to intercept it. When two to three miles astern, he changed his course to the east, ostensibly headed for Africa from whence, if he had been seen, it would be assumed he had come. Eventually, when the ship dropped below the horizon he reversed course and headed off to the northwest on an end run. At 1101, Konrad made radio contact, telling the *Michel* he had been seen by the enemy. Von Ruckteschell replied, stating, "My location is quadrant 4331, and my course is 315°." At 1126 the *Michel* lookouts spotted the Arado bearing 180°. The aircraft touched down at 1145, and was picked up at 1200. The incident was summed up by von Ruckteschell with, "The thought, that in the short time of two and one half hours, another ship would come onto the position of the *Michel* is absurd." To this point, I have not mentioned the World War II *Kriegsmarine* method of position reports by its ships and U-boats. Von Ruckteschell told Konrad the *Michel* was in quadrant 4331. This was the product of a very secret system which by use of gnomic and Mercator projections translated latitude and longitude into a simple two letter, four number code which delineated an approximately six mile by six mile area wherein the vessel was situated. This scheme divided the oceans of the world into blocks lettered AA to YE, called quadrants. As an example, quadrant AC measured 486 sea miles on each side. Each quadrant was divided into nine blocks which would be divided into 81 blocks numbered 11 to 99 with the numbers 20, 30, 40, etc., excluded. Thus, the blocks in AC would be designated as AC11 to AC99. Each of those blocks would be similarly divided into 81 blocks measuring 6 miles to a side and also numbered 11 to 99. Those numbers would be added creating a range of positions in quadrant AC from AC1111 to AC 1199, AC1211 to AC1299, going all the way to AC9999. As the quadrant charts also carried latitude and longitude designations, the navigator would enter the ship's or aircraft's position and then determine which quadrant he was in. Of course in the above Ruckteschell-Hoppe exchange it was not necessary to use the alphabetical designator.

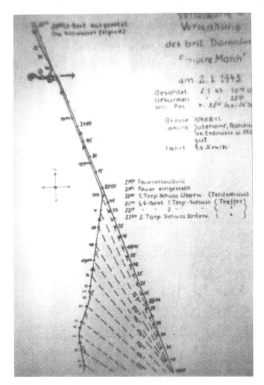

The *Michel's* navigators and lookouts then turned their attention to the enemy vessel, which Konrad identified as an eight-thousand-ton British cargo vessel. She was proceeding on a course of 300°, but at 1300 changed course to 340°, which threw the Germans off the scent for a while. Corrections were made and the hunt was on. At 2115, the motor torpedo boat was in the water, and the *Michel* was on its *Angriff* (attack) course. Open fire was ordered at 2146, cease fire at 2152 when the enemy was burning throughout its entire length. Finally, an hour later, two torpedoes from the *Esau* and one from the *Michel* ended the one-sided fight. This vessel was the 7,040 gross tons, British flagged, *Empire March*, bound for Trinidad from Durban. She was fully loaded with 3,000 tons pig iron, 1,000 tons tea, 4,000 tons peanuts, plus assorted piece goods. Of her crew totaling fifty-eight, twenty-five, including her master, the only officer to survive, were picked up and taken prisoner. Five of these were severely wounded, and of them, one died in the *Michel's* sickbay during the early hours of January 3. He was Able Seaman Robert Barnes McMillan, age 29, of Maryport, Cumbria, England. Von Ruckteschell conducted his funeral service at 0745 in a position close to that of the *Empire March* when it sank. It is his remarks of that occasion which I quoted on pages 231-232. In the area three of the lifeboats from the *Empire March* were found floating, and a small boat manned by sailors armed with hatchets was launched to sink them. Amazingly, another seriously wounded survivor was discovered in one. "He is very weak," wrote von Ruckteschell, "but visibly happy we got to him."

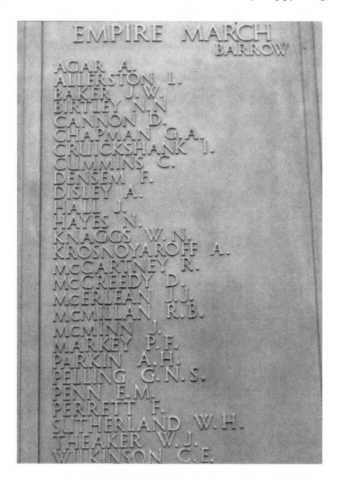

Tower Hill Memorial, London.

On January 5, SKL notified von Ruckteschell of the loss of the *Rhakotis*. "This is a hard blow for us," he wrote in his KTB. He did take comfort in the news that the crew, for the most part, was rescued and none were taken prisoner by the British warship. Also, there was a small glimmer of hope that some of the mail came through the disaster. "That the Norwegian prisoners are in Spain is very unpleasant," he added. "The English intelligence people will soon understand everything." The next day another message from SKL delivered the most cruel news of all. It told von Ruckteschell they saw no possibility at the moment of his continuance on to Germany. Assuming the vessel had sufficient fuel and provisions, he was ordered to return to the Indian Ocean and make for Batavia. So, for the third time the *Michel* and her crew underwent the cold trek below 45° south latitude, and on January 26 the course was set for the long passage to Lombok Strait, the Java Sea, and Batavia. In the afternoon of February 6, the foremast lookout sighted Bali's mountain tops, 117 miles away. The next day, carefully zigzagging and escorted by *Esau*, the eighteen to forty kilometer wide strait between Bali and Lombok was traversed. For the *Michel*'s crew, these lush islands were welcome vistas, the first land they had seen in 324 days. The passage was not without a bit of excitement, however. One of the *Michel*'s many lookouts detected what he thought to be the periscope of a submarine. *Kapitänleutnant* von Schack in *Esau* went on the attack, dropping a single depth charge on what was discovered to be a floating vertical piece of bamboo. The Tandjoeng Priok pilot was picked up at 1010 on the 10th, and at 1526 the *Michel* was secured at Pier 1.

Retrieving the Arado 196.

Konrad flew search flights numbers 43 and 44 on January 4, before the orders to proceed to Batavia were received. From that date onward, however, his two Arados remained in their hatch.

One may wonder at von Ruckteschell's reticence to utilize the aircraft in the long passage across the Indian Ocean. He may not have wanted to find additional victims, or may well have been told by the SKL not to create a disturbance in those waters. The Japanese also might have had a say in what the Germans could or could not do. The chances of encountering an Allied warship were remote, but possible. After all, they were crossing sailing routes from Western Australia to the Red Sea, the Persian Gulf, and to Calcutta, Colombo, and Bombay. Putting Konrad in the air to scout out ahead during the day seems to be a prudent choice. Why wouldn't his commander order it?

It is now known that the British Admiralty was aware of some German activity in the vicinity of Java. On January 4, 1943, HMS *Trusty*, a T-class submarine, departed Colombo for a patrol in Lombok Strait. No details are available as to her specific movements. According to John D. Alden, CDR, USN (Ret), in his *U.S. Submarine Attacks During World War II*, on February 11, the day following *Michel*'s arrival at Tandjoeng Priok, *Trusty* sank a three-thousand-ton motor ship in the Java Sea! Again, facts are missing, but it all seems to be more than coincidence.

CHAPTER TWENTY-TWO

A Few Looks at the *Michel*

When I was clinging to the life raft before the raider picked us up, although it was not a bright night, there was enough visibility for me to see her silhouette. (The scene remains today indelibly impressed in my mind.) So, as soon as we were settled into our new quarters, and armed with the pad of paper and pencil purloined from the doctor, I began reconstructing what I had seen. We were aboard this vessel for four weeks, and not always confined to our quarters, so I was able to gradually embellish my first observation. It should be recalled that we had occasional exercise periods on the foredeck, and I went to the galley three times a day to collect the food for my fellow officer prisoners, all the while keeping my eyes open. And there was a lot to be seen! Also, on the day we left the *Michel*, being transferred by boat in broad daylight to the supply tanker *Uckermark*, I had about fifteen minutes to closely scan her details, resulting in a further refinement of this first rough drawing. There are a few minor errors, such as the misspelling of *schiff* and the indication of "speed 28 knots." The gun in number 2 hatch was not 20 cm, but 15 cm, as in the forecastle and in the stern.

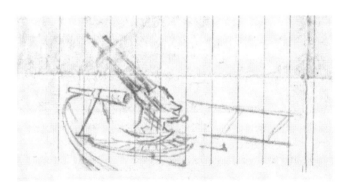

The *Michel's* forward twin 37 mm (3.7 cm) battery. Note "dummy" cannon barrel and tracks allowing unit to be moved a short distance aft.

Also, aft of the stack, there was a single 15 cm, not two as I believed. Worthy of note are the twin 37 mm (3.7 cm) batteries on the after deck house and on the focsl which were disguised as simple 3-inch or 4-inch cannons sometimes carried by comparable merchant vessels in 1942. In reality, the forward 3.7 cm slid back on tracks, as I managed to note on one of my unauthorized visits to the forecastle deck.

Just aft of the focsl and forward of the foremast, I show a wooden box. This was most obvious to me the night I was picked up, and we conjectured about it during our on-deck exercise perambulations. It turned out to be nothing more than a swimming pool set up for the crew's use in tropical latitudes!

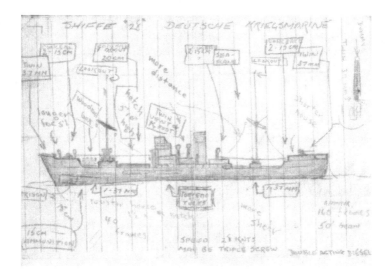

The original "rough" sketch.

After seeing the raider on February 10, and subsequent days at its berth at Tandjoeng Priok, I drew what I call my smooth sketch. There are several details of note here. Basically, my proportions are not true in that I exaggerated the heights of the masts and the stack. Accuracy would make them shorter and the ship longer. As this was a motor ship, not needing a smokestack, the upper portion was removable which, when accomplished, would alter the observer's perception of the vessel considerably. The only other 1943 addition to the original is the inclusion of 2 cm machine gun positions atop the resistor houses at the bases of the masts. All in all, however, when compared to a photo of the *Michel* taken from the Italian blockade runner, *Pietro Orseolo*, when the *Michel* sailed from Batavia, I did produce a fairly recognizable rendering.

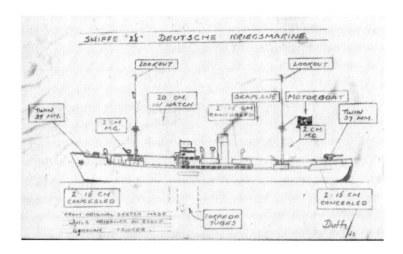

The "smooth" sketch.

Michel departing Tandjoeng Priok on February 15, 1943.
View from *Pietro Orseolo.*

My description of the raider's armament is particularly interesting. From a point of view of over sixty years removed, I cannot recall how I was able to determine gun sizes. Somehow I did learn what she carried and time has allowed me to be proven substantially correct. In fact, in 1987, I attended the annual reunion in Bremerhaven of a number of German naval types who had been in Japan during World War II. They call themselves the *Nippon Gruppe* and include many *Michel* survivors. To that meeting I brought photocopies of my sketches to be distributed to the attendees, but which aroused little comment. Gustav Tober, our guard and constant companion aboard the *Michel*, did question me as to how I was able to see so much of his ship. "You vas officer, Doffy?" he asked. "Yes," I replied. "*Aber* (but) officers go not back here," he said, pointing to the after hatch areas. I told him that I did and there were many places that I investigated. I referred to the sketch of the dummy gun on the focsl that camouflaged the twin 3.7 cm antiaircraft gun. "How about that? I got up there and saw what you had." To which he replied, "Doffy, ve choot you vor dis!"

Later in the year, Wilhelm Osterfeld, who had been the radioman/meteorologist in the *Michel* put out a newsletter as he does after each reunion. In his '87 letter, Osterfeld wrote the big surprise of that year's gathering was the "visit of Mr. and Mrs. Duffy." He went on to review the sinking of the *American Leader* and then devoted many words to my memorabilia, particularly the *Michel* sketches. "George is an exact observer and a good artist," he stated. "Even the main engine is exactly defined: 'double acting Diesel.' It makes me wonder," he continued, "that George reported our gun sizes in centimeters and millimeters. The Americans today still use inches. SOMEONE MUST HAVE GIVEN HIM THAT INFORMATION. WHO COULD IT HAVE BEEN?"

At this point, the reader may be curious as to my original motivation in creating these sketches. You must realize, however, that, first of all, I never thought that I was to be a prisoner for the duration of the war. The Germans would, we believed, put us ashore on a deserted island, or deliver us over to a neutral (Portugal, perhaps), or parole us back to our own people with the agreement that we would not return to sea for the duration of the conflict. Naively, I assumed that I would be able to smuggle my "art work" ashore with me. In retrospect, the whole business was nothing more than an exercise, albeit dangerous. It's difficult to say just what von Ruckteschell would have done had Tober or someone found out what I was doing. Today, it has earned the admiration of one of *Michel*'s officers (notwithstanding what Tober had to say). In 1989, Jürgen Herr, wrote, "Here you receive my respect again, George. You really tried everything to tell your side as much as possible about our ship." And that just about sums it up.

The *Michel*'s fate will be treated in a future chapter. Meanwhile, continuing in her description are several line drawings courtesy of Michael and Christopher Smith whose brother and uncle was lost in the *Lylepark*. These gentlemen found in British archives a copy of a United States Navy Department report on Raider 28, the *Michel*, "based on interrogation of former members of her crew captured from the blockade runners *Weserland*, *Rio Grande*, and *Burgenland*."

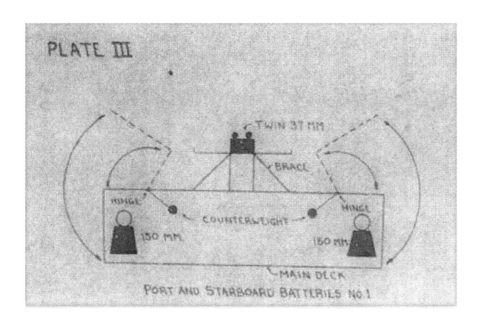

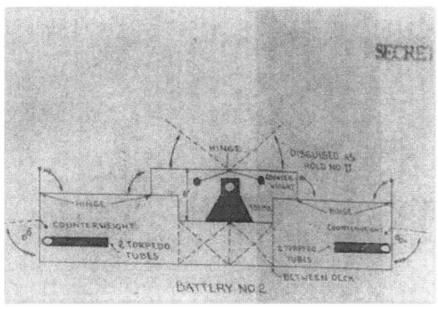

Courtesy of Michael and Christopher Smith from a United States Naval report found in Royal Navy archives. The forward guns and the gun in Number 2 hatch.

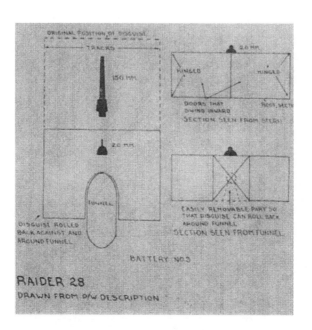

The gun aft of the smoke stack.

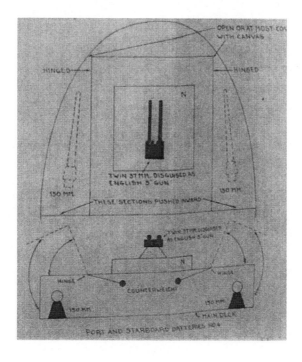

The guns on the after deck.

As written previously, the raider *Thor* was destroyed in the *Uckermark* explosion. Thus, when the *Michel* arrived in Japan in March 1943, a number of her older crew members were supplanted by younger ratings from the *Thor* who had survived its demolition. The three blockade runners, with an unknown number of *Michel* veterans aboard, departed Yokohama at intervals in October. On January 3, 1944, in the South Atlantic, the USS *Somers* (DD 381) sank the *Weserland*. The following day, also in the South Atlantic, the USS *Omaha* (CL 4) and the USS *Jouett* (DD 396), within a five hour time frame, intercepted the *Rio Grande* and the *Burgenland*, which were scuttled by their crews who served out the war, along with survivors of the *Weserland*, in American prison camps.

February 17. Members of the raider crew have been seen ashore. I recognized two men on Sunday, the 14th, but they didn't see me. On Monday, she was supposed to have moved out into the roadstead. I was out again on Tuesday, the 16th, and the ship had evidently sailed.

The *Michel* had departed at 1150 on the fifteenth, bound for Singapore. On the seventeenth, at 0253 she again crossed the equator, and at 1503 arrived at the Singapore pilot station, but no pilot boat appeared. Ultimately she anchored at 1822 off Keppel Harbor from whence von Ruckteschell dispatched Jürgen Herr to inform the Japanese of the ship's arrival. For some time he could find no one. The Japs were partying! Whooping it up for the emperor! Celebrating the anniversary of the city's surrender on February 15, 1942. The raider laid at anchor until 1046 on the 19th, when she moved to a pier for the purpose of taking on fuel. For some unknown reason the survivors of the *Sawokla*, *Eugenie Livanos*, and *Empire March* were not put ashore at Tandjoeng Priok, and were still aboard at this time. Here, however, at 1624 sixty-five of the captives—all the Americans and British and one Canadian—were handed over to the Japanese and became residents of the great Changi Prison at the east end of Singapore Island. Most of them were soon sent to work on the deadly Burma railway. Remaining on board were a mixed bag of seventeen prisoners—eleven Greeks, two British Indians, a Swede, an Argentinean, an Egyptian, and a Maltese. In his KTB von Ruckteschell wrote he was not going to take the chance that any of these men could be considered as neutrals by the Japanese and be repatriated as were the Norwegians and the Swede of the *Rhakotis*. Also not handed over were the four valuable Chinese laundrymen, originally from the *Patella*. The next morning, at 0915, the mooring lines were let go. At 1410 the harbor pilot was dropped, the engine room telegraph swung to *Voll Voraus*, and the *Michel* commenced the last leg of her almost year long voyage, bound for Kobe, Japan.

———

**Engine room Telegraph (ERT) on navigating bridge
of a German merchant vessel, e.g. *Michel*.**

During the time the *Michel* was at Tandjoeng Priok, another hare-brained scheme
was concocted. It may have been Pat Paris's idea. Some of our people were still
wearing the German uniforms issued to them on the night they were rescued.
It was proposed one of us dress as a German sailor and sneak aboard the ship in
order to tell von Ruckteschell about the poor treatment we were receiving from
the Japanese and to request asylum. That "one of us" was me. Good thing the
ship sailed when it did!

CHAPTER TWENTY-THREE

Michel: To Kobe

The *Michel*'s trip to the north was not a pleasant one. Moderate to strong gales were encountered, commencing on February 21, the second day at sea, and continuing until the evening of the twenty-sixth. The winds were generally northerly, ranging from north-northeast to northeast by east. With the courses steered varying between 040° and 060°, the port bow was constantly buffeted by force 6 to force 8 seas, which probably swept the focsl and the fore deck, although the KTB makes no mention of such. Rain showers were experienced from the twenty-first to the twenty-third. These changed to squalls the next three days. On the twenty-sixth, the storm waves were exceeding twenty-five feet, and von Ruckteschell wrote, *Der NO Monsun bläst mit Stärke 9.* (The northeast monsoon blows with force 9.) That's forty-one to forty-seven nautical miles per hour, but by 1900 the wind had dropped to a moderate breeze and they were out of the bad weather. With visibility limited, very little traffic had been encountered. On the twenty-third at daybreak a large tanker was seen, and the next day in the afternoon a convoy consisting of a torpedo boat escorting two steamers was overtaken. Von Ruckteschell estimated their speed at 5 knots. Flag greetings were exchanged with the naval vessel. When the weather cleared on the twenty-sixth, the *Michel* was approaching the southern tip of Formosa (now Taiwan) with the intent of passing to the east. The Japanese navy in Singapore told the Germans this was an especially dangerous area because of the possible presence of an American submarine. At 0400 on the twenty-seventh, in bright moonlight, Yonakuni Island, the westernmost of the Ryukyu Island chain, was sighted. At daybreak, all lookout posts aloft and on the decks were manned. The crew quarters were evacuated of all personnel, only the engine room watch standers remained below decks. The vessel went on to a zigzag plan of steering which, surprisingly, was discontinued at noon. At 0800 next morning, the last day of the month, a large fishing fleet was sighted. In the chance a submarine could be hiding amongst them, the routine of the twenty-seventh was followed. It was 1500 before the raider was clear of the fishermen and zigzagging ceased.

It was not just the east coast of Formosa where submarines of the United States Navy were operating. In this month of February 1943, the *Thresher* (SS 200) hit the Japanese submarine I-62 in Soenda Strait with a dud torpedo; the *Trout* (SS 202) sank a 16,800-ton tanker and a gunboat off the northwest coast of Borneo; the *Tunny* (SS 282) sank two freighters of 6,345 tons and 5,306 tons off Hong Kong; the *Sawfish* (SS 276) mistakenly torpedoed two Russian freighters, running with their lights on, south of the Japanese home islands, and then an 8,000 ton tanker 150 miles southeast of Kyushu. This last sinking occurred on February 21, before the *Michel* reached that latitude, but less than 400 miles from the *Michel*'s projected track. Also, the *Grayling* (SS 209) was patrolling off Corregidor when the *Michel* passed 300 miles to the west on the twenty-fourth. Either the Japanese in Singapore were ill-advised as to what was happening in the waters off Southeast Asia, or they were not being quite forthright with their Axis partner. At a guess it was a dose of both.

During the morning of March 1, Tsushima was sighted and in the afternoon Shimonoseki Strait transited. At 1620, a Japanese patrol boat materialized and somehow or other put itself into a potential collision situation, which von Ruckteschell avoided by calling for full speed astern. "*Unseemännisch* [unseamanlike],", wrote the commander. This was followed by the arrival of a picket boat which instructed the raider to follow it. Eventually, at 1827 an Inland Sea pilot named Higuchi came aboard, and von Ruckteschell was informed a nighttime passage was to be made. No one expected this, but the Japanese had not yet extinguished their coastal navigational lights, and in particular those in the Inland Sea. So, instead of going to anchor and making the scenic passage in daylight, the voyage continued. Von Ruckteschell wrote in his KTB of the anticipated pleasure of the journey and the disappointment felt by all hands. Without further comment, his last entry reads, "March 2, 1943, 1358, anchored in Kobe roadstead, made fast to buoy 6."

CHAPTER TWENTY-FOUR

Last Months at Priok

February 19. Saw a case, contents(?) on the dock. Markings BUENOS AIRES/SS BRAGELAND. (Feb. 25. Jap using case for personal belongings.)

The neutral Swedish *Brageland* was stopped by the German U-164 on January 1, 1943 (just a month and a half before I spotted this case) in the Atlantic Ocean, about 650 miles east of the mouth of the Amazon River. She was "searched and sunk according to prize regulations."

February 22. Working on docks, loading aviation lube oil onto trains. Barrels, still sealed were marked PORT Q'MASTER, FT. MASON FOR ACSO, NICHOLS FIELD, RIZAL, P.I. Dated 10-27-41. All American forces writing radio messages. George B. broadcasts.

My protest and declamations of mid-January seem to have been muffled and/or overridden, as I was working on the docks. I was in charge of the work parties, so something was resolved. As for the radio messages, nothing originating on this date was ever received in the United States. George B. was George Bowens of the *Leader*.

March 3. It is reported that a German naval tanker has been sunk in the N. Atlantic by HMS Sussex.

The source of this information is unknown. At the time, we probably thought the tanker was the *Uckermark*, but of course it wasn't. Incredibly, insofar as my journal entry is concerned, less than a week earlier on February 26, HMS *Sussex*, in a position about 500 miles southwest of Cape Finisterre, indeed sank a German tanker. This was the former Norwegian *Herborg*, captured without resistance in the Indian Ocean by the raider *Thor* on June 19, and taken to Japan by a prize crew. There she was renamed *Hohenfriedberg*, and on November 11 left Yokohama for

Bordeaux. There were in this Tandjoeng Priok camp, undoubtedly, one or more secret radio receivers, but why anyone would have compromised their existence by leaking such innocuous news as the sinking of a single German ship is not understandable.

March 15. Working at Jap Navy station.

This navy station, formerly a yacht club, was manned by a couple dozen Japanese seamen. Once a week they were given a small number of prisoners to perform menial tasks such as grass cutting, raking, sweeping, cleaning, and so forth, in and around the buildings and grounds. The work was no problem, but the Japs were. Slappings and kickings for little or no reasons caused everyone to avoid this detail. It was inevitable, thus, that I, more sooner than later, was handed the assignment. Remember the *Mütze* I stole while on the *Uckermark*? I wore it all the time, and it saved my neck here. The Jap sailors recognized it and when I told them I was a merchant marine officer and my ship had been sunk by a German raider which had taken me prisoner, they were quite impressed. Soon I was teaching them semaphore signaling and the Morse code—in English. I even pulled a few fancy knots from memory and an eye splice they hadn't seen. The job didn't last much more than another month, but it was mine every week. And trouble free!

When returning to station at noon passed close to landing pier where four German Navy officers were waiting for a launch. One of them was the prisoner officer from the Uckermark. Spoke to him and was recognized.

The officer from the *Uckermark* was the counterpart of the *Michel's* Saupe, but he in no way interacted with us in the same manner. He occasionally stopped in to see Captains Pedersen and Scott, nothing else. We had not heard of the Yokohama disaster, but seeing him was no surprise. It is my understanding this fellow was killed while ashore in Singapore, probably not too long after we had exchanged greetings. I cannot recall who told me about this incident. In September 2005, I mentioned it to Heinz Neukirchen and he could not confirm the story, but we did narrow the fellow's identity down to two names, Eugen Lücke, and Kurt Steffens. My guess is Steffens. Neukirchen was a radio operator in the *Uckermark* and escaped injury in the Yokohama explosion. Later, he was in the blockade runner *Weserland* and became a prisoner of war when she was intercepted by United States Naval units in the South Atlantic. He was landed at New Orleans and spent the balance of the war in a place called Papago Park in Phoenix, Arizona.

There are two German ships in the bay at present. One, a three-mast vessel, is painted light gray and may be a raider.

The "two German ships in the bay" had to be blockade runners. In all probability these were the *Burgenland* and the *Irene*. Other than the *Michel* in Kobe, there were no German raiders operational on this date.

March 31. Australians who left here in the latter part of January returned "home" this evening. Also with them are some of the Aussie MG battalions from the Middle East and a few survivors from the Perth. 600 total.

"MG" indicates Machine Gun.

April 1. 11:00 PM, slight earthquake felt here.

April 13. 500 R.A.F. 500 British preparing to leave.

April 15. We are informed this morning that the entire camp is to be cleaned out by the 18th.

April 16. 1250 R.A.F. and British Army left camp.

April 17. All remaining fit men transferred to Bicycle Camp in city of Batavia.

The movement of the various groups of prisoners was quite confusing, and their destinations were never known. It was assumed that when a group left, it was headed for the docks and an ocean voyage to Japan. Long after the end of the war, a Dutchman named Willem Wanrooy, writing under the pen name Van Waterford published an encyclopedia entitled *Prisoners of the Japanese*. This includes statistics, such as the numbers of prisoners carried by specific ships to named destinations. For the January 1 to April 17, 1943 period covered by my journal, as above, no mention is made of any vessel carrying prisoners departing from Batavia or Tandjoeng Priok. So where did these thousands of men go? To Soerabaja, because from April 22 to April 25, eight ships carrying 6,185 British and Dutch prisoners departed from that port city, bound east for the Molucca Islands of Ambon, Ceram, and Haroekoe, and the Lesser Soenda islands of Flores and Timor, to construct airfields for the Japanese.

They had a terrible time as did all prisoners who were unlucky to be chosen for such projects. The work was backbreaking, the Japanese sadistic. There was little food, and medicine was practically nonexistent. Malaria, dysentery, pellagra, and beriberi ravaged the troops, particularly the British. Within seven months it was necessary to return approximately one thousand critically ill men to Java. On November 28, less than a day's run from Soerabaja, the ship carrying them, the *Suez Maru*, was torpedoed and sunk by the USS *Bonefish* (SS 223). The loss of life was enormous—539 prisoners drowned. Eventually, as the work was completed, prisoners were brought back to Batavia. Some, however, remained on their island outposts until the Japanese surrender. Many more never made it all. Succumbing to disease, brutality, accidents, and American and Australian bombing and strafing raids, were 1,549 unfortunate captives, bringing the total to 2,088 of the original 6,185-33.76 percent.

We had been five and a half months at Tandjong Priok. It was a transition period vastly different from that experienced by most people who fell into Japanese hands in the early months of 1942. The hardened fighting troops who led the asssaults on Singapore and the Dutch East Indies, had moved on to the east, leaving the captured territories in the hands of fourth-rate, poorly-trained Japanese soldiers who were nothing more than half animal, half child, and were in no way capable of the brutalities of their predecessors. Oh, they had an attitude, and were quick with a slap to the face for what was sometime a minor transgression. If a prisoner obeyed the rules, however, and kept his mouth shut, not much trouble would come his way.

We learned a little Japanese, enough to understand their orders and to count. We were counted in the evening, we were counted when we went outside to work, we were counted at the work site, we were counted when the work was finished, and we were counted when we returned to camp. The evening count was always the easiest, as we took up our positions in rows of two or three well before the guards arrived. We could then run a preliminary sound-off in English, allowing each front row man to have his Japanese translation on the tip of his tongue. Not all the prisoners were linguists, and when it came to unrehearsed counts there were occasional foul-ups when a prisoner didn't know, for example, when the man to his right shouted *nee-ju-nee* (twenty-two), he should follow with *nee-ju-san*. Occasionally such goofs would be comical, even bringing a grin to the face of the Jap.

Another language or lingo we had to come to grips with were the acronyms used by the British and Australians. There was RSM (Regimental Sergeant Major), BSM (Battalion Sergeant Major), WO (Warrant Officer) OR (Other Ranks), and C of E (Church of England), among others. One evening, before lockup in our early days on Java, a smartly uniformed RAF LC (Royal Air Force lance corporal) came into our area looking for, to my surprise, me. When I was pointed out, he approached and asked if I was Mr. Duffy. I replied, "Yes" to which he queried, "Are you an RC?" Not understanding, I said, "No, I was the Third Officer in that ship." To my embarrassment, this fellow was the Catholic chaplain's assistant. RC meant Roman Catholic, and he was recruiting for Sunday's Mass!

CHAPTER TWENTY-FIVE

Cycle Camp and Soni

April 18. Remaining prisoners in Priok are shifted.

The author's cubicle at the Cycle Camp, which he shared with Frank Stallman.

The round, vertical object at lower left is my sleeping mat. Above, suspended on a wall-to-wall wire, also serving as a clothes line, is a furled mosquito net. On the right wall, a shelf holds a bottle of soya sauce, another bottle of coconut oil, and a jar of salt.

Hanging is my back pack and a cloth bag which was carried on work parties as sort of a forage sack.

Although life in Tandjoeng Priok was at times difficult, it was a veritable picnic compared to what awaited us in our new surroundings. Commanding the Cycle Camp was one Lieutenant Soni Kenichi, an absolute Jekyll-and-Hyde personality. To a few prisoners, notably the previously cited ensign, he was a benefactor. Everyone else regarded him as a maniac. The man would prowl the grounds looking for a reason to administer a beating. One day, as an example, he passed a two-wheeled cart, loaded with sacks of rice, being pulled to the cookhouse by two prisoners. A trickle of rice grains was leaking from one sack, and, as luck would have it, Soni spotted the problem. He stopped the soldiers and sent one to bring the Dutch colonel, the camp's senior officer, to the scene. When the poor man arrived, he was greeted with a stream of Japanese invective, had his face slapped numerous times, and was then forced to get down on his hands and knees to retrace the cart's path and pick up every spilled rice kernel. In Cycle Camp the saluting or bowing ritual was strictly enforced. As we thoroughly disliked bowing to the little bastards, head covers became the rule. I think we even slept in them; for sure nobody wandered about hatless. In addition one had to keep his eyes wide open, which Alex Shershun apparently was not doing one morning when he failed to see Soni and, thus, didn't salute. Soni charged him, screamed the usual invectives, and when Shershun was unable to reply to his Japanese, calmly removed the web belt from his trousers. He wrapped the belt around his hand and then, with the brass buckle on the outside, swung a round house, which caught Alex on the cheekbone inflicting a wide gash as well as knocking him down.

The Japanese soldiers were not immune to their lieutenant's wrath either. On occasion they were assaulted in rank with a full water bottle swung at the end of a belt. During one bayonet practice session using dummy weapons, a particularly incompetent Nip found himself receiving personal instruction from Soni, and when he failed to grasp the technique he was rewarded with having the wooden rifle broken on his head. There was one day when a screaming Soni single handedly attacked the Jap barracks. The little guys, clad only in their white g-strings, came tumbling out the windows and the back door to escape his wrath. Another time, this was late at night, he assembled his troops in full battle gear, and then with his sword in its scabbard, flailed away at their legs and backsides until they had all helped one another scale the camp's barbed wire fence. The ensign, however, enjoyed a strange relationship with Soni. He could visit unannounced, discuss camp matters, drink the Jap's *saki*, and smoke his cigars!

May 13. American merchant marine officers are given corresponding ratings in USNR by Soni, K., Lieutenant, Japanese Army. Pay is still a question.

Officer status was important. Without it we would be reduced to the lowest rank in the camps' pecking order. That Soni agreed to our request is quite interesting. Captain Pedersen undoubtedly initiated the process, which, in any case, would have gone through the Dutch chain of command. The use of the letters USNR indicates the ensign's probable input. Considering his anger toward me, in particular, and the other merchant officers, in general, for some reason he apparently didn't, or couldn't, interfere with this decision.

Our group of Americans, as mentioned earlier totaled one hundred. Of this number, twenty-five were members of the 131st Field Artillery, a Texas-based

National Guard outfit. Several owned stringed instruments: guitars, banjos, and at least one mandolin. Most evenings, they would get together and run through a few numbers of their not inconsiderable repertoire. This music, of course, came to Soni's attention and he liked it. So much that he set up a weekly program of cowboy songs on the local Batavia radio station. Somehow the ensign managed to persuade Soni that this program could also include the reading of American prisoners' letters to their families. In early May I typed out the following:

From/ George W. Duffy #4977
American
Civilian
Java

To/ Richard S. Duffy (Brother),
26 High Street,
Newburyport, Massachusetts,
United States of America.
Birthday greetings from the island of Java.

I am now interned in a military Prisoner of War camp, located in the city of Batavia. It is half a year since we were landed in this part of the world and we are still together—47 survivors of the motorship American Leader.

As you undoubtedly know, the ship was sunk on September 10 by a small merchant raider. During the early part of the engagement we tried to get away but our speed of 14 knots was no match against the 26 knot raider. But then what ordinary freighter is going to stay afloat after she has been sunk with 8-inch shells and a couple of torpedoes? There is not much question regarding the fate of the eleven missing men; some of them when last seen were badly wounded.

Our life since then has not been too difficult. The food here is just what one would expect, consisting mainly of rice plus some meat, and a quantity of vegetables. By means of a camp canteen we may purchase the extra items such as salt, pepper, and sugar, also fruit, eggs, soap, tobacco and so forth. The money for these purchases, we earn. Army, Navy, and Air Force Officers receive a monthly allowance according to their rank while Merchant Officers are paid only for each working day. Officer's details are of a supervisory nature, taking charge of work parties, for example.

Recreation is varied. Sports of all nations are played—soccer, rugby, baseball, football, basketball. We have even had regular track meets. At one time there was an orchestra composed of British soldiers. In this camp the musical unit is a Dutch band.

Study classes, usually for languages, have been organized. I studied French for a while and then German. There, of course, my time in German ships proved invaluable.

Well, I cannot write to everyone, nor as often as I wish. So, I will let you give my regards to all my friends. And to you at home. Don't worry. Things are O.K.

Again Richard, wishing you a happy birthday, and the best of good luck.

This letter was broadcast, apparently on May 18, and may have been heard by an individual on the West Coast of the United States, who did not then contact my family. He could have passed the message to the below mentioned government facility. On the other hand that "facility" may have been an American listening post in Australia. Whatever, on May 31, this is what Richard actually received:

WAR DEPARTMENT
ARMY SERVICE FORCES
OFFICE OF THE PROVOST MARSHALL GENERAL
WASHINGTON

Dear Mr. Duffy:

The Provost Marshall General directs me to transmit to you the following short wave broadcast which was intercepted by government facilities.

Birthday greetings from the Island of Java. I am now interned in a military prisoner of war camp located on Java. It is half a year since we were landed in this part of the world and we are still together, forty-seven survivors of the motorship American Leader.

Author's note: I made several points in this paragraph: (a) that I was writing in May, Richard's birth month, (b) that we had been there since November, (c) that we were being held as military prisoners, and (d) that eleven men did not survive the sinking. I hoped that someone would question the gap between the date of our departure from Capetown and our expected arrival at Punta Arenas with our November arrival on Java. The next paragraph, "As you undoubtedly know . . ." was completely excised.

Our life since then has been not too difficult. The food here is just what one would expect, consisting mainly of rice plus some meat and a quantity of vegetables. By means of a camp canteen we may purchase the extra items such as salt, pepper and sugar, also fruit, eggs, soap, tobacco and so forth. Army, Navy, and Air Force officers receive a monthly allowance to their rank while merchant officers are paid only for each working day. Officer details are of a supervisory nature, for example, taking charge of working parties.

Author's note: What I wanted to emphasize here is that we were not receiving such basics as salt, pepper, sugar, etc. Also, I was complaining about the discrimination against the merchant marine.

Recreation is varied, sports of all nations are played, rugby, baseball, and football and baseball. We have even had regular track meets. At one time there was an orchestra composed of thirty soldiers, in this camp the musical unit is the Dutch band.

Study classes usually for languages have been organized. I studied French for a while and then German. There, of course, our time in German ships proved invaluable. Well I cannot write to everyone as often as I wish so I will let you give my regards to all my friends and to you at home, don't worry things are o.k. Again Richard wishing you a happy, happy birthday and the best of luck. George.

This War Department letter was signed by the same Colonel Breese who belatedly on May 19 reported the content of my April 23 radio broadcast.

Author's note: My insertion of "our time in German ships" solved the question, what happened to them? The *Newburyport Daily News* in its June 2 edition ran the entire letter, adding at the end "Mention of the time spent in German ships could mean that Duffy and his shipmates fell first into the hands of the Germans rather than the Japanese. The exact fate of the American Leader has never been determined. It was lost late last summer or in early fall after a voyage to Iran and elsewhere with war supplies."

They were on the right track, but didn't elaborate. The *News* closed out the report with an "Editor's Note. It is to be understood that the letter was presumably checked by a Japanese censor and that the prisoner would not be allowed to imply that life was anything but comfortable in an enemy prison camp."

The *New York Times* on May 9 did not name our ship, but the *Newburyport Daily News* on June 2 did!

The Japanese rebroadcasted this letter at least twice. The first occasion was from Bandoeng, Java, on July 14, and the second from Jogiakarta, Java, on July 17. Four people heard the July 14 reading, one of whom mysteriously referred to the original May 18 transmission. Why he did not notify my family of his receipt of that is puzzling. A solitary listener picked up the Jogjakarta transmission.

```
                              mission beach
                              San Diego (8) Calif.
                              July 18 1943


mr. Geo. W. Duffy
26 High St.
Newburyport, mass.

Dear mr Duffy:

            Last evening while listening to a
Japanese broadcast from Jokyakarta Java, a
message was given from your son Richard F Duffy
while the broadcaster gives the names and the
addresses slow enough to be copied, the body y
of the message is broadcast too rapidly for one
who is not a stenographer to take down. However
the sense of the message was that your sons is
all right and in good health. He wants you to
write. Did not say where to write, but as these
messages they broadcast each evening are said to
be American prisoners of war on Java, presume a
letter addressed there or through the Red Cross
would reach him. You may have received the
message from another source but thought I'd send
you this little word just in case; I have a son
who is a prisoner in Japan; have had no direct
word from the lad, only through the Red Cross
advising he was held in a camp in Japan, but am
hoping for word every day.

                    Sincerely

                    walter Favorite
                    711 San Jose Place San Diego Calif
```

This is the letter from the sole listener who heard the message to my brother Richard from Jogjakarta. Unfortunately, he managed to confuse us. Nevertheless, it was one more piece of evidence I was alive on Java. Mr. Favorite's son, Robert E., was an Oiler in the *William F. Humphrey* and, of course, had gone to Japan in the *Charlotte Schliemann*.

326

In retrospect, instead of assisting the distressed next of kin, the government was continuing to make things difficult. Beyond notifying my mother, in the case of the first broadcast, twenty five-days after so many civilians had already done so, and intercepting the letter to Richard on May 18 and getting it to him in two weeks, its response to the Japanese radio efforts was dismal. The United States Navy United States Navy Department heard my April 23 letter and wrote to my mother on July 1. The navy was also "copied" by the government facility responsible for intercepting the May 18 message which, remember, opened with the words, "Greetings from the island of Java." It took them until October 2 to pass that along. Not only were they three and a half months late, their navigation was fouled up. The covering letter reported me as being in the Philippines!

May 18. Pat Paris and Mr. Lee left camp in a group of about 50 officers going to camp at Macassauri.

The correct name for this camp was Kampong Makassar.

May 24. Japanese soldiers are making preparations for the coming attack. Curfew commenced in city. One white Dutch and three natives brought into camp. Local newspaper very silent. All prisoners are to take mass gymnastic drill every morning.

This newspaper was named *Asia Raya* and was printed in the Malay language. From it we gleaned bits of information such as locations of sea battles and land fighting, thus being able to measure the progress of the war.

June 2. The Army officers attempted to make Capt. Pedersen, Mr. Hickey, and Mr. Stallman go on outside working party as laborers.

June 5. They tried to put Mr. Kamins out on a party today. I suggested putting a soldier named Jaster in that place, but Lt. Gallienne screamed that Jaster was their batman, but I pointed out that our man was nevertheless on the party. Then to top it off there was a call for eight men to the Artillery Barracks. Now when a gang goes there, they don't want to go back. The Nips beat the hell out of everyone. So, the party of eight men was divided into one soldier and seven merchant seamen. There is more than one reason we'll be happy when we are free and all of them aren't going to be the Japs.

If the ensign was keeping a low profile in his relationship with the merchant marine contingent, the several United States Army Air Force officers certainly didn't. As pointed out earlier, the camps were organized internally without any input from the Japanese. Each barrack was required to supply a daily quota of laborers. The mentioned lieutenant and at least one other were senior to the ensign and convinced the Dutch colonels "running" the camp of their authority over us. It didn't matter that Captain Pedersen and Hickey were commissioned officers in the United States Naval Reserve, or that Soni had classified us as officers. The Army officers, they averred, had been on active duty, Pedersen and Hickey had not. They were to be in charge even if, as it will be later seen, they had to "turn in" their fellow Americans to the Japanese. Of course, this whole debacle could have been avoided if the British colonels at Tandjoeng Priok had recognized our ranks. British merchant seamen were then, and always will be, civilians, and thus it went for us. The Japanese didn't care what we were. They looked at us as the enemy and considered us to be military prisoners. It would have been much easier for us if the British brass had come off their pedestals. Of course, when we came home at the end of the war our own government told us the same thing, in spite of the words "in the service of his country" in our "Missing in Action" telegrams. How this was rectified many years later will be recounted in later pages.

If the rest of the Army and Navy have the same attitude towards the merchant marine as our fellow prisoners show to us, and the merchant marine knows it, these fellow are going to have a hard time getting home.

—Frank Stallman

The "batman" situation is interesting. This is the term used for a British officer's personal servant. Many of that army's units were captured intact, allowing the batmen to continue serving their individual officers in the prison camps. They made tea, stood in line for food, washed uniforms, ran errands, and so on. The Americans didn't carry it to such an extreme, but we had one man for each group of officers—military and merchant marine. These were older men who were supposedly unfit for outside work, but who could earn a day's pay thereby. I doubt if the Japanese knew of this situation, another example of how the camps were run by the inmates!

June 15. During the past few days a number of natives and a few white men (totaling (50) have been taken prisoner. The Japanese guards are all carrying gas masks now.

June 20. Writing postcards again. Same thing as at Christmas.

Another entry elsewhere in my journal states that the date these cards were written was June 26. In any case, my card was delivered at Newburyport on December 9, less than six months later!

June 30. 26 Americans and about 180 British and Dutch leave for Camp Makasura.

Cycle Camp cookhouse.

I still didn't have the name correct! This was a volunteer group composed mainly of officers who chose to take a chance on the unknown as opposed to the unpredictable, terrorizing Soni. I went with this detachment.

I was in the Cycle Camp for a little more than ten weeks and wrote little in my journal during that time. One incident occurred, however, which has remained clear in my memory over all the intervening years. On this particular day, we were told there would be no work parties, but at noon all prisoners must parade in front of their barracks. Because Admiral Yamamoto Isoroku, the commander in chief of the Combined Japanese Fleet had been killed in battle, an empirewide day of mourning had been declared. All over Batavia church bells rang. Jap soldiers and prisoners bowed deeply on cue, and our elation knew no bounds. We had no idea what happened, but it made no difference. The top man in the Japanese Navy was no more. That was the most joyous memorial service ever celebrated.

Why did they do that? Did they think we would feel sorry for the man? Did not they realize what a great spark to our morale such news was?

For the record, Yamamoto was on an inspection tour to the island of Bougainville, the details of which had been intercepted and decoded by United States intelligence. On April 18, 16 United States Army Air Force P-38 fighter aircraft based on Guadacanal caught two Japanese bombers, one of which was carrying the admiral. Both were shot down. Yamamoto's remains were recovered and on

June 5, 1943, a state funeral was held in Tokyo. That is probably the date when we in Batavia silently cheered.

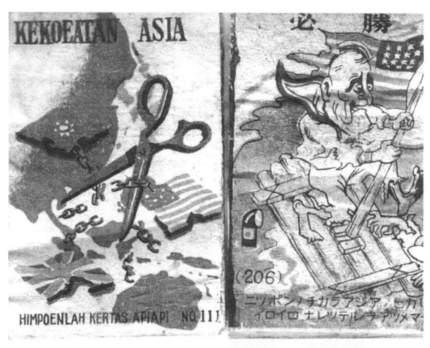

Match boxes. Japanese propaganda aimed at the local Javanese populations.

CHAPTER TWENTY-SIX

A Prison Camp Paradise

Simple diagram of bamboo frame barrack construction, showing sleeping platforms at each side with passage in center. Roof was made of "shingles" using palm frond leaves folded over a thin stick, then loosely stitched together. Resultant roof would be 12 inches or more in thickness.

July 2. Firmly established in our new home. All hands working in garden.

This camp was situated in a grove of coconut palm trees and was composed of a half dozen bamboo-framed, thatched-roof barracks, enclosed with straw mat siding. An aisle ran lengthwise along the centerline. At each side were sleeping platforms made of flattened bamboo. Depending on the camp population the individual prisoner had a space three to five feet wide and about seven feet deep. Other buildings housed the cookhouse, washroom, and latrine. The whole compound was surrounded by a multistranded barbed wire fence, and as one side abutted the main road to Bandoeng, that portion of the fence was covered with the ubiquitous straw matting. Cultivated land surrounded the camp on the other three sides. Outside the perimeter fence there were pens for a number of goats and pigs. The Japanese lieutenant whose name was Tanaka lived in a modern tiled-roof, concrete bungalow. His soldiers had a barrack similar to ours, and a small guardhouse at the camp's main gate.

The senior Allied officer here was Royal Australian Air Force (RAAF) Wing Commander Ron Ramsay-Rae, an imposing figure of a man who towered over the tiny Tanaka. Although from time to time there were problems with the Jap guards, this turned out to be a most remarkable Japanese prison camp. Ramsay-Rae deserves the credit. True, Tanaka was a pip-squeak, completely the opposite of Soni, but the Aussie kept him under control. It was almost a buddy relationship in that the two seemed always together during the day. Thus, without their lieutenant to goad them or provide an unfortunate (for us) example, the guards more or less left us alone.

In addition to the garden areas adjacent to the camp we also worked a large cleared farm within the horseshoe bend of a river about a mile away. This was called Tandjoeng Oost. Here we grew large crops such as peanuts, as opposed to the neatly bedded vegetable plots of Kampong Makassar. Another nearby feature of the landscape was the former Dutch airfield named Tjilitan. We were situated precisely under the approach to a runway and the Jap bombers and fighters came in at tree top altitude. A most interesting experience.

Something occurred in this camp which, in retrospect, had an enormous bearing on my ultimate survival. As mentioned earlier I had been taking French lessons at the Tandjoeng Priok camp where most of the prisoners were British and Australian. Here, although it was an Australian-run camp, the majority of the prisoners were Dutch, many of them former planters. The latter took over the management of the various facets of our agricultural efforts and, naturally, favored their countrymen with work assignments. I found myself digging ditches while Hollanders weeded. The language barrier prevented me from even knowing about the easy jobs. The solution was a no-brainer—learn Dutch. Many of the Hollanders were older men—in their forties and fifties. I was just twenty-one. Some of these fellows had children older than me. In my barrack was a group of seven or eight who, every evening, lit a camp fire and sat around talking, some of them smoking pipes. As they all spoke English to varying degrees, I was invited to sit in, but to each other they spoke their own language. I began to catch on to some of their words and phrases, and soon we dropped the English. For about six weeks, it was a bit of a struggle. After that—no problems. One of these men had, in private life, been a teacher and desiring to improve his English, asked me to tutor him. He had a Dutch language version of a book by Martin and Osa Johnson who were American writers/explorers. About three times a week, this fellow whose name is long forgotten would translate a page into his best English. I would then critique his grammar. In exchange, I would read the same page aloud and he would work over my pronunciations and inflections. It really worked! Later on Sumatra I was able to take charge of mixed nationality work parties, and unless someone told them, many of the Dutch troops didn't know I was American. It saved me from the heavy lifting!

July 12. 60 British ORs, 2 British officers, and 7 Dutch officers leave camp. It is rumored that they, with other prisoners from Bandoeng and Batavia will leave the island. A Jap soldier later told me their destination was New Guinea.

Included in this draft was Geoffrey Sherring, the *Empire Dawn*'s second radio officer. He went to Singapore, became ill there, but later was transported to Nagasaki.

July 16. A nine-day air raid practice period goes into effect tonight. We have only blackout, but it is full moon on the 18th.

July 17. Phil McKeever, Fireman/watertender in the William F. Humphrey, broke his arm yesterday morning. A year ago July 16 his ship was sunk by Schiff 28.

July 23. The Japanese Army announces that at 4 AM on the morning of July 22, two or three enemy bombers appeared over Soerabaja, dropping bombs on the town.

August 5. We have not received any copies of Asia Raya for the past few days. Today the Japs say that no more newspapers will be allowed in camp. Admittedly, Asia Raya has been a good source of information, although a bit late at times. So, the best we can conjecture is that all is not well with the Axis.

———

We were able to follow the course of the war by noting the sites of engagements, attacks, and bombings. The Japanese wrote in glowing terms of their great success in shooting down American aircraft and sinking American ships, but we could see steady progress on the part of our forces through the Southwest Pacific.

August 15. No work today. First anniversary of General Saito's arrival on Java. Several sergeants leave camp to decorate graves. Word from Cycle Camp says that Pedersen, Hickey, and Stallman are still in confinement.

The Japs did silly things like celebrating first anniversaries with a show of compassion for their deceased former enemies. Precisely whose graves these were was never revealed, but could have been in a military cemetery.

The *American Leader* officers stuck to their guns and refused the Army Air Force officers' commands to go on work parties as laborers. As a result, the Air Force officers reported this to Soni, who ordered the three placed in solitary confinement. It appears as though Soni's May 13 actions in giving us corresponding USNR ranks didn't mean anything when it came to work. We were soldiers, plain and simple. According to the *New York Times* of November 18, 1945, Captain Pedersen told Soni, "You can call me a sailor, as I have been at sea thirty six years, but under no circumstance am I a soldier." In any case, Pedersen was incarcerated for sixty days, continuing his argument with Soni, which ended in typical Japanese fashion. The lieutenant added the captain's name to the next draft of prisoners leaving for Singapore. Case closed.

August 23. Captain Scott arrives here.

August 30. Dutch Adjutant awakened last night by Nip sergeant major. Nip says American bombers were here and if bombs were dropped, we would have to extinguish the fires. Actual air raid alarm. This morning rumor says Soerabaja again. Everyone in high spirits.

September 14. Three days ago, our camp radio was removed by the Japs. From what we can ascertain now, all public speakers are also down and no Jap soldier under the rank of Major may keep a set. Rumors are thick concerning Tojo (resigned, then suicide).

Few, if any, Javanese owned radios. By means of the public speakers the Dutch—and now the Japanese—were able to disseminate radio broadcasts of news, announcements, and popular music. We had an actual radio mounted on a platform in the center of the camp. At night when the guards ordinarily would not be inside the camp periphery a wire was run up between a pair of palm trees and, if conditions were right, broadcasts from Australia could be heard. As of September 11, this luxury ceased.

September 20. Japs have admitted capitulation of Italy. All guards are wearing new green uniforms. No liberty for them either. They are being exercised by digging in the garden and are given roadwork in the evening.

The actual date of the signing of the armistice between Italy and the Allies was September 3, and it was announced on September 8.

September 25. For about two weeks now there has been no rain, but this weekend marked the beginning of the rainy season. The rumors of the past few days have put Turkey in the war and Germany capitulated. The general opinion is that Germany will "fold up" within two months of Italy, and that the Japs will be finished six months later. I believe myself that we will be out by May 1944.

September 28. After roll call at 7 PM tonight, all prisoners were marched to the far side of the camp and then the guards searched the barracks. Every person's kitbags, suitcases, etc. were thoroughly gone over. The search was evidently for weapons and most of our garden tools were taken away. I lost only a homemade bread knife which I thought would be a good souvenir. My drawings weren't found at all, however many persons' photographs were taken for inspection and later returned.

October 1. Big native Mohammedan holiday. Drums were beating all day yesterday, and last night when all was quiet in camp, the sound was just a continuous roar. Heavy rain clouds all day, but no rain. Worked in south garden, watering lombok and bajem. Out at 2 PM instead of 3:15 and back into camp at 4:00. No apparent reason. Nip guard barracks searched?

The holiday was Ramadan. *Lombok* is pepper and *bajem* is climbing spinach.

October 2. Preparing bajem plot in morning. In camp at 11:00 instead of 12:30. Nips in city during PM. Regular half-day off for us. Heavy rain at 4:30 lasting about an hour.

October 3. (Sunday). Work as usual. Preparing a plot for bajem. Rumors concerning a draft of prisoners from here. Various totals regarding fit men, old men, etc. requested by Japanese. Lee and Paris still confident of repatriation—letting their hair grow until next week, anyhow. Personally, it was all just a happy dream. Street lights off for about ½ hour after 9 PM.

The Swedish passenger vessel *Gripsholm* was engaged in repatriating diplomatic personnel and certain civilians. We (the American merchant seamen) were interrogated, and, for a while it appeared we were being considered for return to the United States. In fact, so realistic was the situation, I was required by the Australian officers to memorize the names of all the Aussies in the camp (about 400) in the event I did get out, so I could report them to the Australian authorities.

October 4. Out to Tandjong Oost. Wingco and Dutch colonel, also. A very good day. Long rest periods and a fine meal at noon. Signs of the times: we must now march in 2s or 4s all the way out to 'Oost. In camp, the fences are being reinforced, an earthworks being thrown up around the guardhouse, and an order published regarding meetings and gatherings.

October 5. To 'Oost again. Putting compost around jahrak plants. Another easy day. Swimming in the river. Menadonese women claim Timor, Ambon, and other places occupied by the Americans. Much truck activity on the road, mostly lumber.

Jahrak was a castor oil bean plant, to which a large area was devoted. We presumed that these were to be processed into lubricating oil, so did our best to sabotage the project. Beans were planted two to a hill. When we thinned them, the taller sprout was pulled and the smaller received a jab in the roots with a sharpened bamboo sliver.

Although Javanese women were frequently seen bare breasted in the kampongs, full nudity was tabu, so when we would go naked into the river they would call out "naughty, naughty" to us. They also were bathing, but on the opposite bank, and very modestly. The routine was to wear a sarong into the river with a clean dry one around the neck. After washing one's selves and rinsing the worn garments, they would emerge from the water carefully lowering the clean, dry sarongs around their waists.

The Menadonese originally came from the island of Celebes. Much of the camp rumors arose out of these contacts. A woman would call over, for example, "Americans at Timor." Thus, an air raid became an invasion after being retold in several languages.

October 6. Half-holiday, but I had all day off. Timor and Ambon story repeated from hospital. Also, Germany has again capitulated. According to Dr. Burroughs, the draft which left about two weeks ago included Captain Pedersen.

Dr. Burroughs was a United States Navy United States Navy Department doctor who survived the sinking of the USS *Houston*. His practice took him to a central hospital where he picked up news from other locations. Pedersen went to Formosa (now Taiwan), and eventually to Mukden, Manchuria.

October 7. Back in the south garden. Digging holes for eggplant and watering cucumbers. More inquiries from the Nips regarding the 'Leader. Rumors of bombings of Macassar. Two hundred people from there are supposed to be now in 'Cycle Camp.

The inquiries by the Japanese continued to raise our hopes regarding repatriation. The rumors of bombings of Macassar, which is on Celebes, could have come from the same Menadonese women, but if the new arrivals at the Cycle Camp did indeed come from there, then they weren't rumors.

October 8. Working party from 'Cycle Camp tells of 190 officers who have arrived there from Macassar. They are supposed to be of all nationalities and included the commander of the British cruiser Exeter. In a daylight raid on Celebes, two fighters are supposed to have gone up and both were shot down. Plenty of other rumors.

HMS *Exeter*, HMS *Encounter*, and USS *Pope* (DD 225) were sunk in the Java Sea on the afternoon of March 1, 1942. The next day, survivors were picked up by Japanese warships and transferred to a Dutch hospital ship, the *Op Ten Noort*, which landed them at Macassar. The commander of the *Exeter* was Captain Oliver Louden Gordon, RN, who survived the war.

October 9. Harvesting a good crop of spinach in the morning. No work in afternoon. Much air activity. 9 bombers in in morning, and 9 fighters at night. Small amount of mail received in evening. Most of the Australian machine gunners have letters and a few persons whose whereabouts is not known to their next of kin. Capt. Fairbearn, for example, who was taken on Borneo, and Brian Fihelly, shot down over Sumatra. The postmarks, in general, are of June and July, 1942, or over 15 months ago. Capt. Allen, however, has one dated November 1942. The Japs are taking all the goats, it seems, from the camp. Someone has put forward the suggestion that the Indian troops at the hospital are using them.

I don't recall ever getting any goat milk. It probably went to the hospital. Goat meat, however, did occasionally appear in the fried rice and was rather stringy.

October 10. Working in climbing spinach beds all day. Still considerable air activity, all fighters. Rain in afternoon, out to work late. Rain again after dark. Rumor: Germans capitulated as Russians reach Polish border. "Med" fleet bound out to Indian Ocean. Landings in Celebes.

If the British Mediterranean fleet was headed our way, things were going pretty well in Europe and could get better for us.

October 11. Out to Tandjoeng Oost. Very easy day. Cool. Weeding. Continued rumors of Germany quitting and landings in this area.

October 12. Guards here mustered and instructed before taking party. A very miserable day there (Tandjoeng Oost). Japs' usual attitude completely replaced by very sullen actions. They stood over us, watching every move. Officers and men worked together and guards stood at corners of the field. At noon, we knocked off for lunch, then were sent back for our shovels, lined up, and marched "home." Coming back, special care was taken that we kept in 2s or 4s. In camp, everyone worked in the PM, as usual, except us, then came in at 5 o'clock. We all went on parade and a draft of 211 was made up to leave here at 3 AM tomorrow. It included 38 English, and the remainder Dutch. Jimmy Laverick and Roy Neal going. Extreme visibility at Tandjoeng Oost. Gede, Pangrano, and Salak clearly seen.

Ordinarily, we just walked out to Tandjoeng Oost without any formal formation or order. What caused the change in attitude was unknown. That is just the way they were—unpredictable. Nothing of importance occurred in the war in the Pacific around this time. Perhaps it was a delayed reaction to the Italian surrender. Additionally, it is possible the Japs felt we knew of the upcoming draft and some prisoners would attempt to avoid being included by temporarily escaping.

Laverick and Neal were, of course, the third assistant engineer and second officer from the *Empire Dawn*. They were eventually taken to Sumatra where they labored on a Jap air base at Palembang. Both survived the war. I met Roy Neal in Antwerp in 1949 when I was sailing as chief officer in the *American Judge*, and Roy was chief officer in a Houlder Brothers refrigerator ship. Once in the 70s in Sunderland, England, and again in the 80s in Nottingham, England, I caught up with Jimmy. Both have since passed away.

Gede, etc., were prominent mountain peaks fifty to sixty miles away.

October 13. The draft got away in the morning and we later learned they are in 'Cycle Camp. No outside work today: whole holiday. Rain from 6 PM to 8 PM. Parade at about 9 o'clock. All sick personnel counted for the first time I can remember in this camp. Most of the Japanese drunk. The Dutch were told, "Lt. Tanaka says the roofs leak and we all must work very hard." Rumors of another draft and also more people coming here. (Note: This was Wednesday, the usual day off.)

Jimme Laverick and author at Nottingham, England, July 27, 1983.

October 14. Back to work as usual. No Tandjoeng Oost party. Rumors again of Germany throwing in and also that the Jap puppet boss is missing: a fl 2,000 reward is posted. Out an hour late in the afternoon because of rain. The camp is a quagmire. Killed a 3-foot snake, green, slightly poisonous. Sing song with the Australians after supper.

October 15. In front garden, as usual. Plenty of coconuts. Rain in afternoon but not enough to stop work. Continued rumors of peace in Europe and local Germans are supposed to be interned. Nip soldier worrying about other Jap soldiers now prisoners. Had a packet of seeds to be sent home.

These rumors were all wishful thinking. Nothing of any importance was occurring in any part of the worldwide conflict to induce such fantasies.

October 16. Half day. In front garden. One Nip making a bit of a nuisance of himself. Not much doing at all.

October 17. (Sunday) In garden, cutting obie shoots for planting at Tandjoeng Oost. Everyone being moved out of lower end of this hut to make room for a number of people coming in tomorrow.

Obie was the tapioca tree.

October 18. No work in morning for some unknown reason. Out to garden as usual in afternoon. Rain commenced to fall shortly before knock-off and continued well into night. Fifty Dutch from 'Cycle and a dozen Australians from Glodok arrived here at 7 PM. Included two Naval cadets (Dutch) from Celebes. Not much news, though. Soni still raising hell. The draft of the 13th is still in 'Cycle Camp. The Japs were out working on their defenses here when it started to rain, but they couldn't stop. Rain or no rain, they go on until almost 7 o'clock.

Glodok was, in prewar time, a civilian jail in Batavia. The Japanese turned it into a prison camp with the usual deprivations, overcrowding, and so on. The populace, all male of course, was a mix of military and civilian, with the military generally being older or infirm. These people were employed in the hand spinning of jute fiber for the weaving of burlap.

In reference to Soni, while working in the garden at some point during my time at Kampong Makassar one of the Jap guards struck up a conversation with me. He said he would soon be going to New Guinea to fight the Americans. From where we were standing there was a good view of many rice fields extending to more coconut trees, perhaps a half mile away. This little guy then went into a pantomime, imagining himself in New Guinea with the Americans attacking across the fields. He flopped down, pointing his rifle and simulating gun shot sounds. After each volley he would say to me, *"America mati."* Meaning "American dead." This went on for a minute or so when he suddenly turned, aimed to the rear, and shouted out the Japanese equivalent of "Bang, bang." Then with a grin directed at me, he said *"Soni mati."*

October 19. Back to full day routine again. Working in climbing spinach and also picking obie shoots for Tandjoeng Oost. Rumors of landings in Celebes. Timor, Ambon, etc. are supposed to be evacuated by the Japs.

October 20. Fire watch 3 to 4 AM. Half-day work. Still teaching the climbing spinach how to climb. Had quite a talk with the Naval cadets from Macassar in the evening. Rain from 8 to 10 PM.

Because of the high risk of fire due to the bamboo, thatch, and mat construction of the barracks a night watch was maintained. The fellow to my right did an hour, then woke me. After my hour, I called the man to my left, and so it went down the line.

October 21. Another half day off. No work this morning. Nips evidently getting rifle practice. A couple of parties with rifles and gear went out in the morning and afternoon. In garden in afternoon. One of the sows has had 5 pigs and all our climbing spinach has been knocked down by the rain. Started to pluck it but quit at 5 o'clock due to rain. Rain continued for about 3 hours.

Also, on this date, based on what the people who came from Macassar told me, I wrote the following report:

> *All of the crew of the U. S. submarine Perch saved. All the crew of the U. S. destroyer Pope saved except for Yeoman Davis. One American died in the prison camp and one American died on the Dutch hospital ship Op Te Noort. All the officers of the Perch were sent to Japan. All the officers-specialists of the Pope were sent to Japan at the same time. (About April 1942.) Sent to Japan—Lieut. Comm. Blinn (Captain of the Pope), Lieut. Comm. Hurt (Captain of the Perch), Lieutenants Wilson, Bassett, van Buskirk, van der Grift, Schacht, Spears, Michael [sic]. (Last named sent on October 14th with some American ratings.) Left in Makassar—Lieut. A. J. Fisher (Pope). In Batavia—Lieut. Comm. T. A. Donovan (U.S.S. Langley), Lieutenants R. N. Antrim and Lowndes, Ensign Austin (all Pope), Pilot Officer (?) W. D. Haynes (captured in Timor). Flying Officer J. A. Campbell, R.A.F. from Chula Vista, Cal., shot down near Batavia, February 25, 1942. Lieutenant James P. Ferry, [sic] U.S.A.A.C., wounded in Malang, Java, by Jap strafing planes. (To Nippon (?) September 1943.) Lieutenant W. H. Gallienne, U.S.A.A.C., shot down over the island of Bali, February 18, 1942. Buchanen, Sperry Gyroscope Co., Singapore. Ex-Annapolis. Also, connect Major Horrigan, U.S.A.A.C.*

Postwar records indicate the following:

Lieutenant Commander Welford Charles Blinn was repatriated from Mukden, Manchuria at the end of hostilities in 1945. He immediately penned a lengthy report on the *Pope*'s actions up to and including its sinking by Japanese aircraft on March 1, 1942. At the end, he wrote:

> *Part VIII. Lessons learned, conclusion, and recommendations. It is considered that as this report has been delayed three and one-half years and that the installations used are now obsolete, no lessons or conclusions obtained from this action would be of value.*

Lieutenant Commander David Albert Hurt survived the war at Ofuna, Japan, and made a lengthy, formal report of the loss of the *Perch*. His submarine had been badly damaged by Japanese depth charges, and on March 3, 1942 he issued scuttling orders. The entire crew, numbering sixty-two men, were taken prisoner by a Japanese warship. Nine died during their incarceration, most of them on the island of Celebes, in the waning months of the war. Lieutenant William Ritchie Wilson, Jr. (*Pope*), Lieutenant Robert van Rensselaer Bassett,

341

(*Pope*), Lieutenant Beverley Robinson van Buskirk (*Perch*), Lieutenant (jg) Jacob Jay van der Grift (*Perch*), Lieutenant Kenneth George Schacht (*Perch*), and Lieutenant (jg) William Oscar Spears, Jr. (*Pope*) were repatriated from camps in Japan. Lieutenant (jg) John Joseph Aloysius Michel (*Pope*) was found in Mukden. Lieutenant Allen Jack Fisher was, as above, "left in Maccasar," but somehow made it to Batavia in July 1945 from where he was repatriated. Lieutenant Commander Thomas Alton Donovan was also repatriated from Batavia. See below for more information on this officer. Lieutenant Richard Nott Antrim also came home from Batavia as did Lieutenant William Rawlins Lowndes and Ensign Donald Ellsworth Austin. All three were from the *Pope*. See below for more on Antrim. "Pilot Officer," actually Second Lieutenant Walter D. Haines, U.S.A.A.C. had come down from Makassar to Batavia with Donovan and was repatriated from there. John A. Campbell was repatriated from Batavia and returned home to Chula Vista. In 1998, he was still living there. First Lieutenant James P. Ferrey was repatriated from Mukden. Curiously, unknown to the author in 1943, Ferrey was a Canadian citizen, giving his residence as Port Nelson, Ontario. First Lieutenant Winfred H. Gallienne reportedly survived, but no information as to where he was at the end is available. Gaylord A. Buchanen, Jr., graduated from the United States Naval Academy in the class of 1940. Shortly thereafter, he was injured in a shipboard accident which resulted in the loss of a leg. Eventually, he was retired from active duty and found civilian employment with the Sperry Gyroscope Company, reportedly in its bomb sight division. The outbreak of hostilities in December 1941 found him in Singapore from whence he managed to get as far as Batavia. The author was at Kampong Makassar with Buck. After the war, he returned to college, became a medical doctor practicing in Utah. He passed away in 1994 at the age of 77. Major William K. Horrigan, at one point, was shipped to Japan and was in Mukden at the end.

Many years ago, someone told me a story about an American naval officer who had been a prisoner of the Japanese in the former Dutch East Indies and had been awarded the Congressional Medal of Honor. According to my informant, this officer had gone to the rescue of a fellow officer who was being severely beaten by a Japanese prison guard. I had never heard of such an incident. Furthermore, to the best of my knowledge, there were no other United States Navy United States Navy Department officers in the area outside of those few in Tandjong Priok, Cycle Camp, and Kampong Makassar with whom I was acquainted. It was not until the age of the Internet that I learned the truth, for on January 30, 1947, President Harry S. Truman bestowed the coveted medal on the above mentioned then Commander Richard Nott Antrim. The citation reads as follows:

"For conspicuous gallantry and intrepidity at the risk of his life above and beyond the call of duty while interned as a prisoner of war of the enemy Japanese in the city of Makassar, Celebes, Netherlands East Indies, in April 1942. Acting instantly on behalf of a naval officer who was subjected to a vicious clubbing by a frenzied Japanese guard venting his insane wrath upon the helpless prisoner, Commdr. (then Lt.) Antrim boldly intervened, attempting to quiet the guard and finally persuading him to discuss the charges against the officer. With the entire Japanese force assembled and making extraordinary preparations for the threatened beating, and with the tension heightened by 2,700 Allied prisoners rapidly closing in, Cmdr. Antrim courageously appealed to the fanatic enemy, risking his own life to mitigate the punishment. When the other had been beaten unconscious by 15 blows of a hawser and was repeatedly kicked by 3 soldiers beyond which he could not survive, Cmdr. Antrim gallantly stepped forward and indicated to the perplexed guards that he would take the remainder of the punishment, throwing the Japanese completely off balance in their amazement and eliciting a roar of acclaim from the suddenly inspired prisoners. By his fearless leadership and valiant concern for the welfare of another, he not only saved the life of a fellow officer and stunned the Japanese into saving his own life but also brought about a new respect for American officers and men and a great improvement in camp living conditions. His heroic conduct throughout reflects the highest credit upon Cmdr. Antrim and the U. S. Naval service."

Commander Antrim later rose to the rank of Rear Admiral, retiring from the Navy in 1954. He passed away in 1969 at the age of 61. The USS *Antrim* (FFG 20) launched in 1979 was named in his honor.

The recommendation that Commander Antrim be awarded the Medal of Honor came from Captain Donovan who was at Macassar and witnessed the beating incident. Earlier in this account it was noted Donovan had been in the USS *Langley* (AV 3), a seaplane tender. This vessel, once the USS *Jupiter* (AC-3), a coal carrier, had been converted to the Navy's first aircraft carrier, classified as the (CV 1). In mid-February 1942 at Fremantle, Australia, the *Langley* took on 32 United States Army Air Force P-40 fighter aircraft, their pilots, ground crews, stores and equipment. Her destination was Tjilatjap, Java, a small port on the island's South coast. She almost made it, but plans for a night approach and arrival were forestalled by bureaucratic wrangling. Thus, it was 0700 on the morning of February 27 when two escorts, coming out of Tjilatjap, met her. These vessels, the USS *Edsall* (DD 219) and the USS *Whipple* (DD 217) were 1920 vintage, four stack destroyers, ill equipped for modern warfare. Several hours later, a Japanese patrol plane spotted the small convoy and just before noon the bombers arrived. After an hour and a half, the *Langley's* commanding officer passed the order to abandon ship. How many men were lost is not clear, nor is there an accurate count of survivors, although the Internet website History of Ships and Navies says there were sixteen deaths. Dwight R. Messimer in his 1983 *Pawns of War: The Loss of the USS Langley and the USS Pecos*, published by the Naval Institute Press, writes, "There were now 308 officers and men from the tender jammed into the narrow confines of the old four-piper (Whipple). He also wrote, They (*Whipple* and *Edsall*) both were filled to over-capacity with the *Langley* survivors."

Many sources put the *Langley's* crew at 468, and adding 44 USAAC personnel brings the total to 512. From that deduct the 16 killed and the 308 in the *Whipple*, and it appears the *Edsall* had 188 *Langley* people on board. The *Pecos* in the title of Messimer's book was also vintage 1921, a fleet oiler (AO 6) which had been in Tjilatjap since February 6. During that time she had provided bunkers for the USS *Houston* (CL 30) and the USS *Marblehead* (CL 12). Both of these vessels had been damaged in Java Sea actions, and had suffered numerous casualties, but by February 27 the *Houston* was back in the Java Sea and the *Marblehead* in Trincomalee, Ceylon. On the morning of the *Langley's* loss the *Pecos* departed, bound for Ceylon, as well. Her radiomen were soon reading transmissions from the *Edsall* and the *Whipple*, related to the attack on the *Langley*, spurring her commander to ask for all possible speed. Australia was the goal of the destroyers, but that was countermanded by orders for all three vessels to rendezvous at Christmas Island, 260 miles southwest of Tjilatjap. The *Pecos* was to take most of the *Langley* survivors and proceed to Exmouth, Western Australia. This did not please her commander as he, while at Tjilatjap, had embarked many walking wounded from the *Houston*, the *Marblehead*, and the USS *Stewart* (DD 224) which had been damaged by enemy gunfire and then capsized in a Soerabaja drydock. Referring to the commander of *Pecos*, Messimer wrote, "His crew, normally 125, was already swollen to more than twice that number." The USAAC personnel were, however, to be taken from the *Whipple*, placed aboard the *Edsall* and, with others of their detachment already in the *Edsall*, carried to Tjilatjap to fight the Japanese. On the morning of February 28, when the destroyers arrived at Christmas Island's pilot station they learned of the sighting in the vicinity the previous day of a Japanese submarine. A decision was made then to carry out the personnel transfers at sea, with one destroyer performing an anti-submarine patrol while the other was busy with the exchange. The *Pecos* soon came into sight and Lieutenant Commander Donovan was dispatched in the pilot boat to inform her commander of the change in plans. Within minutes, before Donovan could reach the *Pecos*, Japanese aircraft appeared, intent on bombing shore facilities.

The three ships ran for deep water, heading south to get out of the bombers' range. They never returned. On March 31, a whole month later, Donovan was captured by a Japanese landing force.

For the record, the three ships came together the next morning, March 1. According to Messimer, 276 *Langley* survivors were taken off the *Whipple* and put aboard the *Pecos* and 177 came from the *Edsall*. That meant the *Pecos* added 453 men to the estimated 250 men already on board. Within hours, a Japanese carrier-based scout plane found her. The first bomb hit at 1203 and at 1530, his ship having taken numerous hits and close misses, the commander of the *Pecos* ordered her abandoned. Prior to that, radio calls for help had been heard by the *Whipple* which turned back, timing its arrival on the scene to be after dark. She managed to find 232 survivors, only about one-third of those on board, and brought them to Fremantle on March 4. The *Edsall*, after leaving the *Pecos*, ran afoul of a Japanese task force and was never heard from again. The decapitated remains of five of her crew, identified by their dog tags, were found on Celebes in the early 1950s.

So, Lieutenant Commander Donovan was spared this debacle at the price of almost forty-two month's incarceration. On his return to the United States, Donovan was immediately promoted to Commander and 40 days later to Captain. Stan Gorski became acquainted with Donovan and Antrim in Cycle Camp and over the years spoke frequently of them. I don't know how much of the above relating to them he knew, particularly Antrim's Medal of Honor. Also, I believe he never made contact after the war with either man. Unfortunately, Stan passed away in 2003 at the age of 89.

October 25. Remaining in camp. Rain during evening. Blackout.

October 26. Pretty well recovered now, but taking day off anyway. Dysentary [sic] scare. A couple of Nips are sick. Our canteen is to be closed for a period of ten days. Pay day for officers at 6:30 and also regular ten-day pay. Supper at 6:15 to allow for blackout, but then there was no blackout.

The canteen was a small store where one could purchase with our earnings extras such as tobacco, palm sugar, salt, coconut oil, and so on. It was shut down as general punishment for some transgression such as too much singing in the barracks or whistling "Colonel Bogy" while marching to Tandjoeng Oost.

October 27. No work this morning. Parade at about 10 for inspection of stools by Nip doctor. A very silly affair. Each one lines up with his sample on a sheet of cellophane and the Doc walks down the line, rather quickly, at that. Afternoon off as per usual. Light rain in evening.

October 28. Back to work in the climbing spinach. Full day with afternoon light rain. Dysentary [sic] scare still on.

October 29. Working in spinach beds during AM. Japs removing scrap iron from dump. Back to work at 2 PM until 4. Japs have gone uptown. Rumor: Soerabaja bombed again. Tanaka says we'll be free in a year.

October 30. Half day. Cleaning up cucumber beds in morning. Talking to a Jap. He says, "Amerika orang bizar, tidak bagoes. Australia bagoes." (American president no good. Australian good.) Rain in afternoon. Paid. Writing postcards.

This postcard I addressed to my brother Robert whose birthday was on the twenty-eighth. As we couldn't date these cards, this was my method of establishing a time frame for the people at home. This particular card arrived on August 4, 1944, a bit over ten months later.

October 31. Plucking climbing spinach all morning. Raining in afternoon so that we don't get out until after 4. Mix-up with Dutch officers' pay. Their wives won't get any money this month. Rumors of another draft leaving. Russians supposed to have made spectacular gains. Planting spinach.

In mid-August of 1943, Russia launched an attack on a 440 mile wide front which was called the Battle of the River Dneiper. By October, 23 bridgeheads had been established across the river and vast areas of the Ukraine were clear of German troops. So, the "ice cream" was correct.

November 1. Plucking climbing spinach and working on new beds with van Damm. Talk of some sort of a moat being dug around camp. Out again in PM, but heavy rain at 4:30 so we quit for day. Raining at intervals until 9:30. Japs' newssheet in, things looking good.

November 2. Announcement on parade this morning that all persons are forbidden to walk within 5 meters of the outside boundaries unless they are working. In garden, weeding our new beds. Working on peanuts from Tandjoeng Oost in PM. Light rain.

November 3. (Wednesday) All day off for some reason or other. It appears now that it's the Empresses birthday. Various contingents of wog troops marching on road, equipped with bamboo sticks, straw hats, and big Jap flags. One outfit even had a four—piece band. But then to spoil everything we were forced to go to work in the afternoon breaking up sticks. I guess it was punishment, something to do with not saluting. Light rain in evening. It is also Campbell's birthday.

Wog was a not-so-polite generalization for the general populace. Supposedly it was derived from "Worthy Oriental Gentleman," a phrase coined by the British in India many years ago.

November 4. All day off. The usual two-week affair. Didn't do too much. Slept all PM. New Nippon papers in tell of fighting in Philippine Islands. Jap guards have complained that we are not showing the proper respect.

Even the Japs were spreading rumors. The U.S. forces in the Pacific were nowhere near the Philippines.

November 5. Tandjoeng Oost. Fine, cloudy day. Making beds for planting. Slight rain on the way back. Rumors: Americans landing on Ambon . . . Germany capitulates . . . natives given new warnings against U.S.

November 6. Today marked the completion of one year under the Dai Nippon Gun. Lee broke out his long-saved can of corned beef at noon. I was at Tandjoeng Oost in the morning. Half day off as per usual. Rain at 5 PM until well into the evening. Another Nip newssheet is in, but absolutely nothing about Italy or Russia.

November 7. All books, papers, etc. are to be turned into the Nips. So that puts a stop to this day-to-day stuff.

As the reader sees, I did not comply. Actually, I never left any of my papers laying about. Everything was hidden in the atap roof.

November 13. All clear on the books and papers.

November 17. Actual air raid. Single plane heard overhead.

November 26. Surprise draft left for Cycle Camp at 7 PM, having had but 1½ hours warning. Fifteen officers, including Mr. Lee. One hundred Dutch to supplement the building corps came in from 'Cycle.

The camp was being expanded from its 200 troops / 400 officers complement to about 1,200 troops.

November 27. Weight 68 kg. 149.6 lbs

Amazing! After a year's diet of rice, vegetables, and fruit, I weighed more than I ever did! No question, the food at Tandjong Priok was remarkable. Even the morning pap was flavored with nutmeg or cinnamon. The evening meal every Friday included a slice of water buffalo meat for everyone. The camp was, as I mentioned, in a coconut grove and the nuts proliferated. We weren't allowed to knock them off the trees, but fallen nuts often lay on the ground for days at a time. We were growing such produce as tomatoes, cucumbers, eggplants, bananas, and papayas. Understandably, a certain amount didn't get into the Japs' hands. Of course, there was considerable risk in trying to steal the ripened items, so schemes were concocted to flummox the guards. Most of these involved the times at the beginning and end of the work days when the guards had not gotten into their watch towers around the perimeter, or were coming down to escort us back to the barracks.

One day, Pat Paris came up with an idea that would allow the two of us to smuggle fruit into camp where we could casually and safely eat it with our evening meal. The Japs issued to prisoners, who did not possess water bottles, empty coconut shells fitted with carrying straps. A small hole had been drilled in the top through which the meat had been scraped out and a wooden plug inserted. They served the purpose quite well. Pat's brainstorm involved the finding of a large coconut, taking it to the tool shed, and sawing off the top—in the style of a Halloween pumpkin. Henceforth, when we went to work in the morning, one of us carried a shell with water, the other the empty one.

We grew everything in raised beds, so the soil was always loose. In the afternoon, when the guards came down from the towers, we would have a hole ready in a bed, and the fruits or vegetables selected. At the proper moment, the theft would be accomplished, wrapped in a banana leaf, and buried. The next morning, at little risk, we would pop our loot into the empty shell, to be savored in the evening. People did, indeed, wonder how we were putting the produce into our mess tins, but it was not until months later, when I was leaving Kampong Makassar, did I reveal our secret to the wing commander.

December 15. Big change in camp. All officers sent out last night and 600 ORs came in today from Glodok and 'Cycle.

What I meant to say was that all the Dutch and Australian military officers who had been working in the gardens were transferred. Wing Commander Ramsay-Rae and his staff remained, as did the merchant marine officer contingent.

December 20. Search of barracks by Japs. Very complete, evidently looking for arms.

CHAPTER TWENTY-SEVEN

1944 and the "Hell Ships"

February 6. Barracks searched again. All papers and writing materials picked up. Signs of the times: the Jap guards are carrying their rifles in the garden. Trenches and earthworks have been thrown up around the camp.

My foresight again saved this journal and other material. However, the lack of entries indicates that I was being very cautious at this stage. The camp was now occupied by about fifteen hundred men, few of whom were known to me. My friendly Dutch and Aussie officer friends were gone. What had been an easy-going, casual atmosphere was now a work camp.

February 9. Frank Stallman left in a group of 20-odd men over age 50.

February 14. Chief Engineer Young of the Empire Dawn taken to the hospital.

This man had become my "barrack mate." We had our meals together, and generally looked after each other's interests.

February 16. Mail and packages arrived. Pkgs Lee and Hickey.

This was the first indication that word had been received in the States of our being on Java, almost twenty-two months after departing New York.

April 16. More mail for Americans. Pat and Hickey. The news is extremely good. Everyone super-optimistic. General trend of thought is that Java will be finished by July.

April 29. Writing postcards again.

This was the fourth card. It was addressed to my brother Richard, although I made no mention this time of his upcoming birthday. It was eventually delivered. No date of receipt was noted.

May 4. Small number of letters for Americans. Hickey 2, Lee 5.

May 9. Big draft of fit men (350) out and about 900 new people in.

Of all the atrocities, indignities, and inhumanity wreaked upon their captives by the Japanese in World War II, probably the worst single class of mistreatment was the prison ship. Countless groups of men were moved from island to island in the Dutch East Indies, others from the Philippines and Java and Singapore to Japan, still others to Burma and Formosa and even to Manchuria. For the most part, the ships used in these operations were antiquated rust buckets, although, occasionally a fairly modern liner was utilized. All of them shared one common denominator—misery. Prisoners were packed—perhaps "stuffed" is a better word—into cargo holds. Food was limited and sanitary accommodations crude. The unthinkable was in every mind. "What if an Allied submarine or aircraft spots us?" In fact, numerous Japanese ships carrying prisoners of war were sunk with the resultant loss of thousands of lives, the ultimate act in the "we don't care if you live or die" administration of the Japanese. In the previously mentioned *Prisoners of War of the Japanese in World War II*, Willem Wanrooy lists fifty-six incidents of the transport of 68,068 prisoners by sea of which sixteen vessels were lost with total prisoner deaths of 20,920! Wanrooy survived the torpedoing of the *Junyo Maru* by HMS *Tradewind* in September 1944. This will be covered in a later chapter. Hickey and I were originally included in the 350-man group which left on May 9, and we were not classified as officers. We protested and were replaced. These men went to the Cycle Camp, from where they, with 427 additional bodies, on May 19 embarked in a small freighter bound on a three day voyage to Singapore. After ten days in a crude transit camp on River Valley Road, 772 prisoners (five had flunked the routine stool exam) were taken by motorized barges to an anchored freighter which was loaded with bauxite. In that number were eighteen of the *American Leader* survivors:

Yeoman 3/c USN Donald P. Behrendt
Messman George Bowens
Wiper Ernest W. D'Ambrose
Able Seaman Charles J. Delaney
Oiler Herman R. Denzler
Deck Maintenance Man Charles Dickinger
Oiler William A. Grover

Third Assistant Engineer Eric O. Kamins
Wiper Anthony J. Marcinkus
Seaman 2/c USN Alvin P. Mlodzik
Seaman 2/c USN Carl J. Mogenson
Seaman 2/c USN Harold K. Myers
Ordinary Seaman Giovanni M. Porchia
Mess Utility Man Ferdinand J. Potocny
Able Seaman Kenneth J. Pride
Junior Third Officer Alexander Shershun
Engine Maintenance Man Louis R. Williams
Junior Engineer Charles T. Young

Two days later, in a convoy of sixteen ships (as reported by an Australian, Peter McGrath-Kerr) or thirty ships plus escorting naval vessels (according to Eric Kamins) the prison ship headed North. The date was June 3. Kamins later wrote,

1979 Annual Reunion of Australian 2/40ᵗʰ Infantry Battalion.
These four men are survivors of the *Tamahoku Maru*. Left to right,
Frank Fitzmaurice, Peter McGrath-Kerr, Bruce Lean, and Jack Prosser.

It was a very rusty, old, coal burning steamer. As a trained marine engineer, I knew instinctively that she was a death trap. The space allotted to us was in the 'tween deck, forward of the navigating bridge. Beneath us was the cargo hold, full of ore. Our space was barely enough to hold us comfortably standing. Stretching out or sleeping was another horrible matter. Our personal possessions consisted of a spoon, a cup, a tin plate, a toothbrush, and some discarded Japanese army clothing. There was one set of clippers to keep our hair at the decreed 3/8-inch, and we had one razor blade per thirty men. The hatch boards were on, covered with the usual three layers of canvas tarpaulins, wedged tight and battened down. The only way out and up was a two-foot wide ladder to a small hatch on deck. Only five men were allowed on deck at one time for toilet purposes. This was accomplished from a four-plank affair with a small rail around it, hanging over the side. For tissue there was a high-pressure saltwater hose.

All in all, it was a very dangerous situation. There were no life belts, no life boats. No life rafts. This would be our floating home for thirty-plus days, with terrible crowding, bad food, foul air, and Asian rats. Even with zigzagging, many ships were sunk.

McGrath-Kerr says on the second night out of Singapore, in the South China Sea, one of the escorts was torpedoed, probably by a U.S. submarine.

Curiously, postwar sources, Japanese and American alike, disclose only one sinking incident in that entire sea during June 1944. That was a Nipponese naval frigate, the CD 15, torpedoed on the sixth by the USS *Raton* (SS 270) about 450 miles northeast of Singapore. So, Kamins's story is suspect, while McGrath-Kerr's seems closer to the truth.

On the eleventh, the convoy arrived at Manila, where it lay at anchor for three days. On the fourteenth, they sailed, arriving at Takao, Formosa, five days later. There, the prisoners were transferred to a larger ship, the 6,780-gross-ton *Tamahoko Maru*, which also embarked approximately nine hundred Japanese repatriates. On the twenty-first, the convoy was again at sea, and by dawn of the twenty-fourth was in sight of the southernmost Japanese home island of Kyushu and other offshore islands, bound for the great shipbuilding port of Nagasaki.

A few hours earlier that same day, just after midnight, three United States submarines had rendezvoused near the small island of Danjo Gunto, 110 miles southwest of Nagasaki, and a good 100 miles from the convoy's track. An intercepted Japanese radio message indicated that one of its battleships, damaged in the Philippine Sea battle of June 19-21, was attempting to reach either Sasebo or Kobe. This information was passed along to the three subs, which came together to plan a coordinated interception. The USS *Tang* (SS 306) commanded by CDR Richard H. O'Kane won the task of covering Koshiki Strait between Kyushu and the Koshiki Islands. The USS *Tinosa* (SS 283), CDR Donald F. Weise, and the USS *Sealion*, (SS 315), CDR Eli T. Reich, stood out to sea westward from the Koshikis, each patrolling a thirty-mile stretch of the East China Sea. At 2145, the *Tang's* radar screen came alive with a mass of blips, 20,000 yards to the south. As many as two dozen ships were exiting the strait, northbound and directly toward Dick O'Kane and his boat. As the range decreased, the convoy's composition became clear: six large vessels in two columns of three, surrounded by twelve escorting destroyers and gunboats. Running on the surface, O'Kane maneuvered inside of the screening naval vessels and took aim at the first two ships in the right hand column, the *Tamahoko Maru* and the tanker *Nasusan Maru*. He sent three torpedoes toward the tanker and then another three at *Tamahoko*.

Eric Kamins wrote,

> *Our ship was the second to be torpedoed and sunk. The ship just blew apart and sank in less than two minutes, taking all of us down with her. There was no way for escape since we were locked in, and it was pitch dark. By a wonderful miracle, not of my own doing, as there was nothing anyone could do, and there was no direction, I popped up to the surface. I got my first breath of air, said a prayer, and then a third ship blew up. She had much ammunition on board and chunks of steel dropped all around. I recall a Japanese destroyer going by me at full speed, not a hundred feet away. By very great fortune, I found a piece of an ice box door which contained cork and I hung on to this "lifesaver" for sixteen hours until a Japanese fishing boat came along and rescued me. (A seaman at sea will usually help another seaman, war or no war.) I was pretty well dehydrated, sunburned, and weak. The fisherman took me into Nagasaki and put me ashore at the Mitsubishi shipyard where a number of Allied prisoners labored and where I met up with about thirty-five other survivors of the Tamahoko Maru. Then and only then came the realization that so many men had died. It was an incredible feeling of great loss and overpowering loneliness in an alien wartime land. Many of those fine men had been close buddies, sharing almost two years of hardship.*

Peter McGrath-Kerr confirms Eric as far as the tanker being hit first. He continues,

I was asleep when I was awakened by an explosion and the sound of running feet on the deck above. I had risen to my feet when I was staggered by the explosion of a torpedo which hit our ship near the rear of the hold, just under the bridge. Before long, the lights went out and water poured in over the hatch coaming and at the same time flooded up from below. I floated up against the underside of the deck and was trapped there as the ship went down. I found my way to the hatch opening and shot up to the surface, having my pants stripped off by the rush through the water. When I reached the surface, I was alongside a tangle of timbers, so I clambered onto them. After a while, I was joined by an Australian. Later a capsized life boat drifted by, so we climbed onto it. During the night, two more Australians and three Javanese (Dutch Army) soldiers came aboard. A Japanese whaling ship and a seaplane appeared when daylight arrived. Boats picked up survivors. A Jap destroyer was lurking about during the night, probably hoping to see the sub. It picked up several survivors and when the whaling ship arrived made them jump off and swim to it. One non-swimmer drowned. We were eventually picked up at about noon and arrived at the Mitsubishi shipyard at 5 PM.

Peter had a better handle on the statistics of the disaster than Eric. Here are his figures:

	on board	lost	survived
Australian	267	195	72
American	43	30	13
British	196	154	42
Dutch	<u>266</u>	<u>181</u>	<u>85</u>
Totals	772	560	212

Of the eighteen *American Leader* crew members who left Java on May 19, only five made it to Japan: Eric Kamins, Kenneth Pride, Johnnie Porchia, Tony Marcinkus, and Ernie D'Ambrose. What if Hickey and I had not protested our inclusion in the May 9 draft?

According to Clay Blair, Jr., author of *Silent Victory*, published by Bantam Books in 1976, four ships went down that night. "If the records are accurate," writes Blair, "it means that O'Kane sank four ships with six torpedoes, making this the single best attack of the war."

**Work by Fritz Mansfeldt, Torpedoeman, Hsk *Michel*.
George Bowens, lost in *Tomahaku Maru*.**

**Photo courtesy of Deborah Gunther. Alvin P. Mlodzik,
lost in *Tomahaku Maru*.**

Ironically, off the China coast in late October, during an attack on another convoy, the *Tang*'s last torpedo broached, went on a circular run, and twenty seconds after being fired came back and exploded into the aft torpedo room. The only survivors, O'Kane and seven of his crew, were taken prisoner by a Japanese patrol boat.

CHAPTER TWENTY-EIGHT

The Draft

Undated. It is an old story that seamen, on retiring from life at sea, on going ashore invariably try their hands at farming. Now I don't consider myself finished where seafaring is concerned, but, nevertheless, here I am growing spinach on Java. Since becoming a Japanese prisoner of war in November 1942, I have been at other camps in and near Batavia, but have spent the past eleven months here. During this time I have performed all sorts of gardening tasks and grown a variety of vegetables. Right now as I have already stated, I am raising a type of spinach (climbing). In the plot next to me, Capt. Reed has a fine crop of eggplant, and Pat Paris—of all people—is in the pineapple patch.

All of the Americans have recently received shoes and food packages from the Red Cross. When the day's work was finished on the 12th of May, we were called out to the Japanese quarters. There each of us was given a pair of shoes. Special care was taken in regard to size and, mind you, we had our choice of patterns. Then came the packages, so big and heavy that some of the fellows could barely carry them. In each individual box there was soap and cigarettes and cans of meat and cheese; dozens of tins of various sizes and shapes and contents; foods which I had almost forgotten. We returned to camp, so excited, I think, that we nearly neglected to salute the guards.

Now that the novelty has worn off and everything has been sampled, we have all paired up to conserve our supplies. Then, of course, we have our friends to look after. The Chief Engineer of the Empire Dawn has his meals with me. We have a small table outside the hut. Because he cannot eat heavy foods, the butter, cheese, and milk are proving invaluable.

And now, in closing this brief article, I can say that, in spite of the circumstances, things aren't going too badly. My health is good and my spirits high. It is the end of May. Once, more than a year ago, I imagined that by this time we'd be free. My guess was wrong, but by how much? Right now, I believe that these are the important months—May, June, and July—and for the sake of picking a date, I have been saying for the past few weeks that Fourth of July will see us out.

Wow! Such optimism! Also the Red Cross package and the shoes arrived on my twenty-first birthday!

The Capt. Reed mentioned was Owen Harvey Reed, a native of Washington County, Maine. He arrived at Cycle Camp after I had left there in mid-1943, and came out to Kampong Makassar in one of the year-end drafts. His ship, the *William King*, homeward bound from the Persian Gulf, was sunk on June 6, 1943. by the German U-198, 200 miles east of Durban, South Africa. Although the first torpedo badly damaged the Liberty ship, Reed and the gun crew remained on board hoping that the sub would surface and they could get a few shots off. The crew lowered lifeboats, dropped rafts, and abandoned ship. The German commander didn't bite, however, and after a wait of thirty minutes fired a second torpedo which caused the *William King* to settle by the stern. One of the boats took off Capt. Reed and the gunners. About fifteen minutes later the submarine rose to the surface. Approaching Reed's boat the commander asked for the captain. Reed stood up and said that the captain was dead. "Who are you?" asked the German. "I am the first officer," replied Reed. At that point he was invited aboard and taken prisoner. Exactly one month later the U-198 sank the Greek *Hydraios* about 350 miles north of the site of the *William King* sinking and took her chief engineer prisoner. He was C. D. Pithis, from the town of Vrondados on the island of Chios, Greece. Both men were later transferred to a tanker, probably the *Michel*'s old friend, the *Charlotte Schliemann*, eventually sunk by a British task force in the Indian Ocean. It could have been the *Brake* as well. (A bit more on them later.) Reed had an idea the tanker flew the Italian flag, but I have never been able to come up with anything in that vein. The Greek fellow came out to Kampong Makassar in early June.

Understandably, I became quite friendly with Owen Reed. The Americans in Kampong Makassar were few in number, and of them there were only eight officers: me, Hickey, Lee, Paris, Stallman, and Dryer from the *American Leader*, Buck Buchanen, and Doc Burroughs. Lee and Stallman had gone back to Cycle Camp at the end of '43 and early '44, so the six of us remaining naturally banded together. Reed and I were both New Englanders. He came, as I said, from Maine, and had frequently passed through Newburyport on his way to and from home. We had a great deal in common and got along well. I will always remember an incident in which he played a prominent part, but first must provide a bit of background.

———

Our guards on Java were poorly equipped and untrained. We jokingly commented that they were each issued a cap and a rifle and told to go find the rest. Indeed many of them sported green uniforms once worn by Javanese troops in the Dutch army. They were unceasingly drilled in two facets of Japanese infantry fighting: bayoneting and hand grenade throwing. The bayonet drills would be one on one, each participant wearing a fencing-style facemask and a chest protector. Instead of real rifles and bayonets, they were armed with imitation rifle stocks with longer barrels to simulate the length of a bayonet. Facing each other, the combatants would bow and then go into a hippety-hop backward and forward, stabbing and parrying. These exhibitions drew sizeable audiences until one evening one of the guards asked Pat Paris if the American marines practiced this way. To the Jap's surprise, Pat told him the Americans don't use bayonets. "They all have Tommy guns," he said. "*Brrrrrt! Brrrrrt! Brrrrt!*" he mimicked, swinging an imaginary gun from his waist. Guess what? No more spectators at the bayonet practices.

As for hand grenades, the Japs had a silly, stilted routine whereby the throwing arm was kept straight and the delivery was overhand. They were lucky if they could make a toss of more than sixty feet. Owen Reed had played a good bit of baseball in his youth and still had an outstanding arm. On occasion when we were working at the Tandjoeng Oost spread, he'd pick up a baseball sized stone and fling it as though he was throwing a runner out at home from center field. Our fellow prisoners, the Aussies, the British, and the Dutch, were amazed at these feats and kept their eyes out for suitable stones. Soon, the Japs became spectators, oohing and aahing at Reed's prowess—until someone drew the inevitable conclusion. Many Americans could throw baseballs the same distance, but now they were throwing hand grenades at the Japanese. That ended it. No more rock throwing!

May 30. Today is Tuesday. Since Saturday noon I have been kept in bed with a heavy cold or influenza. Events of the weekend were rather curious, however. Yesterday afternoon the entire camp was paraded before the Jap doctor for reclassification. We are all in medical categories: B Class for fit men, A Class for super fit, C Class for light duty, and X Class—no work at all. Well, all that he did was chase most of the Cs and Xs into A! Tanaka has been very friendly with the Wingco, even to the point of coffee and cigars, and has also been doing some night prowling in the camp. Aircraft activity is on the increase. More medicine is to be provided, especially quinine, so that all men will be healthy before the end of June. Rumors are rife concerning drafts to Nippon, but I guess no one knows the true state of affairs. Soerabaja supposed to have been raided two days ago. "Voice of Nippon" of 22nd in. Nothing outstanding, except admissions of raids on East Java on May 17 and 18.

May 31. Back to work again. Considerable unrest and antagonism being stirred up by Dutch troops' goose-stepping antics. It's bad enough if the Japs force us to do it, but if we have to because only the Dutch want to—! Rumors of Japs supposed to be getting ready to go to Nippon accompanied by us. Date is the 5th.

June 1. Order read on parade that we must in the future goose-step on passing guard—house. Usual Thursday work—half day. Six bombers up out of K. No other activity there. Spanish class in PM. Supper at 6:30 before roll call. Hickey, Wright, and Co. had a couple of tins of raisin wine afterwards.

On certain ceremonial occasions the Japanese army used the goose step, for which the German army was well known. Suddenly, the Dutch troops in this camp began goose-stepping when they paraded past the guardhouse on their way to and from work. What instigated this action, I have no idea, but the Dutch had an exasperating tendency to curry favors from the Japs and someone must have remembered the old saw that imitation is the sincerest form of flattery. They did it so well that the Japs established it as the rule. Not everyone obeyed. The *American Leader* and *Empire Dawn* officers plus at least one Dutch skipper went to work as a group, and we decided we would not goose-step. Who ever was in charge hand-saluted the guards, identified us as so many *Kai-gun shoko* (navy officers) and we ambled past. The Japs never reacted! They just sat there! This went on for a few days, and then a group of Australian officers who had gone along with the goose step decided that if we didn't, they wouldn't. There were a few faces slapped and a few heads knocked as a result. From then on, all the garden workers goose-stepped as they passed the guardhouse—except the merchant marine officers!

The K referred to was Kemajoran, the former civilian airport several miles north of us.

Hickey was friendly with of group of officers who socialized evenings. One was named Wright, and I refer to the others as company. Certain of the Red Cross packages contained raisins, mine didn't. Someone knew how to ferment these in coconut milk. Also, there was an alcohol still in camp which produced a certain amount of product, although it eventually exploded. The word "wine" was probably a generic term for whatever beverages we managed to concoct.

June 2. Draft of 800 arrived from 'Cycle Camp at daybreak. Stallman, Cohen, and four other Americans. Also a Greek Chief Engineer. Full day work. Three strange aircraft over at noon. Camp is full of stories. Rumors of a transport of fit men before end of month. Padang bombed. Fighting in S. Sumatra. Cheribon bombed. Eyewitness accounts of Soerabaja attack.

June 3. Very cool at daybreak. Usual day. Little aircraft activity. Informal party for certain officers after supper. Sponsored by American officers. Raisin wine and canapes made up from our Red Cross packages.

June 4. All day off. Long conversation with Stallman in morning. He tells of the prisoners who left Priok on April 12, 1943 and have now returned from Ambon. Also American officers in 'Cycle Camp are maintaining their usual attitude towards the Merchant Marine. Four fighters in at supper time before parade at 7:30.

The name Ambon, which appears frequently in this journal, is one of the Molucca Islands between Celebes and New Guinea. The Ambonese people, prewar, enjoyed their colonial status and many of their men served in the Dutch armed forces. So, it was with perhaps a great deal of wishful thinking that continued rumors of American occupation permeated the camps. The draft that left Tandjong Priok on April 12, 1943 had a terrible experience. They were forced to level a small coral island—with nothing more than hand tools—to create a landing strip for Japanese fighter aircraft. There was little food and hardly any medicine. The voyages from Java took inordinate lengths of time (60 days each way, for example) and many prisoners died on board. Approximately 53 percent of those who left Java did not return.

June 5. Regular day's work. Evidently same four planes out to Eastward early. Draft now going, according to rumor, on 16th. Personally, I'm getting a bit pessimistic that things may not be going as well outside as I expect. Had a talk with the Greek engineer in the evening. Got a "charge" as Hickey calls it. Rumor says Rome has fallen. Rain during night.

The actual date of the entry of American troops into Rome was June 4. Considering that we were six or seven hours ahead of Italian time, some one of us was hearing the Allied broadcasts simultaneously with the rest of the world. Who ever it was, his identity was top secret. I always suspected the radio's existence, but made not a single entry in this journal regarding such notion. It would have been bad enough if the Jap's discovered my writings, but if I had even hinted of a radio receiver hidden in the camp and they read of it, the result would have been an absolute disaster. Radios discovered in the possession of prisoners on the infamous River Kwai railroad project caused the Japanese to murder at least five British officers, according to Gavan Daws in his 1994 book entitled *Prisoners of the Japanese.* It was not until I was safely home did I learn who had our Kampong

Makassar radio when *Liberty* magazine ran a photograph of former prisoner of war, Gaylord A. Buchanan, Jr., with the parts of the radio he had concealed in his aluminum, artificial leg.

June 6. Regular day's work. Several slapping incidents. No rumors of any consequence.

Our usually complacent guards were becoming ornery. Perhaps it was the bad news from Europe, or maybe the fact that the camp population had grown to over two thousand, putting them in a stressful state.

June 7. Work as usual. Rumor says that three U.S. aviators recently captured in E. Java are now in Batavia.

In 1993, I was in Germany visiting Jürgen Herr, the former assistant gunnery officer in the raider *Michel*. One day while perusing his library I came across a photo in a World War II naval history book that startled me. It was an aerial view of Soerabaja under attack by aircraft from the carriers *Illustrious* and *Saratoga*. I knew the *Saratoga* was an American vessel, but *Illustrious* is a British sort of name. Their juxtaposition puzzled me. About a year later, I encountered a fellow named Connie Christuk who had been a year ahead of me at NHS. In the course of our conversation he revealed he had been in an American destroyer which, as part of a joint British/American strike force, had attacked Java and Sumatra in 1944. So, Jürgen's book was correct in its identification of the two carriers. Actually, it was a British Eastern Fleet operation, to which were attached the USS *Saratoga*, Connie's USS *Dunlap*, three other American destroyers and two Dutch destroyers.

My next move was to the National Archives where I easily obtained photocopies of the *Saratoga*'s bridge log book for May 17, 1944. Indeed the *Saratoga* lost an aircraft with three crewmen that morning! The log book entry reads, "1045 At about 0840, Lieutenant W. E. Rowbotham, USN, 79066, of Torpedo Squadron Twelve with crew, Hallock, D.F., ACOM(AA) 223-70-47, USN, and Holmes, J.A., ARM1c, 272-65-42, in TBM-1C Bu.No. 25429, failed to return from raid on Soerabaja, Java. He was seen to make a forced landing with dead engine, 6 miles east of target. Personnel were seen to man rubber life boat."

The *Voice of Nippon* of May 22 was correct and the rumor of the three airman was a fact, but what happened to that unlucky trio will never be known. Certainly, they were delivered to the dreaded Japanese military police, the Kempeitai. Few who fell into their hands survived. Captured aviators, by dictate of Prime Minister Hideki Tojo in 1942, were war criminals automatically subject to execution. At the end of the war, the remains of Duncan F. Hallock and James A. Holmes were recovered and buried in the Philippines, where Hallock still lies. The body of Holmes was repatriated and is buried with his parents in the family plot in Fort Crawford Cemetery, East Brewton, Alabama. William E. Rowbotham is memorialized on the Tablets of the Missing, Manila American Cemetery, Manila, Philippines.

June 8. Half day. Picking spinach with Frank (Stallman). Very cold at daybreak. Kiveron tells me that these months—June and July—are, in the Low Lands (Holland), always cool, accompanied by a clear blue sky. Rumor today talks of landings, full scale, three million men, between LeHavre and Cherbourg. Jap paper of a month ago spoke of possible invasion in the first of May because of favorable tides, etc. A month later, conditions would be the same, which means now. Japs in at night, looking for watches.

Kiveron was an older Dutch officer, perhaps a colonel, with whom I was friendly. I believe he held an important civilian position in prewar Batavia with either the city or the province. At some point in my postwar travels to Holland I purchased a copy of a map of Batavia originally published in 1939. The name of the responsible authority is not given, but its general secretary was J. M. Kiveron.

June 9. Blackout at 1 AM. Regular day's work. A fine day. Six kites out to the east at 2:30 PM. Draft of 350 leaving at 6:30 for work in Batavia. Awful mess of rumors kicking around. Allies 40km from Paris. Ambon occupied. Bombing of Soerabaja.

Kites was Royal Air Force lingo for fighter aircraft.

June 10. Ordinary day. Rather nasty bashing incident late in PM.

June 11. All day off. Nothing unusual. Spanish class in PM. Five suspicious aircraft over at 7:30.

June 12. Back to work again. Not feeling too good. Bad headache.

June 13. Usual day's work. Japs apparently building up a supply of food. Much truck activity at night. New pigpen being constructed to care for 100 more pigs.

June 14. Some sort of an inspection coming off in a day or two. No regular work today. Only inside cleaning parties, but Tandjoeng Oost is out. Rumors Japan bombed. Soerabaja bombed on 10th. Ambon taken. Yap and some of Bonin Group occupied. Special party called at noon to RR station to unload train. Apparently Dutch and English women coming from other parts of the island. Captain Scott back from hospital.

Landings in Europe are apparently a fact. Parade of C and X men at 6:00, resulting in a late meal.

It is probably mere coincidence, but the first American B-29 bomber raids on Japan took place on June 15 when aircraft based in China hit Yawata on Kyushu.

June 15. No work, except Tandjoeng Oost. All huts cleaned and bedding and personal belongings rolled up at head of bed space. A Jap colonel and entourage arrived on the scene sometime this morning, giving the camp a good inspection. We were then paraded on the sports ground in medical categories and inspected. Following this a PT exhibition was given and the big boy left for Tandjoeng Oost. Spanish lesson in PM. Had a talk with DeBart in the evening.

June 16. Back to regular routine. Three aircraft, very high, at about 10 AM. Picked spinach in PM. Supposedly for a German ship which is in port, but that turned out wrong. The stuff is for our own cookhouse. A couple of fighters in to Tjilitan.

June 17. Ordinary work. Picking spinach for cookhouse. Seems to be a firewood shortage, also. A couple of more fighters, may be the same, kicking around. The June 5 issue of "Voice of Nippon" is in. Even less news than before. Japs out at about 9:00 for some sort of excercises. We had another home brew party, but on a slightly smaller scale.

June 18. All day off. Probably the same two fighters up again at daybreak. Spanish class in morning. Dutch S/M Reif gave a violin concert in evening. Rumor says landing in Denmark.

June 19. Back to the old routine again. Jap guards this morning carrying gas masks and tin helmets.

June 20. Usual day. Dutch still trying to make us goose-step. Two bombers and six fighters in to T. at 6 PM. "Voice of Nippon" of the 12th in. Evacuation of Rome by Germans admitted. Rumor says Brussels occupied. Nagasaki heavily bombed. German government supposed to be in Sweden.

June 21. Evidently the same aircraft out in the morning towards east. Rumor says Germany surrendered on 17th. Air raid alarms in Bantam. Had a talk with F/Sgt. Watson in evening. Another bucket of home brew kicking around. Read over Cody's letters.

Watson was a RAF pilot newly arrived in camp. Cody was one of the naval armed guard in the *American Leader*.

———

June 22. Although today is only Thursday, we have all day off for the purpose of some big shifts in camp. We stay in place, however. Spanish lesson in PM.

June 23. Full day. Doing organized PT before work. And that finishes my organized, peaceful life in Kampong Makassar. When we came in from work, the idea was to march on to the sports field for 15 minutes PT. We went on to the field and were kept there. We divided into nationalities and our numbers taken. There was another parade after supper at 8:30 which lasted until midnight.

Bowing to the inevitable prospect of our move elsewhere, Hickey, Paris, and I offered no objection to being included in this draft, although only I would be classified as an officer. Our numbers had come up, and we accepted our unknown fate. What a fortunate collective decision we had made in view of the disaster later incurred by our left-behind shipmates.

June 26. The thing went on for the next two days with parades, inspections, inspections, and so forth. At noon on the 26th, after being on the parade ground most of the morning, the draft was made up. It totaled slightly more than 600 men, mainly Dutch, with 150 English, and a few Aussies (5), Americans (8), a Dane, and a New Zealander. We paraded again in the afternoon for an inspection by a whole gang of Jap officers. Everyone in the draft was required to have a blanket, shoes, and water bottle, among other items. But to make a long story short, our gear was divided into two pieces: A—sufficient for three days, and B—not to be carried with us. Well, it was 6 PM before that parade was over.

The Americans, from the *American Leader*, were Chief Officer Hickey, 1st Assistant Engineer Paris, Ordinary seaman Kalloch, Seaman 1/c USN Parejko, Second Cook and Baker Albert, and me; from the 131st Field Artillery, M. T. Harrelson, and from the USS *Houston*, a Marine named Jack Winters. As for my personal possessions, I had, at this stage, managed to acquire a British Army backpack and an RAF duffle bag which was, surprisingly, full. In retrospect, the constant turmoil and confusion kept us quite off balance and was probably a Japanese ploy to prevent problems with people who didn't want to leave Java. To illustrate how silly the Japs were, when we were out on the sports field in the course of our innumerable inspections, they wouldn't allow us to talk to or come into contact with the other fellows in the camp. When the drill was concluded, however, back into camp we'd go, and mix in with the men they had been keeping us away from!

June 27. The next, and last, parade came at 2:00 AM, ready to march. It was between 2:30 and 3:00 that we marched out into the dark.

Our departure from the camp was unexpectedly emotional. No one had gone to sleep. The barrack lights remained on as people milled about chatting and shaking hands. Men who had been together for years in confinement and perhaps longer in their fighting units were being separated. Knowing what had happened to the drafts that went to the Moluccas, considerable apprehension permeated the scene. I recall saying goodbye to Willie Dryer. We never cared for one another, even in the *American Leader*. Although he had not been directly involved in the Army Air Force vs. merchant marine officer confrontations in the Cycle Camp, he was one of them. So, it was something in the sense of "Goodbye. Good luck. Let bygones be bygones." The march, actually more of a walk, was eerie. The road was smooth and lit occasionally by streetlights. As we passed darkened native dwellings, I had the feeling of being watched. There was no noise other than the low rumble of our footsteps. No one spoke. No one whistled. Everyone had to be wondering about what laid ahead. Just a few Japs monitored the line of prisoners. With the knowledge that there was a bounty on our heads, escape was unthinkable.

At 5:00, after marching without a stop, we arrived at Meester Cornelis (Djatinegara) RR station. Another half hour elapsed before we went on the train, and it was quarter to seven when we stepped out at Tandjoeng Priok and marched directly onto the dock. Another 600-plus arrived later from 'Cycle camp.

When we boarded the train we found the windows covered so no one, even the Dutch, could determine the direction of travel. After a slow, jerky, hour-long ride we came to a stop and were ordered off at what we all recognized as the Tandjoeng Priok rail station, close to the port area. We were marched directly to the port area and onto a broad quay. There was no shade, nor any water. A small, rather decrepit ship of about 1,500 gross tons, was alongside apparently waiting for us. She had a cargo hold forward of the deckhouse and another aft. Two guns were visible, one on the focsl and the other on the raised poop deck.

What was of most interest was a German submarine moored two hundred yards astern of this little freighter. What appeared to be the entire crew was on deck or on the quay, curiously examining us with binoculars. The Japs ignored them. Many years later I learned she was the U-168. One of her officers was Konrad Hoppe! How he came to Batavia is an engaging tale.

CHAPTER TWENTY-NINE

Konrad Hoppe's Many Lives

On February 10, 1943, as related earlier, the *Hilfskreuzer Michel* docked within sight of the Tandjoeng Priok prison camp. Several days later, she departed, arriving at Singapore on the seventeenth. After a brief stay there, she commenced the last leg of her yearlong voyage, bound for Kobe, Japan, where she arrived on March 2. Preceding her to Japan, a few months earlier, were the *Hilfskreuzer Thor* and our old acquaintance, the *Uckermark*. As recounted, both vessels were destroyed when the *Uckermark* exploded on November 30, 1942. Thus, when the *Michel* arrived in Kobe there were a number of unemployed Kriegsmarine personnel cooling their heels in Yokohama, including the *Thor*'s commander, Günther Gumprich.

Hellmuth von Ruckteschell, physically and mentally exhausted, plagued with a variety of medical problems, decided to use Gumprich as his way out. His request to be relieved of command of the *Michel* was quickly accepted by the SKL, and the available and experienced Gumprich took over. He immediately went about creating a composite crew, choosing from his own men, whom he knew well, and those from the *Michel* whose experience in her and knowledge of her he felt would be of value. One *Michel* officer who he had no chance to recruit was Jürgen Herr. Because of Jürgen's mastery of the English language, Admiral Paul Wenneker, the German naval attaché in Tokyo, enlisted him for his staff. One of Jürgen's duties was to learn Japanese, as Wenneker did not trust the Japanese interpreters. Gumprich did bring with him Ulrich Horn, the *Thor*'s flying officer, which made Konrad Hoppe redundant. Konrad's new job, although it lasted a mere two weeks, was observing training operations in the Inland Sea aboard a Japanese aircraft carrier, the *Ryuho*. Although, in December 1938, Germany had launched a carrier, the *Graf Zeppelin*, her designers and planners appear to have had little knowledge of the American and Japanese advances with this type of warship. Beyond that, an aircraft carrier simply didn't fit into the *Kriegsmarine's* tactics as they evolved, and Hermann Göring refused to part with any aircraft. By the time Konrad joined the *Ryuho*, work on the *Graf Zeppelin* had been suspended. His return to Germany to report on the Jap carrier was thus cancelled, and he was sent south to the island of Penang off the west coast of Malaya, where a joint Japanese/German submarine base had been established. This trip was made during June of 1943, in a Japanese Navy DC-2 via Peking, Formosa, Hainan, and Singapore. "I was stared at as some miracle," he wrote, "being the first white man the natives had seen in eighteen months." Although Konrad said he made that trip in a DC-2, it is more likely it was a DC-3. Between November 1937 and April 1940, the Great Northern Airways of Japan purchased fifteen new DC-3 aircraft from Douglass, which had discontinued building the DC-2 in 1936. Was Great Northern actually the Japanese Navy?

On October 17, while Konrad was enjoying the good life of tropical Penang, disaster befell the *Michel*. Returning from a five-and-one-half-month voyage in the Indian and Pacific Oceans, and on her last night at sea, she was torpedoed by the USS *Tarpon* (SS 175). Reportedly, two hundred and sixty-three of her crew and nineteen Norwegian prisoners of war went down with her. Her new commander, *Kapitän zur See* Günther Gumprich, was lost as were the following officers who had been aboard since leaving Germany:

Commander *Esau* and First Torpedo Officer *Kapitänleutnant* Malte von Schacht
Radio Officer *Kapitänleutnant* Götz-Frederick von Rabenau
First Gunnery Officer *Oberleutnant zur See* S. Jacob Schwinn
Prize Officer *Oberleutnant zur See der Reserve* Walter Duborg
Supply Officer *Oberleutnant* Ludwig Stadler
Chief Engineer *Korvettenkapitän (Ing)* Fritz Hanstein
Second Engineer *Oberleutnant (Ing) der Reserve* Eric Bethke
Third Engineer *Leutnant (Ing) der Reserve* Gustav Jördens
Second Medical Officer *Marine-stabsartz der Reserve* Doktor Hans-Christel Pfeiffer
Dentist *Marine-zahnartz* Edmund Scherf

What a Stroke of Luck Saved Konrad Hoppe!

Toward the end of the year, Konrad, still a *Kapitänleutnant*, was relieved of his command by the higher ranked *Korvettenkapitän* Wilhelm Dommes, crew 31, who had left his command, the U-178, because of ill health. From Penang, Konrad went back to Singapore where he joined the former Italian submarine *Reginaldo Giuliana*, taken over by the *Kriegsmarine* on September 10, 1943 after Italy's capitulation, and designated UIT-23. He served as first officer in her for a brief period and then was called back to Penang by *Kapitänleutnant* Helmuth Pich, crew 34, commander of the U-168. Old acquaintances from their navy air force days in Norderney before the war, they had, of course, been together in Penang. Pich had left Penang in early January 1944, headed home, but shortly after departing, his first officer, Hans-Jorg Stenger, was stricken with appendicitis forcing the boat to return to base. Thus, Konrad was summoned to fill in. The U-168 eventually sailed on February 7 with instructions to conduct a war patrol in the Arabian Sea which was done with moderate success. On February 14, in a position about 350 nautical miles southwest of Colombo, HMS *Salviking* was torpedoed and sunk. This was one of twelve King Salvor class salvage vessels constructed for the Royal Navy from July 1942 to February 1944. Displacing 1,780 tons, they were 217 feet in length, with a 37 foot beam, and a draft of 13 feet. The next day, 600 miles southwest of Colombo, the 4,385 gross ton Greek streamer *Epaminondas C. Embiricos* was encountered, east of the entrance to the One and Half Degree Channel in the Maldive Islands. She was dispatched with a single torpedo. Finally, on the fifteenth, the Norwegian motor tanker *Fenris*, 9,804 gross tons, was attacked in the Arabian Gulf about half way between Colombo and the entrance to the Red Sea. She survived hits by the U-168's last two torpedoes.

Actually, in addition to the U-168, the SKL, in the first six weeks of 1944, ordered five Far East boats to return to Europe. All were to be refueled in the Indian Ocean by the *Michel*'s consort of 1942, the *Charlotte Schliemann*. On February 11, she was spotted by a Royal Air Force Catalina flying boat which notified HMS *Relentless* a hundred miles away. Darkness had fallen before the destroyer found the *Schliemann* and with gunfire put an end to her career. Four lifeboats containing the tanker's forty-two man crew were successfully launched. Two of the boats, each carrying ten men were never seen again. A third boat, also with ten occupants, reached Madagascar in twenty-six days. Her men were rescued the next morning by a British freighter. The fourth lifeboat also made it to Madagascar—in thirty days. One of its twelve sailors died during the perilous voyage. The twenty-one survivors spent the remainder of the war in British prison camps. A month elapsed before the tanker *Brake* could be placed on station, and then, on March 12, having topped off U-188 and sent her home to Europe, and with U-168 and U-532 on scene, a Swordfish aircraft from HMS *Battler* appeared. The *Battler*, out of Durban, South Africa, had been searching for the German tanker for seven days so spotting her was no accident. The nearby HMS *Roebuck* was notified, and when she was sighted by the *Brake*'s crew, they set off the scuttling charges and abandoned ship. The *Roebuck*, aware of the presence of the two U-boats, gave the area a wide berth, allowing the U-168 to rescue the *Brake*'s crew who she brought to Batavia. Also in the Indian Ocean at the time were the Europe-bound U-183 and UIT-24, which, along with the U-532, were called back to Penang. The last of the six to leave was the UIT-23, in which Hoppe served at Singapore. On

February 14, on her way from that port to Penang, she was sunk by HMS *Tally Ho*, with the loss of twenty-six of her forty man crew.

Another Close Call for Hoppe!

Allied intelligence was responsible for this entire German fiasco. The considerable radio activity generated by the six U-boats, and the two tankers, was being copied and deciphered, pinpointing the rendezvous locations. Looking back, the Royal Navy was criticized for utilizing the decoded German radio traffic to intercept two unimportant ships. It was felt the SKL would have its suspicions aroused by the loss of the two tankers, but, as so often happened, the Germans believed their codes had not been compromised until it was too late.

But Konrad's Luck Still Held!

When the U-168 returned to Batavia, her first officer, having recovered from his appendectomy, rejoined her, and Konrad was again unemployed. This situation was resolved by the creation of a German U-boat base at the large city of Soerabaja on Java's east end where, prewar, the Dutch had maintained a large naval base. Konrad was placed in charge of this facility. In due course, the U-168 was ordered from Batavia to Soerabaja, which was duly noted by Allied intelligence. The Dutch submarine *Zwaardvisch* (swordfish) was alerted, took up position along the U-168's estimated course, and in a surface attack in the early morning hours of October 6 fired six torpedoes at the hapless *Unterseeboot*. One hit sent Pich's command to the bottom. He was picked up and taken prisoner, along with Dr. Georg Wenzel and twenty enlisted men. Twenty-four men were lost, among them Hans-Jorg Stenger, with whom Konrad Hoppe had swapped berths in January and June. An additional thirteen men were picked up by Javanese fishermen.

Konrad Hoppe relates being notified in the morning by the Kempeitai, the Japanese secret police, of word from the coastal village of Rembang telling of a number of German sailors being rescued by native fishermen and brought ashore. The senior Kempeitai officer decided to go to the scene and investigate the situation. With his chauffeur driven limousine, he picked up Konrad and they raced to the village, arriving to learn from the survivors of Pich's prisoner of war status. The Japanese officer became enraged. He stormed at Hoppe, criticizing Pich because he had allowed himself to become a captive. "He should have gone down with his boat! Surrender is disgraceful!" Hoppe, in turn, berated the Jap and would not return to Soerabaja with him. In fact, according to Hoppe, he rejected any further contact with the Kempeitai. If they wished to speak with him, they had to contact Hoppe's senior in Batavia, who would inform him of their desires.

But Konrad Had Dodged Another Bullet!

There are conflicting reports relative to the personnel losses and survivors of the U-168. Http://www.dutchsubmarines.com/boats/boat_zwardvis1.htm carries the above figures. http://uboatwaffe.net, based in Germany, contains almost 50,000 names and has a much more comprehensive account of the crew of the U-168. It lists by name and rank thirty-four survivors of which twenty-one were taken prisoner, and twenty-two were killed in the sinking. The book *U-boats Destroyed* by Paul Kemp places the number of survivors at twenty-four, of which five were retained by the *Zwaardvisch*: the commanding officer and the doctor, as above, and also a watch officer, the chief engineer, and a severely injured enlisted man. Additionally, Kemp writes that survivors told the submarine skipper three torpedoes had struck their boat, but only one had exploded. He adds this interesting observation: "The German U-boat command in the Far East became convinced that the loss of U 168 could be attributed to 'loose talk' since the crew had taken their Indonesian girlfriends on board the U-boat for a farewell party." Farewell, indeed!

Two of the lucky survivors of the U-168 were twenty-one year old *Machinenobergefreiter* Gerhart Jurkat and twenty-two year old *Matrosenobergefreiten* Huburtus Lammel. Jurkat then joined U-537 at Soerabaja. Just a bit over a month later, that boat commanded by *Kapitänleutnant* Peter Schrewe, crew 34, sailed on a patrol intended to take her to Australia. After having traveled a mere 160 miles, on November 8 she was sighted on the surface by the USS *Flounder* (SS 251). Two torpedoes ended the U-537's voyage and the lives of her fifty-eight man crew, including the suddenly unfortunate Jurkat. Lammel, at some point and location having been assigned to the U-196, met his untimely death when that boat went missing as of December 1, 1944, some two months after he lucked out with the U-168.

The U-188 made it to Europe, delivering about 150 tons of badly needed raw materials to Bordeaux after Allied ground forces had landed in Normandy. According to Clay Blair, in *Hitler's U-Boat War: The Hunted, 1942-1945*, her commander, *Kapitänleutnant* Siegfried Lüdden, attempted to travel to Berlin to make his patrol report to Admiral Dönitz and deliver other secret papers relating to the war in the Far East. Somewhere en route his motorcade was ambushed by partisans. He was killed and his briefcase liberated. Another source, http://www.uboat.net, states Lüdden died on January 13, 1945, in a fire aboard the accommodation vessel *Dar-Es-Salaam* berthed in Kiel. Now, yet another story has surfaced. Http://www.u-boat-archiv.de carries the service record of *Kapitänleutnant* Carl-August Landfermann. This gentleman, who was still living in 2006, reports he was *Leitender Ingenieur* (chief engineer) in several U-boats until April 30, 1944, when he was ordered to join the Twelfth U-boat Flotilla at Bordeaux. On June 26, he and Lüdden accompanied by several *Kriegsmarine* personnel were on their way to Paris when near Limoges they were captured by French Resistance fighters. Three weeks later they were able to escape from their captors. Moving only at night, it took them seven days to locate German forces occupying Limoges and continue their journey to Berlin. Thus, the account of his death in Kiel is probably correct.

U-532 remained in Southeast Asia until January 13, 1945 when she sailed from Batavia with another cargo of raw materials. Germany surrendered before she reached port and her cargo was discharged in Liverpool. Prior to that, on March 28, 1945, she had, in mid-Atlantic, encountered the American tanker *Oklahoma* (9,264 tons) carrying a full cargo of petroleum products, most of which was gasoline. Two torpedoes set the tanker afire, and she sank with the loss of fifty of her seventy-two armed guard and merchant crew. Ironically, six weeks later the Battle of the Atlantic ended.

CHAPTER THIRTY

The *Chukka Maru* and Singapore

12:00 N, embarked on SS Chukka Maru. Makassar group in hold, 'Cycle camp group on deck. 2:30 PM sailed.

We, standing on the quay, didn't know about the *Tamahoko Maru* disaster of less than thirty-six hours previous, nor had we heard of the *Suez Maru* torpedoing of the previous November. So I personally had no concern about boarding this little ship awaiting us. The Japanese eventually lined us up by nationality with, of course, the Dutch predominating. Forty-nine of them and an officer were counted off and directed up the gangway. They were followed by seven similar contingents until four-hundred Hollanders were in the ship, leaving a small number who were sent to the end of the line. Next, one hundred and fifty British prisoners followed. This left about fifty Makassar men on the quay, a mixed bag of Hollanders and British along with the aforementioned small numbers of Australians and Americans, the Dane, and the New Zealander, with me as the designated officer.

On board, we found chaos as the Japanese pushed and shoved and slapped. The first fifty men had been herded into an area under a wooden platform about four feet high that went all around the cargo hold. Each prisoner was allotted enough space to sit with his knees drawn up in front of him with his belongings in his lap. A subsequent group of fifty was jammed up against them, then fifty more and fifty more. When three hundred were packed in, the process was repeated on the platform which offered no more head room than the space below. My group and I ended up under the open hatch where we could, at least, stand upright and get fresh air.

When the Japs had completed cramming us in, the Cycle Camp group was brought aboard in fifties, but they were to make the trip on deck in any place that a person could locate sitting or standing room. No provision was made to protect the prisoners from the sun, rain, or the cold nights. The little ship was a veritable human ant heap. At 2:30 PM, the lines were cast off, and we steamed out of the harbor. We knew nothing of our destination, but we recognized one overwhelming fact. We could be in for many problems and big trouble if this voyage was to last much longer than a few days. That afternoon and evening we moved north. The next day was typical tropical weather, the sea flat calm, the sky bright blue with scattered clouds, the air comfortably warm. The Japs allowed us to move around. Those people originally lodged in the hold could come on deck and those on deck could go below if they wished. We were extraordinarily crowded and in constant contact with other bodies. The Japs did ease the situation by allowing a number of men to go onto the after deck. Following months ashore, and the regimentation of the camps, this ship ride was a real break in the routine and, for me, an absolute pleasure. It was just great to be back at sea with the salt air and the motion of the vessel. There was a feeling of release from the dreary days of Java. In a sense, I was free again.

On the down side, food was limited. Twice a day each prisoner received two sticky rice balls and tea, and this is where the Jap idea of forty nine men and one officer proved of value. Each officer was responsible for seeing that his group received their ration—no more, no less. As related above, I and my mixed bag were the last into the hold and occupied the square of the hatch. That's where the rice and tea were distributed, so I was given the added responsibility of organizing the feeding of the whole six hundred. Of course, I was dealing with the other officers. There was no confusion, nor were there any real problems whether handing out food or controlling sleeping and sitting space. It should be noted the few Americans had various remains of our Red Cross packages, and most of the others had some sort of emergency provisions. Thus, there was no outright hunger.

Another negative existed on deck. The sanitary facilities were simply wooden boxes, with one board knocked out of the bottom, hung over the ship's side. When nature called, one had to climb over the bulwarks and squat to do one's business. As the majority of the prisoners were soldiers—"landlubbers" is a better word in this instance—they knew nothing of such nautical terms as windward and leeward. Not infrequently, the windward boxes would be used, and if the wind was just right (or wrong!) whatever was being let go would be whipped back and deposited amongst the deck sitters. Of particular irritation to the Dutchmen was the American, British, and Australian use of toilet paper which regularly came spiraling up in the breeze. The Dutch used water to clean themselves. Every one of them carried a bottle dedicated to that function, and the spray was in no way as noticeable.

June 28. 6:00 PM, anchored south of Bangka Island.

June 29. 8:00 AM, underway. 5:00 PM, anchored in mouth of Moesi River. 11:00 PM, underway.

June 30. 5:00 PM, anchored near Sumatra coast.

July 1. 3:00 AM, underway. 6:00 PM, docked at Singapore. Everyone ashore and marched to an isolation camp. Here things were in a bad state.

By noon on July first, it was apparent we were approaching Singapore. During the afternoon the city's buildings rose into view. As we entered the harbor we came upon an anchored U-boat. Many of her crew were out sunning themselves. They recognized us for what we were, and there was a great deal of waving back and forth. One accordian playing *Matrose* serenaded us with "The Beer Barrel Polka." Interesting. White race enemies acting like friends in the presence of the little yellow men. This was probably the U-532, which, after the *Brake* was sunk, returned to Penang. She is reported as arriving at Singapore on May 18.

After five days of intermittent travel in waters where the Japanese gunners seemed always to be on the alert, we tied up in Keppel Harbor, Singapore. What the future held we had not the slightest idea, but for now we were relatively safe. Incidentally, this little ship was named *Chukka Maru*. In my post war research I have not come up with a single word about her. It is worth noting that historical sources show the USS *Flasher* (SS 249) sank the 6,079 ton freighter *Niho Maru* (or *Nippo Maru*) and heavily damaged the 14,050 ton naval oiler *Notoro* in the early morning hours of June 29, in a position about ninety miles ESE of Singapore. That could have been the reason for the *Chukka Maru* anchoring on the twenty-ninth and thirtieth.

The *Flasher*, on her third war patrol, was a new boat, having been commissioned on September 25, 1943. At the end of the war, she was credited with sinking 100,231 tons of Japanese shipping, the best record in the United States submarine force. In number of ships sunk, she was rated fourth.

Immediately after docking, we were disembarked and walked through the streets of the city. The inhabitants watched silently and unemotionally. My thoughts ran along the line that the Japanese were using this parade as a propaganda stunt, implying we were newly captured. There had, however, been numerous such spectacles. Also, at the southeast corner of the island was the vast prison camp known as Changi, containing as many as forty-thousand men, mostly British and Australians. I now doubt the native populace was at all impressed by us.

Singapore, 1979. Cleared area in center is site of river Valley camp.

Shortly, we arrived at a dilapidated group of bamboo-frame buildings called River Valley Road camp, consisting mainly of roofs without siding, located in a clearing in the center of the city on the west bank of the Singapore River. Several of the structures were occupied by Allied prisoners, most of them without shirts or shorts, some of them stark naked. The Japanese kept us away from these men, but we soon learned they were survivors of a ship sunk in Malacca Strait several days earlier. What happened is the Japanese had a number of prisoners in the North Sumatra city of Medan who they wished to move to Singapore for use as laborers elsewhere, similar to our situation. We didn't know our destination, nor did our new acquaintances know theirs. All indications showed us bound for Japan. Possibly, this Medan draft was to join us for the long voyage north. Unknown to us, the Japanese had commenced a project on Sumatra. A railroad was to be constructed across the center of the island. Already two thousand prisoners, also from Java, but via Padang on the west coast of Sumatra, labored on the project. If these Medan people were marked for the railroad, it is difficult to understand why the Japs transported them by sea. Roads existed on the island; perhaps there was a shortage of fuel and vehicles. Maybe we had misread the Japanese, and the twelve hundred of us were indeed headed for Sumatra.

In any case, the Japanese took these fellows from Medan to the port city of Belawan on June 25 and loaded them into the old (1910-built) 3,040 ton, former

Dutch passenger ship *Van Waerwijk* renamed *Harikiku* (or *Harukiku*) *Maru*. In 1942, just after the Japanese invasion of Java, her crew scuttled her in an attempt to block the port of Tandjoeng Priok. The occupying Japs had her afloat and back in service four or five months later. At noon, in the company of a freighter, two small tankers, and two gunboats, the *Harikiku Maru* got underway. On board were 720 prisoners of several nationalities—Dutch, Indonesian, British, Australian, and one lone Norwegian. The small convoy moved southward, hugging the coast, and at dusk anchored, having traveled not many miles. The next day, still only sixty miles from Belawan, and in a position two hundred and sixty miles northwest of Singapore, the slow moving vessels came into the periscope sight of Lt. R. L. Alexander R.N., in command of HMS *Truculent*. Two torpedoes quickly put the *Harikiku* on the bottom, where, according to the Dutch historian Henk Neumann, she still sat in 1983, masts above the surface. Eye witnesses stated the *Truculent* also sank the accompanying freighter and one of the gunboats, but postwar sources do not give such credit. Of the 720 prisoners, 542 were rescued by the tankers and the gunboats and native fishermen working nearby. The count of the lost was

Dutch	113
English	48
Australian	12
Indonesian	4
Norwegian	1
	178

Three survivors, picked up by a fisherman, told of being well treated and brought ashore, from whence they journeyed back to Medan. They related their rescuers had told them the Japanese occupying officials had instructed local fishermen, in the event of a sinking, to pick up swimmers. Japanese were to be given first priority, followed by Indonesians, Dutch, English, and Australians. The rescue of Americans was not necessary! These three fellows had a rather difficult time when they arrived in Medan, being beaten by their captors for no more reason than they had survived. A day or two later, the Japs provided them with clothing, food, and money, and sent them by truck to Pakan Baroe, thus deepening the mystery surrounding the original destinations of the *Harikiku Maru* and *Chukka Maru* prisoners. Along the way, their guard, at gunpoint, robbed them of their money.

As a sidelight, to illustrate the difficulty of maintaining records in those days, between 1976 and 1985 three books were written which contained chapters relating to the *Harikiku Maru* sinking. Henk Hovinga authored the first two: *Dodenspoorweg Door Het Oerwoud (Death Railway through the Jungle)* and *Eindstation Pakan Baroe 1944-1945 (Last Stop Pakan Baroe 1944-1945)*. The latter is essentially an expansion of the earlier volume. In 1985, Henk Neumann and a coauthor, E. van Witsen wrote *De Sumatra Spoorweg (The Sumatra Railway)*. Neumann was born on Sumatra, educated in Holland, and had returned to Sumatra in time to be captured by the Japanese. As opposed to the Neumann and Van Witsen style of lists, tables, and statistics, Hovinga presents narratives. Numbers are numbers, however, and Hovinga astoundingly shows the *Harikiku Maru* as having embarked 1,174 prisoners, 454 more than Neumann and Van Witsen counted. All three books agree on the number of lost men, but of the total, Hovinga says 156 went down with the ship and 22 died subsequent to being brought into the River Valley Road camp. Neumann and Van Witsen name the entire 178, and say nothing of survivors dying in Singapore.

July 16. Left River Valley Camp in a draft of 280 men. Marched to docks and boarded river steamer Elizabeth. 10:30 AM, sailed.

I, for one, was happy to be out of River Valley. As written earlier, the barracks were in disrepair. The food was meager, and we had absolutely nothing to do all day long. One diversion was watching the well-dressed Singaporese on the nearby streets. The ladies were, of course, of particular note. We hadn't seen anything like them on Java. Tall, slender Malayan and Chinese ladies in tight-fitting long gowns with slit sides were a common sight. We had been poorly fed for so long, they had no physical impact on us.

CHAPTER THIRTY-ONE

Pakan Baroe, Sumatra

July 17. 2:30 PM. Arrived at Pakan Baroe, Sumatra. Waited several hours, then boarded train which took us to the new camp. Arrived there footsore and weary at 7:00 PM. We're going to build a railroad.

Having been given no clues as to our destination or what we would do when we arrived, this was a shocker. Everyone knew of the horror stories from the Moluccas. Railway construction could be a repeat. Our new camp site was on the south bank, about fifteen feet above a river called Kampar Kanan. The rail line terminated at the north bank; we crossed over by foot on an unfinished bridge. The camp buildings were similar to those at Kampong Makassar. Other than several hundred men who had preceded us from Singapore, and were in this camp, we saw no other Allied prisoners. The two thousand who had left Java on May 17 were in the vicinity, and had probably put up these barracks and three other sites in

Remnants of railroad bridge over the Kampar Kanan, 1979.

and around Pakan Baroe. Thus, this was designated as Camp 4.

View of Kampar Kanan. Camp number 4 was situated on opposite bank approximately at cleared area to right. Material floating in river is bundles of rubber. 1979.

A fifth camp was located further out on the projected line and was soon occupied by others of our group from Java and Singapore.

Our guards were a very unpleasant surprise. Koreans! They wore Japanese Army uniforms, carried rifles and bayonets, but were considered to be inferior by the Japanese railroad troops. The Japs had come from Burma, where postwar estimates of the total loss of life in the construction of the railway there were placed at 12,600 Allied prisoners and 80,000 indigenous and imported laborers. These hard-line troops cared not if we lived or died. The Koreans were the meanest Orientals we had experienced. They and the Japs really didn't get along, so the Koreans took their frustrations out on us. All in all, we couldn't have had a worse combination of wardens. Food was dismal and scarce. Work on the railway would be a killer.

July 30. A Dutch soldier named Jenxis, age 47, died in camp this morning from heart failure caused by over work. And I came down with malaria.

July 31. Jap clouted Dutchman on work party with a piece of timber causing a concussion.

August 17. Dutch soldier Schipper, age 50, died today.

August 18. Dutch Sgt. Preiss, age 33, and Dutch Lieutenant van der Spek, also 33, died today.

August 23. Dutch Adjutant Slikker, age 42, died today.

It didn't take very long—less than two weeks—after my arrival on Sumatra for the stark reality of our situation to be illustrated by the death of Jenxis. On Java, I had been very friendly with van der Spek. He came up with us in the *Chukka Maru*, but something happened to him in Singapore. He came into Camp 4 on a stretcher, and really did not recognize me. This was the first acquaintance I lost out there, and his death was troublesome.

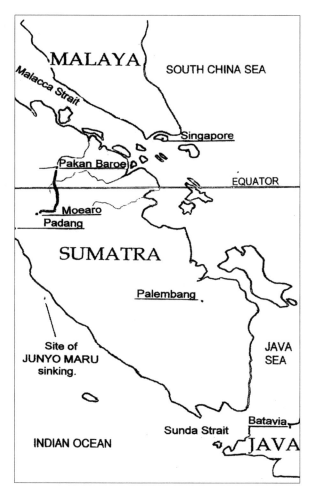

Loci of Pakan Baroe to Moearo railway and sinking of S.S. *Junyo Maru*.

Into this scenario in late September arrived several hundred British, Dutch, and a few American prisoners, some of them naked. All were without possessions. They came on foot, having been carried by truck from Padang to a nearby point. None could relate their route, but the stories poured out.

The west coast of Sumatra—the Indian Ocean side of this tremendous (more than a thousand miles long) island—is steep. Green clad mountain peaks in excess of 9,000 feet are only forty-five miles inland. Off shore, pinnacle islands thrust up from 3,600 foot depths, creating thirty and forty mile wide channels between them and the main island, through which a swirl of the Indian Ocean, swinging clockwise from northwest to southeast produces a strong two to three knot down current. For centuries sailing vessels made this their way to Sunda Strait and the Java Sea.

In 1944, in these waters, British submarines were cautiously engaging the Japanese. Basically, it was not much more than hit and run. Grab a prau. Board a small coaster. If there was cargo aboard that could be considered of assistance to the enemy, the vessel would be disposed of. One of the by-products was the enlisting of disenchanted Malay crew members who could be turned into coast watchers after a training stint at Trincomalee on Ceylon. So, that is what it was all about with HMS *Tradewind* in September. No Jap carriers to seek out. No Jap cruisers or battleships. Nothing but the nineteen-ton *Bintang Pasir* anchored close to shore, which was left unharmed on the sixteenth after a boarding party found its cargo consisted of nutmegs and cinnamon bark. A few hours later, the twenty-four-ton *Sinar Boelan*, under sail, was hailed and stopped. In her hold were four hundred bags of cement, which were soon on their way to the bottom, courtesy of a pair of demolition charges, while seven of her crew paddled toward shore. One crewman opted for the *Tradewind*. In the meantime, a closer examination of the *Bintang Pasir*'s manifest disclosed that under the nutmegs and cinnamon could be 300 bags of cement. A return visit confirmed the fact, and the still-at-anchor two masted prau was set afire.

The *Tradewind* was a Repeat T-Class boat built at Chatham Dockyard in England, and completed on October 18, 1943. She carried a bow salvo of eight 21-inch torpedoes with a reload of a further six, and a stern salvo of three. At Trincomalee on May 21, 1944, she joined the Royal Navy's Fourth Submarine Flotilla. The *Tradewind* was under the command of Lieutenant Commander S. L. C. Maydon, DSO, RN. His mission on this particular patrol, which originated at Trincomalee on September 8, was twofold. Primarily, he was to conduct two clandestine operations, *Caprice* and *Ripley II* involving coast watchers. And, of course, he was to interdict the Japanese controlled sea commerce. His patrol area was the Sumatran coast, outside the ten-fathom curve, from 2° south to Soenda Strait. Just to the north of this area is the port of Padang, from whence the two unfortunate coasters had departed with their miniscule loads of cement. Completely unknown to *Tradewind* and her commander, as they searched for prey and did what they were supposed to do just offshore, less than two hundred miles away we were toiling and starving and dying.

In early September, at about the time *Tradewind* was preparing for this particular patrol, on Java the Japanese were readying another draft of prisoners. For some unknown reason, this draft was announced as destined for the cement factories at Padang. In reality the 2,200 prisoners were marked to join us on the railway, the completion of which was of the utmost urgency to the Japanese. It is probable that in some state of desperation, the Japanese authorities reached back into Java and ordered the draft to be readied. Tragically, many of these men were over age forty-five, having been born in the nineteenth century. In addition, and this is almost mind-boggling, a number of teenaged Javanese laborers, estimated to be as many as 4,300, were to accompany the prisoners. There were no records kept of these unlucky young men. The usual manner of conscription was for the Japanese to announce an unusual event, e.g., a movie, a soccer match, or free food—but only for youths. Once the Nips had their quota, it was off to the coal mine or the ship or whatever was the manpower requirement. They went with nothing, no extra clothing, no eating utensils—nothing.

S.S. *Junyo Maru*.

Previous drafts from Java to Sumatra had, as in my case, consisted of as many as 1,200 men traveling in a small coaster, but to move 6,500 men, plus the accompanying Japanese or Korean guard force called for a sizeable vessel.

Sizeable—not necessarily suitable. Somehow, an old crock of a ship named *Junyo Maru* was available. The *Junyo Maru* was also built in Britain. One source says at Liverpool as early as 1908, and first named *Deslock*. Other information indicates that she was out of the yard of Robert Duncan & Co., Ltd., Port Glasgow, in 1913 as the *Ardgorm*. The latter appears to be the correct information. *Ardgorm*: 405 feet long, 53 foot beam, 8,310 deadweight tons, burned coal under her Scotch boilers. She was later known as *Hartland Point, Hartland, Sureway,* and *Zyunyo* or *Junyo Maru.*

Late on the afternoon of September 15 she left her berth at Tandjong Priok. It had taken almost the entire day to embark the POWs and the Javanese, known as coolies or *"romushas."* Then after moving out into the roadstead and anchoring for twenty-four hours or so, she picked up the hook and headed for sea, only to come to a stop while her crew lowered a boat to chase down a Dutchman who had decided to swim for one of the Thousand Islands that dot the bay north of the harbor. Eventually, in the early evening of the sixteenth, escorted by two gunboats, the *Junyo Maru* began her voyage. The route would be through Soenda Strait into the Indian Ocean, then north to Padang. The seventeenth found them out of sight of land, but on the eighteenth, the Sumatran coast was visible, maybe fifteen to twenty miles off. As the day drew to a close, those on board, if they gave it a thought, could check off more than seventy-two miserable hours away from Tandjong Priok.

Ahead, aboard the *Tradewind*, September 18 was quiet. She had dived at 0530 and patrolled during the day on a line 145°/325° keeping outside the ten-fathom curve, but within eight miles of the coast. What follows are unedited excerpts from the HMS *Tradewind* commanding officer's patrol report on September 8-October 4, 1944 (Patrol Number 3).

18th September

1516   *I was called to the periscope by Sub. Lieutenant P. C. Daley, Royal Navy Volunteer Reserve, the Officer of the Watch, who had sighted through the low power periscope, at a range subsequently estimated to have been over 13,500 yards, a very small plume of smoke to the Southward. The success of the attack which followed was in large measure due to the excellence of the lookout kept by this officer, whose first operational patrol this is and who is a Special Service officer and not, strictly speaking, a Submarine officer.*

The smoke was first sighted bearing 173° degs., course was altered to 190 degs. and HMS Tradewind ran in, mostly at full speed, on courses between 190 degs. and 226 degs. I decided that handicapped by the lack of a high power periscope, it was essential during the early stages of the attack to get into a position whence a close range attack could be delivered, as range taking and hence estimation of speed through a low power periscope is very inaccurate over 4,000 yards. In fact, only one range, 3,000 yards at 1545½, when the target bore 184 degs., was taken during the attack just six minutes before firing; target's speed was assessed by counted revolutions from the asdic.

The first estimation of course at 1530 gave 295 degs. About five minutes later, the target zigged to 340 degs. and at about 1545 she was seen to be escorted by two M.L.s, one on her starboard beam, the other on her port quarter. Their H.E. and, later, asdic transmissions, were reported by asdic. The target was an old-fashion merchant vessel of four to five thousand tons, of the three island type. two masts, single, tall, thin funnel and counter stern. She was about two-thirds fully loaded.

1548   *I decided to turn onto a 40-degree Track Angle (course 200 degs.; at that time I was steering 225 degs.) and had just started to turn when the target obligingly zig-zagged back to her original course of 295 degs., putting me almost on a 95-degree track.*

1551½   *Four torpedoes were fired at 15 second intervals, with the submarine still swinging to port, courses 209½ degs., 207 degs., 204½ degs., and 202 degs. Intended spread was 600 feet, one length and one half of the target, but was, in fact, considerably increased by the swing on firing. The point of aim was a quarter length ahead of the stem. Estimated speed eight knots. One minute thirty seconds and one minute forty five seconds after firing, two explosions were clearly heard, between six and nine minutes later three depth charges were dropped. By this time, HMS Tradewind was deep and retiring on a course of 270 degs. Target's H.E. ceased after the explosions of the torpedoes and was not subsequently heard.*

1613½   *On a bearing 120 degs., loud crackling noises were heard by asdic—probably the target breaking up. There was no further counter-attack and spamodic H.E. was heard until 1630, as if the escorts were picking up survivors. Had it not been for the lack of the high power periscope denying me the opportunity of seeing how heavily armed the escorts were, it might have been profitable to have waited until they were well laden with survivors and then to have surfaced and gunned them. Under the circumstances this was not considered prudent.*

1702   *HMS Tradewind was back at periscope depth and one M.L. only was in sight, bearing 084 degs., distance three miles. I am fairly confident that the target sank.*

1709   *Altered course to 180 degs. and reloaded Nos. 2, and 3, and 4 tubes.*

1938   *Surfaced in position 03 degs. 00 mins, S., 101 degs. 09 mins. E. Proceeded to the South East. Very heavy rain in the night.*

What if Maydon had indeed surfaced with his intent to gun what he thought were Japanese crewmen off this "old-fashion merchant vessel" and instead found literally thousands of desperate human beings floundering in the wreckage?

What if?

But he didn't, and night fell.

Maydon hit the *Junyo Maru* with two torpedoes. The first struck forward, and hardly any one on board really knew what it was. A voice from the bridge called down in English to the prisoners on the after deck, shouting that there was engine trouble. Within seconds another explosion occurred. This was in the after hold, outrightly killing many men, and throwing hundreds into the air and overboard. It should be noted, however, that a few prisoners—mainly merchant seamen and naval types—had immediately gone into the ocean when they realized that the first blast was a torpedo hit. These people, thus, escaped the carnage, and as the vessel continued underway for some distance, were somewhat apart from the mass of humanity that ended up in the water around the doomed ship. The Japanese crew and prisoner guards managed to get the two lifeboats into the sea, plus a few rafts or floats which were strictly for their own use. They all carried Jap flags and, after dark, displayed small lights on their life preservers. One of the escorting vessels made a half-hearted attack on the *Tradewind* by dropping three depth charges, but then, after the *Junyo Maru* went down by the stern, both escorts turned to rescuing survivors. At first, there seemed to be little or no discrimination, and although the gun boats kept away from the great mass of swimmers, some of the above-mentioned merchant and navy types were picked up. Of course, the flag-wavers were first priority. After dark, there appears to have been little rescue effort, and it was not until the following morning that the two lifeboats were located and their occupants taken aboard. Soon thereafter, both escorts departed the scene, headed for Emma

Haven, the port for Padang, a good ninety miles away. It is unclear if any further life saving effort was made by the Japanese. One (and maybe both) possibly returned to the disaster site, but that could not have been until the twentieth.

The full extent of this sad story will never be known. There is no exact count of survivors, nor of deaths. For example, two 1985 Dutch publications fail to agree on the number who succumbed to the *Tradewind*'s torpedoes. The previously mentioned *De Sumatra Spoorweg* by Neumann and Van Witsen at one point places the deaths (including seventeen who were rescued but died shortly after reaching Padang) at 1,477. However, they name only 1,431. The second book, *Eresaluut boven Massagraf* (*Honorable Salute Above a Mass Grave*) by Ed. Melis and W. F. van Wamel lists the names of only 1,381 Hollanders. Neumann and Van Witsen show 32 British losses; Melis and van Wamel do not, nor do they include the seveteen who were rescued but died at Padang. Neither book includes the eight Americans and a lone Australian officer who died. Accepting *De Sumatra Spoorweg* as the definitive tome, some interesting numbers are revealed. Of the 1,477, 648 were age forty-four or over, 290 were over fifty, one was sixty and another sixty-two. Those 648 were born in the nineteenth century and were probably at or near their life expectancy. A few years ago, I learned persons born in the United States during 1921 or 1922 (my year of birth) had a life expectancy of fifty years. Imagine what it was for those 648 born before 1900, and probably in the tropical East Indies. What railway building production could the Japanese expect to receive from such a group? What a callous waste of humanity!

A highly probable recap looks like this:

	prisoners	*romushas*
embarked	2,200	4,300
killed/drowned	1,477	4,100
survivors	723	200

Definitely, fifteen Americans were on board, and eight were lost. Five of these eight had been taken prisoner when their ships had been sunk by the *Michel* over two years earlier:

Ensign William H. Dryer, USNR	MS *American Leader*
Able Seaman Moody H. Harrison	MS *American Leader*
Second Officer Walter H. Lee	MS *American Leader*
Fireman/Watertender Philip P. McKeever	SS *William F. Humphrey*
Second Engineer Frank E. Stallman	MS *American Leader*

Also lost were

Captain Owen H. Reed	SS *William King*
Gordon R. "Brodie" Miller,	131ˢᵗ Field Artillery, United States Army
J. R. Sokolowski	131ˢᵗ Field Artillery, United States Army

Survivors were

Bosun Stanley E. Gorski	MS *American Leader*
Able Seaman William Hosey	SS *William F. Humphrey*
Corporal William Miller, United States Marine Corps	USS *Houston*
Able Seaman Frank Patocka,	MS *American Leader*
Ordinary Seaman Steve Pekich	MS *American Leader*
Chief Cook Neville Sutherland	MS *American Leader*
Messman Christopher Walsh	MS *American Leader*

These seven eventually found themselves working on the Death Railway, which claimed the lives of Pekich (December 26, 1944) and Hosey (May 4, 1945). One other American casualty (who was not aboard the *Junyo Maru*, having arrived on Sumatra with me on the *Chukka Maru*) was Sidney M. Albert, second cook and baker in the *American Leader*, who succumbed on May 28, 1945.

As for Commander Maydon, his *Tradewind*, and his crew, they saw the war to its victorious conclusion. He retired from the Royal Navy at his own request on March 1, 1949. HMS *Tradewind* was scrapped in 1959. For many years, I conjectured as to the identity of the submarine that sank the the *Junyo Maru*. After the war whenever talk turned to submarines, I would inquire as to who sank a ship off the west coast of Sumatra on September 18, 1944. For years, there was never a clue until 1961 when the United States Naval Institute directed me to Capt. F. Kent Loomis, USN (Ret) of the Naval Historical Foundation. Capt. Loomis, on December 21, 1961 wrote, as follows:

> *We believe that the ship you have referred to as being sunk on 18 September 1944 was the cargo ship Junyo Maru (5,065 tons). HMS Tradewind reported the sinking of this ship on 18 September with two torpedoes in the approximate location 2-35S, 101-10W. However, from the limited information that we have available on this attack it appears that the commanding officer of Tradewind had no idea either before or after the sinking that the Junyo Maru was carrying prisoners of war.*

———

From here the trail led to Historical Section, Admiralty, Whitehall, London, which invited me to write to the commanding officer, *HMS Tradewind*, via their offices. In due course, I did so, and on February 19, 1962 received the following:

Dear Mr. Duffy:

I was most interested to receive your letter of 10 February and to learn that you were in the vicinity and might have been an eye-witness of the sinking of the motor vessel, Junyo Maru, 6065 tons, on the afternoon of 18 September 1944, not far from Benkulen in southern Sumatra.

Yes, I was the Captain of Tradewind, the British submarine responsible.

I shall be interested to hear from you again if you have any more details of this incident . . . while you were a prisoner-of-war. Do you know what was the cargo of this vessel? Did she have onboard any allied prisoners-of-war? We were often anxious that we might scupper our own people but you could not stop to ask!

I occasionally visit America and I would very much like to meet you . . . . I am now a member of Parliament, representing WELLS Division of Somerset.

Yours sincerely,
[signed] *Lynch Maydon.*

Commander Maydon never made it to the United States, and nor did I get to England. Over the next few years we corresponded occasionally. Frankly, I did not wish to tell him of the enormity of the disaster his torpedoes caused, but in my reply to the above letter I did say, "It is incredible that you have learned nothing of the Junyo Mary. For, you see *Junyo Maru* was carrying prisoners of war." He never picked me up on that.

Stan Gorski, the *American Leader*'s bosun, and, as listed above, a survivor of the *Junyo Maru*, was living at that time in Racine, Wisconsin. Stan and I visited, corresponded, and telephoned each other frequently, so he was well aware of my efforts to identify the *Junyo Maru*'s nemesis. Therefore, I decided to let Stan relate his story of the sinking and survival to Maydon. On January 2, 1963, Maydon complained that, although he had written to Stan, he had not received a reply. I guess Stan was reluctant as well to break the news to him, although he promised to send Maydon a vivid audio tape of his personal experience that late afternoon of September 18, 1944. For the next four years, nothing transpired between us.

All the while I had been pursuing another angle in this story. Maydon's first letter to me, also included this paragraph:

> We had carried out a number of patrols off the coasts of SUMATRA and JAVA in connection with some special operations in which two Americans, BOB KOKE . . . and RAY KAUFFMAN . . . were concerned.

> Should you know any means that might enable me to get in touch with them, I shall be very grateful. I have not heard from either since 1949.

On July 18, 1967, I reactivated our correspondence with the news, "I've found Kauffman for you!" By pure chance, I had run across an article in *Yachting* about Ray Franklin Kauffman of Williamsburg, Virginia and his yacht *Radian*. Maydon had mentioned that Kauffman was a yachtsman who had sailed around the world before the war, and this article thusly described Kauffman. A letter to *Yachting* produced an address, and a letter to Kauffman elicited the response I had hoped for: Ray Franklin Kauffman was an OSS officer involved in the training of Malayan coast watchers in Ceylon for eventual insertion onto Sumatra from the *Tradewind*. Maydon immediately replied (July 26) with thanks, and then, once again, the lines of communication broke down. Earlier in the month, Stan Gorski and I recorded several hours of conversation which Stan was to edit and send to Maydon. In November 1968, we traveled to Williamsburg to meet Kauffman, and still another recording was made.

By this time, another individual had come onto the scene, as the result of a chance encounter on July 11, 1968 in a Norwalk, Connecticut boatyard. Karel Rink was a yacht broker, and I was working for a Marblehead, Massachusetts sail making firm. Rink had been a pilot in the Royal Dutch Air Force, and he had a brother, a lieutenant in the Dutch army, who—and this is almost unbelievable—was killed in the Japanese prison ship *Juno Maru!* Rink knew little of the circumstances surrounding the sinking. Of course, as I told him, I knew *all* about it. This led to a Rye, New York free-lance magazine writer and former World War II merchant seaman named Mark Walker, a tenant of Rink. Walker immediately jumped into the story, proposing that he write a book. In early 1969, we gathered in New York—Gorski, Kauffman, Rink, Walker, and I. Walker went to work on a manuscript and eventually desired to go to England to interview Commander

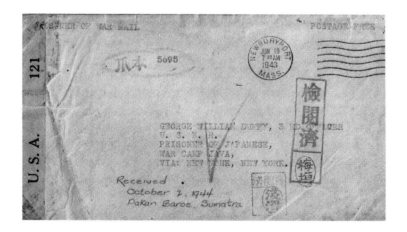

The envelope which held the first letter received by the author after over two years imprisonment. The two square stampings indicate the letter has been censored, and the oval stamps therein are the censors' individual identification. Top left is my official number and the two characters indicate where I was. These were applied in the office at the Cycle Camp in Batavia. Blank paper for any use was in short supply, so the author used envelope backs and the reverse side of letters from his mother for sketching and journal purposes.

Maydon, so I on May 16 knocked out an introductory letter. At this point I had not heard from Maydon for almost two years. Walker did meet Maydon that summer and interviewed him. Two years later, on a return trip to England he was informed that the Commander had passed away. The fact that Maydon's family had not notified me of his passing bothered me to some extent, and I wondered if his learning of the sinking and its immense loss of life had a bearing on his death. It was not until mid-2003, when I received a copy of a Dutch-language TV show entitled "Sinking of the *Junyo Maru*," which had been telecast on February 25 that year, did I learn what happened. In June 1970 Maydon was diagnosed as having leukemia. He resigned from Parliament, and nine months later at the age of only 57 passed away.

Of the estimated 723 prisoner of war survivors of the *Junyo Maru*, there were in late 1991, according to one of them—Willem Wanrooy of Palmdale, California—only twenty-five living. As of mid-2003, I was aware of only three—Stan Gorski, and two Hollanders, W. Punt and A. Bloem, who appeared in the above mentioned "Sinking of the *Junyo Maru*." In the video, however, a son of Commander Maydon relates his father's receipt of a tape from America. So, Gorski had indeed sent it, and it was not the cause of Maydon's demise.

One bit of good news came out of this *Junyo Maru* tale. Stan, who had been working in the Jap office at Cycle Camp, told me the latest batch of mail in at Batavia included letters for me. This was the first indication I had that my family knew I was alive. Twenty-nine months had elapsed since the *American Leader* departed New York

October 2. Received today, 9 letters: 6 from Mother, 2 from Eleanor, and 1 from Madelyn. They are postmarked from June 19 to September 7, last year. I really get a big kick out of them, but also a twinge of homesickness. I wonder what has happened there in the last 13 months.

Fortunately, my mother made carbon copies of everything she typed to me, and numbered and dated each. I noted the date of my receipt in the camp. Thus, I have been able to reconstruct her entire correspondence. In total she sent fifty-one messages, of which I received twenty-one. To her dismay, letter number 1 was returned to her, not having made it past the U.S. Censor. She filled two pages with single-spaced copy, without indents or paragraph breaks, which undoubtedly caused its rejection. Additionally, she provided detailed information concerning the radio monitoring network and personal information, which the censor probably felt should not be revealed to the Japanese. An edited version of that letter is provided herewith.

Newburyport, Mass.
May 21, 1943.

My dear George:

Our joy and happiness at receiving your message is hard to describe and now to be able to write to you surely is grand. We think of you constantly, hoping and praying that you are feeling fine, will be treated good, and will come home soon. Everybody here is so happy and more people than we will ever know said they never gave up praying for you. People everywhere have been truly wonderful during these months of sadness and now are glad to share our joy. Since Easter Sunday nearly forty people from all parts of the U.S. wrote to me as they heard your message too, and wanted to do their bit in bringing comfort to me. The one on Easter came from a man in Pennsylvania and we were so elated about it that we could hardly believe it to be true, so during the afternoon Colley telephoned to him and we both had a talk with him and he told us about getting these messages over his short-wave radio, so many every day, and that we would without doubt get others and sure enough we did, the letters came thick and fast for several days. And each one was read over and over again, then on the 11th of May a broadcasting station in California sent us the record of your message which seemed to bring you closer to us and needless to say we listen to that many times each day. We have an electric record player which Dot and Madelyn gave Eleanor for Christmas. Your twenty first birthday will be one you will always remember or maybe one you will want to forget. I had a Mass said for your safe return as well as in Thanksgiving for God's kindness in sparing you to us.

At this point in the letter she reported in great detail on my brothers and sisters, aunts and uncles, cousins, friends, schoolmates, shipmates, families, and so on. Dot and Madelyn, mentioned above, were my father's sisters, thus my aunts.

Well, my dear, I am getting close to the bottom of this page, and feel that I have written enough, even though I was told to make it brief the censor may think I don't know the meaning of the word. Now that the Provost Marshall General in Washington says I can write I will do so as often as possible and sincerely hope you will have the liberty to write to us. So, with heaps of love and kisses and the best of luck from all of us I'll say so long and God bless you.

Lovingly,
Mother.

Letters numbered 2 to 7, which were the six I received, were shorter (just a single page), much less emotional, and similar in content, with reports on everyone's activities. On September 18, she wrote again, but that wasn't delivered to me until January 27, 1945, seventeen months in transit. Her next three letters never left the United States, each being returned with a small printed slip of paper. This stated,

> *This communication is returned since the Japanese government has refused delivery of any mail to American prisoners of war and civilian internees held by Japan unless it complies with all of the following conditions:*
>
> 1. *Letters must be less than 25 words in length.*
> 2. *Letters must be typewritten or legibly block printed.*
> 3. *Subject matter must be strictly personal; no military or political matter or opinions may be included.*
> 4. *The name of the Internment Camp must appear in the forwarding address.*

THESE CONDITIONS HAVE BEEN IMPOSED BY THE JAPANESE GOVERNMENT AND NOT BY THE UNITED STATES GOVERNMENT.

From here on the entire mail situation became a fiasco, though neither of us knew it. She sent her first twenty-five word message, number 12, on October 13, 1943. Number 45 went out on February 12, 1945. Of that thirty-four, I received nine, four after we knew the war was over. One, number 30, was returned to her. Of interest, that had been opened and censored by the German *Oberkomande der Wehrmacht!* Her last three letters, numbered 49 to 51, mailed between May 26 and July 6, 1945 were returned. Everything else was swallowed up as the American forces rolled on to Tokyo.

CHAPTER THIRTY-TWO

Working on the Railroad

*October 27. Topics of the day: . . . where is Mountbatten and what is he doing . . .
what is happening in the Pacific . . . the election is coming up next week; how will
that directly influence the war? . . . just how will things break here (if and when they
break) . . . and, damn it t'hell, we are all getting pretty impatient . . . I had an idea
once that I'd be a Jap POW for just about two years, thus being able to say that I was 2
months with the Germans and 2 whole years with the Japs . . . Bode has set November
4 as the concluding date, and Hickey says October 31 . . . rather coincidental . . . Pat
Paris also says October 31, but that is because it is his wedding anniversary—13th,
this year.*

Bode was Australian, a lieutenant in the British Army, and my barrack mate at
that particular time.

*November 1. Well, the war isn't over yet, and today we are transferred to Camp #5
from Camp #4.*

Reflections on Camp 4. The work details here were primarily involved in completing
the bridge, a key link in the supply of materials to the whole project. Some rails
and ties were being hand-carried through the construction, but progress was slow.
Also, the monsoon rainy season had begun, the river rose, and trees and logs and
other debris occasionally became caught on the upriver side of the bridge pilings.
This necessitated the formation of a swim party. I had been telling the Japs I was
captain of the *American Leader*, thus they figured I could swim and was put in
charge. Actually, it was fun, and we were fed out of the Japanese cookhouse.

Several memorable experiences occurred. First of all, we were counted twice
a day, morning and evening. Once I was in charge of a rail laying party which
returned after dark. We would march as far as the Jap barracks, where we would
be turned over to the Koreans. They, in turn, would escort us to our huts where a

count was made. In this instance, as the Koreans turned away, several of the Japs indicated I was to go into their barrack building to have a drink and something to eat. I did and probably spent an hour, getting a shot of saki and a couple rice balls. Meanwhile, down in the camp, the count, of course, came up one man short. The Dutch officers had a contingency plan which involved shuffling a few people around allowing one man to be counted twice. The recount satisfied the Koreans until I, with one of the Jap soldiers as an escort, sauntered out of the darkness. Oh, was there hell to pay? The whole camp was turned out for another count. The Koreans knew they had been hoodwinked. The Dutch commander was slapped around, as were a few other officers. Fortunately, no one blamed me, and I escaped unscathed. The Japs, I think, treated the matter as a practical joke on the Koreans.

An example of the bad blood between them was a comical "fight" one evening involving King Kong, a huge Korean, and one of the Jap railway soldiers. They were kicking at each other and when King Kong missed with a wild one, the Jap grabbed him by the ankle, and started running around in a circle. The Korean hopped up and down, flailing away with his fists but unable to reach the Jap. Everyone roared with laughter—Japs, Koreans, and prisoners, until the two were separated.

Another incident is strong in my memory. I was in charge of a group of prisoners who, with a Jap sergeant and a few soldiers, were aligning the tracks. The prisoners were using crowbars to nudge the sections of previously laid track into a reasonably straight line. At the end of the day, as we were walking back to camp, we came across a crowbar that someone had decided not to carry any further, or perhaps had been left behind by the previous day's crew. The sergeant told me to pick it up, and I said, "*Tidak*" (no). We communicated out there with a prison lingo of sorts, a mixture of Malayan, English, and Japanese, with a big dose of sign language. I told him I was *shoko* (officer) and he was *gunso* (sergeant). He told me I was *gila* (crazy), and that was the end of the argument. Neither of us lost face, and as far as I know the crowbar is still there.

The lack of decent food was beginning to affect everyone. The unchanging menu looked something like this: In the morning, we received a dollop of what was called *ongol-ongol*, a jellylike concoction whose only ingredient was tapioca flour. At noon, it was a cup of rice leveled off. That is, the cook swiped a flat stick across the rim of the serving cup, assuring everyone an equal ration. In addition to the rice, there was generally a watery soup containing grasses and tree leaves. In the evening, the cup of rice was humped up, and the soup had a little more body to it with the addition of chopped up carrots, okra, tapioca root, and so on. Green tea was the only available libation. This was barely enough to keep us alive, never mind support a day's work on the railway. A fair distribution system was adhered to in each barrack by lining up according to each man's living space. For example, to begin with, if the building held one hundred men, fifty to a side, the men on one side were numbered 1 to 50, and the others 51 to 100. When all 100 had been fed, whatever was leftover went to number 1 man, number 2 man, and so on. When the leftovers were gone, the number of the first man who didn't receive any was noted, and the next day the leftovers would start with him. We called them "laggies" from the Malayan word *lagi*, meaning more.

Wire-guided barge serves as vehicular ferry across Kampar Kanan, 1979. A modern steel trussed bridge in now in place.

The officer status situation resurfaced for Pat Paris and me as soon as we arrived at Camp 4. (Hickey, for some reason, maybe his poor health, ended up in Camp 2, headquarters.) I reported to the Dutch commanding officer, speaking Dutch, informing him I was Mijnheer Duffy, and I expected to be accorded proper officer recognition. Some debate ensued, but I won my case and retained the officer designation awarded me back on Java by the explosive Soni. On August 20, a few days over a month after our arrival on Sumatra, RAF Wing Commander Patrick Davis, the senior Allied officer on the project, addressed a letter to one Dorré, confirming Pat's, Hickey's, and my officer status. That a copy went to Lt. Fred Sparks, officer commanding British troops, No. 4 POW Camp, Pakan Baroe, Sumatra, indicates I was, at least, under British jurisdiction even though the camp itself was Dutch. Of the eight Americans who came up from Java in the *Chukka Maru* and the seven American survivors of the *Junyo Maru*, all but two were at Camp 4. As mentioned, Hickey was in Camp 2, as was Harrelson.

Occasionally, on Java, the Japs would throw a great party for themselves to celebrate a supposed victory over the hated Americans. The saki would flow liberally, which led to the singing of patriotic songs, cheering, and the like. In actuality, a battle had taken place, but in 1944 their navy, in particular, was being seriously mauled. Toward the end of October one of these drunken orgies erupted to mark their navy's success in Leyte Gulf where they sank an American light cruiser, two escort carriers, two destroyers, and a destroyer escort. What they didn't know were the Japanese Navy's losses: four aircraft carriers, three battleships, six heavy cruisers, four light cruisers, and eleven destroyers. (These figures are from *The Times Atlas of the Second World War*, copyright Times Books, London, 1989, 1994.) At the height of all the whooping, the Royal Navy's Lieutenant Commander Upton remarked to me, "Georgie, it sounds as though they're mourning another victory."

There had been about five hundred of us in Camp 4 and about mid-October, the bridge was completed. We abandoned that camp and joined a similar number of prisoners, who had come up from Java with us in the *Chukka Maru*, in Camp 5. Of the approximately one thousand, half were Dutch, and the other half British, Australian, at least one New Zealander, and eleven Americans. The work consisted of widening an existing cross-island road, in order to accommodate the rail line but still allowing vehicular traffic.

November 6. This is our second anniversary of becoming Japanese prisoners. Corned beef for supper, if I can get the can open! Pat went into the hospital last night with a light attack of dysentary [sic]. Betting, not too serious, has the odds even on the war finishing before Christmas, and 4-1 on it ending before March 1, 1945.

The corned beef was hoarded from the Red Cross package of May 12. The camp didn't have a hospital, but a rather isolated barrack to keep the ill prisoners away from the healthy. Furthermore, there were no trained medics out on the line, and there were little or no personnel to spare in the camps for assignment to such work.

November 13. 100-odd sick sent in to Camp #2, including Pat Paris. Received a note from BJH. Says according to Roosevelt, war will finish this year. Jap Sgt/Major states war can be over any day now. Also same statement from Jap guards and soldiers. Stories on large fleet and troop concentration in Colombo.

Camp 2 did have a large hospital and a staff of doctors and medical orderlies, but without medicine and equipment. Thus, Camp 2, unfortunately, was where the seriously ill were sent to die. "BJH" was Hickey.

November 19. The war in Europe is supposed to have ended on November 13.

November 26. Raining all morning. No work party out. Stayed on my bed. Rather a wasted day, but, then, most of our days are wasted. Had a run in with a Jap guard yesterday and have a very sore left hip now. He clipped me three times with his rifle, mainly because I am an American. Plenty of so-called news kicking around. Some of it rather hard to believe, such as landings at Nagasaki and other places in Nippon.

This rifle-beating was again an instance of my stretching the limits. This time I didn't get away with it. I was in charge of a group of about one hundred Australians who were loading gravel into small, open top rail cars. A spur track had been brought in to an open area which sloped upward and as the digging proceeded an embankment had been created. So, they were simply knocking down the banking and shoveling the sandy soil into the cars. When the string of cars was full, a truck fitted with flanged wheels would pull them out to the main track and move them down the line to be dumped. On this work party this particular day, was a British soldier who was to care for any prisoners who became ill, and before noon he had five or six casualties sitting or laying in the shade of a tree. A lone Jap was assigned to supervise the job, and he decided to determine if these fellows were indeed unable to work. When I saw him approach the group, I quickly moved over to the scene and told him that the men couldn't work. This irritated the Jap, and he asked me if I was Australian. (On Sumatra we didn't wear the identification tags required on Java.) I told him I didn't understand him, and he asked, "*English-ka?*" Again I didn't understand, and he queried, "*Blanda-ka?*" *Blanda* is the Malay word for Dutch. When I again said I didn't understand, he moved his rifle from his right hand to the left, and I sensed a roundhouse coming. I quickly leaned toward him, pointed my finger at my chest and said America. He was absolutely startled. I believe he had no idea any Americans were within a thousand miles. He quickly waved me off and told me to go back to the job. Soon, though, the word came down the line, that he was working up a rage and I should be careful.

When it was time to return to the nearby camp for the noon meal, the Jap told me to get everyone out on the road and formed up. While I was in the process of doing so, he decided to demote me and pushed me into the ranks. When I protested, he grabbed his rifle by the muzzle and using it like a baseball bat whacked me on my left side, just below the ribs. The force of the blow knocked me down, but because I had seen other people in such a situation receive a few kicks, I scrambled to my feet. He leveled me two more times before deciding I had enough. The other officers in the camp attempted to persuade me not to go out in the afternoon, but I persisted, because I did not want the guy to believe he had injured me. Strangely, it was he who didn't show up for the shift. In fact, I never really came into contact with him again. On occasion, he was on duty in the guard-house, but he seemed to avoid me.

November 27. Russia is supposed to have declared war on Japan, and Germany has capitulated.

November 29. What we wouldn't give for an up to date newspaper, or to be able to sit down and listen to news broadcasts.

December 1. Staying inside doing absolutely nothing today. Was on work party yesterday. Very warm. Men are getting very run down by this day after day business. Several passed out during yesterday's work. Heavy rains have caused the river to rise considerably and the RR was washed out at one point. It rained practically all last night, right up to the time the work party was called out this morning. No more "news" kicking around except that a Jap cook is supposed to have said that the war is over and they are simply waiting for word from HQ. The spirit here in camp is extremely optimistic, and Gorski and I were discussing what should happen to Japan on December 8.

The reader will recall my account of the happenings in Manila on December 8, 1941.

December 5. I'm down with malaria. Niet zoo best [Dutch for "not so good"].

December 9. Well, the old war is in its fourth year now. I don't admit it but I'm getting impatient. The fighting in Europe evidently has ceased. Russia has declared war on Japan, but in regard to actual fighting there is little known. Korea probably has been invaded. Sakhalin, Bonin, Riu Kius, Philippines, Formosa, Hong Kong, and Shanghai in Alled possession. Kyushu, Shikoku (the two southernmost of the Japanese group) are also occupied and there is fighting on Honshu, with Osaka being mentioned. Really we're existing here simply day to day, and it is a very pessimistic person who gives it yet three months. A few months ago I had hopes that this business would finish up in time to be home for Christmas. Well, even if the war did end up today or tomorrow, I wouldn't be able to make it now. So, for the sake of another date, I'll take April 14 which marks the completion of 3 years on the American Leader articles.

Looking back, April 14 was an important date in my life. Not only did this perilous journey in the *American Leader* begin on April 14, 1942, but another of life's journeys commenced on the same date in 1921 when my parents were married. Astoundingly, Margaret and I were married on April 14, 1951!

December 17. Five months have elapsed since we first saw Pakan Baroe. The bridge repairs have finished and an enormous amount of rails and sleepers are being shipped out the line. It appears as though they are in a big hurry to complete this railway. Today was sort of a yasumay day. The bridge party was free and rain in the morning prevented the other parties from going out until 1:00 PM. I have been with the jungle wood gang for the last few days and we worked through the rain, taking the afternoon off. News or rumors extremely scarce and a rather pessimistic feeling has pervaded the camp. It is not preventing everyone from discussing what we will do when we get out, though. Really, food comes before everything else when a conversation gets started.

"Sleepers" was British for "railroad ties," *yasumay* Japanese for "rest period." The wood gang cut down large trees, trimmed them, and hauled them out of the jungle for use as pilings. This was a very difficult operation.

December 20. Story yesterday that the Americans hold four big airfields on Honshu, or something to that effect. A Jap on the bridge said that the Americans were at Nagasaki. I wish that I could believe these reports: I do in a sense, but more on the wishful thinking side.

December 24. "Christmas Eve in the Workhouse." Steve Pekich off to Camp #2 this evening. Saw tracks of a wild animal, perhaps a tiger, close to camp today. The print was about as large as the palm of my hand. Previously there have been tracks seen in this vicinity, but I had never gone to look at them.

Camp 5 was at the twenty-three-kilometer pole, and Camp 6 was thirteen kilometers farther down the line. According to the two Dutch authors, Henk Neumann and Henk Hovinga, sometime between October 12 and December 12, a Japanese soldier known as Pig Head was attacked and killed by a tiger in the vicinity of Camp 6.

Christmas Day, 1944. Breakfast—5 Ongol Balls and coffee. Lunch—Ikan Daging Nasi Goreng, Corned beef, and coffee. Dinner—Rice, Brown Beans and Meat, Sambal Katjang, Trassie Balls, coffee.

Coffee was supplied by the camp in the morning and evening. Luckily, Bode and I had just enough sugar to last out the day. The breakfast Ongol balls were very tasty, flavored with sugar and cinnamon. The Corned Beef was my last tin from the Kampong Makassar Red Cross issue. For the evening meal, I made up the Trassie Balls, consisting of tapioca flour, katoel, oedang, currie powder, and trassie. I could eat only two with the meal, and Bode managed a single one. We saved the remainder for the following day.

Translations. *Ongol* was the flour which, when mixed with water and heated, was the standard morning meal. The *ongol* balls were more like doughnut holes. *Ikan daging* were tiny, dried, salted fish. *Nasi* is the word for cooked rice, and *nasi goreng* is cooked rice which has then been stir fried. *Sambal* is a hot pepper paste, and *katjang* is the generic word for bean. *Trassie* is an ill-smelling, but very tasty fish paste. *Katoel* at this stage in time escapes me, but it appears to have been a clump of rice. *Oedang* are small shrimps.

December 26. The war is supposed to have ended.

December 27. Natives taking over all jobs on RR, such as engineers, firemen, brakemen. Saw tracks of a big elephant which had come though the bath place last night. A single print measured from the tip of my fingers to be elbow. He had cut quite a swath through the jungle, also.

It was necessary to maintain a bonfire near the camp cookhouse throughout the night to ward off predators. The absence of barbed wire fences out on the line should also be noted.

December 29. On the move again. Tomorrow, 100 English speaking leave for a camp further along the line. Report from Camp #2 says that Steve Pekich died in that camp on the 26th of December.

December 31. Settled in our new camp, Lipat Kain. The move came off very uneventfully, the 50km train ride taking about 5 hours. I had an argument with Rosier when I arrived concerning my status and the work question. He evidently went to the Japs, but the reply was in my favor.

This was Camp 7 near the kampong named Lipat Kain. I cannot recall seeing many natives, however. Rosier was a Dutch army captain who commanded the camp. Although I showed the letters delineating my status, I was alone without any support from Paris or Hickcy. Of course, Rosier was under a great deal of pressure to produce numbers for the working parties, and I was to him, just another body.

CHAPTER THIRTY-THREE

1945

January 1. Down with malaria again, but not so bad as last time. The people here are not as optimistic as those in Camp #4, some of them figuring at least another 6 months. May be, but I don't see myself a prisoner 2 months from now. I am always of the belief that it can finish up any day. There are also stories here concerning the return of all English POWs to Singapore, and the Dutch to Fort de Kock. More coolies arrive every day. Bode figures that jealousy is the cause of all the trouble we Americans are having here. Yet, it is still, "When are the Yanks coming?"

Fort de Kock, also known as Bukit-tingi, was a small Dutch settlement in the west central Sumatran highlands, first fortified in 1825. In the Dutch scheme of things, it was considered to be quite important. Under today's Indonesian regime, its name is spelled Bukittingi.

January 10. A couple of Japs told one of the Dutchmen that yesterday a B–29 appeared over Pakan Baroe. Padang has evidently been bombed recently, and the Japs on the trains are all carrying rifles, tin hats, and gas masks. The Jap Lt. figures on a landing here by March. The work parties are really catching hell, too. Reveille here is at 7:15 AM, and tonight the main party came in at 10:10 PM. That means the work party which paraded at 8:15 AM was out 14 hours. Lights out at 11:30 PM. After the men come in they have to wash and eat, etc., so they're lucky if they get to sleep before midnight, giving them seven hours rest for the next day.

These work parties were engaged in laying the sleepers and tracks. Since mid-May, only about seventy-five kilometers of the line commencing at Pakan Baroe had been completed, with almost twice as much to be done. At that rate, Moearo would not be reached until the end of February 1946. The Japanese panicked, and the prisoners suffered. Also, it should be noted Camp 7 was located just five kilometers north of the Equator, and it was summer time in the Southern Hemisphere.

January 14. Camp splits up. 500 going down the line to establish a new camp. The RR runs about 145km from there to Moearo. Looking things over, Lord "Looie" had better get a move on or most of us will be wearing grass skirts or leaves or something. I have, to my name, two pairs of shorts. One is patched and threadbare and won't stand any more repairing. The other pair is just patched, but the condition is pretty good. In addition, I own an Australian tunic, short-sleeved, which Cocky Watts gave me when I left Java, and the sweater which I wore overboard from the American Leader.

Lord Looie was, of course, Louis Mountbatten, supreme Allied commander for Southeast Asia, and Cocky Watts was one of the 2/40th officers who had befriended us on Java.

Hats, I have but one, the little black cap I stole on the Uckermark. My socks consist of four odd ones, two darned and two undarnable. My shoes are Dutch Army, canvas-topped, a present from Captain Rosier. They're in fair shape for a POW, at any rate. Also in my kit is a ragged bath towel and a flimsy Japanese hand towel. To sleep on, I have two straw mats and a burlap bag; the blanket, probably the best piece of gear of all, is Jap issue. Also in the footwear line is a pair of crepe rubber slippers. Then, for eating equipment there is a china plate, an aluminum pan, a tin cup, spoon, knife (stolen from the Uckermark), and a sheath knife. To carry all this barang I have a big sea bag and a British Army side-pack. I think the food situation, though serious, is really laughable. Some of the concoctions—man-oh-man!—we call them delicious, but I can imagine eating them in peacetime. On the other hand, a lot of the stuff is really first class. The idea is this: in addition to the regular cookhouse issue, it is considered a necessity to have our own extras. For example, last night, Bode and I fried up a mess of small fish. One of the Ambonese came in during the afternoon with a pan full, for which Visser paid 6 gulden. Our kongsie took half, and split four ways, meant 75¢ a portion. The cookhouse meal consisted of a stew made up of varied vegetables and quite a good amount of grated coconut. It was sufficient, but the fish made a meal out of it.

Visser was a Dutch officer who spoke passable Japanese and acted as the camp's interpreter. *Kong* is a Chinese word for "business." We modified it to *kongsie*, meaning a small group which had come together for the mutual benefit of its members. Generally a *kongsie* consisted of three, four, or five people who helped each other by sharing money and food, and caring for ill members.

Another tasty bit that I make up is fried cake. This is simply oedang, salt, and tapioca flour, mixed with water, and fried in deep coconut oil. Local vegetables, such as squashes and melons, are available at rather high prices. Still, they provide that needed extra. A couple of POWs were watching a Jap aircraft the other day when one of the guards came along and said, America shikoki, tidak. Nanti-nanti. (Translation: That is not an American plane. They will come later.) Doc Wyatt remarked last evening that people back home would probably be very skeptical if they could suddenly see us or a picture of us entitled, "Life on the Equator." I put a jacket on every evening before supper, and afterwards we sit around the fire in the fore part of the barracks with a pot of coffee. I took the wood party out today: Jew rokko may. Ambil kayu. Kitchen. Three languages to say six words.

Jew rokko may is Japanese for "sixteen men." *Ambil kayu* is Malayan for "carry wood."

By cripe, it's going to be great to get out of this business. I'm fed up. Absolutely. Imagine being able to sleep in a single bed and not have to worry about mosquitoes or mosquito nets and not to be worried about bedbugs and lice. And to have my own job and be able to do it without someone thinking he's doing me a favor by letting me work inside the camp. And to get away from these weak-sister, so-called brother officers, Dutch and English alike, and meet up with some two-fisted Yanks, who, if they've got something to say, tell you right to your face. There are only two of us here, Ski and I, and Ski with only one good arm can't be allowed to cut veg in the kitchen. No, he's got to burn rubbish, carry logs, lug sand and clay. And then there is this baloney of telling Bode to tell me what they want—that certainly takes the prize.

Gorski had dislocated his shoulder in an accident while driving pilings on the bridge at Camp 4.

January is drawing to a close, and we're still here. News, we have none. Bode came in a couple of nights ago with an "authentic" report on American landings in Japan. I don't believe it though. It does appear that fighting is going on in Germany, and my opinion is that the Allies are taking things easy, more or less, in preparation for a Spring offensive to finish the war. Here, I believe the same strategy holds forth. The possibility of being freed by a landing on this island is, also to my way of thinking, very much in the books. Plenty of mail coming in lately, but, as usual, tidak for Mrs. Duffy's boy.

Tidak is Malayan for "nothing."

January 27. Received this morning a letter from Mother, postmarked August 30, 1943. Rather heavily censored and the envelope all cluttered up with hash marks.

January 29. Because I am a "Warrant Officer" who will not work I left Camp #7 today for Camp #2. Perhaps I should better say that I was kicked out.

Although my January 14 mention of receiving a pair of shoes from Capt. Rosier hinted at better relations between us, such was not the case. He continued to complain to the Japanese about my status, so the Japs in their usual manner solved the problem by making no decision and sending me back to headquarters. A dozen or more "unfit to work" prisoners, including Stan Gorski, rode with me on an empty flatbed railway car. When we arrived at Camp 2, the Japs told us to empty our kit bags for inspection. I did not and got away with it by simply refusing. Again, I played the *shoko* role, calling their bluff. A large percentage of the material contained in this book could have been destroyed, and severe punishment inflicted on me had I not challenged the little bastards.

Here, we were reunited with Hickey, Paris, Kalloch, Albert, and Parejko from the *American Leader*, and Hosey from the *William F. Humphrey*.

February 6. Looking over the situation from this angle, the climax is nearing (I hope). News, and I think that it is really straight, tells of large-scale landings during last month from Akyab, in Burma, southward. Here, the evacuation appears to be underway. Daily, truckloads of equipment are going past the camp towards Pakan Baroe. Also, I have seen a few tanks and some field artillery. This is the headquarters of the area camps, situated on the main road from Pakan Baroe to Pajakoembo, about 4.5km from Pakan Baroe.

Road from Pakan Baroe airport to city, 1979. Camp number 2 was situated at curve, behind wooden fence.

The Akyab news was correct. British forces had taken that city on January 4, and in February, three infantry divisions, the 25th, 26th, and 82nd West African moved southward along the Arakan coast.

February 7. Down again with malaria, and a real good whack, too.

February 12. Feeling fairly decent today, so I'll try and get a few notes down. There have been rather strange occurrences around here lately, the strangest being the passing by of an extremely high Japanese personage in the evening of the 10th. All work parties came in at 4 PM, and we had to remain in the barracks after 4:30, and no bedding or clothing was allowed on the outside lines. In any case, several cars flying various official flags came in to Pakan Baroe about 6:00, and as they passed, the guards turned their backs to. The next day, there were no work parties out at all. Sometime during the day, the cars returned, but whether they had the same flags and received the same treatment (honors), I don't know. Today, shortly before noon, we were given a concert in camp by a Jap military band. The opening number was Sousa's "Washington Post" march. Anyhow, to continue looking over the situation, everybody here is feeling pretty happy and optimistic. There was somewhat of a letdown after Christmas and New Year, mainly, I think, because many had built up hopes of being free by that time. Now, we kind of look on March as being THE month. The evacuation, or perhaps better called "reinforcement move", has in the past week or ten days tapered off to practically nothing. Our food situation is becoming rather bad due to transportation difficulties. Also, fire wood.

Close-up of Camp number 2 site.

———

In retrospect, it was not until 1979, when I again visited Pakan Baroe, I discovered the road running past Camp 2 connected to a road from the airport. I believe I thought in 1945 this important personage came from central Sumatra, whereas, in fact, he probably landed on the tenth and flew out on the eleventh. Also, those musicians were a real feeble lot.

February 15. We receive some good news. Jap guards very nervous. Nothing officially admitted nor even rumored. I wonder if, at home, they are saving any magazines or newspapers. I am on the wood party, as usual, day after day. Boy! If we could get just one decent meal in 24 hours, this work would be a snap.

I have no idea what this good news could have been. As for the "wood party," this was a group of thirty officers (of which perhaps twenty would be able to go to work on a given day). We were involved in cutting down a large grove of trees which produced liquid latex. In plantation style, the trees stood in rows and we knocked them down, row by row. We were organized into two groups: choppers and carriers. The choppers toppled the trees, which were tall and branchless except at the top, and then cut them into suitable lengths. Pairs of similar sized men, using burlap padding to protect their shoulders, carried the logs into camp where other prisoners sawed them into eighteen-inch sections for splitting. This wood, although quite wet because of its latex content, burned very well in the cookhouse fires and in the boilers of the locomotives. It did cause problems on the trains, however, as large burning cinders would rain down on the prisoners riding in the open cars behind.

February 20. Strong rumors of occupation of Java. Japs here busy building and having air raid shelters built.

February 22. Malaria again.

February 23. Searched.

February 24. Snake soup for our kongsie tonight.

Snakes were occasionally encountered in the brush around the rubber trees. Killed, skinned, and cut into small chunks, and boiled in a small amount of water, the result had a remarkable resemblance to chicken soup.

February 28. February has passed into memory, and March is at hand. March, the long awaited and anticipated month in which big things should happen. We shall see what we shall see. 31 days to go.

March 9. The 10th yasumay day since Christmas, and we're still here.

March 22. Springtime. Increase in aerial activity lately. Scarcity of Japanese troops around Pakan Baroe. Many deaths in camp: three yesterday and three more today. Personally am feeling very fit. Graduated from the wood-carrying department to the tree choppers. Went today to Pakan Baroe on a special job.

"Downtown" Pakan Baroe had changed very little from 1945 to 1979.

First time I've been there since July 17. Money giving me a bit of worry; right now I owe 75 gulden. Trying to sell my sweater and knife. We're doing a lot of talk lately about post-war plans. Another attempt to raise contributions for our (merchant marine officers) salaries has fallen through. Just as happy though.

We had a few people, mainly Australians, who wanted to set up a tax scheme whereby every officer would contribute a few cents per month into a pool which would then be distributed to the merchant officers. The idea was probably scuttled by the Dutch, with whom we were always in disagreement.

March 24. Big air raid drill this afternoon.

March 25. Hickey into hospital with dysentery.

April 1 . . . well, March certainly went by quickly.

April 3. Tuesday. The end doesn't seem any nearer. I am officially sick in quarters at present. Rather amusing. Wanted a day off a couple of days ago and went to Colonel Hennessy with quite a story. He sent me to have a blood slide taken and, be damned if it didn't turn out positive—malaria!! The rest will probably do me good since I worked about 27 straight days last month. The trouble with remaining inside, however, is that one thinks too much of this business—the war and food and so forth.

The colonel's name was actually spelled Hennessee. He was the senior British medical officer in the camp.

April 4. The RR line has been broken. On Good Friday, a hurry-up call was received here for 100 men to go to an unknown destination. 41 men eventually left. Last night they returned. It seems that floodwaters had damaged the bridge (3rd) out on the road from here and an attempt was being made to save it. Shortly after the arrival of the 41 POWs, though, the thing collapsed. Luckily, no prisoners were on it, but a large number of coolies were swept away. The expedition ended up as a complete success. In spite of the confusion, etc., the group lived exceptionally well. The quarters were poor, but the food in quantity and quality was as good as any of them have had since becoming POWs.

The Japanese had access to sufficient food for us. Yet in spite of our dire straits, they were simply not interested in seeing we had enough to maintain a minimum standard of health.

April 7. Last month, 41 men died in this camp and 8 in the outlying camps. Today, 6 have already been buried; 2 and maybe 3 will be buried this evening. The total for these 7 days is over 25.

April 9. Am on a draft of 50 leaving for a new camp along the line, but was later replaced. And I was not going as an officer, either.

The Dutch, who were the administrators of this camp, were certainly adamant in their efforts to put the merchant marine officers out on the work parties as laborers.

April 10. Deaths still occurring at a fast rate. Buried 7 this afternoon. That makes 35 in 10 days. They can't get people to carry the bodies to the cemetery, so the wood party is detailed as bearers. The other day, the 7th, I carried a Dutchman up the hill and I don't even know who he was. Today, it was an English fellow named Hobson.

According to *De Sumatra Spoorweg* by H. Neumann and E. Van Witsen, four men died at Camp 2 on April 6, and eight on April 7. I have no idea which of these I carried to his grave. Hobson was Stanley George Hobson, aircraftman 1st Class, Royal Air Force Volunteer Reserve, whose date of death was April 9. He was 29. Following the war, his remains were recovered and reburied in the Jakarta War Cemetery, Indonesia. Jakarta is the modern name for Batavia.

April 18. Another yasumay day. A very optimistic feeling has pervaded the camp. News is scarce, as usual, but here is what we know at present: Stalin has recently been in the United States; a Russ-Jap non-aggression treaty expires this month; landings in Japan; Roosevelt dies suddenly.

April 19. Continued stories on landings and death of Roosevelt. Official camp attitude is that former is false, but latter is true. Doc Simonz, Sims, and Kraal attempting to throw cold water on extreme optimism. Jap tells of sinking of King George V. Other news exists, but he is not allowed to tell it until after the war is over. Malayan newspaper reports that the conference in San Francisco will begin on the 25th.

April 21. Roosevelt died at Warm Springs on April 12. Landings on Kyushu took place on March 23, and on Honshu on April 1 and succeeding days. Roosevelt's successor is a certain Trumann.

April 23. Beginning today and continuing for 6 days, the rations have been reduced to 270gr rice and 200gr flour (tapioca) per day for workers, and 100gr rice and 200gr flour per day for sick in quarters. That means, in fact, a loaf of bread for breakfast and lunch, and rice for supper. We can, at this stage of the game, ill afford a reduction in food. Again today, the wood party was pressed into service to deliver 4 unknown bodies to the graveyard.

When a man died, his remains were taken to a preparation area, where he was washed and wrapped in a straw mat. If he had four friends in camp, they could request a formal interment service which would be conducted in the evening or on a *yasumay* day. It was required that a Jap guard accompany such a burial detail. If one died without the requisite four companions to give him a proper service, then the body was placed outside the makeshift morgue. The wood party returned to camp each day at lunch time and, going back in the afternoon, would swing by the morgue, pick up any bodies, and deliver them to the grave diggers who would unceremoniously bury them.

April 24. S.I.Q. today. Perhaps malaria again. No result as yet on blood slide. And I wonder what the Yanks are doing today.

April 26. Blood slide returned yesterday—positive. Total deaths for the month, so far, are 79. I have finally got my debts paid off by selling my jacket and my sweater, and I'm still broke. Automobiles and trucks—not all, but some—passing the camp in the past couple of days have been displaying the Jap flag horizontally, i.e. visible from the air. Malay paper tells of bombing of Padang on the 10th.

April 27. Everyone wondering about this San Francisco conference. Short rations still carrying on. Had carbow for supper last night. Not bad. Drinking a good deal of coffee lately. The canteen received a supply of green beans which have been roasted in the oven. We crush or grind them ourselves. Rumor has it that the war in Europe is finished. Things had better finish here dam' quick. Another two months and they'll not be able to bury the dead fast enough. At present 4 graves are being dug in advance. Talk of another draft out to the bridge. Hickey, Ski, and I are not on the list, but Pat, for various reasons, is.

Pat Paris, as I have written previously, was a cantankerous, strong-minded individual, whose mental state was somewhat suspect. His personal hygiene was not the best either, causing his barrack mates considerable concern. Thus, he was an early choice for transfer.

April 29. The Emperor's Birthday. 10 deaths, including Lt. Thompson and Pop Malcolm. Another carbow meal. Rumors very scarce.

April 30. Yesterday, the Japs presented the camp a pig. We haven't even seen pork for a couple of months, and a fine feed of fried rice was planned. This morning, the bastards took the pig back again. They did condescend to leave the head and guts, though. We have all recently been issued with new POW numbers and have again signed papers that we will not under any circumstances attempt escape. Deaths in this camp for the month totaled 106, and in the outlying camps 14.

May the first. How is it possible? The war in Europe is filling out its sixth full year, and this business out here has been going on almost three and a half years. Of course, everyone looks into the future with complete confidence and full optimism. As one Dutch officer remarked this morning, Een mai. Wat zult deze maand ons geven? [One May. What shall this month give us?] On the other hand, regarding things seriously, if conditions do not improve and we don't get out of here within 6 months, half the present camp strength will die. And now, to be a bit more cheerful, there is mail recently received. Some of the Dutch post cards have been delivered; the English stuff will come in in a couple of days.

May 4. What a day this has been. The first event was the death of Bill Hosey, Able Seaman from the William F. Humphrey. He died of beri-beri at about 9:15 AM. The funeral was held at 2:30 PM with Mr. Hickey reading the service. The bearers were Lt. Corley, Gene Parejko, Paddy Walton, and myself. He was extremely swollen and made a terrific load. The burning sun didn't help things at all. The sweat just streamed out of us. At noon, I received some mail—6 letters from Mother and one each from Eleanor and Madelyn. They are all 30 word affairs dating from March 27 to June 7, last year. Then in the evening, two birthday cards came from Richard and Natalie. They were dated April 25, last year, and, curious enough, arrived just in time this year.

Corley was British, and my partner on the wood party. Walton's identity has escaped from memory. Natalie was, of course, my younger sister.

May 9. Another yasumay day. It seems that the only time I have the opportunity to put something down here is on these afternoons or when I am S.I.Q. In any case, we know about Hitler and Mussolini.

May 16. Haven't been feeling too well lately, but am still working every day. Celebrated the birthday with a good nasi goreng from the galley, then Hickey found out it was the "famous" day, so the following evening we had a private feed—hard boiled egg, fried brown beans.

May 25. This is the first opportunity I've had for a couple of days to put something down here. We have had about a week of extremely hot weather and chopping down rubber trees wasn't exactly a pleasant occupation. News is extremely scarce and even the Japs aren't saying much. Since my last entry, though, we have learned of the finish of the European war.

June 8. I am just recovering from the worst attack of malaria that I've had yet. I worked for 31 days without a break, most of the time axe work, and when the "old bug" hit I went down for the count. Yes, the whole packet—fever, chills, and sweats. I never imagined it could be so bad. And the damned quinine is a case of the cure being worse than the disease.

Quinine is a product manufactured from the bark of the chinchona tree. All that we had was the bark or strippings off the branches. These were dried thoroughly and then ground into an extremely bitter tasting powder, which was almost impossible to ingest. One solution was to mix the powder with a cup of tea, another was to use the morning *ongol-ongol* paste as sort of an emulsifier. Both methods introduced the stuff into the system, at a price of a great deal of gagging and retching.

On May 28, 10 PM, Sidney M. Albert, Second Cook and Baker in the American Leader died in the hospital here. It was the same story again, malaria, beri-beri, swollen body, dysentery, vitaminosis of the intestines. I buried him at 7:30 PM on the

29th. Gorski, Miller, an Englishman named Blaycock, and I were the bearers. Kalloch carried the cross and the shovels. I read a short service and the Lord's Prayer. (Note: My exertion in carrying Albert up the hill led to the malaria attack.)

One could survive repeated malaria attacks, but if dysentery hit simultaneously, trouble loomed. The malnutrition-spawned beriberi caused a fluid accumulation, commencing in the lower extremities, leading to an immense swelling of the entire body. In combination, thus, these ailments resulted in death, usually by heart failure.

There is quite an amount of POW movement between camps lately. The only point that appears definite is that all non-essential officers are being brought in from the outlying camps. There are many rumors concerning eventual centralization of all POWs at Fort de Kock, Moerawa, Singapore, or someplace. As regards the war? Well, that's just it—a big question mark. What is happening? Is there going to be a landing here? How far has the fighting in Japan gone? Why are the Japs holding out? And so on and on. I get so disgusted with the futility of it all. If we could only say that we had another two weeks to serve, or still a month, it would be something to look forward to. But now we work until we are sick, recover, return to the labor; hoping against hope that maybe tomorrow, or at least the day after, the thing will finish. Everyone is "on edge" and we argue and complain over the slightest trifles. Roll on, the end.

June 15. Received today another half-dozen letters.

June 23. It is summer time now, and we await the end every day. Many strange occurrences are taking place. Nothing really important, but just actions and words of the Japs. There is something intense in the air. I fixed up our spending accounts yesterday, for the first 20 days of the month. The total actually consumed was fl 407.23 worth. Not bad going when one considers that our combined effort (salaries—3 men) received from the Japs for last month's work was fl 16.35.

June 27. Just a year ago today we left Java. One whole year ago. And we thought then that this business was almost finished. Still we go on, day after day, hoping and waiting. Sometimes we become depressed and dejected, but for that there is a solution, and that is the fact that the war in Europe is finished.

One of the perks attached to membership in the wood party was the opportunity to contact the local inhabitants. As a rule, we had a single Japanese soldier accompanying us, and the axe men, maybe as many as ten, would be spread out over the plantation. So the guard simply stayed in one place where we would have built a small fire for him. The log carriers, unsupervised, went in and out of the camp through a small gate in the barbed wire. As mentioned, we used burlap sacks to cushion our shoulders against the logs, and these sacks easily hid items being smuggled in both directions. The natives wanted cloth, and our need was food. I have no idea how many of the wood party were involved, if any others, but Hickey, Gorski, and I ran a nice little black market operation in the time we were in Camp 2. They would purchase, or take on consignment, whatever a fellow prisoner saw fit to dispose of. I did the bartering, although prices for shirts and trousers were pretty well stabilized, as were the prices for the foodstuffs.

I haven't mentioned much about money. The Japanese came into the East Indies with a baseless currency, which immediately replaced the Dutch gulden.

"Invasion money" issued by the Japanese, supplanting the pre-war Dutch currency.

Although we dealt in Gulden, an equal value Malay Rupee was also in circulation.

When we first came to Java, if we went out on a work detail, we were paid ten cents a day and a duck egg cost four cents. In June 1945 at Camp 2, we were being paid thirty-five cents a day, and a duck egg was three gulden. In that month, the three of us were paid 16.35 gulden, and we purchased 568.36 gulden worth of edibles. I was selling clothing items for upward of sixty gulden, taking a commission which in turn bought coconuts, peppers, peanuts, beans, coconut oil, eggs, salt, salted fish, fresh fish, bananas, goat meat, water buffalo meat, even tobacco (although I didn't smoke, the other two did). In addition, we sold a small quantity of the salt fish and the tobacco and a few other items, increasing our cash flow to almost 100 gulden. I still have the records of that month! In the meantime, in that thirty-day span in the very same camp, fifty prisoners expired from starvation and lack of medicine, eleven died in the other camps in the Pakan Baroe area, and seven passed away out on the line. What an indictment of the Japanese inhumanity!

Our black market dealings clearly illustrated the *kongsie* style of life. One man could not survive on his own. Hickey, although down with malaria three-quarters of the time, worked on the camp administration to keep Stan and me in the cookhouse and wood party, respectively. This kept us off the debilitating railway work gangs. In addition, Stan's personality provided insurance for his job in the cookhouse, the benefits of which cannot be overstated. I, the third party in the *kongsie*, more fit and less prone to the malaria which plagued the three of us, was the chameleon, slithering in and out with my goodie-laden burlap sack. What we had, we shared, equally and without rancor or disagreement. It worked this way: other than the tobacco, whatever our efforts netted was divided into three portions. One of us turned his back, another chose a particular portion, and the fellow who could not see indicated to whom that portion would go. Then the routine was repeated for the two remaining portions. Fair and square, it worked.

July 15. A Dutch truck driver returned from Lipat Kain today with a story of having seen an American aircraft flying at low altitude there. A strange sounding plane, unseen, passed overhead here shortly after noon. Speculation is that it was the same aircraft.

July 16. The same plane was overhead at the same time today.

The moment I heard the aircraft on the fifteenth, I knew it was not one of theirs. It wasn't exactly ours either, because we belonged to no one. Anyway, I stepped out of the bamboo barrack to take a look. Whoever he was, he was flying high and fast. The glare of the noon sun kept me from staring very long. On the sixteenth, we came in for lunch about quarter to twelve. I asked Hickey to draw my rice, and offering no explanation headed down toward the bath place. I had walked beyond the cookhouse and was near a small grassy plot on the slope when I heard what I was listening for. It was a strange aircraft. I casually sat down on the grass, clasped my hands behind my head and laid back. I looked and looked, yet again saw nothing.

"I can't be wrong," I told myself. *"It has to happen some time."* After so many disappointments, though, I refused to allow my emotions any freedom. We had been prisoners over thirty-four months—almost a thousand days and it seemed we had heard a thousand rumors of the war's ending. Something occurred on the work party that next day causing us to be a few minutes late returning for lunch. As we marched past the sentry box and entered the main gate, with a high whine and a deep drone an aircraft came out of the south and faded into the north.

By the eighteenth, I had told Hickey of my suspicions, and that day, at noon we saw him. That evening under the mosquito nettings in the dimly lighted shack, the two of us discussed the events. Were they reconnaissance flights? Or did the Allies have an airfield closer than we knew? Why weren't the Nips alarmed? There hadn't been any air raid warnings. Were we actually nearing the day of going home after what seemed an eternity behind the barbed wire? For answers we could only guess. Who was the pilot? Where did he come from and where was he going? For him, we had only envy. He never knew we were down below him. The thought of us, or anyone in an enemy prison camp, probably never came to his mind. He couldn't help us if he wished. He was lucky. We knew it. He was free. Free to go the canteen and buy a bar of soap and take a bath when he pleased. Free to drink a glass of pure water or a Coke or a ginger ale. Free to receive mail less than a year old, and to read a newspaper, and listen to today's news on the radio. Imagine the proper meal awaiting him on his return to base, with maybe a beer or two. Picture the decent, bedbug-free bunk he slept in that night. He probably took his good fortune for granted, at the same time griping about his particular situation. In our squalor and despair we waited.

CHAPTER THIRTY-FOUR

The Last Month

July 24. All sorts of things happening lately. We lost our jobs on the wood party a couple of days ago and went out to work on the RR. This morning at 8AM, a draft of 100 men left Camp #2. Included were Hickey, Ski, and I. Our destination was pretty well unknown. Traveling by train, we reached Lipat Kain at 1 PM and stopped for lunch. It was almost 8 o'clock when we departed, and about midnight when we reached Koda Baroe. Here we transferred to trucks and rode to Logas prison camp. Here, at about 3 AM, we ate our previous evening meal.

Lipat Kain was my old Camp 7, Koda Baroe was Camp 8 at the 111 km pole, and Logas was Camp 9, 31 km further out.

July 25. After about a half-hour stop, the journey by truck was continued. Then it began to rain. Luckily, my truck was equipped with a large rubber sheet and we managed to remain dry. It must have been 2:30 PM before we reached Moearo, after a wonderful ride through the mountains. Here we boarded another train and after about 20km came to our new camp.

Moearo was the southwestern terminal of the Pakan Baroe to Moearo railway, where it would connect to the existing line to Padang and other West Sumatra communities. Our new camp was number 12. Hickey and I, and the British merchant officer Bromley were able to maintain our officer status there. On certain days I was in charge of working parties laying the rails. All along my fluency in Dutch stood me in good stead. We had about eight hundred men in this camp, and the work party was a mix of Dutch, English, and Australians. The Japanese were quite amused at my ability to shout commands and numbers in Dutch and English. The Japs also knew the British and Aussies were not happy to work under Dutch officers, just as the Dutch troops wanted little to do with the limey and pommie officers. When I was not involved with the railway, I worked in camp with other "surplus" officers. I say surplus because the Japs had a firm policy regarding the proportion of officers to soldiers on the work details: one officer for every forty-nine men, as was the case aboard the *Chukka Maru*. Thus, we always had surplus officers in the camp, and these people were assigned to nonproductive jobs, such as barrack repairs, or as in Camp 2, wood chopping.

Back in 1943, in my days at Kampong Makassar, I noted in my journal on July 12, the departure of a small draft including Geoffrey Sherring, one of the *Empire Dawn*'s radio officers. At this point in time, early August of 1945, he had been in Nagasaki for almost two years.

Geoffrey Sherring, 1989.

At first, he was employed as a riveter in the Mitsubishi shipyard located some distance outside the city, but now was working in the yard's foundry in the city itself. The prisoners' quarters were adjacent. In 1993, at Geoff's home in Stockport, England, I videotaped his account of what happened in Nagasaki on August 9, 1945. Here is what he said:

> *On the first of August, we had a very big area bombing by the American Air Force which damaged the city a great deal, but none of it was incendiary, and therefore the town had very few fires, if any. We were still mopping up after this, when suddenly the Japanese began to take a very different view of air raids. The first thing we knew about it was when a different air raid warning occurred at night. We would all be gotten out of our beds and marched out of the town to lie along side of the road on the grassy verges. This was a very unusual thing and, of course, it wasted a lot of the*

time we had for sleeping. Because our work was twelve hours a day, we needed the sleep. This, we felt, couldn't carry on for very long. Fortunately, it didn't, because on the morning of the 9th of August we had the usual air raid warning. Since it was daylight, we were merely recalled from the foundry. This would have been about eight o'clock. It was the weather plane. Everyone knew this. The warning was obeyed even though it was a single plane reconnaissance. We all waved good morning to the aircraft and went back to work when it was gone.

When we arrived at the foundry, strangely, there was absolutely no one there! We didn't understand this. We had come to realize the Japanese were now very jumpy about air raids, but had not picked up any rumors or knowledge of the atomic bomb dropped three days earlier on Hiroshima. Be that as it may, we couldn't do any work and our soldiers, very disgruntled, took us back to camp. In a sort of diffident manner, they gave us a few jobs to do, and then went off to get a bit of shut-eye after the previous night when they had taken us out into the hinterland.

An Australian friend, Bernie O'Keefe, and I were detailed to pump some rainwater out of a shallow air raid shelter. I said to him, "When we've done this, we shall go in there and have a cigarette." I had a magnifying glass with which I could light a cigarette on the quiet. The Japanese were very strict on the use of cigarettes and fire, because they are a very fire conscious nation. So we pumped the place dry and went in and lit up. This shelter was basically a trench, about four feet deep, with slabs of four-foot thick concrete for a roof. It was designed really to stop falling debris and certainly would not have stopped the smallest bomb any air raid would have brought. Whilst we were there, Bernie said to me, "I can hear a motor car on the road." Naturally, I said to Bernie, "Don't be ridiculous. First of all, there aren't any motorcars. Secondly, they've got no petrol." However, he said, "I'm going to crawl along to see if I can see anything." He wouldn't have been able to see anything because we had a very high wooden fence all around the camp. As I looked at his retreating behind going toward the opening in the trench, I could see the sunlight coming in, in a slanting direction from the south. It was about eleven o'clock, and Bernie was silhouetted against the sunlight and suddenly to my amazement, a very, very brilliant and powerful light shone in from the opposite direction, completely eclipsing the sun, and of an entirely different color. It was the color of a welding flash, a blue, mostly ultra-violet flash. Fortunately, Bernie had not got to the hole and was not exposed to this flash, because, we were later to find out, anybody who was exposed to that flash, got very, very severe burns indeed.

**Photo courtesy of Peter McGrath-Kerr. Nagasaki, showing estimated
epi-center of nuclear explosion over city. Concentric circles are 500 meters
apart, indicating Fukuoka 14 prisoner of war camp was about
1, 750 meters from epi-center, or 1.1 statute miles.**

After it there was a silence, a noticeable silence. There hadn't been any sound connected with the flash. Almost immediately as I began to wonder at the silence, there was a rolling crash of thunder over the top of our shelter. This was the shock wave from the bomb, which had been discharged to the north of us. Bernie and I quickly scrambled out into what we found was a choking fog of brown smoke and dust. As this rolled back a little we felt very large drops of rain which were as big as grapes and composed of dirty mud. This did not last very long, and the astonishing sight of the flattened city almost defeated our comprehension. The camp fence, probably ten feet in height, and made of wooden planks, was completely blown down. We could see all the way around over it, and as we turned to look at our own building, it had collapsed and seemed to be almost kneeling.

It is not the author's intent to relate further details of Sherring's interview, but merely to interject this as a chronological event which had an important bearing on future events.

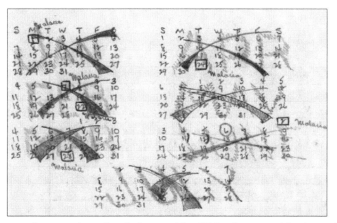

August 17. Made a new calendar today, the third this year. The first one consisted of only three months and at the end of March I had to add a couple of more months. Now, I've brought it up to the end of November. I wonder. Certainly, three and six months ago I never imagined that we'd still be here at this date. And what does the next quarter year hold in store?

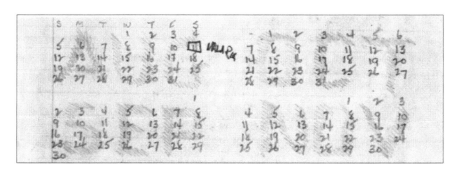

In any case, the damn RR is finished. On the 14th, our gang met, at a point 40km from Moearo, the rail layers from the other end. Now, the whole stretch, after probably three year's work, is completed from Pakan Baroe to Moearo. We broke camp on the 9th and 10th, moving to a site 35.6 km from Moearo. Hectic is no word to describe the shift—it was a real madhouse. In the afternoon of the 9th, the first contingent left. The baggage and stores were piled on the train and we went on top, hanging on to the man who was hanging on to the man in the middle. Everything happened—the engine ran off the track, and we arrived after dark, and a previous derailment forced us to walk the last 2km loaded high with packs and bags and sacks. Crossing one of the high, narrow bridges, a young Dutch fellow had either a dizzy spell or tripped in the dark and fell 50 feet to his death.

Of course, on the date I wrote the above paragraphs, the war was over. We didn't know it, and life (and death) went on. On August 2, Bromley and I did not go out on the rail line, and were put to work doing odd jobs around the camp. Although we slept side by side, I knew nothing about this fellow. He was an utter mystery. In fact, after the war I scribbled this about him:

Among the assortment of odd characters incarcerated in the numerous Japanese prison camps of the Far East in which I lived, Bromley was, in my eyes, the oddest. He had come to Java in October 1943 from Celebes, and came out to Tandjong Priok, where I was, at the end of the year. Y. C. L. Bromley, a typical "lime juice" style name. That is all I ever knew. No first name, no middle names. He had a bunk space across from me, but he kept his mouth shut, except when there was food around. Could that guy eat! Anything and everything. No one had any information on him. As I said, he was close-mouthed. Not even his own countrymen got much out of him. He claimed to have been Chief Mate in a Fleet Auxiliary tanker, yet others who came from Celebes said the real Chief Mate was still over there and this fellow was a phony. He sure looked the part: close, deepset, dark eyes; full beard; swarthy complexion. "He's nothing but a Singapore beachcomber," remarked one Dutchman.

In June, 1944, when I went to Singapore in the *Chukka Maru*, and then over to Sumatra to work on the railway, Bromley was in the same draft. I don't recall him in any of the camps along the line, but he is mentioned in the "Merchant Officers' Status Letter" sent by Wing Commander Davis to Camp 4 on August 20, 1944, so he must have been in that camp. Also, he probably was in the group of 100 prisoners who made the long trek from Camp 2 to Camp 12 on July 24-25, because his bunk space was next to mine in the latter camp. Red Hickey, the *American Leader*'s chief officer, also made that journey, and he slept next to me on my left. This barrack was a double-decker with a second layer of sleeping spaces about five feet above the lower level. Also, our mosquito nettings were communal, each covering about eight prisoners.

At this stage, the Japs were in an absolute frenzy in their attempt to finish the line. Work parties went out with as little as four or five hours rest; some groups spent twenty-four hours (and longer) away from camp. I had my share of these and remember one night, well after darkness had fallen, when returning "home," the locomotive derailed. The Japs took everyone off the train and attempted to force the prisoners to assist in getting the engine up on the tracks. It was raining, we were hungry, and absolutely drained of any energy whatsoever. That was the closest to rebellion I ever experienced under the Japanese. We just sat there in the mud and the drizzle and did nothing. They telephoned one of the camps which resulted in the appearance, somewhat later, of a number of Nip soldiers who managed to get the locomotive back on track and us to our barracks. Curiously, there was no retaliation.

The food situation along the railway was atrocious, but at Camp 12 we subsisted on what has to be called a starvation diet. It was the same old *ongol-ongol* for breakfast, a small amount of rice and the grass and leaves stew for lunch, a bit more rice with vegetable stew for dinner, but all in diminished quantities. There were a few supplemental items available from the occasionally encountered native traders: dried fish, duck eggs, beans, dried peas, etc., but nothing to compare with the variety and quantity available to the wood chopping party at Camp 2. The jungle itself offered a few edible delicacies, most memorable of which are the nuts of the rubber trees.

Rubber trees, from which latex is harvested, are tall and slender and easily cut down. The nuts grow in green pods, somewhat similar in appearance to tangerines. When ripe, these thumb-sized nuts exude a gas which when heated by the sun causes the pod to pop open. We diligently searched for the nuts in the undergrowth. The trick then was the treatment. Generally, each nut was cut length-wise into quarters, soaked in fresh water for at least 48 hours, and dried in the sun for a week or more. This removed what the Dutch called *blauwzuur* which I, in my notes, have translated to cyanide. This was the explosive agent in the nutshells. The end product was indeed tasty, resembling a walnut. The cooks chopped up the treated nuts which, mixed with tapioca flour, resulted in a nut bread of sorts.

On August 2, Bromley and I were not on the rotation to go out on the line, and were assigned to cut down several rubber trees just outside the camp perimeter for use as firewood. By midday, Bromley had gleaned a substantial amount of nuts from the felled trees—maybe a kilo. When we came in for our meager lunch of rice and watery stew, we were told an older (age forty-six) Dutch soldier was breathing his last and he was not expected to live many more hours. That put an end to the axe work as a grave was needed. Before our arrival at Camp 12, three men had died and were buried a short distance away, alongside the tracks. As this location was out of sight of the camp, a Jap had to accompany us. I suppose it was his day off, but he gave us no trouble, even helping out for a while. Oh, it was tough going. The ground was almost like shale, and, to be honest, we didn't get down too far. When I dug, Bromley continued his rubber nut collecting. After a while, the guard decided we had done enough and we returned to the camp.

A little sidelight of camp life which I have neglected to mention here is our "hobo stoves." We all had some manner of a small bucket or can rigged up to burn wood scraps under a wire grate in order to cook whatever we had managed to steal or scrounge from the Japs, or buy from the natives. Around suppertime of this day of which I have been writing, I noticed Bromley stewing up a pot full of the green nuts he had harvested. "Hey," I said, "I hope you're not going to eat those." In response I received a look and a grunt that told me to mind my own business. Indeed, he did wolf down the entire pot.

At sometime during the ensuing night, I crawled out under the wall of the communal mosquito night on my way to the latrine. Bromley was sitting at the edge of the platform. He didn't look at me, and I said nothing to him. In the morning, the day began with the usual *clang-clang! clang-clang! clang-clang!* from a Jap whacking a piece of suspended piping, and the "Kurah! Kurah!" of another one stomping down the barrack aisle. I arose and began furling the protective netting. Hickey had malaria and wasn't getting up. There was no motion from Bromley either. I probably gave him a shove with my foot and when that drew no response, I leaned over to say something. His eyes were partially open, and there was a dark liquid seeping out of the corner of his mouth.

In some alarm, I called across the aisle to Doctor Bessom, a Hollander, who had come out from Camp 2 with us. "Doktor! Doktor! Komt U hier!" He quickly came over, took a look, went back for his stethoscope, and returned. After administering to Bromley for a minute or two, or whatever it was, he looked up and said, "Hij ist dood." We covered the body with Bromley's blanket, after which Bessom cautioned me about telling the troops. He felt it would be a serious blow to their morale if they learned before they went out to work that the apparently healthy Englishman had succumbed. Better to let them know in the evening when they could sleep on the news. In the meantime, Hickey, eyes wide, observed the startling sequence. Almost as an afterthought, I turned and said to him, "He's dead." Without a blink, he hissed, "Get his beans and his money."

In due course, the work party departed, and I reported for another day of in-camp labor to learn that the Dutch fellow had also passed away during the night. Another grave had to be dug, and the superstitious Japs wouldn't come out with me, and there was no one else in camp to help, so they let me out by myself. I managed to get down to about the same depth as the previous day, and before supper, with the assistance of several administrative people, buried the two bodies. A search of Bromley's sparse belongings disclosed nothing, not a clue as to his identity. Not a letter, or a card, or anything. We never even ascertained what the *Y* or the *C* or the *L* represented. He died the way he lived. An ironic note is three days later, August 6, 1945, the United States dropped an atomic bomb on Hiroshima, and nine days later Japan surrendered. Bromley almost made it, but the mouth that he had kept closed for so many months ultimately betrayed him.

In 2001, I discovered the web site of the British Commonwealth War Graves Commission, which carries an entry concerning Ythil Charles Lewis Bromley, chief officer of the SS *Francol*, who died on August 3, 1945 at age 41. The entry lists his parents and his wife, and states he is commemorated on panel 51 of the Tower Hill Memorial in London.

Tower Hill Memorial. London.

This memorial is dedicated to those men of the British Merchant Navy and fishing fleets who have no known graves. An e-mail from me, dated November 10, 2001 to the commission, providing the details of Bromley's death and burial remains unanswered.

The *Francol* was a 2,623 ton Royal Fleet Auxiliary tanker which, along with the depot ship *Anking* and Mine Sweeper 51 was attempting to escape from the Dutch East Indies in early March 1942. They were being escorted by HMAS *Yarra*, a Grimsby class sloop armed with three 4-inch guns and four 3-pounders. At first light on March 4, in a position about 285 miles South of Java, the convoy was sighted by a Japanese force consisting of three cruisers and two destroyers. The Allied ships were quickly destroyed with most of their crews killed. Reportedly, only Bromley and an able seaman from the *Francol* survived to be taken prisoner.

The Dutch fellow who fell off the bridge during the move of August 9-10 is identified in *De Sumatra Spoorweg* as K. A. van Affelen van Saemsfoort, a civilian, age twenty. I refer to him as being young, but at the time I was just past my twenty-third birthday. I didn't know him, but I do recall seeing his body at the scene. (*Was I involved in the attempted rescue?*) In a further irony, on the morning of the ninth, 2,520 miles to the northeast, a B-29 of the United States Army Air Force had dropped an atomic bomb which detonated over the city of Nagasaki. Van Saemsfoort was the first of seven—three other Hollanders, two Britains, and a Norwegian—who died in the next eighteen days at Camp 11. How unfortunate!

August 19. Now we're wondering what will happen in the near future. Everything seems to be—well—out of order. There are no work parties out on the line; no sign of any activity at all. The camp had rice and tapioca flour rations on hand for the period up to September 18, and now rations for three more weeks have been delivered. The Jap lieutenant is away and the administration has been told not to reckon on vegetables for the next 3 or 4 days. One of the guards and a native on the line have told stories of Russia declaring war on Japan. And there was, a few days ago, a bit of a rumor stating that the war is over. Damn it, its GOT to end some day and what, just what are these Japs thinking of? How can they hold out?

Russia had in fact declared war on Japan on August 8.

August 22. The word this morning is that our rice ration is increased to 600gr per man per day, and that in 10 days we are returning to Pakan Baroe.

Well, it certainly was a stupendous work when one thinks of the coolies and prisoners and sees what has been done. But if you try to consider the worth or value of the project—man, it has been nothing but stupidity on the part of the Japs. I have never written much of anything regarding the RR—it's trials and difficulties, swamps and jungles, hills and curves, bridges and rivers, derailments and landslides, washouts and collapses—that will be just as impossible as the line itself. If you could but see some of the cuttings, some of the fills, some of the bridges, the avenues hewn out of solid jungle, you would think it unbelievable that such a fantastic project could ever have been performed by man alone. Man, working almost barehanded. No trucks or tractors, bulldozers or steam shovels, pile drivers or power saws, but shovels and patjols and baskets.

A *patjol* was an adzelike tool used in the Far East as a shovel. Essentially, it is utilized in a chopping motion between one's legs, something like an overgrown hoe.

A patjol display along with a section of the original Pakan Baroe railway at the National Memorial Arboretum at Alrewas, Staffordshire, England. The author feels the staff or handle on those used along the railway was shorter than this model, as they were usually swung between legs.

The latest is that the meat ration shall be increased from 50 to 150gr per man per day. Of course, this may all be a sort of reward, but with the little bit of news which we receive pointing to the cessation of hostilities any day now, the camp is quite agog. Not that anyone really believes in the idea of the business being finished, but just that it may be.

It becomes rather laughable, though. For instance, one of the Dutch doctors, in viewing the circumstances, remarked that the war certainly was over. Why? Well, when wars are over, the first thing that happens is an increase in the prisoners' rations.

Typical of some of the thinking we contended with over the years. I don't know what history books he had been studying.

August 23. The payment of salaries earned during July was finally made today. The tardiness was due, of course, to various inter-camp changes, etc. I had 11 gulden and 50 cents coming, and Hickey, 10 gulden. Back in Camp #2, we had run up a joint debt of about 100 gulden with Doc Simonz. The idea was to pay off this debt with the profit from a watch deal. To make a long story short, the deal fell through and before we had time to get things straightened out, we came away to Moearo. On the evening before leaving, we talked the matter over with Simonz and came to an amicable agreement that would, so far as possible, repay the money as soon as possible. If circumstances prevented this before the end of the war, payment in U.S. currency was acceptable. Now today, when the payroll came, our salaries had been withheld at, mind you, the request of Dr. Simonz—the dirty bastard. In the first place, what right has he to attach another POW's money? Doesn't he trust us now; does he prefer Jap invasion paper to U.S. dollars? O.K. He'll get them. When I am good and ready. Among items of local and more public interest is that our Korean guardians left suddenly this noontime. They were relieved by a handful of Jap soldiers, some of whom had served as guards in Camp #2.

I cannot recall ever seeing Simonz again. Certainly, he received no money from us, because we had none. So, all he had from the 100 gulden debt was 21.50.

August 24. Everyone's spirits were a bit dampened by the changeover, but the yasumay goes on. Odd things are still happening, however. The Jap lieutenant sent in cigarettes for the officers last evening, and today, soap arrived for all hands—soap which Visser (the camp commander) had, 3 days ago, requested. One of the new guards is supposed to have said that the Koreans have gone to Pakan Baroe and, of all things, will be interned there. The latest order received this afternoon is that no longer may POWs be employed by the Japanese—not even as cooks or water carriers.

August 26. Three Dutch doctors arriving from a coolie hospital in Moearo tell of the end of the war on the 14th or 15th of this month. Most of the POWs don't believe it, but I am convinced. Tomorrow, the first contingent leaves for Pakan Baroe.

That afternoon, I had been wandering around the camp, visiting here and there, when I heard a clamor from the direction of the front gate. It sounded as though people were cheering, but I was not so sure. With some caution, I walked to the far side of the last hut and peeked around the corner to discern about fifty, rather agitated, Dutch prisoners gathered around several men in full Dutch Army uniforms. Deciding it was safe to become involved, I joined the crowd, and soon learned these men were saying the war was over! It was impossible to get close enough to talk personally to any one of them, so I went back to my own building to tell Hickey and Gorski the news. At that juncture, we just couldn't convince ourselves. It certainly was a strange and unexpected manner for things to end. Later in the day, actually after the evening meal, I sought out the doctors and introduced myself to one. Speaking in Dutch, he told me what he knew. I have forgotten the details, but his story made sense. Now a believer, I returned to Hickey and Gorski. Carefully reconstructing what I had heard, we agreed, shook hands in congratulations, and talked on into the night.

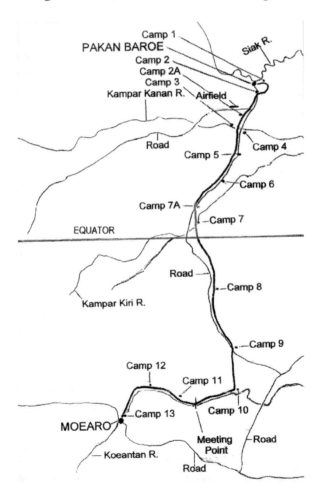

The completed railway. The author labored in the areas of Camps 4,5,7,2,12, and 11. He was one of the very few prisoners who actually traversed the entire line, from Camp 13 to Camp 2.

August 27. Didn't get to sleep until well after 4 AM this morning. Up at 6:45 getting ready to leave at 9:00. Departure then delayed until 5 PM. Eventually left, 250 of us, at about 3 PM. Took one-third of all stores and equipment. Everyone quite happy. Japs still disorganizing everything, but quite changed. We sang for a couple of hours as we rode along in the moonlight.

August 28. Arrived at Logas prison camp at about 7 AM. Impossible to sleep a wink all night. We rode on a carload of rice and my rear end became mighty sore. At Logas, they had been officially notified a couple of days ago. Received some mail. Everyone issued with shorts, shirt, chowat, hat, towel, and cigarettes. Now, there is no doubt in anyone's mind. Resumed the terrible journey after having eaten breakfast—dry rice and coffee. Two men died during the day. Very hot, crowded. "The Ride to Freedom." It hardly seems worth it. After a while, we reached Camp #2. Delays and stops. The Japs seemed insistent to disagree and cause disruptions. At least in Camp #2 we were given some rice and bouillon.

That train ride was slow, very slow. In the first place, the engine was pushing, not pulling the cars, preventing the driver from seeing the tracks, which ordinarily would be illuminated by the small headlight. The distance from Camp 12 to Camp 9 was 58 kilometers, about 36½ miles, and it took 16 hours. We covered the 140 kilometers between Camps 9 and 2 in 12 hours or so. Two incidents remain strong in my memory. At one point in the afternoon, we were attempting to climb a long grade, and the little engine just was not up to the task. The driver, a Jap, then backed all the way down with us remaining sitting on top of the bags of rice in the roofless cars. Then they told us to get off and walk to the top of the hill. Typical Japanese thinking! In due course the driver built up a head of steam and managed to resolve his problem and successfully negotiated the crest. I had worked with this particular Jap on numerous occasions, and he was not too bad a guy. Hustling to the head of the column, I attracted his attention. He jumped down out of the cab and in prison camp jargon told me the war was over, I was headed to New York, and he was going into the prison camps. Somewhat later, we were climbing another slope and it appeared we would make it. I leaned over the side of my car, which was just in front of the engine. He had his head out, as well. Our eyes met. I gave him a grin and a thumbs-up. He replied with the same.

The rail line was basically a single track with strategically placed sidings. Earlier in the day, one of our frequent stops was caused by having to wait on a siding for an oncoming train. This proved to be a Japanese troop train, and what a sad looking bunch they were. I was sitting next to an older Jap, a corporal. He motioned toward his countrymen, then pointed a finger to his heart. *Sakit*, he said, the Malay word for sick.

The *chowat* mentioned with the clothing was a Japanese g-string made up of a piece of cloth twenty four to thirty inches long, eight to ten inches wide. with a tape or string fastened across one end. A person would hold this, hanging down behind him, pull the tape around his waist, tie it, and pull the cloth up between his legs and flap it over the tape, apron-like.

Five men died on August 28, three Hollanders and two British, and were buried in the Camp 2 cemetery. There is no indication as to the identity of the two persons who died on the train.

August 29. What an awful mess. The Wing Commander must be insane. Chaos indescribable. More men arriving tonight. Food poor and slight. Most of the officers leave at 8 PM for another camp. Some day we may catch up on all this lost sleep. Large unidentified a/c over in afternoon. Bode tells of National Anthem.

"Another camp" was a decently constructed building which had been used as a school. About one hundred of us were lodged there, sleeping on our mats on the hard packed dirt floor. As a British officer, Bode was privy to much of the activity amongst the British and Dutch concerning which faction would be in control until the occupation troops arrived. Every issue erupted in an argument, even as to whose anthem would be played if or when a band appeared!

August 30. Somewhat settled in new camp. Wing Commander told Ski last night occupation begins today. Just let me out of this. Man oh man. What an awful mess. Wing Commander and Jap Captain visit camp. Hickey asks about money. Wing Commander wants to know what we did with our savings.

To have made such a statement, Wing Commander Davis must have gotten into the Japanese saki. He couldn't have been sober! The Jap Captain's name was Miyazaki. He had known for almost two weeks of the surrender, but publicly refused to acknowledge it. He had his reasons, the main one being concern for an uprising by the prisoners and/or the native population, both of which harbored an intense hatred toward him and his charges. Unknown to Miyazaki, secret radio receivers existed in Pakan Baroe from whence many of the past year's "rumors" had emanated. On August 20, the Japs burned their records. On the 23rd, Wing Commander Davis ordered the few men in camp who possessed musical instruments to gather and play *"Wilhelminus,"* the Dutch anthem, and "God Save the King." There was no reaction from the Japs. Out on the line, on the same day, my old "friend" Rosier at Camp 9 at Logas was called to the Jap commander's office and told a cease fire was in effect. Thus it was when I, in the first Moearo to Camp 2 group, arrived there on the twenty-eighth. Very much a standoff by both sides existed.

Much earlier, on July 3, a British major named Lodge and three Asian soldiers had been put ashore by submarine at Bagan Siapiapi, about 110 miles north of Pakan Baroe on the Strait of Malacca coast. Learning in August by radio from their base of the Japanese emperor's surrender, they courageously approached a Japanese outpost, accepted its occupants' surrender, and learned of the thousands of us on the Pakan Baroe railway. In the meantime, a Royal Marine Corps major named Gideon Francois Jacobs, about my age, and from South Africa, had been deputized to be dropped by parachute into the city of Fort de Kock to accept the surrender of the entire one-thousand-mile long Sumatra! He was soon flown to Pakan Baroe where he met Wing Commander Davis, Colonel Hennessee, and other ranking officers. I don't recall this, so it must have happened before I arrived at Camp 2 from Camp 12. In his book *Prelude to the Monsoon*, Jacobs wrote,

> *Later the* (greeting) *committee took me on an inspection of some of the huts. It was an unforgettable experience. Nearly all the men were suffering from beri-beri, the disease caused by malnutrition and which takes a number of different forms. In many cases, the men's bodies had become swollen to grotesque proportions, their limbs looking like water-filled balloons. In others the swelling had subsided and with the water drained away only the skeletons remained.*

August 31. Odd items. Today is the birthday of the Dutch queen . . . The Wingco's title is now "Officer Commanding British troops in the Pakan Baroe Area" . . . What's that make us? . . . Olie balls, cheese, and coffee at 11 o'clock . . . Flags being flown at all camps today, according to the nationalities of the officers commanding the camps . . . Johnson's buying party returned this noon in a hired truck . . . All the Dutchmen doing a lot of flag-waving, wearing the color of the House of Orange, etc. . . . Johnson just came by—the buying party was a drunken success . . . There was a flag raising scheduled for 11 AM, but by 12 the flag had not been delivered, so they'll giver 'er another try at 5 PM . . . Nice white bandages and adhesive tape being sported . . . Some people still walloping the rubbish heap . . . Renesser tells how the 2nd Moearo contingent, after having been issued new clothing at Logas, went and sold most of it before they reached Pakan Baroe . . . Everyone damnably cheerful, but where are the relieving troops? . . . Singapore presumably occupied . . . Allied HQ there commands Jap secret police who pass latest information on to Jap secret police in occupied areas . . . They, in turn, communicate with POWs, internees, etc. . . . Quite a system . . . Orders being issued from HQ by the basket full . . . Everyone, ex-POWs, Japs, and all, confined to camps . . . The only way one can get out is by means of a pass in the form of a red armband . . . As a matter of fact, it appears that in order to do anything from leaving the barracks to taking a nap necessitates a red arm band . . . Guards are posted at all camps . . . Here they are British Indians . . . Well, the flag finally did go up and with a surprisingly short ceremony . . . Had a community sing and concert in the evening . . . Not bad at all . . . Opened with the American, British, and Dutch national anthems . . . Ransom did a couple of decent solos and Bartels provided a couple of good comic tunes . . . Rain kind of dampened the affair, though . . . Doctors say that it doesn't matter how much food we eat as long as we spread it over the day . . . Hickey and I had five meals today.

A few of the above items require explanation. "Olie balls" were palm-sized clusters of steamed rice, recooked in coconut oil. Johnson was a British civilian who, I believe, had been a planter in Malaya before the war. Thus, he was fluent in that language and why he was chosen to head this buying party which had gone into Pakan Baroe to purchase much needed food items. Also, he is the Johnson named in the letter of August 20, 1944, where he was denied officer status. This incident illustrates the callowness of the Japanese administration toward the prisoners. There was plenty of food in the countryside. They simply chose to allow us to starve.

There were British Indian soldiers in camps near the railway, but I never saw them, and I don't know what they did for work. In any event, to forestall the possibility of trouble between the ex-prisoners, and the Japanese, and the locals, Major Jacobs requested the Japanese bring a number of these men to the Pakan Baroe area, and, at the same time move their soldiers away. These Indians were fitted with Japanese rifles. No ammunition, though! Their only real duty was to keep us from straying. Actually, those of us who gave the matter any thought had no desire to investigate any area previously inhabited by the Japs. Being booby-trapped was a stark possibility. Ransom was a captain in the Australian Army. Bartel's identity is, unfortunately, forgotten.

One problem of ours—Hickey and me—was solved at this juncture. Finances. The highest ranking Dutch officer in Camp 2 was a medical doctor named Haga with the rank of colonel. In fact he was the commander of the Cycle Camp who Soni punished because of the leaky rice sack. I have forgotten the details, but the paper work survived. Somehow or other Haga agreed to loan us 500 guldens! I am sure we never repaid him because such payment was to be made in American dollars. This gave us spending money, as we were no longer on work details for the Japs.

September 1. Odd items continued. Vitamin pill for breakfast . . . Cookhouse gang still doing a marvelous job . . . The food really has a taste . . . Still no official action as regards funds for the merchant marine officers . . . This camp was formerly a native school . . . Plenty of Jap books kicking around, plus the famous wooden rifle . . . The books are being smoked or written on, as in this case, and the rifles make good firewood.

What a difference three days and Johnson made. On the twenty-ninth I wrote the "food was poor and slight" and on the first it was "marvelous."

September 5. Time rolls on and apparently nothing happens, but the voyage home will take so long that a few days here and there are not going to matter much. By the time I return, over 3½ years will have elapsed. That seems almost impossible to realize. 3½ years! Why I was only 2 years in the Nantucket. How everything must have changed. I'll be a foreigner—an alien. I'll have to learn how to live all over again. It will be strange and maybe difficult. You will never completely know what these years have been, because I will never, never be able to describe it. In civilization, so much is taken for granted. Radios, telephones, newspapers. Bathtubs and running water. Electric lights. We are all Rip van Winkels. There is so much to relate. Two books could never contain it. There are funny stories and tragic stories, and stories that are unbelievable. I have made hundreds of acquaintances and many friends—Dutch, English, and Australians. Important people, common people. Soldiers and sailors. Politicians, planters, and pilots. People with a wealth of knowledge and experience. I have learned several languages to varying degrees of proficiency—Dutch, German, French, Spanish, Malayan, even a little Japanese. And I still have to go on telling myself that it is all over.

September 9. The machine is beginning to move. Day before yesterday, a British Major, two Chinese, and a Malayan put in their appearance.

These are the men mentioned above, as having been infiltrated at Bagan Siapiapi on July 3, and it took them almost a month after the surrender to find us. They had to be, by nationality, Lodge, Lam Kie Tjong, Lam Ah Njauw, and Sie Kang Gie. From them we learned of the nuclear bombs dropped on Hiroshima and Nagasaki.

At about this time in September, Wing Commander Davis sent a New Zealander named Claude Thompson, in charge of a small party of men, out to the Pakan Baroe airstrip. Thompson, who had been an aircraft pilot before being captured on Java in February 1942, was instructed to mark a runway and set up small bonfires to be lit on the approach of Allied aircraft. The first arrival did not land, but dropped half a dozen parachutists, including a doctor, his orderly, and a RAF radio officer. On September 14, three Australian Douglas C-47 Dakotas, all carrying food supplies, arrived. Strangely, with the exception of one seriously ill Aussie ex-prisoner, the aircraft returned to base empty. On the fifteenth, a lone, uncamouflaged Dakota came in and disembarked Lady Louis Mountbatten and an entourage of senior British officers. The word of our existence and the terrible conditions in which we were living had spread rapidly. After August 15, 220 deaths were recorded, 42 in camps along the railway, and 178 in the three camps around Pakan Baroe! On the two days of Lady Mountbatten's stay, two Royal Navy men, twenty-four-year-old Able Seaman John Williamson, of Nottingham and twenty-five-year-old Leading Telegraphist Elfred C. Drake, of Manchester, passed away. Also dying were five Hollanders, A. H. F. Bertling, age thirty-seven; E. F. V. Willemsen, age fifty-six; G. Lonker, age forty-three; A. H. Lefebre, age forty-seven; and A. A. M. Luymes, age forty-seven.

Eventually, the visitors were escorted to our "schoolhouse" where we were lined up for inspection. The military people who had salvaged their rank designations were wearing them, and so she addressed each individual as major, captain, etc. She asked what unit they had belonged to, where they came from, and so on. When it came my turn, and I was not showing any identification, she said, "And where do you come from, young man?"

"Boston, Massachusetts," I responded.

Surprised as she had seen only English and Australian officers to that point, she blurted, "What are you doing here?"

"At the moment, Ma'am, trying to get back to Boston," I quipped. She laughed, and asked something about how I got to Sumatra, and when I quickly began telling her our story (Hickey was standing next to me), the inspection came to a halt. She turned to the accompanying officers, and said, "Did you hear that? The Jerries captured these men and brought them all the way out here." I had a small bench in my space, and she sat down and chatted with me for fifteen minutes or so. Then telling Wing Commander Davis to "put the Americans on the top of the list" of the repatriates, resumed her walk down the line.

The following day I wrote:

> For 3 years I have been kicked around, booted from pillar to post, stopped at every corner. It didn't make any difference who they were—Japs or Dutchmen or Limeys or, and sad to say, our own people. No matter what we wanted to do, or they attempted, it was screwed up. Food, transport, a spot to sleep on. Let me out.

All I want is to live my own life, go where my fancy takes me, eat what I like and when I like, wear what I please, and tell anyone who is interested to go RIGHT STRAIGHT TO HELL! I am fed up. Ab-so-lutely. Sure, it's a result of the 3 years. Call it a personal defeat, maybe. I admit I'm changed and different. I can't help it. I'm lucky I'm not mad. Ambition? Gone—higher than a kite. I don't want anything—gold braid or a polished desk or anything. Give me a boat—if not that, a small cottage far off, then let well enough alone.

And I'm not standing in line, be it for the movies or food or what have you, ever again.

Is this all a lot of disjointed rubble? Most probably. One's thoughts jump around so, from one subject to another. I talked to Lady Mountbatten yesterday and she told me of "Spec" Wheeler and old Dan Sultan. But where is Stillwell? Round and round the mulberry bush. Time writes of the boredom of war. Holy cow, sonny! You ain't seen nothin'. There is a lot that I want to see and do, though. Cross country by air and train. See Washington again. And the Planetarium. Chicago. Hear some good music. Modern stuff, too, but no dancing. I want to wander down Times Square and stop and read the news on the Times Bldg. Florida ought to be pretty good and New Orleans. Even walk along the beach. It is pretty good in the wintertime, I think.

Coconut trees and Dutchmen. What a life. And when I think of coconut trees. I think of Pat. (He suffered a direct hit from a green nut.) He's crazy—can't say that the nut did it. Well this will be all over sometime. In the meantime, I'm going to take a nap. A couple of the gang have gone out to buy some chickens. Who wants chickens? Kampong chickens. They'll bring 'em back and then expect us to clean and cook. Its like the beans that Joe decided would taste good fried. I asked Johnny if he was going to fry them and he said "No". I said, "I'm not going to either, so that means we have no beans." Chicken is so dam' much trouble to eat in any case. Let 'em buy some eggs. Then they can put the whole lot in the galley boiler. Voila! Food with a minimum of effort. And away we go on the starboard tack. Aw well, let's go to sleep.

I did keep a calendar of sorts covering the ensuing days which shows the following:

16th No go. 17th In camp.

Following the departure of Lady Mountbatten and her accompanying brass on the sixteenth, no one offered any information as to what was planned for our small group of twelve Americans. That is probably what ticked me off and triggered my diatribe. Apparently, Davis intended to ignore her instructions concerning us. Photos in the Australian War Memorial in Canberra taken on September 17 show former prisoners on stretchers about to be loaded into a RAAF flight to Singapore. It is unclear if we knew about that. What did seem quite plain is we were stuck in Sumatra. Our only course, thus, was to strike out on our own. So, on the morning of the 18th, Hickey and I walked out. No ceremony. No good byes. No payback of Haga's five hundred guldens. Transportation was available and we hitched a ride to the airstrip, figuring sooner or later an American detachment would make an appearance. Gorski and the others were still in the Camp 2 compound, and in our agitated states of mind we left them to their own means.

18th On airport all nite.

Things were quiet and remained thus until the afternoon of the nineteenth when an Australian Dakota landed. We all gathered around in the shade provided by the wings, chatting with the air crew. The pilot told us he was bound for Palembang, about 330 miles to the southeast, but it appeared he didn't have any firm orders and was looking for an excuse to return to Singapore. The fellow killed some time until Palembang was no longer an option, and then invited anyone who wanted to go to Singapore to climb aboard. I had never been in an airplane in my twenty three-plus years, but I was the first up the steps on that one! After 1,106 days of confinement, I was headed home! Before we left, to illustrate the volatile state of affairs from which we were escaping, those paratroopers who dropped onto the airstrip a few days earlier were still there, heavily armed, and making their presence known. At one point when I was conversing with the pilot, I glimpsed a Japanese officer, sword dangling at his side, approaching the area on a bicycle. The pilot hadn't seen him, so I asked if he would like a souvenir Jap sword. He said he would, but when pointed in the direction of the cyclist, he changed his mind. I guess he preferred to get home in one piece rather than chance starting another war.

CHAPTER THIRTY-FIVE

The Journey Home

On arrival at Singapore we were met by United States Army Air Force ground crew personnel and taken to the famed Raffles Hotel where they were lodged. These fellows told us a shuttle flight from Calcutta was due the next day, and after the crew rested overnight it would head back to India. The basic reason for this flight was to repatriate former prisoners of war and civilian internees who were, like us, trickling back into civilization. We must have been the first such American ex-prisoners of war these fellows had seen because they treated us royally. It seemed as though each one of them had a small, private hoard of non-government-issue food snacks, which they unhesitatingly broke out and gave us whatever we wanted. And the beds! After years of sleeping flat on our backs on straw mats on concrete or bamboo slabs, these were absolutely luxurious.

20th "Raffles" Singapore.
21st Left Singapore Arrived Saigon.

There were a number of women and children with us, and a few male civilians. The aircraft was a four-engine DC-4 with bucket seats facing each other along the length of the cabin. At Saigon, we were bussed into the city to what had been, before the Japanese occupation, a hospital. What they used it for is unclear, but the complex was protected by Japanese soldiers with rifles and fixed bayonets standing in front of guardhouses, bowing and screaming as we passed by.

22nd Left Saigon for Rangoon via Bangkok
23rd Left Rangoon for Calcutta.

Upon arrival in Calcutta, late on the twenty-third, we were taken to the United States Army's 142nd General Hospital. There we underwent tests and examinations, anti-Cholera and anti-Typhus shots, and a Smallpox vaccination.

My eyesight was 20/20, but I needed dental care. The food was designed to fatten us up; there was even a case of beer under each hospital bed. After about a week, I was declared fit for travel and was released into the custody of the local War Shipping Administration (WSA) representative, a man named Roger K. Smith, who, happily, was also a graduate of the Massachusetts Nautical School. He treated me like a long-lost grandson, obtained a room for me at the Calcutta United Seamen's Service (USS) facility, and began the process of arranging my transportation to the United States. Most importantly, he gave me a cash advance of $100 enabling me to purchase a couple sets of chino shirts and trousers, a nice pair of half Wellington boots, and the necessary accessories and toilet items. I was the first of the twelve Americans from Pakan Baroe to be treated and released from the 142nd. At that point, I weighed 144 pounds. Two years earlier in Kampong Makassar my weight had been 149.6 pounds and, at a guess, when I returned to Camp 2 at the end of August, I probably was down to 115 or less. Also, most importantly, about this time the USS notified its New York headquarters of my presence in Calcutta. On September 26, New York dispatched a Western Union telegram to my mother notifying her I was out.

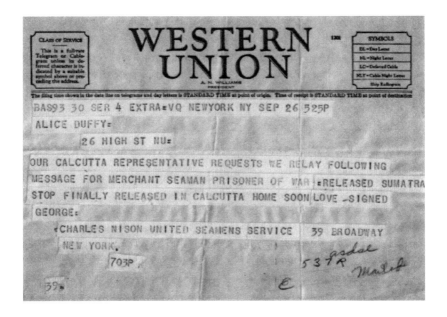

Telegram received by author's mother indicating he had survived the war.

Amazing! It took six weeks of waiting after the Japanese surrender for word to reach Newburyport telling her I had survived and was headed home.

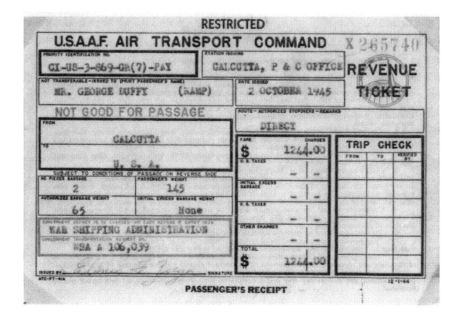

The ticket home!

The trip to New York in a United States Army Air Force Air Transport Command aircraft took five days, covered 10,868 miles, and cost the War Shipping Administration $1,244. Day one was in a DC-3, going from Calcutta to Agra to Karachi. I was the only passenger. The pilot, a fellow from Massachusetts, cajoled someone at the Agra base to take him, his co-pilot, and me out to the site of the Taj Mahal, giving the flight an auspicious beginning. After an overnight in Karachi, it was into a DC-4 for considerably longer jaunts to Bahrein and Cairo. The third day we stopped at Tripoli, then on to Casablanca. Following that, the course led to Santa Maria in the Azores and ended at Stephenville, Nova Scotia. The flight path from Stephenville to New York passed directly over the small town of Newbury, which is adjacent to my home city of Newburyport, Massachusetts. I was able to recognize features I hadn't seen in over forty one months.

Upon reaching Mitchell Field on Long Island, I was handed over to the American Red Cross, which in turn provided a car and driver to take me to a USS hotel in Manhattan. I have forgotten its name and the exact address, but it was on Fifty-fifth or Fifty-sixth Street near Sixth Avenue. After registering, I figured I'd better call home. The problem with that was I couldn't remember their telephone number. The people at the desk came to my rescue and I was soon talking with my jubilant mother. Among other things she told me Colley Court, my benefactor, was in New York at the Waldorf-Astoria Hotel. I told her I was tired and hungry and would find him in the morning. It was Saturday evening, the lights were bright, many people were on the streets, and I felt as if I had been on the moon. In seventeen days I had been transformed and transplanted from an unbelievable, life-threatening existence to an awestruck state of wonderment. Colors! People! Traffic! Wow!

We had been warned about overeating, and I had been quite careful at the various air bases where we stopped on the trip. Fortunately, as I walked down Sixth Avenue, I came across a Chinese restaurant. Beautiful! Just what was called for, and that's where I had my first meal back in the United States of America after an absence of 1,259 days. The next morning, early I think, I walked down to the Waldorf and called Colley Court from a lobby telephone. He told me to come up to his room, and he was waiting at the door when I arrived. He greeted me, shook my hand, and without another word reached for the telephone and put in a call to his wife Dorothy, my aunt. When she answered, he said, "I've got him. I don't know yet where he's been or what happened, but he looks great. We'll be home Tuesday afternoon." What transpired during the balance of the day, I cannot recall. I do remember Monday, quite vividly, because I went down to the United States Lines' offices on the Hudson River piers at the end of Twenty-third Street. A feature of the marine superintendent's office was a long wooden counter, which separated visitors from the secretaries' and clerks' desks. It was here where aspiring officers filled out their application forms before being interviewed. The office manager was a trim, businesslike woman named Marjorie Downing whose lilting brogue instantly defined her Irish origin. I approached the counter and she came over, asking, "May I help you?"

In a matter of fact tone I replied, "I'm George Duffy."

"Glory be to God," she gasped, and turning toward Marine Superintendent S. J. Topping's office called, "Captain! Captain! Come quickly! It's George Duffy from the *American Leader!*" There was not much work done in that office for the remainder of the morning. Topping called in all his assistant superintendents and other important personages, and for the first time they heard the dreadful saga. Eventually, I was given an advance against my final accounting and I went across the street to a haberdashery specializing in merchant marine uniforms. They fitted me out with a stripe and a half on my jacket's sleeves and the United States Line's insignia on my cap. That evening Colley Court threw a party in my honor. The next day's trip to Boston was by train in the reserved seating Club Car, and we arrived at Boston's Back Bay Station in the late afternoon, perhaps 5:30 or so. My mother was there with Colley's driver. If there was anyone else, I cannot recall. She was quite excited. Not agitated, but beaming with joy, feeling my face, looking at me from side to side, searching for injuries she was sure I had suffered. We were a spectacle and many people paused briefly to smile and take in the picture. With my tropical complexion and crisp new uniform there was no question I was returning from the war. For some reason, my brother Robert was awaiting us at South Station, the end of the line. We went there and found him, but the details are forgotten. We then went to Dot and Colley's home in the Bradford section of Haverhill for a reunion with Dot and her two sons, David and Colley, Jr., Aunt Madelyn, and, most surprisingly, my sister Natalie, who was just approaching her fourteenth birthday when I last saw her and was now a junior in high school. The celebratory meal was steak, and I still recall the dismay when I declined it in favor of vegetables only. The day (it was October 9) ended at 26 High Street in Newburyport, where I was warmly greeted by my father.

My happy return home was jolted by the seemingly endless reports of the war-caused deaths of old acquaintances.

Second Lieutenant Gerald Boner, United States Army Air Force.

I learned about Gerald Boner, my first cousin, who was the son of my mother's twin sister. Gerald, less than a month older than I, had become an Army Air Force fighter pilot flying a P-51 Mustang. He was lost on a mission over Europe on January 17, 1945. A memorial Mass, which I was able to attend, was celebrated shortly after my return. Roland Adams, a friend and neighbor, who graduated from NHS four years before me, was captured in the Philippines in 1942 and died of diphtheria at Cabanatuan Prison Camp on July 12, 1942. Out of Margaret's and my 1939 high school class, four did not survive the war: Charlie Anderson, Cliff Kent, Bob Melvin, and Ruth Pike. Of the 1938 class, Bob Drew, Henry Reilly, and Bob Simmons didn't come home, and the 1940 class also lost three members: Bob Donahue, Jim Ryan, and Howard Zabriskie. Only one person in the 1941 class was killed: Bill Farrell, and the 1942 class counted just two: Sweets Chatigny and Harold Coombs. Two other friends from that era, Richie Patterson and Peter Lawton, were also killed in action.

Fortunately, all twenty-six of the fall 1941 class out of the nautical school came through the war, but not quite unscathed. Charlie Stevens had three ships shot out from under him, the SS *Quaker City*, MS *Staghound*, and MS *West Honaker*. Ed Donohoe and Bro McLean were together in the SS *Leslie* when it was torpedoed by the U-123. Bob Curtin and Joe Foley were aboard the SS *Charles Morgan* at the Normandy beachhead when she was sunk by an aerial bomb. Ed Hutchinson's SS *Tivives* was sunk in the Mediterranean by an aircraft torpedo. Other cadets who had been in the *Nantucket* with me, in classes either ahead or behind, who lost their lives were Concetto J. Auditore (SS *Harry Luckenbach*), Charles H. Doell (SS *Caddo*), Austin L. Dougherty (MS *Wichita*), Albert H. Farrell (SS *La Salle*), Edgar S. Malone (SS *John Winthrop*), Alexander Shershun (MS *American Leader*), Joseph T. Subocz (SS *James McKay*), Newell Sweeney (SS *Atlas*), and Herbert W. Trowbridge (USS *Samuel B. Roberts* DE 413). Add to those names the additional twenty-nine *American Leader* crew members, notably among them Charlie Feeney, Walter Lee, Felix Nordfors, George Schabel, and Frank Stallman, all from voyage 2, who had been yearlong, or more, acquaintances. Then there were those friends from the camps who, like van der Speck, didn't make it, and Maxwell Brown, the beloved Australian doctor who went down in the *Junyo Maru* along with the rock-throwing Owen Reed, and Phil McKeever, and the two 131st Field Artillery soldiers, Miller and Sokolowski. Bill Hosey of the *William F. Humphrey* and Bromley, the Englishman, died on Sumatra. Of the U.S. Army and Navy United States Navy Department people who joined us in the early days at Tandjoeng Priok, sixteen died in the *Tomahaku Maru*: Joe Alleva, Paul Glatzert, Harry Hamner, Jim Harrison, Adolph Jaster, Tom Lawson, Frank Looney, Bob McMahon, Ardell Redwine, Melvin Salzman, Lucien Shults, Harold Sewall, Leon Sparkmen, Bob Willerton, Tom Wilson, and Ed Wismann.

Only as late as 2005, did I learn of the death on September 18, 1944 (the date of the *Junyo Maru* sinking) of my barrack mate at Kampong Makassar, the *Empire Dawn*'s chief engineer, James Young. It is presumed he was in the *Junyo Maru* as there is no record of him being buried in the Far East. Dutch records of the *Junyo Maru* disaster omit most non-Dutch losses. For example, there is no mention of the eight American victims in any postwar publications by the previously mentioned Hovinga, Melis, and Neumann. Young is listed as a casualty on the *Empire Dawn* plaque at the Tower Hill Memorial, thus being considered by the Commonwealth War Graves Commission as lost at sea. The assumption is he was indeed in the *Junyo Maru*.

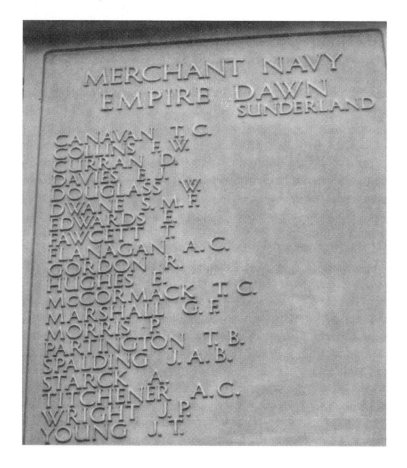

Tower Hill Memorial, London.

What an incredible statistic! Eighty schoolmates, classmates, shipmates, and barrack mates!

Author's mother with her five children, 1946.
Left to right, Richard, Natalie, the author, Robert, and Eleanor.

CHAPTER THIRTY-SIX

The Aftereffects

At some point of time while in Calcutta I was debriefed by United States intelligence officers. To be honest, there was little I could tell them concerning the identities of the Japanese perpetrators of our misery. I knew the Jap soldiers only by nickname: Horse Face, Donald Duck, and so on. Rarely did we see an officer close up. Other than Soni, back on Java, I could name not one. In a sense, I didn't care. I didn't want to get involved. I just wanted to go home. Everyone, I believe, was of the same mind. Thus, by default, it was up to the Hollanders to gain revenge. Java, however, fell into chaos. Between the two world wars, a militant young (born in 1901) engineer named Sukarno was instrumental in the formation of the *Partei Nasional Indonesia*, which was devoted to passive resistance against, and noncooperation with, the Dutch colonial government. In 1929 he was arrested, tried, and found guilty. After two years imprisonment he was exiled to the island of Flores and later transferred to Sumatra. With the arrival of the Japanese in 1942, Sukarno was freed and in 1943 the occupiers allowed the formation of a people's power—*Putera*. Sukarno, who used only one name, became chairman and Mohammed Hatta, vice chairman. This government raised a small, voluntary army, called "hi-ho's" by us prisoners. As the war wound down, the Japanese began talking independence to the Javanese, and Sukarno, a practiced orator, fed the fires. Two days after the surrender of the Japanese, Indonesia declared itself independent. Sukarno became president of the republic and Hatta, vice president. The hi-hos and undisciplined gangs of youths took to the streets. Dutch women and children, after more than three years of internment were attacked and forced back into their camps. White people of any nationality were endangered. At first, small detachments of British troops, bolstered by Ghurka soldiers from India, managed to create a semblance of order. The Javanese, however, were adamant. *Merdeka!* (Independence!) No colonial rule! Dutchmen, stay out! *Merdeka* became their war cry. In November, the British attempted to occupy the city of Soerabaja, and in the process lost one of its generals, assassinated in his squad car. The instability continued until 1949 when finally the Dutch realized the futility of the situation, relinquished their claims of governance to all of the former Dutch East Indies, except for a portion of New Guinea, and handed everything over to the Indonesian Republic.

At the end of the war when the Americans, Australians, and British prisoners were repatriated, the Dutch could not go back to devastated Holland. A large percentage considered the Indies to be their homeland, and desired to reestablish their lives in their original environment. Although the Javanese, particularly those in the eastern portion of the island, centered in Soerabaja, were fanatically pursuing *merdeka*, residents of other areas were less belligerant toward their former rulers. Northern Sumatra—Atjeh Province—was one of those pockets, and so became a haven for former Dutch prisoners of the Japanese, particularly those who called Sumatra home. Earlier, in recounting the makeup of the work force on the Pakan Baroe railway, I mentioned the Atjeh Party, a group of close to five hundred Dutch soldiers who traveled overland from North Sumatra to the railway site. This contingent was headed by a *Kapitein* J. J. A. van de Linde, *Koninklijke Nederlands Indische Leger* (KNIL), Royal Dutch Indies Army, who, at the cessation of hostilities, headed back home to Medan, the province's capital. There, order prevailed, and the survivors of the railway began to consider the enormity of the crime perpetrated by the Japanese on the hundreds of men who died in its construction. In time, a Temporary War Crimes Council was established for the purpose of investigating all war crimes committed by the Japanese on the island. Van de Linde became its prime sleuth, charged with tracking down the officers in high command who oversaw the lower ranked officers on the Pakan Baroe railway construction project and their soldiers. In the end, he named Singapore-based Lieutenant General Tanabe Morotaki, who headed the twenty-fifth Imperial Japanese Army in Singapore, Malacca, North Borneo, and Sumatra, as being responsible for all war crimes committed against the prisoners of war and civilian internees in those areas. The previously mentioned Captain Miyazaki Ryohi, who was at Camp 7 on August 15, 1945, was fingered as the senior officer in charge of the railway. Lt. Minure Toji was his assistant. Both were charged with carrying out Tanabe's orders, which resulted in the deaths of 692 men from June 16, 1944 to October 23, 1945. Ultimately, twenty-eight Japanese officers and soldiers were found guilty of the charges brought against them. On May 30, 1948, Captain Miyazaki was sentenced to death. At a later date, General Tanabe received the same punishment. Exactly when, how, and in what order their executions were conducted is not clear, but the last did not happen until October 11, 1949. Lieutenant Miura and another officer received sentences of life imprisonment. Twenty-four soldiers were given prison sentences of between five to twenty years. To what extent these were imposed, or if they were eventually commutated, is lost in the passage of the years. It is highly possible they served only a few years because Amnesty International, commenting on prosecutions for crimes committed during the Second World War, has issued the following:

> *Surprisingly, the United States General, Douglas MacArthur, Supreme Commander for the Allied Powers in the Far East, as a result of popular opposition in Japan to war crimes trials of Japanese, took the incentive in mid-1947 to urge Allied governments not to hold further war crimes trials. In response to MacArthur's request, the United Kingdom took the lead to stop further trials. On April 12, 1948, the Overseas Reconstruction Committee of the British Cabinet decided "no further trials of war criminals should be started after August 31, 1948." Three months later, the British Commonwealth Relations Office sent a secret telegram to Australia, Canada, Ceylon, India, New Zealand, Pakistan and South Africa suggesting that no new trials should be started after August 31, 1948, partly on political grounds: "In our view, punishment of war criminals is more a matter of discouraging future generations than of meting out retribution to every guilty individual. Moreover, in view of political developments in Germany envisaged by recent tripartite talks, we are convinced that it is now necessary to dispose of the past as soon as possible."*

> *Canada sent a secret cable in response on July 22, 1948 saying that it had no comment to make and the British government sent a subsequent note on August 13, 1948, warning "no public announcement is likely to be made about this." A series of similar political decisions were taken by Japanese and American officials to bring to an end trials of Japanese accused of war crimes and to release those convicted, commute their sentences or pardon them. At the same time that the trial of senior Japanese civilians and military was taking place before the Tokyo Tribunal, Japanese Emperor Hirohito promulgated a secret imperial script pardoning under Japanese law all members of the Japanese armed forces who might have committed crimes during the war, which was later tacitly approved by the United States General MacArthur, as Supreme Commander for the Allied Powers. As a result, there never were any prosecutions in Japanese courts of Japanese for war crimes. The Far Eastern Commission issued a formal advisory in 1949 to the 19 Allies in the Far East that trials of Japanese for war crimes should take place no later than September 30, 1949. Two years later, the Treaty of Peace with Japan provided in Article II that all Japanese who had been convicted of war crimes would be returned to Japan to serve the rest of their sentences under the authority of the Supreme Commander for the Allied Powers, with the aim, as it later became known, to ensure early release on parole or commutation of sentences.*

How unfair!

What a dishonor to the memory of the thousands of Allied soldiers who perished on the railway jobs in Southeast Asia, in the mines and factories of Japan, on the airfield construction projects in the Moluccas, and on the unlucky hell ships sent to the bottom by bombs and torpedoes loosed by their own countrymen. But what confounds me is the United State's and Great Britain's about-face so soon after the cessation of hostilities. In September 1944, the *Rakuyo Maru*, carrying 1,318 prisoners of war (601 British, 716 Australian, and 1 American) from Singapore to Japan, was torpedoed by the USS *Sealion* (SS 315) in the South China Sea. Only 152 (60 British and 92 Australians) survived to be rescued by the *Sealion* and three other submarines: *Barb* (SS 220), *Pampanito* (SS 383), and *Queenfish* (SS 393). After the first contingent of those 60 survivors reached England in November, the secretary of state for war, Sir James Grigg, reporting their arrival and their accounts of life in the Japanese camps said, "It is a matter of profound regret that these disclosures have to be made, but we are convinced it is necessary the Japanese should know that we know how they have been behaving and that we intend to hold them responsible." Three and a half years later the British Cabinet, as above, agreed to discontinuance of war crimes trials of the Japanese. So much for "responsibility."

This same attitude toward the Japanese came to the surface in San Francisco where on September 8, 1951, the Treaty of Peace between the Allied powers and Japan was signed. Article 14, subparagraph (b) states, "Except as otherwise provided in the present Treaty, the Allied Powers waive all reparation claims of the Allied Powers, other claims of the Allied Powers and their nationals arising out of any actions taken by Japan and its nationals in the course of the prosecution of the war, and claims of the Allied Powers for direct costs of occupation."

Bluntly speaking, the Japanese owed me nothing, and the United States government agreed!

Another area in which the *American Leader*'s crew, and crews of a few other vessels, were unfairly treated was our wages. Frequently, after the war, I was asked "Did you get paid for all those years as a prisoner?" The answer is "Yes, but." It takes a bit of explaining. Maritime law stipulates that in the event of the loss of a vessel, the crew's wages cease. War or no war, that is the law, and it varies little if one is a British seaman or an America seaman. From the outbreak of war in September 1939, even though it could take weeks or even months for surviving crew members to return to Great Britain and find new employment, all the while they earned not a penny. This went on until May 1941 when the Ministry of

Labour issued an Essential Work Order dictating many changes including the proviso that wages would be paid until shipwrecked seamen were repatriated. For years, an American writer/activist, the son of a British merchant officer who had survived a September 1941 sinking, routinely proclaimed the "no pay for torpedoed seamen" line. It is possible the older man didn't know about the work order. Also, it is difficult to believe, perhaps the owners of his ship simply ignored the work order.

Shortly after the United States entered the war, an entity was formed in Washington under the name War Shipping Administration (WSA). This agency is mentioned briefly on page 439, relative to my repatriation. This bureaucracy confiscated the entire United States merchant fleet not already taken over by the army, navy, and coast guard. These ships continued to be operated by their owners who were compensated for their efforts. The ships' crews ostensibly became federal employees, and an entirely new set of rules governed their compensation, based somewhat on the British model.

Martin J. Norris in his *The Law of Seamen* (4th edition, published by Clark, Boardman, Callaghan, located in Deerfield, Illinois, 1948) writes as follows: "The loss or wreck of the vessel which terminates the seamen's services prior to the period contemplated in the shipping articles entitles them, under present statute (46 USCS 593—now 1031b) to wages for the time of service prior to the termination."

Presumably, this is the law affecting American merchant seamen as of December 7, 1941. One of the WSA's early actions created a War Emergency Board to deal with seamen's issues, which it did in a series of decisions. Its first, made on January 23, 1942, circumventing the law, ordered payment of Benefits to *seamen employed on American flag vessels, where the vessel had been destroyed or abandoned by reason of war risk, or where the seamen had been interned by the enemy.* I was aware of this order, but on board the German ships and in the Japanese prison camps, no one believed me. Not Captain Pedersen, nor Chief Officer Hickey. The latter had been in the *City of Rayville*, sunk by a German mine off Australia in November 1940. End of voyage, end of wages, end of argument. He knew it all. That didn't deter me, so I scribbled my journal and maintained the records. In New York after the war, therefore, I was able to provide United States Lines with the accurate information to create a three and a half year payroll. Still the myth exists. I am acquainted with one person who went through an experience similar to ours, and he cannot remember collecting his three years' benefits which would have exceed $5,000! Maybe he didn't. So, the full answer to the question is "Yes, but we were shortchanged." One of the terms of the shipping articles, the employment contract we signed, called for war bonus payments to be made if the ship entered particularly dangerous waters. These were a percentage of wages, as high as 100 percent. As wages ceased on the date of the sinking, to be replaced by benefits, there was nothing on which to base any bonus. Could anything have been more threatening, more dangerous, than life as prisoners of the Japanese? Nevertheless, article VI of the Emergency Board's decision, specifically cut off bonus pay to internees. Conversely, the board did decree bonus pay "until the seaman arrived at a port where he was no longer exposed to maritime perils." This resulted in 100 percent bonus for the *American Leader*'s crew for the approximate two months spent in the German vessels, and for whatever time certain of them were being transported in Japanese ships! Other unfortunate victims of the well-intended benefit ruling were the next of kin to whom some crew members had allotted payments out of wages. I had done so and the company sent my mother a check every month. That process came to a halt when we were reported lost and it could not be reinstated out of my benefits.

Following the war, the surviving crew of the *President Harrison* who were captured on December 8, 1941, and other West coast seamen who had been interned or held as prisoners of war, sued the WSA for payments of applicable Bonuses. According to David H. Grover and Gretchen G. Grover, authors of *Captives of Shanghai*, the cases were heard in 1947 in the United States District Court for the Northern California District, Southern Division. "The court ruled," according to the Grovers, "that no voyage could occur on land; therefore no war bonuses were authorized for the time spent in internment. Thus, the action was denied. Two years later," wrote the Grovers, "the cases were continued by the United States Court of Appeals, Ninth Circuit. This Court ruled that the findings of the lower court was in error. So, in 1949 the seamen could get their payments, but it was a hollow victory. Legal fees and expenses ate up most of the money."

Unbelievably, the news of those suits and the favorable result of the appeal never reached the twenty-five *American Leader* survivors and the next of kin of the twenty-four lost men. Frankly, this came to my attention only in February 1996 when I purchased the Grovers' book! Why were we not informed? Why did whatever bureaucracy in Washington, which funded the *Harrison*'s crew judgement, not inquire as to other possible beneficiaries? What about United States Lines? In 1949, Pedersen, Hickey, and I were employed in their vessels. Why didn't their legal department catch this West Coast action? One possible reason for United States Line's disinterest was the unlicensed *American Leader* crew members (with the exception of bosun Stan Gorski) who were, at that period of time, suing the company on the grounds of negligence on the part of the captain and the chief officer. This negligence, they claimed, led to the loss of the ship. If United States Lines was not interested in the crew's well being, at the very least, they could have acted on behalf of the three of us who were once again sailing in their vessels. And what about the crew of another United States Lines vessel, the *Vincent?* They were captured by a Japanese surface raider soon after the war began. The Grovers mention them as being associated with the bonus suits. At least two of her officers were back in the company's service. Why didn't they tell us?

In retrospect, the War Emergency Board did a good job in putting together a very complicated set of rules and regulations acceptable to the ship owners and labor unions alike. However, it appears never to have addressed the question of merchant seamen being employees of the United States government, i.e., the WSA. Also its policy regarding no bonus payments to captured and interned seamen proved eventually to be illegal. An additional flaw was the lack of compassion for the cut-off allottees. All in all, it was not the best treatment the merchant seamen prisoners/internees could have anticipated.

Which begs another question, prisoners or internees? Why did the Japanese consider some merchant seamen to be prisoners of war and placed them in camps populated by military prisoners and placed others in civilian camps along with women, children, husbands and fathers, clergymen, nuns, and businessmen? The crews of the *American Leader, Sawokla, William F. Humphrey,* and *Connecticut,* all victims of the *Michel,* were, upon being handed over to the Japanese, lodged in military camps. The names of the survivors of the sunken *Capillo,* the left behind people from the *President Grant,* and deserters off the *Ruth Alexander,* for the most part, may be found in the roster of the Los Baños civilian internee camp. Yet, the United States Coast Guard, in the final analysis, lumped us together and considered us to be of one category. To say those of us who were taken prisoner after our ships were sunk were no different than the seamen who deserted or simply missed their ships' sailings is patently wrong.

Yet another injustice was the United States government's refusal to grant to merchant seamen the benefits derived from the Servicemen's Readjustment Act of 1944, otherwise known as the G.I. Bill. All members of the Armed Forces, including those men and women who never served overseas and never saw combat were beneficiaries of this legislation which offered free college educations, low-cost, guaranteed home loans, and medical care at veterans' hospitals. For many years, World War II merchant seamen attempted to persuade Congress to pass legislation making them eligible for such benefits. Because of the opposition mounted by the Veterans of Foreign Wars (VFW) and the American Legion, no action was ever taken. One of the most influential men in the United States, Lane

Kirkland, president of the AFL-CIO, a Kings Point graduate and a merchant marine officer during the war, could never sway the politicians.

In 1977, a number of women, who had been hired during the war to fly United States Army Air Force aircraft from the builders' factories to overseas bases not in combat areas, managed to convince Congress to pass legislation giving them veteran's status. The United States Air Force was handed the task of deciding who would be eligible. Immediately, to the dismay of the air force, other similar groups climbed onto the bandwagon, were deemed to be veterans, and required processing. Merchant seamen, though, individually or collectively, continued to be denied. The author, with three years prisoner of war time behind him, considered by both the Germans and the Japanese to have been a soldier, was rejected by the air force.

Ultimately, that course was abandoned in favor of the judicial approach. If the politicians couldn't see the injustice of our situation, perhaps logic would prevail in another venue. Funded primarily by the maritime labor unions, the air force was sued. In instance after instance, the court was shown how the army and navy had arrested merchant seamen, court martialed them, and jailed them. It was proven that the army and navy had violated the shipping articles signed by the seamen by sending vessels on voyages unspecified in the articles. Day after day, the air force dug itself deeper and deeper into a hole from which it could not extricate itself. Finally, on January 19, 1988, Air Force Secretary Edward C. Aldridge, Jr., signed a document reversing earlier denials of the merchant seamen's petitions. United States District Court Judge Louis F. Oberdorfer had ruled earlier such denials were "arbitrary and capricious."

For most surviving seamen it was forty-odd years too late, and a hollow victory at that, earning nothing more than a flag for one's casket and a marker for his grave. There was no need for a college education and the mortgage was nonexistent. For some, though, who financially were not well-off, treatment at their local Veterans Affairs Medical Center became indeed a life saver.

The VFW and the American Legion fought to the end and decried the judge's verdict. To their credit, the American Legion then changed their stance and sent membership applications to all eligible merchant seamen. To this day, the VFW refuses to recognize World War II merchant seamen as veterans and denies them membership. In view of their longtime opposition, the author, who spent all but forty-five days of the war outside the United States, wonders why any self-respecting seamen would even think about joining such an organization.

It should be noted, the air force was not required to process our applications. As the United States Coast Guard maintained all our records and could easily verify our credentials, the task of issuing our DD 214 forms fell to them. One interesting tidbit is that all honorable discharges issued to eligible merchant seamen were dated August 15, 1945, the day the Japanese surrendered. Mine, however, is dated October 2, 1945. Why, I wonder?

CHAPTER THIRTY-SEVEN

Reunions, Memories, and People

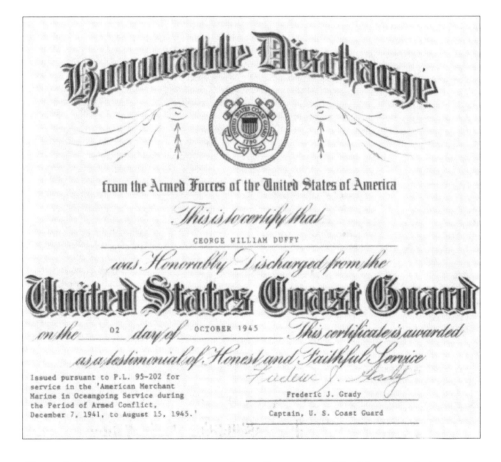

Honorable Discharge

from the Armed Forces of the United States of America

This is to certify that

GEORGE WILLIAM DUFFY

was Honorably Discharged from the

United States Coast Guard

on the 02 day of OCTOBER 1945 This certificate is awarded as a testimonial of Honest and Faithful Service

Issued pursuant to P.L. 95-202 for
service in the 'American Merchant
Marine in Oceangoing Service during
the Period of Armed Conflict,
December 7, 1941, to August 15, 1945.'

Frederic J. Grady

Captain, U. S. Coast Guard

Over the intervening years, a number of war-related incidents and situations have arisen and are worth relating as I bring this project to a close. Of most importance, I believe, is the relationship which developed between Gorski, Hickey,

Pedersen, and myself. I married Margaret in 1951 and never went back to sea. Hickey and Pedersen remained with United States Lines until their retirements, Pedersen in the early 50s and Hickey about twenty years later. I saw both of them frequently as Boston was a major port of call for United States Lines vessels in the North Atlantic general cargo trade and the wool business out of Australia. Hickey was on the Australian run which brought him to Hobart two or three times a year where he managed to connect up with Russell Piggott. This led to a prolonged correspondence between Russell and me. Stan Gorski, who after the war declined to go back to sea, had come onto the scene in the mid-1960s when he decided to go to New York from his home in Racine, Wisconsin, to look for me and Hickey and found Hickey who was temporarily working in the United States Lines' pier offices.

Boston, October 23, 1963. The first reunion. Gorski, Duffy, and Hickey.

In 1972, Russell, because of his postwar work as head of the Tasmanian branch of the Returned Services League, was honored by the Queen of England with the award of Officer of the Order of the British Empire. He and his wife Mildred traveled to London and following the ceremony continued westward, stopping in Newburyport to visit us.

Hickey, who happened to be ashore because of a maritime workers strike, came up from New Jersey, briefly, and Gorski flew in from Racine.

Four of the would-be escapees from Tandjoeng Priok, reunited at Seabrook Beach, New Hampshire twenty-nine years later. From left to right: Piggott, Hickey, the author, and Gorski.

Following their visit with us, the Piggotts went to New York and thence Racine. I managed a few days off and joined the festivities there. All the while, Russell was beseeching me to make the trip to Australia so as to attend an annual reunion of the 2nd/40th Battalion. This we did in 1979 when I was inducted into their Old Comrades Association and delivered the response at the closing dinner.

2/40th Old Comrades Association lapel pin.

In planning the trip, I discovered we could go around the world for the same price as a trip to Australia and back. This allowed us to visit Java, Sumatra, and Singapore, acquainting Margaret with the smells and sounds, heat and humidity, so reminiscent of my prisoner of war days. I was able to find the old Tandjoeng Priok camp, the site of the Cycle Camp, and on Sumatra, Camp 2 and the location of Camp 4, and the remains of the nearby bridge on the railway line.

Stan Gorski and I became close friends. At one stretch, spanning a dozen years, he alone, or sometimes with his wife, Gen, visited us at our Seabrook Beach summer home to celebrate Independence Day. The partying was endless. As Margaret would say, "I love to see him, and I love to see him go home." In turn, I frequently visited them in Racine. Gen passed away in January 1999, whereupon Stan sold their house and moved to Shelton, Washington, where Gen's son, Jay Dunham (Stan's stepson), was living. He was able to find an assisted living complex with a medical facility for Stan. In May 2002, the American Merchant Marine Veterans held their annual convention in Seattle. We attended and one afternoon Jay brought Stan over to see us and Kenneth Pride of the *American Leader* crew, who was also present.

American Leader **survivors at American Merchant Marine Veterans convention in Seattle WA, September 2003. At left is Able Seaman Kenneth Pride, in center is Bosun Stanley E. Gorski, and the author is at the right.**

Seventeen months later, Stan passed away. He was five months past his eighty-ninth birthday. For the record, Captain Pedersen in retirement returned to his home town of Arendal, Norway, where he died on March 20, 1969 at the age of seventy-seven. Hickey passed away in Shelburne, Vermont, on February 7, 2000, a few weeks shy of his ninety-first birthday.

When I came home in 1945, I commenced a search for information on the *Michel*, and eventually learned of her torpedoing by the USS *Tarpon* (SS 175). Then in May 1947, I was chief officer aboard the Liberty ship *Ethan Allen*, discharging a cargo of grain in Hamburg, Germany. On arriving, I had questioned the ship's agent about the *Michel*, and the next day he produced a newspaper carrying a story about von Ruckteschell being tried that day by a British court. The article's translated heading described him as being "severely charged." Cargo operations went very quickly. We sailed and I was unable to learn anything further. Eventually, the news reached me that von Ruckteschell had been found guilty of war crimes and sentenced to ten years in prison. He died on June 24, 1948.

In later years, I became aware of two surviving officers of the *Michel*, Konrad Hoppe and Jürgen Herr, and the existence of a loose organization known as the *Nippon Gruppe*, composed of those Germans, military and civilian, male and female, who had spent time in Japan during the war. Commencing in 1979, these people have held annual weekend reunions. At the same time, a young writer from North Carolina named Ian Millar, whose father was an officer in the British Merchant Marine during World War II, struck up a correspondence with Hoppe and Herr. They sent him photos of the *Nippon Gruppe* gatherings, and Ian passed them along to me. Needless to say, these were zipped back to him with the comment, "I am inclined to let them go down their own road." After all, these men took part in the destruction of my ship and the deaths of eleven of my shipmates, never mind the losses of nineteen others while in the hands of the Japanese. They had not participated in the decision to transfer us, but that hardly ingratiated me to the German navy.

Shortly, a circumstance arose which fundamentally altered my attitude. I was working for a shipping agency in Boston called Boston Overseas, Inc. We represented a number of shipping companies, domestic and foreign, in the New England states. Our function was to solicit import and export cargo for those companies' ships. In December of 1978, Hapag-Lloyd, the large German container ship operator, inaugurated a service whereby cargo containers from Europe consigned to New England customers were transferred from oceangoing ships at Halifax, Nova Scotia, to a small feeder ship. This vessel called weekly at Portsmouth NH and Boston, where the inbound containers were discharged and export containers loaded to be delivered to the next eastbound transatlantic ship in Halifax. The obligation of handling the port details of this operation fell upon me. Once again I was aboard a German ship. Of course, it wasn't the same, and I quickly adjusted my feelings toward Germany and the German people.

Then, several years later came a surprise.

One day in mid-1985, my old friend Bill Wallace and his wife, Irene, visited me and my wife, Margaret. He was carrying a letter from Konrad Hoppe, which closed with the words, "Whenever you see George Duffy, please give him my best regards." I was jolted by that and reacted. It so happened Margaret and I had plans to go to Belgium and Germany a few weeks hence. Locating Voerde, the town where Konrad lived, I determined our schedule would not be disrupted by a brief visit. A letter suggesting a meeting was sent, followed by a telephone call from Belgium. Konrad and his wife Louise invited us to stay at his residence, but I demurred, offering acceptance at a later date. On July 19 we met. After the greetings and introductions, he picked up from the dining room table and presented to me the following hand-lettered declaration:

> *To Captain George W. Duffy*
>
> *In memory of the wartime encounter on September 11 [sic] 1942 in the South Atlantic, 1,000 [sic] miles west of Capetown, presented to the former 3rd officer of the "American Leader" an involuntary shipmate of the German auxiliary cruiser "Michel" at the peaceful meeting in Voerde, Germany, on July 19, 1985, in deep regret for the distress and torture inflicted by the "Michel" to the crews of the sunken merchantmen and in great delight that the fateful enmity has changed into sincere friendship.*
>
> *Voerde, Germany, July 19, 1985.*
> *(Signed) Konrad Hoppe,*
> *former "flying officer"*
> *of the German auxiliary*
> *cruiser, "Schiff 28, Michel"*

What an amazing statement of remorse—and trust! I could have been coming as a troublemaker or even worse. In the evening we dined as guests of the Hoppes at an expensive restaurant overlooking the Rhine. The next morning when I asked the owner of the hotel for the bill, she indicated Herr Hoppe had paid in advance.

Konrad Hoppe and author, at first meeting, July 19, 1985.

One thing Konrad did extract from me was a promise to attend a future *Nippon Gruppe* meeting. In 1987, on September 10, exactly forty-five years to the day I clambered aboard the *Michel*, I again met up with Gustav Tober and became acquainted with many of his former shipmates. Following are five photographs of the author and *Michel* and *Uckermark* crew members who have been previously mentioned in this narrative.

Jürgen Herr

Gustav Tober

Wilhelm Osterfeld

Carl Cords

Friedrich W. Bruns.

Jürgen Herr, Bill Wallace, the author, and Konrad Hoppe at the
German War Memorial at LaBoe (near Kiel). Germany, September 1988.
The u-boat is the Type VIIc/41 U-995, built by Blohm & Voss, Hamburg, 1943.

A year later, I introduced Bill and Irene Wallace to the *Gruppe*. Margaret didn't attend that meeting. In 1991, I was in Germany for the delivery ceremony of a new ship, and Konrad and Louise entertained me for several days. Following that, I made the 1993, 1995, 1997, 2000, 2005, and 2007 meetings. Unfortunately, Konrad's beloved Louise passed away in 1996. He moved into a small apartment and continues to travel as they did before her death. In the fall of 1998, he spent two weeks with us, his first trip to the United States. Earlier that year, we had embarked on a two-week motor coach tour of Italy. And who met us when we landed in Rome? Konrad!

Konrad Hoppe and the author in Rome, June 12, 1998.

His last trip to the United States was in August 2002, when he spent eight days with us, the highlight of which was his appearance at a Massachusetts Maritime Academy Alumni Association luncheon meeting where he was the featured speaker.

Sincere friendship? Indeed!

**Konrad Hoppe, J. Revell Carr, and the author at the author's residence
on Seabrook Beach NH, August 2002.**

Photo courtesy of Christopher Robert Smith. At meeting of *Nippon Gruppe* at
Unna, Germany, September 2005. Left to right: **Engelbert Nalepa**, Quartermaster
Michel. Survived sinking. **Konrad Hoppe**, Flying Officer *Widder* and *Michel*. Was
not aboard *Michel* at time of sinking. **Herman Becker**, Radioman *Michel*. Survived
sinking. **Heinz Weitzel**, Radioman *Thor*. Survivied *Uckermark/Thor* explosion,
although severely injured. **Wilhelm Osterfeld**, Radioman/meteorologist *Widder*
and *Michel*. Was not aboard *Michel* at time of sinking. **Heinz Fritze**, Radioman
Michel. Survived sinking. **Heinz Neukirehen**, Radioman *Uckermark*. Survived

explosion. Was in *Weserland* when it was intercepted by U.S. Navy task force in S. Atlantic in early 1944. Spent remainder of war as prisoner in the United States, mainly in Arizona. **The author.**

In the summer of 1942, Charlie Kelleher was a radio officer in an American freighter on a voyage similar to the *American Leader*'s. At some point, he became ill and was hospitalized in an Indian port. Upon recovering, he was placed in the aforementioned *Sawokla* for repatriation to the United States. He survived her sinking, became a prisoner in the *Michel*, and was in the group of sixty-five turned over to the Japanese on February 19, 1943 at Singapore. Most of this group were soon sent up to Burma to work on the railway made famous by the movie *The Bridge on the River Kwai*. After the war when I met Dennis Roland, he told me about Charlie, who he thought was living in the Boston area. I never did locate him until after the court case granting us veteran's benefits was decided. I had gone to Manchester NH to begin the application to the Veterans Administration. When the clerk learned of my German/Japanese experience, he said he had never heard of such a situation until the previous day. I asked him who the person was, and he replied, "Charles Kelleher." So, he gave me Charlie's phone number. I called him that evening and he was as surprised to hear from me as I was when I learned he was alive and living in New Hampshire. In due course I visited him, and when he met me at the door, he remarked, "George Duffy! Who would ever imagine that forty-six years after I found your hidden note in the German raider, you would walk into my kitchen!"

Charles Kelleher.

The author receiving the Prisoner of War Medal from Rear Admiral
William J. Flanagan, Jr. USN. Applauding is Rear Admiral John F. Aylmer,
USMS, a 1957 graduate, who was President of the Academy at the time.

Daughter Maryellen, author and wife Margaret, daughter Geraldine, on
occasion of award of Prisoner of War medal, 1989.

With my honorable discharge in hand, several avenues, which had been hitherto closed, now opened up. I was able to apply for the Prisoner of War Medal and asked that it be sent to the Massachusetts Maritime Academy for award at a suitable date. Thus, at the November 1989 Annual Meeting of the Massachusetts Maritime Academy Alumni Association, Rear Admiral William J. Flanagan, Jr., USN, a 1964 graduate of the academy, performed the honor.

A short time later, Capt. Thomas J. Hudner, USN (Ret), a Congressional Medal of Honor recipient and director of the State of Massachusetts Veterans Services Division, requested my presence at the Veterans Day service at the State House in Boston. I was, thus, the first merchant marine veteran to ever appear at the podium at that prestigious event. Of note is the action of the authorities at the maritime academy to provide a color guard for my presentation and the attendance of the academy's glee club, which offered numerous musical renditions during the morning affair.

**The author addressing the Veterans Day assemblage
at the Massachusetts State House in 1989.**

This activity resulted in my being nominated for, and named, the Massachusetts Maritime Academy Alumni Association's 1990 Alumnus of the Year, This honor brought with it an inscribed Chelsea Ship's bell clock, and the invitation to address the 1990 class at its graduation ceremony.

June 1990. Graduation ceremony, Massachusetts Maritime Academy.
Rear Admiral John A. Moriarty, USN (RET), Class of 1959, and
George M. Steinbrenner III, owner of the New York Yankees,
congratulate the author.

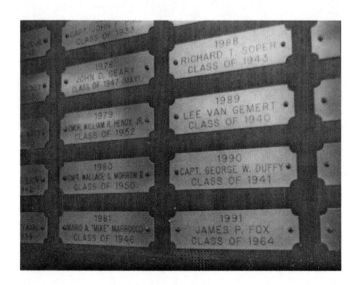

Alumnus of the Year plaques in Hurley Library
at Massachusetts Maritime Academy.

The reader will recall how, when we were prisoners in the tanker *Uckermark*, her captain asked his crew to donate to us whatever spare reading material and game sets they had. One day, I was perusing the tabloid magazine *Berliner Illustrierte Zeitung* (No. 27, 1942), a publication comparable to what we now receive with our Sunday newspapers. A slick production, it contained many photographs. This particular edition carried a photo essay reporting the sinking of an American oil tanker by a U-boat commanded by *Kapitänleutnant* Hardegan, whose photograph was included.

Translation

THE LIFEBOATS BURN!

The great fatal stroke:

A gigantic column of smoke rises into the Heaven from a USA tanker, which a German torpedo has just hit amidships. A tongue of fire shoots out from the lost ship. To the left, near the pillar of smoke, three smaller ones rise up: the oil that was thrown up and ignited by the explosion has fallen like a deadly rain, setting the lifeboats on fire.

Saved from the deadly realm of the burning sea:

Men of the tanker crew who reached an emergency raft. The German U-boat proceeds toward them.

A head emerges with a two-week beard:

It is Lieutenant Commander Hardegen, a wearer of the Knight's Cross with Oak Leaves, one of the most successful leaders of the German submarine force in operation against the US.

Seven men survive!

The horror that they have just lived through has marked and stained their oil-besmeared faces.

Another picture showed seven men of the tanker crew on a life raft, facing the enemy with looks of fear, desperation, and, perhaps, a little defiance. Blithely assuming some day I would be able to find these men and they would enjoy seeing how things looked from another perspective, I tore the page out, folded it, and hid it away.

I was literally haunted by the specter of these drifting men and upon my return to the United States three years later began a search for their identities. The first step was to loan the page to the United Seamen's Service, whose personnel took it to all the oil tanker companies in and around New York City. Immediately a pattern was established: a great deal of interest, but no answer. Thus it would go over the years. Occasionally, I would resurrect the sheet from my files to show to some old shipmate or interested acquaintance, and that was about the extent of it. There was no question in my mind these seven men were Americans.

They were dressed like Americans, and two of them wore life jackets of the type we had on board in those days. Furthermore, the raft is identical to what had been placed on American ships in the early 40s. Clues, but not enough. One tantalizing bit of evidence was just out of sight. Stenciled on the life jacket worn by the fellow in the middle of the group is the vessel's name. Alas, even with a glass it is unreadable. One may imagine a pair of EEs, or at least assume so. Additional assumptions are, for one, the attack took place in warm weather because of the men's light clothing. Secondly, the date had to be late March or early April or even sooner for the U-boat to return home, the photos processed and captions written, censored, published and circulated in July. Regardless how diligently I searched library after library, or how deeply I delved into list after list, nowhere could I obtain a complete record of United States flag merchant vessels lost during World War II. I went through Lloyd's Register and I purchased book after book, hoping somehow I'd be able to recognize the name of a ship sunk early in 1942 in warm or tropical waters, possibly having two EEs in its name. If I could, then I would have the beginning of the identification of the men on the raft.

The break came in 1981 when I received a letter from Capt. Arthur R. Moore, a United States Merchant Marine Academy (Kings Point) graduate, who now lives in Hallowell, Maine. Captain Moore told me he was "compiling a history of all U.S. flag merchant ships lost or damaged from enemy causes during World War II. Also compiling a list of merchant marine personnel lost or taken prisoner." He had numerous questions for me. Needless to say, I telephoned him. "Arthur," I said, "if you are doing what you say you are doing, then you are going to answer questions I have been asking for almost forty years." I told him about my *Illustrierte Zeitung* page, sent it to him, and in a matter of a few days we had the first answer. These fellows, according to the FBI, which enhanced the photo and read the name on the life jacket, were from a ship called *Muskogee*. German records in Arthur's possession identified Reinhard Hardegen in the U-123 as the attacker of the *Muskogee*, and, as above, Hardegen was named and pictured in the *Illustrierte Zeitung* spread. But now the crusher: the *Muskogee* was lost with all hands!

All hands! And I had a paper containing a photograph of seven of her crew on the day she went down!

Captain Moore published this photograph in his monumental (originally 522 pages, latest printing 706) pictorial history entitled *A Careless Word . . . A Needless Sinking* under the heading "CAN YOU IDENTIFY ANY OF THESE MEN?" As has been the case since 1945, no one came forward with any hint of an answer. One evening some months later I tackled a project I had

AMBUSHED UNDER THE SOUTHERN CROSS

been contemplating ever since Arthur's book made its appearance. There is at Massachusetts Maritime Academy (formerly the Massachusetts Nautical School from which I graduated) a plaque commemorating those alumni who lost their lives in World War II. *A Careless Word . . . A Needless Sinking* contains a listing of all seamen who perished between 1941 and 1945, along with their positions and the names of the vessels in which they sailed. Imagine my astonishment when I cross-referenced the name of Morgan J. Finucane on the plaque with Finucane, Morgan J., Chief Mate, SS *Muskogee*, in the book. As the *Muskogee* carried a crew of thirty-four, the chances were a little better than one out of five that Finucane was in the photograph taken from the conning tower of the U-boat. Eventually, with the assistance of two men who had been in the nautical school in 1928: Captain John Cusick, of Sun City West, Arizona, and Chief Engineer Mario "Lou" Guidette of Livingston, New Jersey, a 1928 snapshot of Morgan Finucane came to light. Comparing that snapshot with the German news magazine picture leaves no doubt that the man in the center of the group on the raft, the one wearing the life jacket with the illegible ship's name, is indeed Morgan J. Finucane. Tentative identification has been made of the third person from the left. He is probably Third Mate Nathanial D. Foster. The man standing right rear with his hands to his mouth may be Able Seaman Anthony G. Sousa. The other four faces remain nameless.

It has now come to happen that this *Muskogee* story is much more than the saving of the news magazine page, and the search for the identity of the men and the vessel. In 1976, under the leadership of Captain Thomas A. King, Eastern Region director for the United States Maritime Administration, an organization was created to raise the funds needed to develop and maintain a memorial dedicated to all American merchant seamen lost from 1775 to the present. With that act, the *Muskogee*'s abandoned men and the American Merchant Mariners' Memorial began converging. Ultimately, the American Merchant Mariners' Memorial Inc. formed a subcommittee, the Art Advisory Committee, for the purpose of selecting the memorial's design. The chairman of this committee, an individual worthy of note in this narrative, was Charles Dana Gibson, a self-employed marine consultant specializing in historical research and analysis, and a former fellow licensed master mariner. Captain Gibson was personally committed to a memorial that would not only impress the public in general, but would particularly appeal to the seafarer. It is quite clear that he favored the castaway concept prompted by the photo of the seven men on the raft. He was drawn to it, as he said in his March 20, 1987 letter to his Art Advisory Committee, because it represented a "theme common to all periods." He felt "(it) is the starkest portrayal ever caught on film depicting the toll the sea can extract from a ship's company. It is a circumstance that spans the ages."

This improbable story finally came to a conclusion on October 8, 1991 with the dedication at Battery Park at the Southern end of Manhattan in New York City of the American Merchant Mariners' Memorial. Remembered on that day were the 1,554 American merchant vessels lost, 733 of them being one thousand tons or more, and their 9,497 crewmen killed in the great sea battle of 1941-1945. Remembered specifically were the *American Leader* and the *Muskogee* and the men who manned them.

Marisol, the Memorial's sculptress with author at unveiling ceremony.

We held the course: Tom King, with his dedication to the Memorial; Dana Gibson, with his vision of the seven men on the raft; I, with the German news magazine photograph of the *Muskogee*'s lost mariners; they, on their endless voyage.

In 1943, Congress authorized the War Shipping Administration to issue War Zone Ribbon bars to those merchant seamen who had actively served in three specific war zones, who had served between September 8, 1939, and December 7, 1941, and who had experienced actual combat conditions. No medals were provided at the time. In fact, the only merchant marine medals awarded during or after the war were the Distinguished Service Medal, the Mariner's Medal, and the Victory Medal.

American Merchant Mariners' Memorial.

WAR SHIPPING ADMINISTRATION

This is to certify that

George William Duffy
_____

HAS BEEN AWARDED THE

MARINER'S MEDAL

16—40219-1

ADMINISTRATOR

U.S. DEPARTMENT OF TRANSPORTATION
MARITIME ADMINISTRATION

This is to certify that

GEORGE W. DUFFY
_____

HAS BEEN AWARDED by the War Shipping Administration the

The Merchant Marine Defense Bar

indicating active service in THE UNITED STATES MERCHANT MARINE
during the National Emergency — September 8, 1939 to December 7, 1941.

FORM MA-881-L

Maritime Administrator

U.S. DEPARTMENT OF TRANSPORTATION
MARITIME ADMINISTRATION

 (STAR)

This is to certify that

GEORGE W. DUFFY
_____

HAS BEEN AWARDED by the War Shipping Administration the

The Merchant Marine Combat Bar

confirming active service with THE UNITED STATES MERCHANT MARINE
in a ship which was engaged in direct enemy action.

FORM MA-881-G

U.S. DEPARTMENT OF TRANSPORTATION
MARITIME ADMINISTRATION

This is to certify that

GEORGE W. DUFFY

HAS BEEN AWARDED by the War Shipping Administration the

Atlantic War Zone Bar

confirming active service with THE UNITED STATES MERCHANT MARINE *or* MARITIME SERVICE *during* WORLD WAR II.

Form MA-881-F

Maritime Administrator

U.S. DEPARTMENT OF TRANSPORTATION
MARITIME ADMINISTRATION

This is to certify that

GEORGE W. DUFFY

HAS BEEN AWARDED by the War Shipping Administration the

Pacific War Zone Bar

confirming active service with THE UNITED STATES MERCHANT MARINE *in that war area.*

FORM MA-881-M

Maritime Administrator

U.S. DEPARTMENT OF TRANSPORTATION
MARITIME ADMINISTRATION

This is to certify that

GEORGE W. DUFFY

HAS BEEN AWARDED by the War Shipping Administration the

Mediterranean Middle East War Zone Bar

confirming active service with THE UNITED STATES MERCHANT MARINE *in that war area.*

FORM MA-881-K

U.S. DEPARTMENT OF TRANSPORTATION
MARITIME ADMINISTRATION

This is to certify that

GEORGE W. DUFFY

HAS BEEN AWARDED BY THE WAR SHIPPING ADMINISTRATION THE

VICTORY MEDAL

confirming active service with THE UNITED STATES
MERCHANT MARINE *or* MARITIME SERVICE *during*
WORLD WAR II.

MA 881B
(10-81)

Maritime Administrator.

U.S. DEPARTMENT OF TRANSPORTATION
MARITIME ADMINISTRATION

This is to certify that

GEORGE W. DUFFY

HAS BEEN AWARDED by the War Shipping Administration the

Philippine Defense Ribbon

confirming active service with THE UNITED STATES MERCHANT MARINE
in that war area.

FORM MA-881-I

Maritime Administrator

On May 19, 1992, National Maritime Day, over forty-six years after the end of World War II, the United States Department of Commerce, through its Maritime Administration, unveiled four new medals for service in that war: the Atlantic War Zone Medal, the Pacific War Zone Medal, the Mediterranean—Middle East War Zone Medal, and the Merchant Marine Defense Medal. Also, the Korean Service Medal and the Vietnam Service Medal were introduced to be awarded to the seafarers who served in those conflicts. Six veteran seamen, two of whom had been taken prisoner, whose backgrounds personified each of the medals, were recognized and received the first of each of the six awarded decorations. The author, who was in Manila on the war's first day and spent almost three years in the former Dutch East Indies and Singapore, was honored by being the recipient of the initial Pacific War Zone Medal. The presentation was made by Secretary of Transportation Andrew H. Card, Jr., assisted by Maritime Administrator Captain Warren G. Leback. Fittingly, the ceremony was held on board the SS *John W. Brown*, one of the two remaining World War II Liberty ships, which steamed under her own power from Baltimore to Alexandria VA for the occasion.

Secretary of Transportation Andrew H. Card, Jr., Maritime Administrator Capt. Warren G. Leback, and the Author.

Philip P. McKeever was a fireman/watertender in the *William F. Humphrey* when she was sunk by the *Michel*. Seriously wounded, he was taken prisoner and, as recounted earlier, when his shipmates were transferred to the *Charlotte*

Schliemann, he remained aboard. Thus, he shared our sojourn into the hands of the Japanese. In September 1944, after twenty-six months as a prisoner, he was lost in the *Junyo Maru* disaster. Phil left a wife and a daughter named Elizabeth, who was born in 1942 and, thus, never knew him.

More than forty years later, this girl, who had become the wife of James Gardner and the mother of two sons, began having strange dreams relating to stars and planets and her lost father of whose fate she knew nothing. Inspired by her dreams, she and Jim embarked on a search for Phil McKeever's history. Their first approach was to the United States Merchant Marine Academy at Kings Point, New York, a few miles away from New Hyde Park where they lived. That should have been enough, but their contact was unbelievably stupid and ignorant and turned them away. Next, they tried the seamen's unions in the city. After several false starts, they reached Carmelo Guastella of the National Maritime Union (NMU). This gentleman had in his office a copy of *A Careless Word . . . A Needless Sinking* by Capt. Arthur R. Moore, which has been mentioned earlier and was published by the American Merchant Marine Museum at the United States Merchant Marine Academy! In this encyclopedia is a photo of the *William F. Humphrey*, an account of her loss, and names and details of her crew members, some of which I had provided to Captain Moore. By luck and perseverance, the Gardners had the basic story, but I still wonder at the ineptness of the person who answered the telephone at the academy and the perspicacity of the NMU's Guastella.

Stan Gorski, Jim Gardner, Elizabeth McKeever Gardner, and Karel Rink, at King's Point, November 1990.

A letter from the Gardners to Captain Moore elicited a quick response wherein he told the Gardners about Stan Gorski and me, and that we would be able to provide further details. Within weeks, my wife, Margaret, and I visited them, and Carmelo Guastella, at their home. Later in the year, I acted as master of ceremonies at the Merchant Marine Academy (we had their attention by this time) when Elizabeth McKeever Gardner was formally presented her father's certificate of honorable discharge signed by the secretary of transportation, and her father's various decorations, including the Mariners Medal and the Prisoner of War Medal.

On April 8, 1994, at the Calverton National Cemetery on Long Island, the book was closed on Philip P. McKeever when the Department of Veterans Affairs emplaced his memorial plaque. "We have now come full circle from the original dreams to the final resting place of a wandering spirit," wrote Elizabeth and Jim. "We believe that Phil McKeever is now at rest. His story has been told."

In 1988, a group of World War II merchant mariners created the American Merchant Marine Veterans Memorial located on South Harbor Boulevard in San Pedro, California. On May 22, 2003, by plan, an expansion of the original memorial was dedicated. This consists of a number of black, stone panels inscribed with the names of every United States merchant vessel lost in World War II, accompanied by the names of those crew members who did not survive the incident. Also listed are the 706 men and women who were taken prisoner, with emphasis on those who died while in enemy hands.

General layout of addition

American Leader section.
Only those lost at time of sinking appear here.

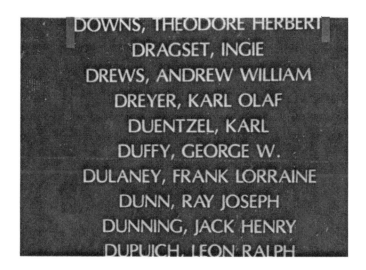

DOWNS, THEODORE HERBERT
DRAGSET, INGIE
DREWS, ANDREW WILLIAM
DREYER, KARL OLAF
DUENTZEL, KARL
DUFFY, GEORGE W.
DULANEY, FRANK LORRAINE
DUNN, RAY JOSEPH
DUNNING, JACK HENRY
DUPUICH, LEON RALPH

A portion of the Prisoner of War section.

Following the dedication a largely attended luncheon was enjoyed. It was the author's pleasure and privilege to address the gathering.

Author addressing the luncheon guests.

A direct result of the latter convocation was the invitation to the author to be the keynote speaker on Veterans Recognition Day at the Arizona State Fair, on October 3, the same year. The United States Merchant Marine, as a whole, was the honoree, with the Desert Mariners Chapter of the American Merchant Marine Veterans in charge of the arrangements.

At some point in recent years, perhaps late 2003 or early 2004, the author was contacted via the Internet by a young lady named Amanda Farrell whose home is in New Zealand. She was at the time, however, living on Sumatra where her father manages a lumber operation. They had learned from the local population of the railroad built in 1944-45 for the Japanese by the Allied prisoners of war. An Internet search located me, and I was able to provide the family with a limited amount of information and suggestions as to where to look for specific artifacts. The results have been fantastic, as seen herewith.

**One of the locomotives used in the construction of the railway.
It is set on a platform decorated with stone panels depicting the location
of the line and other art work. Curiously it is located in a cemetery in
Pakan Baroe. In our 1979 visit to Sumatra, Margaret and I did not see this,
although we queried many people as to the existence of any railway artifacts.**

Amanda Farrell inspecting derelict locomotive near the old Pakan Baroe railway line.

Jamie Farrell at same locomotive.

Jamie Farrell and lumber mill Foreman Bambam inspecting
abandoned and stripped Japanese Army tank.

After sixty years, the path of the railway through the jungle
is still descernable.

Jamie Farrell and Amanda on the embankment approach at the site of the old Lipat Kain railway bridge. This was built by the prisoners in WWII in order to elevate the tracks above the river's flood-stage level.

The modern-day bridge over the Kampar Kiri
at Lipat Kain.

The author and Margaret, 2006.

THE END

ACKNOWLEDGEMENTS

Although I had long professed the desire to do this book, it really didn't gain any solid impetus until 1994 when I began writing a monthly editorial page column for the *Daily News* of Newburyport, Massachusetts. The tacit support given me by Merrily Buchs, presently news editor of that publication, encouraged me to commence expanding my *Nantucket* journal and prison camp diary. In 2002, David W. Graham, LCDR, USN (Ret.), a fellow member of Boston's prestigious Wardroom Club, who has practically memorized my World War II escapades, told me he had a close friend whose acquaintance I should make. Interestingly enough, this fellow worked in Newburyport. A luncheon meeting was arranged, and I met Mike Meehan. To my utter surprise, Mike was a literary agent, working with the Moore Literary Agency on High Street, about a half mile from where my family lived for many years. Mike and Claudette Moore introduced me to the publishing industry's facts of life and the book slowly took shape, culminating in the finished product five years later.

Most of the information contained herein relating to the German navy comes from my attendance at a half dozen *Nippon Gruppe* meetings ranging from 1987 to 2005, and numerous visits to the homes of Konrad Hoppe and Jürgen Herr. Konrad translated for me his occasionally kept wartime diary, and a daily diary written by a noncommissioned enlisted man in the *Michel*. I am not sure of this man's identity, but have been told he was Werner Stöhr, the assistant to the vessel's administration officer, Otto Saupe.

Christopher Smith of Nottingham, England, and his uncle, Michael Smith of London, in recent years embarked on a search for information concerning the sinking of the SS *Lylepark* by the *Michel*. Mike's brother Charles (Chris's uncle as well, of course) was Assistant Steward in the *Lylepark* and was killed at age seventeen in the attack. These fellows found me on the Internet. I told them what I knew about the raider, and later they graciously shared with me pertinent material found in British archives relating to the *Lylepark*, HMS *Archer*, HMS *Alcantara*, and Hellmuth von Ruckteschell.

On the home front, no one can be happier at the completion of this effort than Margaret. Of necessity, I have spent many, many hours at the word processor and the computer while she passed the time away in front of her television set, or watching classic movies from Netflix. Recently, she took up knitting, making fancy-colored stockings for the daughters and granddaughters, thus reaping some benefit from her solitude. As for the daughters and granddaughters, they have always been aware of the project and have, on occasion, been of assistance. For the record, they are Maryellen Duffy, Ed.D.; her husband Jerry Cabana; and their three daughters, Caitlyn, Marilyn, and Andrea; Geraldine and her husband Fred Carter; and their daughters, Christine and Anne. Of particular note is Christine's work as my proofreader.

In closing, I must call the reader's attention to the outstanding cover design created by John and Sarah Raleigh of Newburyport.

Thanks to all.

BIBLIOGRAPHY

Books

Alden, John D. *U.S. Submarine Attacks During World War II.* Annapolis, Maryland: United States Naval Institute, 1989.

Blair, Clay, Jr., *Silent Victory. The U.S. Submarine War Against Japan.* Toronto, New York, London: Bantam Books, 1975.

Blair, Joan and Clay, Jr. *Return From the River Kwai.* New York: Simon and Schuster, 1979.

Blair, Clay. *Hitler's U-Boat War. The Hunters, 1939-1942.* New York: Random House, 1996.

Blair, Clay. *Hitler's U-Boat War. The Hunted, 1942-1945.* New York: Random House, 1998.

Carr, J. Revell. *All Brave Sailors. The Sinking of the Anglo-Saxon, August 21, 1940.* New York: Simon & Schuster, 2004.

Daws, Gavan. *Prisoners of the Japanese. POWs of World War II in the Pacific.* New York: William Morrow and Company, Inc., 1994.

Flanagan, Lt. Gen. Edward M., Jr. *The Los Baños Raid. The 11th Airborne Jumps at Dawn.* Novato, California: Presidio Press, 1986.

Gibson, Charles. *The Ship With Five Names.* London, New York, Toronto: Abelard-Schumann, 1965.

Gleichauf, Justin F. *Unsung Sailors. The Naval Armed Guard in World War II.* Annapolis, Maryland: Naval Istitute Press, 1990.

Grover, David H. and Gretchen G. Grover *Captives of Shanghai. The Story of the President Harrison*. Napa, California: Western Maritime Press, 1989.

Herlin, Hans. *The Survivor. The True Story of the Sinking of the Doggerbank*. London: Leo Cooper, 1994.

Hovinga, Henk. *Dodenspoorweg door het oerwoud. Het drama van de Pakan Baroe-Spoorweg op Sumatra*. Amsterdam: Buijten & Schipperheijn, 1976.

Hovinga, Henk. *Eindstation Pakan Baroe 1944-1945*. Amsterdam: Buijten & Schipperheijn, 1982.

Krug, Hans-Joachim; Yoichi Hirami, Bertold J. Sander-Nagashima, and Axel Niestlé. *Reluctant Allies. German and Japanese Naval Relations in World War II*. Annapolis, Maryland: Naval Institute Press. 2001.

Krancher, Jan A. *The Defining Years in the Dutch East Indies, 1942-1949. Survivors' Accounts of Japanese Invasion and Enslavement of Europeans and the Revolution That Created Free Indonesia*. Jefferson, North Carolina and London: McFarland and Company, 1996.

LaMont-Brown, Raymond. *Kempeitai. Japan's Dreaded Military Police*. Gloucesterchire, England: Sutton Publishing. 1998.

Lane, Tony. *The Merchant Seamen's War*. Manchester Manchester, England and New York: University Press, 1990.

Langelo, Vincent A. *With All Our Might. The U.S.S. Boise (CL-47)*. Austin, Texas: Eakin Press, Austin Press, 2000.

MacIntosh, Jim. *The War Diary of a POW*. Los Altos, California: Mansell Publishing, 1999.

Marvel, William. *Andersonville. The Last Depot*. Chapel Hill, North Carolina and London: The University of North Carolina Press, 1994.

Melis, Ed. *Eresaluut boven massagraf. Junyo Maru de-vergeten-scheepsramp*. Nijmegan, The Netherlands: Self-published, 1984.

Messimer, Dwight R. *Pawns of War. The Loss of the USS Langley and the USS Pecos*. Annapolis, Maryland: Naval Institute Press, 1983.

Moore, Arthur R. *A Careless Word . . . A Needless Sinking. A history of the Tremendous losses in ships and men suffered by the U.S. Merchant Marine during World War II 1941-1946.* Kings Point, New York: American Merchant Marine Museum, 1983. Revised editions, 1984, 1985, and 1988. Seventh printing, 1998.

Muggenthaler, August Karl. *German Raiders of World ar II. The first complete history of Germany's ocean marauders—the last of a great era of naval warfare.* Engelwood Cliffs, New Jersey: Prentice-Hall, Inc., 1977.

Neumann, Henk and van Witsen, E. *De Sumatra Spoorweg.* Middelie, Holland: Studio Pieter Mulier, 1985.

O'Kane, Rear Admiral Richard H. *Clear the Bridge. The War Patrols of the U.S.S. Tang.* Novato, California: Presidio Press. 1977.

Olson, Wesley. *Bitter Victory. The Death of HMAS Sydney.* Annapolis, Maryland: Naval Institute Press, 2000.

Parkes, Meg. *Notify Alec Rattray . . . A Story of Survival 1941-43.* Wirral, England: Krangi Publications, 2002.

Parkes, Meg . . . . *A. A. Duncan is OK. A story of one war and two captivities.* Wirral, England: Kranji Press, 2003.

Prange, Gordon W. with Goldstein, Donald M. and Dillon, Katherine V. *Pearl Harbor. The Verdict of History.* New York: McGraw-Hill Book Company, 1986.

Prange, Gordon W. with Goldstein, Donald M. and Dillon, Katherine V. *The Day the Japanese Attacked Pearl Harbor.* New York: McGraw-Hill Book Company, 1988.

Rohwer, Jürgen. *Axis Submarine Successes of World War Two. German, Italian, and Japanese Submarine Successes, 1929-1945.* Annapolis, Maryland: Naval Institute Press, 1999.

Schmalenbach, Paul. *German Raiders. A history of auxiliary cruisers of the German Navy 1895-1945.* Annapolis, Maryland: Naval History Press, 1977.

Tanaka, Yuki. *Hidden Horrors. Japanese War Crimes in World War II.* Boulder, Colorado: West View Press, 1996.

Thomas, Lowell. *Count Luckner, The Sea Devil.* Garden City, New York: Doubleday, Page & Company, 1927.

Thompson, Claude. *Into The Sun.* Warkworth, New Zealand: Self-published, 1996.

Tischer, Heinz. *Die Abenteuer des lezen Kapers. Hilfskreuzer Thor's Reise in die Katastrophe.* Grosshansdorf, Germany: Self-published, 1983.

United States Navy Hydrographic Office. *American Pactical Navigator.* Washington, D.C.: Government Printing Office, 1943.

Veenstra, J. H. W. *Als krijsgegevangene naar de Molukken en Flores. Relaas van een Japans transport van Nederlandse en Engelse militairen 1943-1945.* 's-Gravenhage, Holland: Martinus Nijhoff, 1982.

Waterford, Van (a.k.a. Wanrooy, Willem). *Prisoners of the Japanese in World War II. Statistical History, Personal Narratives ands Memorials Concerning POWs in Camps And on Hellships, Civilian Internees, Asian Slave Laborers and Others Captured in The Pacific Theater.* Jefferson, North Carolina and London: McFarland and Company, Inc., 1994.

Wolter, Tim. *POW Baseball in World War II. The National Pastime Behind Barbed Wire.* Jefferson, North Carolina and London: McFarland and Company, Inc., 2002.

Woodward, David. *The Secret Raiders.* New York: Avon Publications, Inc., 1955.

Internet

American Merchant Marine at War. www.usmm.org

Amnesty International. web.amnesty.org

Ascension at War. www.websmith.demon.co.uk

Bocing Douglas "Havoc". www.boeing.com/history/mdc/havoc/htm

Center For Research Allied POWs Under the Japanese. www.mansell.com

Children of Far East Prisoners of War. www.cofepow.org.uk

City of Cairo. www.sscityofcairo.co.uk/index.php

Commonwealth War Graves Commission. www.cwgc.org

Das Ktb der U-Bootwaffe. ktb.ubootwaffe.net

Fepow Community. www.fepow-community.org.uk

German Naval Maps of the Second World War. www.geocities.com/germangrid/eindex.htm

Holder of the Knights Cross With Oakleaves. www.feldgrau.com.hkcwo.html

Hyper war: U S Army in the Philippines. www.ibiblio.org/hyperwar/USA-P-PI/index.html

Kriegsmarine and U-boat History. www.ubootwaffe.net

Medal of Honor Recipients. www.army/mil/cmh-pg/html

Norwegian Merchant Fleet WW II. www.warsailors.com

Official Chronology of the U.S. Navy in World War II. www.ibiblio.org/hyperwar/USN/USN-chron.html

Port Chicago CA Explosion. www.history.navy.mil/faqs/faq80-1.htm

———

United States Naval Institute. www.usni.org

World War II U.S. Naval Armed Guard and World War II U.S. Merchant Marine. www.armed-guard.com

Compact Disks

Hovinga, Henk. *Final Destination Pakan Baroe. Railroad of Death Through the Jungle. 1943-1945.* Translated from Dutch by Bernard J. Wolters, San Gabriel, California 91776.

Mansell, Roger. *Untitled.* Listing of all United States servicemen and civilians captured and imprisoned in the Far East by the Japanese during World War II. Provides, where applicable, name, rank, service number, branch, unit, where held, and if deceased, date of death, location, and cause.

Microfilm

von Ruckteschell, Hellmuth. *Kriegstagebuch, Hsk Michel. 8 Oktober 1942 bis 2 März 1943.* United States National Archives and Records Administration, College Park, Maryland.

Miscellaneous

Massachusetts, The Commonwealth of. Department of Education. Massachusetts Nautical School. Schoolship *Nantucket.* Regulations 1935.

Private Publication

Dorgan, Mary Jane. *The Family of Edward Lanen (1826-1877). More Than a Century in America 1855-1978. A Genealogical Report by a Great-granddaughter.* Photos, family trees, news clippings. Self-published and not for sale. (Note: Edward Lanen was also the great-grandfather of George W. Duffy.)

INDEX

Addendum

Marshall (Mike) Roberts Soper, Killed in Action during sinking of *American Leader* on September 10, 1942. Photo courtesy of Jeannine Peters, a niece.

Captain Duffy's Decorations

Pins

United States Lines' house flag flanked by United States Merchant Marine emblem and Merchant Marine Active Service lapel pin.

Medal bars

Row one: Mariner's Medal, Merchant Marine Combat (star indicates vessel was sunk)

Row two: Pacific War Zone, Atlantic War Zone, Mediterranean Middle East War Zone, World War Two Victory

Row three: Prisoner of War, Asiatic Pacific Campaign, Philippine Defense, Philippine Liberation.

Row four: Philippine Independence, New York State Conspicuous Service with star, Federation des Combattants Alliies en Europe (FCAEE) Croix Alliés, Distinguished Service Medal of the Interallied Military Order Sphinx

Row five: Philippine Presidential Unit Citation

Medals

Row six: Prisoner of War Medal, Mariner's Medal, Merchant Marine Defense Medal, Pacific War Zone Medal, Atlantic War Zone Medal, Mediterranean-Middle East War Zone Medal, World War Two Victory Medal

Row seven: Philippine Defense Medal, Philippine Independence Medal, New York Conspicuous Service Cross, FCAEE Cross, Order of the Sphinx Medal, Soviet Union Medal commemorating the fortieth anniversary of Victory in the Great Patriotic War of 1941-1945 (not shown, a similar Soviet Union medal commemorating the fiftieth anniversary)

CPSIA information can be obtained at www.ICGtesting.com
Printed in the USA
BVOW070016201112

305959BV00003B/6/P